**SVEC**
**2011**
**01**

# Joseph de Maistre
# and the legacy of Enlightenment

*SVEC* (formerly known as *Studies on Voltaire and the Eighteenth Century*)
is dedicated to eighteenth-century research. *SVEC* welcomes work across a
broad range of disciplines and critical methodologies.

www.voltaire.ox.ac.uk

# Joseph de Maistre
# and the legacy of Enlightenment

*Edited by*

CAROLINA ARMENTEROS

*and*

RICHARD A. LEBRUN

VOLTAIRE FOUNDATION

OXFORD

2011

ISBN 978 0 7294 1008 3
ISSN 0435-2866

The Voltaire Foundation is a department of the University of
Oxford. It furthers the University's objective of excellence in
research, scholarship and education by publishing worldwide.

Voltaire Foundation
99 Banbury Road
Oxford OX2 6JX, UK
www.voltaire.ox.ac.uk

A catalogue record for this book is available from the British Library

History of ideas / political history / religion
Histoire des idées / histoire de la politique / la religion

Cover illustration: Portrait of Count Joseph de Maistre (1753-1821), engraved by
Francois le Villain (litho, b/w photo) by Pierre Bouillon (1776-1831) (after).
BnF, Paris / Giraudon / The Bridgeman Art Library.

FSC (the Forest Stewardship Council) is an independent organization established to
promote responsible management of the world's forests.

This book is printed on acid-free paper
Printed in the UK by Page Bros (Norwich) Ltd

To the memory of
Emile Perreau-Saussine (1972-2010),
our friend and colleague.

# Contents

# Acknowledgements

The articles contained in this volume, with the exception of Carolina Armenteros' piece on 'Maistre's Rousseaus', were first presented at *Reappraisals / Reconsidérations*, the Fifth International Colloquium on Joseph de Maistre, held at Jesus College, Cambridge, on 4 and 5 December 2008. We owe our warmest thanks to Pierre Glaudes and Michael Kohlhauer for the invaluable advice they offered at the beginning of our editorial venture.

We would like to express our deepest appreciation to all the contributors of this volume, who responded promptly and graciously to our many questions and suggestions for revisions to their work. We are also grateful to the anonymous reviewer of *SVEC* for very helpful suggestions for improving our manuscript.

Lastly, this volume is dedicated to the memory of one of our authors, Emile Perreau-Saussine, who died suddenly in February 2010. His chapter in this book is one of the last pieces of scholarship that he completed before his untimely death at the age of 37.

# Introduction

CAROLINA ARMENTEROS *and* RICHARD A. LEBRUN

## I

If any one thinker had to be chosen to represent the Counter-Enlightenment, Joseph de Maistre (1754-1821) would be a favourite candidate. His attack on the philosophy that he considered responsible for the French Revolution was overwhelming. The anger and desperation that he felt at the crumbling of a whole world were admirably served by a clear and logical mind, an enormous erudition and a lively and memorable style, all devoted to constructing a replacement for *philosophie*. For the intensely emotional Maistre, the memory of the upheaval that had demolished the *ancien régime* became an obsession, impelling him to measure moral phenomena empirically, to re-found politics on historical grounds, and to become one of the earliest theorists of social violence. More than two centuries on, his pages still tremble with the anxieties of the Terror.

Isaiah Berlin set Maistre up for the role of paradigm of the Counter-Enlightenment in the thrice-printed piece that he devoted to the Savoyard as a forerunner of fascism.[1] In it, the Counter-Enlightenment as represented by Maistre became symbolic of the horrors that derive infallibly from denying the generous ideals of the Century of Lights. By the same stroke, it transmuted into the onerous and perfect antithesis of eighteenth-century philosophy.[2]

Berlin's concept of Counter-Enlightenment has since been extensively enlarged and critiqued. Contrary to the philosophic and Germano-centric phenomenon he initially portrayed, the Counter-Enlightenment now has French origins in a discontented Grub Street[3] hostile to the *philosophes*.[4] And it is no longer the mere antagonist of a monolithic and

---

1. For the definitive version, see Isaiah Berlin, 'Joseph de Maistre and the origins of fascism', in *The Crooked timber of humanity: chapters in the history of ideas*, ed. Henry Hardy (London 1990).
2. For an assessment of Berlin's depiction of Maistre, see Graeme Garrard, 'Isaiah Berlin's Joseph de Maistre', in *Isaiah Berlin's Counter-Enlightenment*, ed. Joseph Mali and Robert Wokler (Philadelphia, PA, 2003), p.117-31.
3. See Robert Darnton, *The Literary underground of the old regime* (Cambridge, MA, 1982).
4. Darrin McMahon, *Enemies of the Enlightenment: the French Counter-Enlightenment and the making of modernity* (Oxford, 2001).

well-defined intellectual movement.[5] In fact scholars now suggest that Rousseau himself was a founding representative of the Counter-Enlightenment – rather than the slightly odd *philosophe* of Berlinian memory.[6] They point out that the Counter-Enlightenment lacked a single identity and had multiple incarnations;[7] and some even intimate that its enemy – and therefore itself – might not even have existed in the first place.[8]

The historian of ideas interested in the recovery of writers' intentions can also ask how thinkers as diverse – and even as antagonistic – as, say, Herder and Maistre could be related. Maistre, for one, disliked Herder intensely, seeing in him a champion of the noxious dreams it was so urgent to shatter.[9] The idea that he himself advanced the same cause as the German preacher would have shocked and grieved him. The suspicion has likewise grown that, in being so dismissive of historical context, Berlin's highly selective reading of Maistre and his posterity was tendentious. A recent study has gone so far as to argue that Berlin had a hidden agenda.[10] This volume, however, does not aim to add to the critique of the concept that has come to be associated with Berlin more than any other. It seeks, rather, to reflect on the implications that Maistre's historical relationship to eighteenth-century philosophy has for Enlightenment, Counter-Enlightenment and Maistrian studies, as well as for political debate in our own time.

In raising the historical profile of the Counter-Enlightenment, current scholarship has reconceptualised the movement as a plural phenomenon that thrived both within and on the fringes of the Enlightenment. The Counter-Enlightenment now appears in two different guises – as an attitudinal phenomenon, and as a family of thought fragmented according to intellectual filiation and historical circumstance. This latter identity places it in a precarious position, revealing it as an intimate relation of the very philosophy it denounces.

---

5.  Robert Wokler, 'Isaiah Berlin's Enlightenment and Counter-Enlightenment', in *Isaiah Berlin's Counter-Enlightenment*, p.13-32.
6.  See Arthur Melzer, 'The origin of the Counter-Enlightenment: Rousseau and the new religion of sincerity', *American political science review* 90, 2 (1996), p.344-60 and Graeme Garrard, *Rousseau's Counter-Enlightenment: a republican critique of the philosophes* (Albany, NY, 2003).
7.  Graeme Garrard, *Counter-Enlightenments: from the eighteenth century to the present* (London, 2006).
8.  James Schmidt, 'What Enlightenment project?', *Political theory* 28, 6 (2000), p.734-57.
9.  See Robert Triomphe, 'Joseph de Maistre et Herder', *Revue de littérature comparée* 7-9 (1954), p.322-29.
10. See Cyprian Blamires, 'Berlin, Maistre and fascism', paper presented at *Reappraisals/Reconsidérations: Fifth International Colloquium on Joseph de Maistre*, Jesus College, Cambridge, 5-6 December 2008.

But, to ask once more Kant's classic question, what is Enlightenment? Here again, the field lies upturned by debate. John Robertson has challenged postmodernity's plural Enlightenments differentiated by circumstance and context, with an account of the Enlightenment as an international movement embracing all of Europe and permeating the intellectual life of regions as mutually remote as Scotland and Naples.[11] This volume does not take sides in this debate: rather, the articles it contains reach conclusions on Maistrian thought that are consistent with the arguments of both. Together, they suggest that Maistre was involved in various strands of Enlightenment that are distinct without being separate.

Maistre's case supports Robertson's contention insofar as he was an ardent reader of both Hume and Vico, the two paradigms of the Scottish and Neapolitan Enlightenments, respectively. Maistre condemned the former as a philosopher and used him as a historian. And he harboured both curiosity and praise for the latter: he was one of his first non-Neapolitan readers[12] and found in his writings materials useful for building his own epistemology and political thought.[13] A fluent reader of six modern and two ancient languages who devoured works written from Madrid to Moscow, Maistre was a *de facto* if late participant in the cosmopolitan movement *par excellence* that the Enlightenment has been traditionally portrayed as being, and that Robertson has reawakened after some two decades' slumber.

Yet Maistre is also undeniably close to the conservative and religious, and especially to the Catholic Enlightenments that have come to prominence in scholarship since the beginning of the postmodern age. Like John Pocock's English conservatives, Maistre shared a taste for gradual reform and a desire to leave room for religion in politics. But he was less congenial toward the Arminian Enlightenment described by the same author and to the Jansenist Enlightenment that prepared the French Revolution.[14] While Maistre knew and used Port Royal's masters extensively, opposition to Jansenism consumed much of his last polemical energies, partly inspiring his Ultramontanist *magnum opus*, *Du Pape* (1819), as well as *De l'Eglise gallicane* (1821), originally written as Book V of the first work.

The Jansenist Enlightenment was but a portion of the theological Enlightenment, a movement that encouraged the advance of reason

---

11. Robertson, *The Case for the Enlightenment: Scotland and Naples 1680-1760* (Cambridge, 2005).

12. See Elio Gianturco, *Joseph de Maistre and Giambattista Vico: Italian roots of De Maistre's political culture* (unpublished Ph.D. dissertation, Columbia University, 1937), p.vii.

13. Victor Nguyen, 'Maistre, Vico et le retour des dieux', *Revue des études maistriennes* 3 (1977), p.243-55.

14. See Dale Van Kley, *The Religious origins of the French Revolution: from Calvin to the Civil Constitution* (New Haven, CT, 1996).

within the limits of religion alone.[15] Maistre inherited the Jesuit-sponsored current of it that was inimical to the Jansenists, and that Jeffrey Burson has recently described.[16] Most notably associated with the Abbé Jean-Martin de Prades (1720-1782) and his ill-starred thesis defence at the Sorbonne, this unashamedly apologetic Enlightenment combined obedience to the authorities of church and state with the determination to spread itself through publication. The Jesuits were its bastions, and their *Journal de Trévoux* the principal organ of its diffusion. Maistre had a lifelong and familial attachment to the Society of Jesus that he expressed with the cadences of a verb conjugation: 'mon grand-père aimait les Jésuites, mon père les aimait, ma sublime mère les aimait, je les aime, mon fils les aime, son fils les aimera'.[17] It was a liking that explains what otherwise appear as strange, lonely features of his thought – like his ability to reconcile empiricism with Malebranche's reformulation of Descartes' rationalist and intuitionist epistemology.[18]

But Maistre and the Jesuits differed on a crucial point. The empiricism the latter championed was that of Locke, a sensualist whom one may be now surprised to discover in such pious company, but who had only begun to acquire his theologically scandalous (and rather tendentious) reputation as a materialist in Voltaire's *Lettres philosophiques* of 1734. Until mid-century, Locke the providentialist empiricist was exceedingly help-ful to the Jesuits, explaining humanity's postlapsarian corruption and the consequent need for revealed truth[19] in the wake of the theological crisis inaugurated by Descartes.[20] Later, things changed: the precursors of Jonathan Israel's radical Enlightenment were massively successful in popularising their invention of a materialist Locke, while the Jansenists decried his sensualism loudly and blamed the Jesuits for adopting it. Inheriting these positions in the latter half of the century – that is, accepting as his own the image of Locke propagated by the *philosophes* and the Jansenists – Maistre rejected the English philosopher.[21] He replaced his empiricism with another, derived from Hume, which he

---

15. Dale Van Kley, Foreword to Jeffrey Burson, *The Rise and fall of theological Enlightenment: Jean-Martin de Prades and ideological polarization in eighteenth-century France* (Notre Dame, IN, 2010), p.ix.

16. In Burson, *The Rise and fall of theological Enlightenment*.

17. Maistre to the Chevalier de Saint-Réal, September 1816, *Œuvres complètes de Joseph de Maistre* (henceforth *OC*), 14 vol. (Lyon, 1884-1887), vol.13, p.426.

18. On Maistre's adherence to Cartesian innatism, see, in this volume, Philippe Barthelet's article, 'The Cambridge Platonists mirrored by Joseph de Maistre'.

19. Burson, *The Rise and fall of theological Enlightenment*, p.22.

20. Burson, *The Rise and fall of theological Enlightenment*, p.41.

21. On Maistre and Locke, see E. D. Watt, '"Locked in": De Maistre's critique of French Lockeanism', *Journal of the history of ideas* 32, 1 (1971), p.129-32.

found in the writings of the Abbé Nicolas-Sylvestre Bergier (1718-90),[22] an heir of the theological Enlightenment and the most respected Catholic apologist of eighteenth-century France.[23] Indeed the distaste for Locke was one of the few themes common to Maistrian and Jansenist thought – another being the admiration of Descartes.[24]

Maistre had ties both to the Jesuits' theological Enlightenment and to what we now call the Counter-Enlightenment. This latter was the synthesis that emerged from the theological Enlightenment after the mid-century scandals surrounding the *Encyclopédie*. Adopting a far more combative stance than its predecessor, the Counter-Enlightenment defended revelation against the same thinkers with whom the Jesuits and other clerics had dialogued, and even collaborated, during the much more intellectually open first part of the century.[25]

Theological Enlightenment, Jansenist Enlightenment and Counter-Enlightenment are distinct from the more familiar Catholic Enlightenment first described by Sebastian Merkle in 1908.[26] Associated with the desire to improve Catholic institutions with the help of Catholic states in the wake of the Jesuit expulsions of the 1760s, this movement derived partly from the reform-oriented work of Ludovico Muratori (1672-1750) and more specifically from his insistence that charity should be not only a matter of belief, but also of widespread social and institutional practice.[27] Maistre's reformism approved of these ideas, but expressed them in theoretically more abstracted ways. The articles in this volume suggest that his Catholic advocacy of reform was expressed by a post-revolutionary historico-mystical philosophy that modelled the waning of violence, the perfection of social institutions, and the angelisation of humanity through time.[28] Platonism, and especially Origen's Alexandrian Neoplatonism, was crucial to this project. In fact, one innovation of

22. On Maistre's valorisation of experience, see, in this volume, Carolina Armenteros' article, 'Maistre's Rousseaus'.
23. On Bergier, see Robert Palmer, *Catholics and unbelievers in eighteenth-century France* (Princeton, NJ, 1939), p.46, 87, 96-101, 157, 198, 215-18.
24. On Maistre and Descartes, see, in this volume, Philippe Barthelet's article 'The Cambridge Platonists mirrored by Joseph de Maistre'.
25. For an account of how the theological and radical Enlightenments at first converged and later became inimical, partly as a result of Prades' thesis, see Burson, *The Rise and fall of theological Enlightenment*.
26. See Sebastian Merkle, *Die katholische Beurteilung des Aufklärungszeitalters: Vortrag auf dem Internationalen Kongress für Historischen Wissenschaften zu Berlin am 12. August 1908* (Berlin, 1908).
27. Samuel J. Miller, 'Introduction: Enlightened Catholicism on a European scale', in *Portugal and Rome c.1748-1830: Aspects of the Catholic Enlightenment* (Rome, 1973), p.1-27.
28. On Maistre's vision of history, see, in this volume, Jean-Yves Pranchère's article, 'The negative of the Enlightenment, the positive of order and the impossible positivity of history'.

this volume is to demonstrate how very central the Platonic tradition was to Maistre's thought, and especially to his ability to engage with and appropriate the Enlightenment.[29]

If Maistre can step into new light that shows him no longer only as an enemy, but also as an heir and practitioner of the Enlightenment, his thought can suggest ways in which current Enlightenment studies may be revised. Although the many Enlightenments that have emerged in recent scholarship are exceedingly varied, they all share one feature in common. When marrying preceding traditions, the Enlightenment appears as the active, giving and generative force, while tradition plays the role of the passive and welcoming receiver. The articles gathered in this volume challenge this view. How they do so becomes apparent on reflecting that the philosophy of the eighteenth century – as Maistre himself highlighted in the *Examen de la philosophie de Bacon* (1809) – derived from the very traditions it subverted, and that, as Maistre again emphasised, it was the firstborn of Christian theology. Unsurprisingly, Catholicism and Enlightenment converged precisely on those ideas that the Enlightenment held to be most dearly its own: the conviction that reason is the major vehicle of a truth accessible by all; the identification of liberty as a fundamental human attribute that moral education must direct rightly; the belief that human nature is self-perfection over time; and the insistence that moral knowledge must have social benefits and yield practical results.

Whether these themes prevailed in Maistre's thought in their Enlightenment or traditional versions is often difficult to tell. The two streams fuse so easily and frequently under his pen that the question itself sometimes seems stripped of meaning. What is certain is that Enlightenment and tradition tested each other on the pages of Maistre's works. On the one hand, in combating the Enlightenment with its own weapons, Maistre subjected religious truths to worldly standards. For him, a government proved the legitimacy of its rule over a people not by exercising justice, but by simply enduring – since, as the ancients observed, only that which does more good than evil survives time's ordeal. Pronouncing history to be the measure of politics, these arguments helped to inaugurate historicism's reign over the Restoration. But they were not arguments invariably consistent with the prescriptions of

---

29. On Maistre's Platonism, see, in this volume, Philippe Barthelet, 'The Cambridge Platonists mirrored by Joseph de Maistre'; Douglas Hedley, 'Enigmatic images of an invisible world: sacrifice, suffering and theodicy in Joseph de Maistre'; Aimee Barbeau, 'The Savoyard philosopher: deist or Neoplatonist?'; and Elcio Verçosa Filho, 'The pedagogical nature of Maistre's thought'.

Catholic orthodoxy, which, following Augustine, often sealed off the City of God and the City of the World as mutually impenetrable realms.

On the other hand, the Enlightenment stood condemned as a moral failure in the court of tradition. Modern philosophy, wrote Maistre, made men and women callous and self-interested; it constricted the heart; it located wisdom in an unfeeling reason that served only abstraction or its own interests; it drove people, in all, to sloth, ill will, selfishness, revolt and every variety of vice, thanks to its unspoken creed that inventive ideas are an adequate substitute for compassionate conduct. That such darts were often thrown at Rousseau, a critic of rationalism and the consummate symbol of philosophical sentimentalism, may strike the reader as unjust; but from Maistre's viewpoint, Jean-Jacques' own pride and the mass violence unleashed by his revolutionary offspring offered ample evidence for the soundness of the analysis.

Tradition and Enlightenment thus met, attacked and formed each other in the pages of Maistre's works. The articles in this volume suggest that one cannot always know who moulded and transformed whom, or even which streams of thought generated certain opinions or ideas. But the extent to which the two enemies conspired and bonded in the Maistrian synthesis makes it possible to understand what otherwise seems downright weird: for example how, as Aimee Barbeau and Elcio Verçosa Filho suggest in their articles, Maistre could keep Origen's company while reconciling religion with modernity; or how, as Darrin McMahon recounts, the concept of genius so beloved of the eighteenth century could transform in Maistre's hands into a gently portentous warning against the dangers of starting 'an insurrection against God'.[30]

The possibility that Maistre was not only an heir but also a representative of the Enlightenment must therefore be entertained. For if the Enlightenment ended with the Napoleonic wars, as many chronologies allow, Maistre was not too late to contribute to it. And as soon as one stops thinking of the Enlightenment as a strictly secular phenomenon, as soon as one allows that some of its strands were fundamentally theological in character, it becomes difficult to continue to perceive Maistre as the apotheosis of Counter-Enlightenment. This is especially the case when remembering that this latter concept has been rendered fragile in the process of being specified and expanded.

This collection is the first large-scale attempt to assess Maistre's debt to the Enlightenment, and to discuss the ways in which he appropriated and transformed its major themes. If any common impression emerges from

---

30. Maistre, *Essai sur le principe générateur des constitutions politiques*, in *Joseph de Maistre: Œuvres*, ed. Pierre Glaudes (Paris, 2007), p.399.

reading the articles, it is the versatility, the creativity and, paradoxically, the openness that characterised Maistre's approach to Enlightenment and tradition alike. His position on both displays that undefinable ambiguity, that ability to slip away and never be firmly seized, that renders writers lastingly compelling across the centuries. Indeed for all his reputation as the archetype of the Counter-Enlightenment, Maistre, when well known, resists categorisation. This volume tries to show how, and to ask why.

It also tries to reflect on the special relevance that Maistrian studies have for our own time. We live in an age when religions are increasingly putting themselves forward as legitimate sources of public and political reason. From Barack Obama's dialogue with the Catholic Church over abortion and world poverty to the French and Belgian governments' ban on the *burqa*, the democratic states that emerged during the Age of Revolution are now continually confronted with the reinvigoration of tradition, and with the growth of religious populations on their territories whose moral and social ideals often challenge their own. In this context, it is thought-provoking and instructive to examine the relationship that Maistre, as a religious conservative, bore to the intellectual trends commonly associated with the rise of secular politics and the making of the modern world.

## II

To appreciate the significance of the interpretations of Maistre's relationship to the Enlightenment to be found in this volume, it is helpful to review the historiography of this issue. Although Maistre has long been recognised as one of the most important and influential theorists reacting to the Enlightenment and French Revolution, general agreement on his importance has been accompanied by a wide range of disagreement on the exact nature of this relationship.

The primary division, naturally enough, has been between those who treasured the heritage of the Enlightenment and approved the French Revolution, and those who condemned both these historical developments. As early as 1852, the *Edinburgh review* provided an apt characterisation of the divergent interpretations of the two schools:

> By the one party he has been reviled as the apologist of the headsman, the advocate of the Inquisition, the adversary of free inquiry, the virulent detractor of Bacon, the friend of the Jesuits, and the unscrupulous perverter of historic truth for his own controversial purposes; by the other, he is extolled as an austere moralist reacting against the sentimentality and philosophism (to use his own word) of the age, a steadfast believer and an unshrinking upholder of all he believed, an elegant scholar, a powerful logician, a disinterested statesman, and the unflinching advocate of a

persecuted order, which reckoned among its members the friends and instructors of his youth.[31]

The fundamental dichotomy between liberal critics and conservative admirers has cut deeper than mere rational considerations. A remark by a well-known nineteenth-century French liberal, Charles de Rémusat (1797-1875), nicely captures the emotional reaction Maistre has often provoked. Rémusat acknowledged to his readers that 'I have never read ten pages of Comte de Maistre without feeling a profound joy at not thinking like him'.[32] For far too long and far too often, much that has been written about Joseph de Maistre has been one-sided and polemical in nature – written to prove his validity and relevance or intended to discredit him and the ideas and institutions he defended.

It must be acknowledged as well that the nature of Maistre's writings has in some ways contributed to the difficulty of arriving at a fair assessment of his thought. Most of his writings were occasional pieces, written for a particular audience, and not political, philosophical or theological treatises *per se*. They usually lack the organisation and compartmentalisation by discipline that might be expected of a scholarly theorist. In fact, it can be argued that much of his literary production can be best characterised as pamphlet literature.[33] The occasional nature of much of Maistre's work also makes it difficult to depict and evaluate his views on any particular subject without studying all his writings. The polemical nature of the Savoyard's prose has created additional problems. It is too easy to be offended or misled by the mordant sarcasm of his style, and to mistake the substance of his thought.

It is perhaps not surprising then that given the continuing controversial presence of both the Enlightenment and the heritage of the French Revolution in the political and intellectual life of the West, and given the provocative and problematic nature of Maistre's works, the fundamental dichotomy between uncritical admirers and hostile critics discerned by the *Edinburgh review* in 1852 persisted for well over a century. With few exceptions, French and English interpreters alike continued to characterise his thought primarily on the basis of their own sympathy for or dislike of the whole Enlightenment project.[34] It was not

---

31. Anonymous, review of the 1851 edition of Maistre's *Lettres et opuscules inédits*, *Edinburgh review* (October, 1852) 96:290.
32. Charles de Rémusat, 'Du Traditionalisme', *Revue des deux mondes* 9 (27th year, 2nd period), (May 1857), p.245, 15.
33. See Richard A. Lebrun, 'Joseph de Maistre as pamphleteer', in *The New enfant du siècle: Joseph de Maistre as a writer*, ed. Carolina Armenteros and Richard Lebrun, *St Andrews studies in French history and culture* 1 (St Andrews, 2010), p.19-46.
34. For an assessment of English and American readings of Maistre from the 1840s through the 1990s, see Richard A. Lebrun, 'Joseph de Maistre in the Anglophone world', in Lebrun

until the post-World War II years that more balanced and nuanced assessments of his relationship to the Enlightenment began to appear, mainly in the form of doctoral theses, some of which were subsequently published as monographs.

A brief review of those dissertations that saw publication in whole or in part should begin with the thesis that Robert Triomphe defended in Paris in 1955, but did not publish until 1968.[35] Systematically hostile to his subject (blaming him or at least his intellectual descendants for the Vichy regime), Triomphe both challenged Maistre's received status as an authentic Catholic champion of the Counter-Enlightenment and provided a great body of new factual information about Maistre as well as provocative reflections on Maistre's relationships to a great many intellectual traditions from Greek antiquity to his own time. It was in large part Triomphe's work that stimulated Jean-Louis Darcel's lifetime of scholarship on Maistre, a work that included his own *doctorat d'état* thesis (defended in 1984), negotiation of access to the Maistre papers still in the hands of his descendants, and the founding and editing of the *Revue des études maistriennes*. Although Darcel never published his thesis as a monograph, his scholarly articles and his editorial work (including critical editions of some of Maistre's major works) were key contributions to Maistre scholarship, ultimately enhancing our understanding of Maistre's relationships to both the Enlightenment and the Counter-Enlightenment.

Richard A. Lebrun's 1963 doctoral thesis for the University of Minnesota, published in 1965,[36] was undertaken and completed without knowledge of either Triomphe or Darcel. Lebrun's study found a somewhat paradoxical relationship between Maistre's Catholicism and his political thought. He concluded that though Maistre was a sincere Catholic reacting with moral indignation against what he judged to be the irreligion of his time, he produced a political theory that owed as much to the assumptions, influences and circumstances of his own era as to traditional Catholic thought. Although the ultimate basis of his opposition to the Enlightenment was his firm adherence to essentially Catholic beliefs, the content, as well as the form and expression of his

---

(ed.), *Maistre: life thought and influence*, p.271-89. There is no equivalent brief review of French interpretations of Maistre; however reference should be made to Philippe Barthelet's massive volume, *Joseph de Maistre*, Les Dossiers H (Lausanne, 2005), which includes material drawn from a host of French writers from Maistre's time to our own. Barthelet's Prologue to the volume, p.17-23, is quite helpful.

35. Robert Triomphe, *Joseph de Maistre: étude sur la vie et sur la doctrine d'un matérialiste mystique* (Geneva, 1968).

36. Richard A. Lebrun, *Throne and altar: the political and religious thought of Joseph de Maistre* (Ottawa, 1965).

reply, was conditioned by his immersion in the thought world of his opponents. Lebrun suggested that this paradoxical relationship between Maistre's sincere Catholicism and his political theory helps explain why his thought had been the object of such contradictory judgments. Liberal critics, shocked by some of his illiberal conclusions, jumped to the conclusion that the objectionable features of Maistre's thought were the result of his Catholicism, his Jesuit training or the calculation of a class-oriented aristocrat. On the other side, Maistre's Catholic admirers, recognising the writer's religious sincerity and high moral purpose, too readily assumed that his thought was sound and orthodox. Lebrun concluded: 'Critics and admirers alike, blinded perhaps by the violence of Maistre's attack on the *philosophes,* failed to recognise the extent to which Maistre too was a man of the Enlighenment'.[37]

Provocatively entitled *A Modern Maistre,*[38] Owen Bradley's 1999 book is a revised version of a 1992 Cornell University Ph.D. thesis that portrayed Maistre as a subtle social theorist whose critique of the Enlightenment bears an uncanny resemblance to the central claims of postmodernist thought. The guiding thread of Bradley's analysis is Maistre's theory of sacrifice. One of Maistre's central concerns, Bradley contends, was how human disorder is shaped and managed by ritualised behaviors and symbolic forms. Maistre, in this view, was less an irrationalist than a theorist of social irrationality. Sidestepping the traditional dichotomy between Maistre's admirers and critics, Bradley aimed to depict Maistre as 'the ambiguous, equivocal, undecidable figure' he believes he ought to be for modern thought. If Bradley focused on the sociological and anthropological dimensions of Maistre's thought, not the least of his contributions to Maistre scholarship was to inspire others to probe more deeply and to reassess the philosophical and theological aspects of Maistre's thinking about sacrifice and violence.[39]

Jean-Yves Pranchère's 1996 *thèse de doctorat* in philosophy for the Université de Rouen, *L'Autorité contre les Lumières. La philosophie de Joseph de Maistre*[40] was published by Droz in 2004. While not denying Maistre's status as a Counter-Enlightenment thinker, it showed that although Maistre had denounced the ideas of the *Lumières* he had nevertheless participated in its dialectic. Taking Maistre seriously as a philosopher Pranchère explored how Maistre expressed and took to their logical conclusions the paradoxes inherent in the Enlightenment itself. He seeks

---

37. Lebrun, *Throne and altar,* p.157.
38. Owen Bradley, *A Modern Maistre: the social and political thought of Joseph de Maistre* (Lincoln, NE, 1999).
39. See, for instance, Douglas Hedley, 'Enigmatic images of an invisible world: sacrifice, suffering and theodicy in Joseph de Maistre' in this volume.
40. Subsequently published in a revised version by Droz (Geneva, 2004).

also to analyse how Maistre articulates his historicism according to a rationalist metaphysics.

Graeme Garrard's 1997 Oxford D.Phil. dissertation on the relationship between Rousseau, Maistre and the French Enlightenment was never published as a monograph. But his central contention that Rousseau is best read as a precursor of the Counter-Enlightenment, with Maistre understood as Rousseau's ally against *philosophie*, had already appeared in an important article in *History of political thought* even before the dissertation was defended.[41] Garrard subsequently supplemented this pioneering contribution to our understanding of Maistre's relationship to both the Enlightenment and the Counter-Enlightenment with a broad-ranging study that situated Maistre's position in the context of other 'Counter-Enlightenments'.[42]

*The More moderate side of Joseph de Maistre: views on political liberty and political economy*[43] is a revised version of the thesis Cara Camcastle defended at Queen's University (Kingston, Ontario) in 2001 for a Ph.D. in political science. Camcastle's contribution is that of a well-trained political scientist who was able both to delineate the main features of Maistre's political thought and to place his positions in the context of contemporary thinkers addressing similar problems. In particular, her treatment of Maistre's views on money, taxes and commerce, based on documents other scholars had largely ignored, demonstrates that he held the views of an economic liberal whose position was close to that of Montesquieu and Adam Smith.

The thesis Carolina Armenteros defended in 2004 for a Ph.D. in history from the University of Cambridge, entitled 'Joseph de Maistre and the idea of history, 1794-1820', has not yet been published as a monograph. However some of her key findings about Maistre's contributions to new historical ways of thinking about nature, politics and society – ways that transformed Rousseau's thought and went beyond negating Enlightenment philosophy to work out a new relationship between political and historical thought, a distinctive kind of historicism – have appeared in articles in *History of political thought* and the *Journal of the history of ideas*.[44] For Armenteros, Maistre's thought is founded on the

---

41. Graeme Garrard, 'Rousseau, Maistre, and the Counter-Enlightenment', *History of political thought* 15, 1 (1994), p.97-120.

42. Garrard, *Counter-Enlightenments*.

43. Cara Camcastle, *The More moderate side of Joseph de Maistre: views on political liberty and political economy* (Montreal, 2005).

44. Carolina Armenteros, 'Parabolas and the fate of nations: the beginnings of conservative historicism in Joseph de Maistre's *De la Souveraineté du peuple*', *History of political thought* 28, 2 (2007), p.230-52, and 'From human nature to normal humanity: Joseph de Maistre, Rousseau, and the origins of moral statistics', *Journal of the history of ideas* 68, 1 (2007), p.107-30.

historical propositions that he elaborates in the process of refuting Rousseau.

The direction taken by the recent academic scholarship reviewed above suggests that the interpretations offered here of Maistre's relationship to the Enlightenment are anything but idiosyncratic or perverse. All enrich our understanding by exploring diverse and even surprising aspects of a complex and challenging thinker.

## III

This volume is presented in three parts. The first, which explores some of the polemics of the Counter-Enlightenment, opens with an article by Darrin McMahon on 'The genius of Maistre'. The word 'genius' recurs throughout Maistre's works and the concept of genius figures prominently in his thought. This article defines Maistre's concept of genius and puts it in the context of a tradition of thought going back to antiquity. It also argues that the Enlightenment at once borrowed from this tradition and subverted it.

The second article in Part I, by Joseph Eaton, examines Joseph de Maistre's commentary on the United States. Most scholarship on Maistre's views of America has focused on his denial of the possibility of natural rights as embodied in the American Declaration of Independence and on his views on the folly of the American use of deliberate reason to found a new constitution. A closer look at Maistre's writings on America, however, offers a richer view of his social philosophy. Eaton argues that denying America's viability was central to Maistre's critique of the Enlightenment. For Maistre, the American republic was infantile but also impossible – as was suggested by the impracticability of plans for a new federal capital. Eaton concludes that Maistre's comments on America were polemical rather than systematic. For him, America was a symbolic battleground for European controversies; his real targets were naturalists, republicans and Rousseau's naive idea of the noble savage.

The last article in Part I, Jean-Yves Pranchère's study of the 'negativity of the Enlightenment', is a philosophical study that examines the relationship between Maistre's concepts of order, history, and the Enlightenment. Pranchère argues that Maistre's ideas of time, and especially of prophecy, are inextricably bound up with his vision of order. A historical-prophetic perspective is thus crucial for understanding his thinking on sovereignty, which evolves from a prediction of the return of monarchy in the *Considérations* to a vision of the intensification of Catholicism in *Du Pape*.

Part II of our volume, 'Makers and heirs of the Enlightenment', explores the intellectual affinities between Joseph de Maistre and two important currents in eighteenth-century thought. In the first, Philippe Barthelet examines the relationship between Maistre, the Cambridge Platonists and Plato himself. The article argues that Maistre's reading of Ralph Cudworth and Henry More was part and parcel of his critique of the *Encyclopédie*, which denigrated these two authors for upholding views very similar to Maistre's. Gathering together the references to Cambridge Platonism in Maistre's works, Barthelet concludes that Maistre was especially interested in their innatism. More broadly, Cudworth and More's transcendental Christianity helped Maistre to lay the foundations of his political morality – although he never shared in his predecessors' ultimate refutation of Descartes.

In the second article in Part II, co-editor Carolina Armenteros examines the topic of 'Maistre's Rousseaus'. In his works, manuscripts and notebooks Maistre repeatedly criticised Rousseau, whose philosophy he condemned for having led to the French Revolution. Armenteros, however, demonstrates how Maistre's harsh criticism of Rousseau masked not only the great intellectual debt that he owed to the Genevan, but also the philosophical attitudes that he drew from his thought. This was an intellectual relationship that, throughout Maistre's life and even across the revolutionary divide, revolved around the problem of religion. Using Maistre's notebooks, correspondence and published works, this article assesses the breadth and character of Rousseau's legacy in Maistrian and, by extension, nineteenth-century French thought.

The last article in Part II, by Yannis Constantinidès, compares the ways in which Maistre and Schopenhauer critiqued the Enlightenment. The author's purpose is to demonstrate the uncanny convergences between the worldviews of these two thinkers who seem never to have read each other. The exercise constitutes an original contribution to Maistre and Schopenhauer scholarship alike that questions the status of both thinkers as representatives of the Counter-Enlightenment.

According to Constantinidès, Maistre and Schopenhauer both criticised the Enlightenment illusion that humanity can emancipate itself on its own and progress morally through history. They substituted for blind faith in the critical power of reason a firm commitment to the irresistible force of quasi-mystical illumination. Yet, as Constantinidès emphasises, this does not mean that either of them was an irrationalist: for both, reason plays an important role. It is simply subordinate to intuition.

Part III of our volume offers explorations of Maistrian 'afterlives' of the theological Enlightenment. In the first article here, Douglas Hedley provides a careful depiction of the philosophical and theological features of Maistre's theodicy. Treating Maistre's concepts of sacrifice and suffering within the broader concerns of his thought, Hedley argues that Maistre is a distinctively Romantic thinker in that he exhibits both a sensitivity to cultural specificity and to the significance of history (i.e. modern) and yet an insistence upon the ineluctably transcendent dimension of the human (i.e. traditional). He concludes that Owen Bradley was quite wrong to see Maistre's reflections on sacrifice as essentially sociological, even though the Savoyard was a genuine precursor of the sociologists of religion.

The second article in this section, by Emile Perreau-Saussine, attempts to explain 'Why Maistre became Ultramontane'. The argument goes back to the great Gallican theologian, Bossuet, who seems to have taken it for granted that the French monarchy could proclaim its independence of the papacy in temporal things (as it did with the Gallican declaration of 1682) without endangering religion in France. With Bossuet's theology of national sovereignty in mind, one can understand why Maistre became an Ultramontane after a Revolution that challenged the Catholic character of the French state and nation. Perreau-Saussine demonstrates how the authority of confessional states is constrained by their confessional nature. The deconfessionalisation of the state accomplished by the Revolution freed it from the controls previously imposed by its religious identity. That is why, in *Du Pape* (1819), Maistre argues that, to avoid tyranny, European peoples should turn to the papacy.

The next article in Part III, by Aimee Barbeau, explores Maistre's very significant relationship with eighteenth-century deism. In an elegantly developed argument, Barbeau explores the ways in which Maistre engaged eighteenth-century deism, whose vocabulary and ideas he often used for his own purposes – even to the point of sounding like a deist at times – by drawing on the faith and speculations of Origen, the famous third-century Alexandrian theologian, to address what he perceived to be the inadequacies of the Enlightenment.

The concluding article in our volume offers a new global perspective on Maistre's religious thought, insisting on his primarily pedagogical purpose. Elcio Verçosa Filho argues that Maistre's religious perspective is expressed in two different but complementary dimensions, Providence and established religion, and that all of his thought springs from these twin concerns. The first is the primary subject of most of Maistre's major works, in particular *Considérations sur la France* and *Les Soirées de Saint-Pétersbourg*. It serves as a general framework for most of his later work. The latter appears throughout his writings, beginning with the seminal *Mémoire au duc de Brunswick sur la Franc-Maçonnerie*, where Maistre states the religious nature of man and history from the point of view of education. Verçosa Filho argues that Maistre's providentialism is best understood as a divine education of humanity that encompasses and goes beyond the education provided by the religious institutions discussed in the *Mémoire*.

Thus Maistre's dual focus on Providence and religious tradition (sometimes identified with the 'conservative verities') constitutes a two-fold concept of education and makes of him a pedagogue in a double sense. With a view to explaining exactly how Maistre works out this divine educational perspective throughout his *œuvre*, this article considers three of his major works, the *Mémoire au duc de Brunswick*, *Les Soirées* and his translation of Plutarch's treatise on divine justice. The aim is to disclose the similarities between the great pedagogical project at the heart of Maistre's thought, and the ultimate goal of the Enlightenment that he so fiercely fought.

In all, this volume aims to fill in the grey shades in Maistre's portrait, so long and so often drawn only in black and white. In this sense, it is a contribution to our knowledge of the sources and nature of Maistrian thought. At a deeper and more general level, however, this book also aims to show how the Enlightenment and traditional thought could meld, conspiring unwittingly with one another, and using each other to make similar arguments or even pursue the same ends.

# I

## Polemics of the Counter-Enlightenment

# The genius of Maistre

DARRIN M. MCMAHON

I am not myself a Maistre scholar.[1] And although I have written on Maistre, on the genesis of conservative thought, and opposition to the Enlightenment more broadly, it has been some time since I have worked closely on these materials.[2] And so when I was contacted about participating in this enterprise, I asked if I might have license to write about what I have been working on more recently, the representations of genius and the genius figure in European thought. But I did so without really knowing, at that stage, what Maistre himself had to say on the subject.

It turns out that Maistre has quite a lot to say about genius, which was somewhat surprising at first, but probably should not have been, given that genius was a central, and in many ways a novel, concept in the eighteenth century, and that Maistre generally has something interesting and provocative to say about important eighteenth-century concepts. So what I would like to do here is to consider Maistre's thoughts on genius. What one comes away with – or at least what I'd like to suggest – is a picture of Maistre in this light that accords very well with the portrait that people like Richard Lebrun, Pierre Glaudes and Jean-Louis Darcel, among others, have drawn for us. That is of a Maistre who, though a critic of his time, is very much a product of it, a thinker imbedded in contexts – be they Catholic, Conservative, Counter-Enlightenment or indeed En-lightenment contexts – and who draws on discourses shared by a good many other Europeans in the late eighteenth and early nineteenth centuries. Maistre, in other words, does not somehow miraculously think outside his time as a fascist *avant la lettre*, as Isaiah Berlin would have it, or as a postmodern thinker as Owen Bradley has argued more recently, if provocatively.[3]

1. I would like to thank Carolina Armenteros, who shared with me early on her fine article, 'Parabolas and the fate of nations', p.230-52, which contains an illuminating discussion of Maistre's understanding of genius. I also would like to thank Richard Lebrun, who very kindly placed his vast knowledge of Maistre's writings at my disposal, and pointed me in the direction of fruitful passages. Finally, I am grateful to my graduate assistant, Maureen Macleod, who helped gather materials and organise my references.
2. McMahon, *Enemies of the Enlightenment*.
3. Isaiah Berlin, 'Joseph de Maistre and the origins of fascism', in Berlin, *The Crooked timber of humanity*, p.91-174. Bradley, *A Modern Maistre*.

To make a case for the importance of context in assessing Maistre's thought is no longer, of course, controversial. But I do also want to reaffirm the point that Maistre had an uncanny ability to put his finger on issues that would re-emerge in later, more modern contexts, and that genius – and the genius – is a fine example. In this respect, at least, Berlin was on to something when he characterised Maistre as a profoundly 'modern' figure who was in certain ways a visionary, a man who had an intuitive sense of many of the subsequent dilemmas modern societies would face.[4] In addition to being a man of his time, Maistre was farsighted about problems that lay on the horizon of the future.

So what does Maistre have to say about genius, and what does genius have to say about the long eighteenth century and its aftermath? I want to start with the latter point, because genius is really one of these ubiquitous concepts in the eighteenth century, invoked by a great many people, in France, in the United Kingdom, in Germany and elsewhere. And while historians, philosophers, literary scholars and others have necessarily written a good deal about this widespread interest, they have not in my view sufficiently explained it, or more precisely, sufficiently explained the critical innovation that occurs in the eighteenth century in the way that Europeans and their dependents in the New World talk about genius. That innovation being that they speak about *the* genius as a human being, and indeed almost exclusively as a man. Genius is a gendered concept from the outset, which is an interesting line of inquiry in its own right.[5] But what I want to emphasise here is that the genius is a modern creation, and indeed prior to the eighteenth century, the word 'genius' would never have been applied in any of the Indo-European languages to a human being of either sex as a predicate. It was, rather, exclusively an object. One had a genius, one was not a genius.

What was it that one had? That is a large subject. But the easy way to answer the question is by looking at European dictionaries in the seventeenth and eighteenth centuries in a sort of abbreviated *Begriffsgeschichte*. And given that we are dealing with a Francophone writer, let me give you here the definition of the *Dictionnnaire de l'Académie française* of 1694, which is rather typical: 'Genie. S. m. L'esprit, ou le demon, soit bon, soit mauvais, qui, selon la doctrine des Anciens accompagnoit les hommes depuis leur naissance jusques à leur mort. *Bon genie. mauvais genie. le genie de Socrate. le mauvais génie de Brutus. Le genie d'Auguste etoit plus fort que celuy d'Antoine*'.[6]

4.   Berlin, 'Joseph de Maistre', *The Crooked timber*, p.96.
5.   See, for example, Christine Battersby, *Gender and genius: towards a feminist aesthetics* (Bloomington, IN, 1990).
6.   *Dictionnaire de l'Académie françoise*, 2 vol. (1694), vol.1, p.517.

This is the first definition, and it is really the oldest, being the ancient idea of a tutelary spirit or god that accompanies men – and again it was exclusively men – from birth to death, acting as a conduit to the sacred, a divine 'companion', as Horace describes it, a *comes*. The idea is primarily Roman – *genius* being a Latin word, from the verb *gigno/gignere*, to father or to beget, genius originally being thought of as a god of birth – but there were important Greek precedents, too, in the idea of the personal *daimon* or spirit, like that said to have accompanied Socrates (*daimonion*). And in fact the Greek and Roman notions tend to get conflated in the late Republic and into the Empire by people like Varro, Plutarch and Apuleius, among others. 'Il se dit aussi, de ces esprits ou demons qui, selon la doctrine des Anciens, president à de certains lieux, à des villes, &c. *Le genie du lieu, le genie de Rome, du peuple Romain*. On dit, *Le genie de la France*, pour dire, *L'Ange tutelaire de la France*.'[7] The Romans thought of 'genii' not only as deities who watched over the birth and development of men – and to whom one sacrificed on one's birthday, the origin in fact of our birthday cake – but also as deities who watched over places (the *genius loci*) and corporations, which were likewise 'born' and 'founded' by fathers and looked after by 'patrons'. By the late Empire, according to the fourth-century Roman grammarian Maurus Servius, there was 'Nullus enim Locus sine Genio'.[8] Virtually every place and corporation in Rome, from the Senate, to the baker's guild, to local springs and army posts, had their own genius, the devotional statues of which still stand in the thousands in museums around the world.

We are lucky to have them, for Christians made a concerted effort to smash them in the late fourth and fifth centuries, outlawing the practice of sacrificing wine to genius in the Codex Theodosianus of 392. Yet genius, not surprisingly, does not really go away, but lives on in other forms – in the idea of the patron saint, as Peter Brown has shown, but even more importantly in the notion of the guardian angel – both of individuals and of places, and even of countries, and you get a hint of that in the Academy's third definition, which observes that *L'Ange tutelaire de la France* was sometimes still called 'Le Genie de la France.[9]' Others were even more explicit in connecting the two. Robert Cawdrey's *First English dictionary*, of 1604, for example, defines genius simply as 'the angell that waits on man, be it a good or evil angell', and Furetière's *Dictionnaire universel* of 1690 does the same, pointing out in its second definition of the word that 'Genie se dit dans le Christianisme des bons Anges qui

---

7.  *Dictionnaire de l'Académie françoise*, vol.1, p.517.
8.  Maurus Servius Honoratus, Servii grammatici in Vergilii Aenidos, 5.950.
9.  Peter Brown, *The Cult of the saints: its rise and function in Latin Christianity* (Chicago, IL, 1981).

accompagnent les hommes'.[10] One could cite many similar definitions and examples where this same parallel is made, beginning with the early Christian Neoplatonists.

So we have the genius as a classical figure, a tutelary spirit of people and places, and we have genius in its Christianised form as the guardian angel. There is another main meaning, introduced in the late fifteenth and early sixteenth centuries, which essentially blends the Latin *genius* (and in due course the various Indo-European vernacular terms for *genius*) with that of the Latin *ingenium*, a word that meant to the Romans something like innate ability or talent. Now that is an interesting conflation, explored in a classic book by Edgar Zilsel.[11] And it shows up in the Academy's fourth definition, which puts it this way: 'Il signifie aussi, L'inclination ou disposition naturelle, ou le talent particulier d'un chacun. *Beau genie. grand genie. puissant genie. vaste genie. genie universel. il a un merveilleux genie pour telle chose. suivre son genie. forcer son genie. faire quelque chose contre son genie...*'[12] We are beginning to get here something that resembles a more modern understanding of genius as not just a natural inclination or talent, but a *special* talent – a *vaste génie*, a *puissant génie*. But note that genius in this definition is still an object of the individual, something one *has* rather than something one *is*. I have a genius: a spirit, or an angel or a natural inclination. I am not a genius.

That is where the second edition, the 1718 edition, of the Dictionary of the Académie française is particularly revealing. It includes all of the definitions that I have just given from the 1694 edition, with only minor alterations. But it adds this one: 'On dit, qu'Un homme *Est un beau, un grand genie, un genie superieur*, pour dire, qu'*Il a un beau, un grand genie*'.[13] A man *is* a great genius when his genius is great. What one witnesses here is really the birth of a new type of being, who would subsequently play a very significant role in European culture: *the* genius.

The birth was by no means unique to France. In England it came a little earlier, if we can believe the *Spectator*, which observes in 1711 that 'There is no Character more frequently given to a Writer, than that of

---

10. Robert Cawdrey, *A Table alphabetical of hard usual English words* (1604), a facsimile reproduction with an introduction by Robert A. Peters (Gainesville, FL, 1966), p.61 and *Dictionnaire universel, contenant généralement tous les mots français tant vieux que modernes et les termes de toutes les sciences et des arts* (1690), Slatkine reprint edition, 2 vol. (Geneva, 1970), vol.2, np.
11. Edgar Zilsel, *Die Enstehung des Geniebegriffes* (Tübingen, 1926).
12. *Dictionnaire de l'Académie françoise*, vol.1, p.517.
13. *Nouveau dictionnaire de l'Académie françoise*, 2 vol. (Paris, J.-B. Coignard; 1718), vol.1, p.722-23. This was not, it should be stressed, the first such usage. Note, for example, that one finds buried in the third entry of 'genie' in Furetière's 1690 *Dictionnaire universel*, the following usage, 'cet homme est un vaste genie, qui est capable de tout', *Dictionnaire universel*, vol.2, np.

being a Genius'.[14] In Germany, where the term and the notion was originally borrowed from France and England, it comes a little later, in the second half of the eighteenth century, with the literary and philosophic flowering often referred to tellingly as the *Geniezeit*.[15] But giving or taking a few decades on either side, the phenomenon is a general European one.

This is not, in itself, a new discovery or claim. A number of scholars have pointed out the birth of the genius in this period, and the classicist Penelope Murray has edited a fine collection of essays entitled *Genius: the history of an idea*, which makes this point, among others, very nicely.[16] But what these scholars have not done, in my view, is sufficiently explain this shift, explain *why* the genius is born in the eighteenth century and what that birth ultimately meant.[17] That is the question I am wrestling with at the moment, and I think Maistre has something very insightful to say on the matter.

Maistre uses the term *génie* in virtually all of his writings, and in every one of the senses I have sketched for you just now, and a few others as well, speaking for example of 'le génie de l'Orient', or 'le génie Européen' or – like Chateaubriand – of the 'Génie du Christianisime', to signify the particular ethos or spirit of a people or a religion or a culture.[18] He also speaks of Malebranche, in *Les Soirées de Saint-Pétersbourg*, of 'a flash of genius', 'cet éclair de génie',[19] or the 'coup-d'oeil d'aigle' and 'l'impétuosité créatrice' of the 'génie vigoureux' of Victor Amadeus II, as a way to indicate inspiration, epiphany, a piercing thought or capacity for brilliance.[20] And, finally, he uses genius in the new eighteenth-century sense of a specially gifted or talented individual – the genius – and in fact he is surprisingly liberal in his usage of the epithet, speaking not only of someone like Bossuet as a genius, as we might expect, but also

---

14. Joseph Addison, *Spectator* 160 (3 September 1711).
15. See the rich article 'Genie', in the *Historisches Wörterbuch der Philosophie*, ed. Joachim Ritter, 13 vol. (Basel, 1971-2007), vol.3, p.279-309.
16. Penelope Murray, ed., *Genius: the history of an idea* (Oxford, 1989). G. Matore and A. J. Greimas, 'La Naissance du "génie" au dix-huitième siècle: étude lexicologique', *Le Français moderne* 25 (1957), p.256-72.
17. The most probing discussion of the matter to date may be found in John Hope Mason's rich and insightful *The Value of creativity: the origins and emergence of a modern belief* (Aldershot, 2003). See also Peter Bürger, *Überlegungen zur historisch-soziologischen Erklärung der Genie-Ästhetik im 18. Jahrhundert* (Heidelberg, 1984).
18. See, for example, Maistre, *Du Pape*, ed. by Jacques Lovie and Joannès Chetail (Geneva, 1966), p.327.
19. Maistre, *Les Soirées de Saint-Pétersbourg: Entretiens sur le gouvernement temporel de la Providence*, in Glaudes (ed.), *Maistre: Œuvres*, p.732.
20. Joseph de Maistre, *Quatrième lettre d'un royaliste savoisien*, in *OC*, vol. 7, p.174.

of Bacon and Rousseau, Locke, and even Robespierre, an evil genius, a man in possession of 'un génie infernal'.

But what does Maistre really mean when he calls someone a genius, or when he describes him as *un homme de génie*, in possession of this powerful force? He gives us the fullest treatment of the subject in the second chapter of *L'Examen de la philosophie de Bacon*:

> Fénelon a dit une chose remarquable sur l'attrait divin. *Il ne se prouve point*, dit-il, *par des mouvements si marqués qu'ils portent avec eux la certitude qu'ils sont divins*. Et il ajoute qu'on ne le possède point, lorsqu'on se dit à soi-même: *Oui! c'est par mouvement que j'agis*. (*Œuvres spirit.* tom IV, lettre CLXII, p.155, 166 d l'édit. in-12)
>
> Il y a un grand analogue entre la grâce et le génie; car le *génie* est une *grâce*. Le véritable homme de génie est celui qui agit *par mouvement* ou par impulsion, sans jamais se contempler, et sans jamais se dire: *Oui! c'est par mouvement que j'agis.*[21]

He goes on later in the chapter to speak again of 'l'analogie de la grâce et du génie, qui est une grâce'.[22] And he speaks elsewhere, in other writings, of genius in very similar terms, noting for example, in *De l'Eglise gallicane*, in the context of a discussion of Condé, that 'Le génie ne SORT d'aucune école; il ne s'acquiert nulle parte et se développe partout: comme il ne reconnait point de maître, il ne doit remercier que la Providence'.[23]

So genius cannot be taught, it is often unconscious even to the possessor, and it is conferred divinely. The first thing one might say about this is that it sounds rather familiar. It is true that in certain respects Maistre's thinking about genius merely repeats eighteenth- and early nineteenth-century commonplaces. The idea, for example, that the man of creative brilliance or deep insight is divinely inspired is a very old one, tracing back at least to Plato: in dialogues like the *Ion* and the *Symposium* where Plato speaks of the 'divine furor' or the '*furor poeticus*', as his Latin translators called it, a notion that is revived and Christianised in the Renaissance by people like Marsilio Ficino, who makes much of the divinely inspired artist, seized by the frenzy or ecstasy of God, his creativity literally breathed into him by divine *afflatus* or breath. And that continues to be quite a familiar notion well into the seventeenth and eighteenth centuries, where the *afflatus*, interestingly, is often likened to 'enthusiasm'.

Similarly, the idea that genius is natural – unlettered or unschooled – is hardly original to Maistre. It comes to prominence in the late seven-

21. Maistre, *OC*, vol.6, p.54.
22. Maistre, *OC*, vol.6, p.58.
23. Maistre, *De l'Eglise gallicane dans son rapport avec le souverain pontife*, in *OC*, vol.3, p.34.

teenth and eighteenth centuries and gradually wins out – in England and
Germany especially, but in due course in France as well – over concep-
tions of genius that place a greater emphasis on cultivation, training, on
learned technique, on taste or *goût*. Addison calls the latter 'artful genius'
or 'imitative genius', a 'second class of Genius', as opposed to the 'first
class', the natural genius, who by 'mere Strength of natural Parts, and
without any Assistance of Art or Learning', produces works that are the
'delight of their own Times and the Wonder of Posterity'.[24] It is this
conception that gains prominence and leads to the cult of original or
natural genius in the eighteenth century around people like Pindar and
Homer and Shakespeare – all deemed to be men without formal learning
or training, who are 'prodigies of mankind', through force of their nature
alone. The emphasis here is on one's given nature, one's *ingenium*, and
one might argue that there is a different genealogy at work, tracing to
Aristotle, by way of Longinus, whereas the idea of divine inspiration
traces to Plato, a distinction that the musicologist Peter Kivy describes as
the difference between the 'possessor and the possessed' in a nice little
book of that name.[25] There is certainly something to that, though I would
want to insist that even in his natural guise, the genius could still lay claim
to a divine calling or function, for even if his power was not thought of as
directly infused via inspiration, it could be understood as divinely
conferred by birth. So, for example, a proponent of natural genius like
Edward Young can describe genius in his *Conjectures on original composition*
of 1759 as 'the god within', a sort of modern gloss on Ovid, who calls
*Genius* 'deus in nobis', a force, Young reckons, to be worshipped and
honored and reverenced.[26]

And that, in a word, is my point. That genius as both power and person
in the eighteenth century continued to serve a divine function and role,
even – and perhaps especially – when that role is not explicitly
acknowledged as such. Voltaire, in his article on genius and genii in
the *Philosophical dictionary*, for example, observes 'Je n'ai jamais vu de
génie; aucun homme de ma connaissance n'en a vu'. He is speaking of
angels and tutelary spirits, and adds, 'je ne crois donc pas une chose dont
il n'y a pas la moindre preuve'.[27] If seeing was believing, then Enlightened
men and women in the eighteenth century simply did not believe, and
were often pat in their dismissals of a whole host of mediators that had
served human beings in the West for thousands of years as companions,

24. Addison, *Spectator* 160 (3 September 1711).
25. Peter Kivy, *The Possessor and the possessed: Handel, Mozart, Beethoven and the idea of musical genius* (New Haven, CT, 2001), p.26.
26. Edward Young, *Conjectures on original composition in a letter to the author of Sir Charles Grandison* (London; A. Millar, 1759).
27. Voltaire, 'Génies', in *Dictionnaire philosophique* (Paris, 1838), p.539.

intercessors to the divine, messengers and translators to the gods. They ridiculed the cult of the saints, they did away with demons and angels, both good and bad, and they scoffed at genii in all forms. If we are to believe Jonathan Israel, a good many of them did away with God as well.[28] I am not so sure that the numbers are as great as Israel would have it, though I do think it is clear that even for those, the great majority, like Voltaire, who continued to believe in a Creator of some kind, God was nonetheless increasingly remote, distant, withdrawn. And that, as Marcel Gauchet has argued forcefully in *The Disenchantment of the world*, created an opening, a space for a new type of agency in a more autonomous and malleable universe in which, as Gauchet puts it, the 'human community is left to itself'.[29]

What I would like to suggest – and what I think Maistre intuited and understood – is that this same withdrawal created a space in which a new type of mediator could step to take up, or if you prefer, usurp, some of the essential functions of those that were being swept away. Human beings had never, in the history of the world, lived without mediators to the divine, without spiritual companions of one sort or another, and I do not think they were entirely ready to do so now, whatever they might say to the contrary. To live in a world alone with a distant God, or alone altogether was, after all, lonely, and it should hardly surprise us that men and women who scoffed at the genii might look for a genius of a new kind. That figure, I am suggesting, was *the* genius, whose incarnation and apotheosis in the eighteenth century can be understood as an instance of what Gauchet has called the 'religious after religion'.[30] In effect, the genii became the genius.

Maistre understood this, understood the Promethean transfer of sacrality by which men were robbing the gods and God of their powers, expropriating them for themselves. And so, while on the one hand he speaks of genius in the language of his time, he also possesses an insight, a prophetic one, that escaped many of his contemporaries. For if the man of genius was a man who was filled with grace – and I should stress that despite this long tradition of divine fury, I am not aware of anyone else, least of all a Catholic, who refers to genius specifically as grace – if a man of genius is filled with grace, he is, in effect, a kind of saint who, like the saints and prophets and genii of old, serves as a companion and inter-

---

28. Jonathan Israel, *Radical Enlightenment: philosophy and the making of modernity* (Oxford, 2001) and *Enlightenment contested: philosophy, modernity, and the emancipation of man 1670-1752* (Oxford, 2006).
29. Marcel Gauchet, *The Disenchantment of the world: a political history of religion*, trans. Oscar Burge (Princeton, NJ, 1997), p.159.
30. Gauchet, *Disenchantment of the world*, p.200-207.

cessor, a messenger and translator of the sacred world.[31] That may seem a strong claim, but it becomes less so when we think for a moment of the pantheonisation of Voltaire or Rousseau, or indeed of the peculiar cult of the relics of geniuses: from Voltaire's heart, Marat's body or Schiller's skull to – purportedly at least – Napoleon's penis.[32] Now of course Maistre himself hardly saw these men or their various preserved appendages as saintly; he saw them rather as idols and the worship of them as idolatry. They were, yes, imbued with genius, but they had perversely squandered their gifts in their 'insurrection contre Dieu', a phrase he uses in the *Essai sur le principe générateur* in pointing out that 'Les hommes de ce siècle ont prostitué le génie à l'irréligion, et, suivant l'expression admirable de Saint Louis mourant, ILS ONT GUERROYÉ DIEU DE SES DONS'.[33] They had, in effect, like fallen angels, converted their grace to diabolical power.

Now Maistre was clear, in his own estimation, as to who were the sinners and who were the saints, the fallen geniuses and the truly holy ones, though he does acknowledge in *De la Souveraineté* that 'Ces mots de *talent* et de *génie* nous trompent tous les jours; souvent ces qualités ne sont pas où nous croyons les voir, et souvent aussi elles appartiennent à des hommes dangereux'.[34] And therein lies the rub: one man's saint was another man's sinner. One's man good genius, another man's pretender. There was a danger, in short, to ascribing genius to mortal men.

It needs to be stressed that Maistre allows himself on occasion to yearn for one of these human saviors – the genius – who will make us right in the world, with God and with ourselves. There will come a time, he hopes out loud in the *Les Soirées de Saint-Pétersbourg*, when 'l'affinité naturelle de la religion et de la science les réunisse dans la tête d'un seul homme de génie: l'apparition de cet homme ne saurait être éloignée, et peut-être même existe-t-il déjà. Celui-là sera fameux, et mettra fin au XVIIIᵉ siècle qui dure toujours; car les siècles intellectuels ne se règlent pas sur le calendrier comme les *siècles* proprement dits'.[35] There are other such

31. There is, however, an older tradition in Renaissance and neo-classical aesthetics of associating genius with an artist's grace and the mysterious 'je ne sais quoi' that confers beauty. On these themes, see Annie Becq, *Genèse de l'esthétique française moderne: de la raison classique à l'imagination créatrice 1680-1814*, 2 vol. (Pisa, 1984), vol.1, p.97-114, and M. H. Abrams, *The Mirror and the lamp: romantic theory and the critical tradition* (Oxford, 1953), p.193-95.

32. On the reliquary interest in the brains of geniuses, see Michael Hagner, *Geniale Gehirne: Zur Geschichte der Elitegehirnforschung* (Munich, 2007).

33. Maistre, *Essai sur le principe générateur* in Glaudes (ed.), *Maistre: Œuvres*, p.399.

34. Maistre, *De la Souveraineté du peuple: un anti-contrat social*, ed. Jean-Louis Darcel (Paris, 1992), p.228.

35. Maistre, *Les Soirées de Saint-Pétersbourg* in Glaudes (ed.), *Maistre: Œuvres*, p.765.

passages, and they move from the intellectual to the political. Listen to
how he speaks of the 'veritable elect', the founder of a nation in *De la
Souveraineté*:

> L'instituteur d'un peuple est précisément cette main habile; doué d'une
> pénétration extraordinaire, ou, ce qui est plus probable, d'un instinct
> infaillible (car souvent le génie ne se rend pas compte de ce qu'il opère, et
> c'est en quoi surtout il diffère de l'esprit), il devine ces forces et ces qualités
> occultes qui forment le caractère de sa nation; il devine les moyens de les
> féconder, de les mettre en action et d'en tirer le plus grand parti possible. On
> ne le voit jamais écrire ni argumenter: sa manière tient de l'inspiration; et si
> quelquefois il prend la plume, ce n'est pas pour disserter, c'est pour
> ordonner.[36]

This is a wistful, admiring portrait, which as Carolina Armenteros has
pointed out, bears an interesting resemblance to Rousseau's legislator.
And yet, as she also stresses, Maistre's genius here is a man of the past ('a
man of primitive times destined to fade with time') – a founder, a father,
who established nations, and hence order, long ago.[37] He is not a man of
the future, and though Maistre perhaps flirts at times with a certain
longing for a return of this human vehicle of God's will, I think that for
the most part he is, on the contrary, sensitive to the tremendous danger
of investing human beings with this kind of power. The genius, this
modern creation, this idol, who assumed the power of gods to wage war
on God, was a man to be feared. It may be true, as Maistre says famously
in the *Considérations sur la France*, that 'le sang est l'engrais de cette plante
qu'on appelle génie'.[38] But whatever else it may bring, war had given
birth to the *génie infernal* of Robespierre, and it was not at all clear that a
more saintly genius, a man who would completely overthrow the eighteenth century, stood on the horizon.

Coleridge, in the *Biographia literaria*, points out that 'In times of
tumult', men of what he calls '*commanding genius*' 'are destined to come
forth as the shaping spirit of Ruin, to destroy the wisdom of ages in order
to substitute the fancies of a day, and to change kings and kingdoms, as
the wind shifts and shapes the clouds'.[39] What I am suggesting is that
Maistre saw something similar on the horizon of modernity, and in so far
as the modern genius was its herald and prophet – its false god – the
picture was not at all encouraging. For the modern genius – full of
reckless power – was a human creation, and when human beings invested
men with the power of gods, they could do terrible things. The Revol-

---

36.  Maistre in Darcel (ed.), *De la Souveraineté du peuple*, p.122.
37.  Armenteros, 'Parabolas and the fate of nations', p.235.
38.  Maistre, *Considérations sur la France*, in Glaudes (ed.), *Maistre: Œuvres*, p.217.
39.  Samuel Coleridge, *Biographia literaria*, ed. J. Shawcross, 2 vol. (Oxford, 1907), vol.1, p.15.

ution, after all, in Maistre's estimation, *c'était la faute à Voltaire*. Perhaps others would do worse.

Let me close, on that note, with one final thought. Careful scholars have devoted a good deal of energy to debunking Isaiah Berlin's infamous and unjust link between Maistre and fascism. But let me just hazard that, at least where genius is concerned, we might consider re-establishing it, although in a very different way.

As early as 1920, in a speech delivered on 27 April of that year, Hitler insisted that Germany needed a 'dictator who is a genius', and his writings and speeches from that point on are filled with allusions to genius.[40] Thus, in *Mein Kampf* (1924), Hitler observes in one of his many passages devoted to genius that although '[t]rue genius is always inborn and never cultivated, let alone learned', it nonetheless takes a 'special cause' to summon it forth. That cause, it will come as little surprise, was war.

> It nearly always takes some stimulus to bring the genius on the scene. The hammer-stroke of Fate which throws one man to the ground suddenly strikes steel in another, and when the shell of everyday life is broken, the previously hidden kernel lies open before the eyes of the astonished world. The world then resists and does not want to believe [that it now beholds] a very different being.[41]

That Hitler considered himself to be such a being is fairly clear. Others certainly did. Georg Schott's *Das Volksbuch vom Hitler*, which appeared in the same year as *Mein Kampf*, includes a chapter heading, 'the genius', as well as others on 'the prophetic person', the 'religious person' and the 'man of will'.[42] Goebbels hailed Hitler shortly after their first meeting as a 'genius' and he repeated the claim to his death, sustaining Hitler's own view that, as he explained in a speech in the mid 1920s, the people formed a pyramid with 'the great man, the genius' at its head. 'The people are for the statesman what stone is for the sculptor', Goebbels observed chillingly in his novel *Michael* in 1931. He added shortly thereafter that *Genies verbrauchen Menschen. Das ist nun einmal so.* 'Geniuses use up people, that is just the way it is'.[43] Maistre might well have agreed that God made use of people in this way, sculpting them for his greater ends.

---

40. Cited in Ian Kershaw, *Hitler, 1889-1936: hubris* (New York, 2000), p.151.

41. Adolf Hitler, *Mein Kampf*, trans. Ralph Mannheim (London, 1969), p.266. The critical discussion occurs in vol.1, ch.9, 'Nation and race'. I have consulted the German edition for comparison. *Mein Kampf: Entstehung, Aufbau, Stil, Änderungen, Quellen, Quellenwert, kommentierte Auszüge*, ed. Werner Masser (Munich, Esslingen, 1966).

42. Georg Schott, *Das Volksbuch vom Hitler* (Munich, 1924).

43. Goebbels cited in Jochen Schmidt, *Die Geschichte des Genie-Gedankens in der deutschen Literatur, Philosophie und Politik 1750-1945*, 2 vol. (Heidelberg, 2004), vol.2, p.207.

But that mere mortals should usurp that divine role he would have denied. In this respect, Maistre was a prophet not of fascism, but of the terrible danger of investing mortals who would not bow down to the Lord, with power that was not rightfully theirs, the power of God.

# 'This babe-in-arms': Joseph de Maistre's critique of America

## JOSEPH EATON

Though Maistre's comments on the New World are scattered throughout his works, his views on America are noteworthy for the insights they provide into his broader political philosophy and as a portent of later European anti-Americanism. Maistre's critique of the fledgeling American republic serves as a lens to understand the use of the New World in European polemics. Denial of America's viability was a necessary component of Maistre's critique of the French Revolution and republicanism.

Maistre's critique of America combined severe Christian pessimism,[1] echoes of the Enlightenment critique of America, and revulsion of the American experiment with republicanism. One can divide Maistre's commentary on America into two parts: remarks on indigenous peoples throughout the Americas, and observations on the fledgeling North American republic.[2] According to Maistre, both America's natives and the United States' experiment in representative government were doomed – the Indians from some unknown yet terrible crime committed by an ancient chieftain, the European Americans through their audacious attempts at building some components of their national government from scratch.

## America's natives

Maistre's portrait of America's natives refocused the eighteenth-century quarrel on the New World around his own perceptions regarding the causes for the regression of European civilisation. Enlightenment naturalists had concluded from Europe's mostly disastrous encounter with

1. For an account of Maistre's Christian thought, including its more Pelagian aspects, see Douglas Hedley's article in this volume, 'Enigmatic images of an invisible world: sacrifice, suffering and theodicy in Joseph de Maistre'.
2. Having no first-hand experience in America did not disqualify Maistre from speaking on the subject but instead gave him a claim to objectivity. As he explained of his second-hand expertise of France, 'Parfaitement étranger à la France, que je n'ai jamais vue, et ne pouvant rien attendre de son Roi, que je ne connaîtrai jamais, si j'avance des erreurs, les Français peuvent au moins les lire sans colère, comme des erreurs entièrement désintéressées'. Maistre, *Considérations sur la France* in Glaudes (ed.), *Maistre: Œuvres*, p.253.

the Americas that the New World was a mistake; the degeneracy of animals and humans, a reduction in the size and fertility of both and corresponding abundance of poisonous plant and animal life, were indicators of a harsh climate. The French naturalist Georges-Louis Leclerc, the Comte de Buffon (1707-1788), explained that, in America, 'La Nature vivante y est [...] beaucoup moins agissante, beaucoup moins variée, et nous pouvons même dire beaucoup moins forte. [...] Tous les animaux qui ont été transportés d'Europe en Amérique, comme les chevaux, les ânes, les bœufs, les brebis, les chèvres, les cochons, les chiens, etc. tous ces animaux, dis-je, y sont devenus plus petits'.[3]

According to Maistre's schema, American degeneracy was due to causes other than climate. He instead posited a more sinister agent for the New World's inferiority; some long forgotten chieftain had brought horrific consequences upon the indigenous Americans by some terrible sin.[4] Maistre replaced Buffon's tableau expressing the relative slightness of animals with a damning moral critique of New World savagery. Rather than being primitive, the Indians were ancient, separated from the mainstream civilisation by a second dose of Original Sin. The vagabond hordes of the Americas were a brutalised people. America was not the Eden thought by European republicans and radicals but rather a Bosch-like landscape of sin and suffering. America's vast reaches 'recèlent encore une foule de hordes sauvages si étrangères au grand bienfait [de la révélation], qu'on serait porté à croire qu'elles en sont exclues par la nature en vertu de quelque anathème primitif et inexplicable'.[5] Of Rousseau's natural man, Maistre wrote, 'Tout homme moral et sensible est révolté par l'abrutissement et par la cruauté de ces sauvages d'Amérique dont Rousseau ose nous vanter l'existence heureuse'.[6]

Maistre's shift from climatic causes to moral causes is consistent with his broader view of historical causation, particularly with regard to Europe's moral catastrophes. Moral degeneration destroyed a race in the Americas, a reminder of the terrible precipitants of the Enlightenment and French Revolution. Maistre blamed America's decline on a single, unknown ruler, not surprising considering his emphasis on biography and the dominance of great men. The eighteenth century had asked if America was a 'mistake'; to Maistre, America was worse than

---

3.   Georges-Louis Leclerc, Comte de Buffon, *Histoire naturelle, générale et particulière, avec la description du cabinet du roi*, 36 vol. (Paris, l'Imprimerie royale, 1749), vol.9, p.86, 103.

4.   Though Maistre did cite Buffon as an authority, Maistre's quotation of eighteenth-century naturalists was selective. Maistre, for example, remarked that 'Buffon a fort bien prouvé qu'une grande partie des animaux est destinée à mourir de mort violente. Il aurait pu, suivant les apparences, étendre sa démonstration à l'homme; mais on peut s'en rapporter aux faits'. *Considérations sur la France*, p.216.

5.   Maistre, *Les Soirées de Saint-Pétersbourg* in *Maistre: Œuvres*, p.766.

6.   Maistre, *De l'Etat de nature*, ed. Yannis Constantinidès (Paris, 2008), p.16.

a mistake.[7] The people of an entire continent had degenerated into an inferior race.

One should not take Maistre's accusations against the indigenous peoples of America literally but instead consider his broader purposes. Maistre's racism was polemical, not systematic. The Americas were a choice battleground for European controversies, the naturalists and Rousseauian believers in the idea of the noble savage being the prime targets of Maistre's comments. The idea that a horrific sin, rather than climate, was the cause of American degeneracy undermined the scientific pride of the natural scientists and the political fantasies of the primitivists. In attacking America's natives, Maistre cast doubt on notions of the goodness of man and reminded that sin could contaminate an entire continent. He wrote about America while thinking about Europe.

A revisionist reading of Maistre allows for a more complex view of his opinions of America's natives. In her recent work, *The More moderate side of Joseph de Maistre* (2005), Cara Camcastle refers to Maistre's defense of American Indian culture in connection with Western impatience with Russia's slow embrace of science. Camcastle explains that Maistre believed that both America's natives and the Russians should enjoy a separate path from that of Western Europe. In Russia's case, rapid adoption of modern science might have its disadvantages; reference to the distinctiveness of American cultures helped to make that point.[8] Camcastle sees Maistre's comments on Russia and indigenous Americans as evidence of a 'pluralistic approach to politics'.[9] Maistre was capable of adding examples from non-Western civilisations to his repertoire in order to make valuable points regarding the shortcomings of contemporary Europe, though his purpose most often had less to do with showing the relativity of civilisations than the arrogance of his intellectual opponents.

America's natives were particularly violent, according to Maistre, but perhaps that was not such a bad thing in his violence-strewn world. The savages had no revealed religion but were no more violent than the French revolutionaries who had brazenly forsaken Christianity. The French had shown 'la barbarie savante, l'atrocité systématique, la corruption calculée, et surtout l'irréligion'.[10] Indians, in their relative

---

7.  Henry Steele Commager and Elmo Giordanetti, *Was America a mistake?* (Columbia, SC, 1968).

8.  Camcastle, *The More moderate side*, p.126-27.

9.  Camcastle, *The More moderate side*, p.126. I see Maistre's occasional tolerance of America's natives, which, according to Camcastle includes an endorsement of cannibalism, as ammunition for debates about Europe.

10. Maistre, *Considérations sur la France* in Glaudes (ed.), *Maistre: Œuvres*, p.225.

innocence, could hardly be as guilty as the French who had deserted revealed religion. Their situation left America's natives less culpable for their violent tendencies. Maistre parallelled the bloodbath of the French Revolution with the violence of American Indians:

> Mais nous qui pâlissons d'horreur à la seule idée de sacrifices humains et de l'anthropophagie, comment pourrions-nous être tout à la fois assez aveugles et assez ingrats pour ne pas reconnaître que nous ne devons ces sentiments qu'à la *loi d'amour* qui a veillé sur notre berceau? Une illustre nation, parvenue au dernier degré de la civilisation et de l'urbanité, osa naguère, dans un accès de délire dont l'histoire ne présente pas un autre exemple, suspendre formellement cette loi: que vîmes-nous? en un clin d'œil, les mœurs des Iroquois et des Algonquins; les saintes lois de l'humanité foulées aux pieds; le sang innocent couvrant les échafauds qui couvraient la France; des hommes frisant et poudrant des têtes sanglantes, et la bouche même de femmes souillée de sang humain.
>
> Voila l'homme *naturel*! ce n'est pas qu'il ne porte en lui-même les germes inextinguibles de la vérité et de la vertu: les droits de sa naissance sont imprescriptibles; mais sans une fécondation divine, ces germes n'écloront jamais, ou ne produiront que des êtres équivoques et malsains.
>
> Il est temps de tirer des faits historiques les plus incontestables une conclusion qui ne l'est pas moins.
>
> Nous savons par une expérience de quarante siècles *que partout où le vrai Dieu ne sera pas connu et servi, en vertu d'une révélation expresse, l'homme immolera toujours l'homme, et souvent le dévorera.*[11]

Maistre measured the savagery of America's natives relative to the declension of European civilisation. Such comparisons allowed Maistre to emphasise the brutality of the French Revolution. Whether the subject was the false opinions of Rousseau, the relativity of Russian civilisation or the unique guilt of French radicalism, Maistre's comments about American natives were really an extension of his opinions on post-1789 Europe. Maistre's focus was Europe's inhumanity, not America.

Maistre only saw one vehicle to civilise/humanise a savage people – the Church: 'Jamais les nations n'ont été civilisées que par la religion. Aucun autre instrument connu n'a de prise sur l'homme sauvage'. Of secular efforts to change America, Maistre wrote, 'Depuis trois siècles nous sommes là avec nos lois, nos arts, nos sciences, notre civilisation, notre commerce et notre luxe: qu'avons-nous gagné sur l'état sauvage? Rien. Nous détruisons ces malheureux avec le fer et l'eau-de-vie'. The *philosophe* admirers of the American savages had failed Europeans and Indians alike: 'Ils ont composé de beaux livres pour prouver que le sauvage était l'homme *naturel*, et que nous ne pouvions souhaiter rien de plus heureux

---

11. Maistre, *Eclaircissement sur les sacrifices* in Glaudes (ed.), *Maistre: Œuvres*, p.823-24.

que de lui ressembler'.[12] By a twist of interpretation, Maistre had connected New World violence with the carnage in Europe and made the Church the solitary agent for the salvation of the New World.

The *philosophes* had lamented the consequences of America's discovery – imperialistic wars, syphilis, and the vast expansion of slavery. Maistre shifted the debate over the New World, decrying the use of America in philosophical debates to prove the inherent goodness of man while making the American Revolution a catalyst for Europe's disasters. Recent history was a better guide to the real nature of humankind than were European fantasies about America's natives, or even North America's republicans.

## The dangerous new republic

While America's natives embodied an old, degenerate civilisation, North America's republicans were representatives of a nation that might fail to survive to full maturity. Maistre linked the American and French revolutions, making the former a cause for the European cataclysm. The thirteen British North American colonies shared some of the blame for the French Revolution: 'Après quinze ans de repos, la révolution d'Amérique entraîna de nouveau la France dans une guerre dont toute la sagesse humaine ne pouvait prévoir les conséquences. On signe la paix en 1782; sept ans après, la révolution commence; elle dure encore; et peut-être que dans ce moment elle a coûté trois millions d'hommes à la France'.[13]

Maistre brought up the subject of America within a polemic regarding Europe's political situation in the *Considérations sur la France*. He asked, 'La république française peut-elle durer?' His answer was a resounding 'NON!' Maistre gave a memorable rejoinder to those who thought otherwise: 'Ainsi, il n'y a rien de nouveau, et la grande république est impossible, parce qu'il n'y a jamais eu de grande république'. Maistre dismissed the notion of representative government entirely: 'Cette représentation est une chose qu'on n'a jamais vue, et qui ne réussira jamais'.[14]

Having linked the Atlantic revolutions, Maistre needed to answer

---

12. Maistre, *Essai sur le principe générateur*, in Glaudes (ed.), *Maistre: Œuvres*, p.384. Maistre compared the Jesuits with the god who taught agriculture to the Egyptians: '*A L'OSIRIS CHRÉTIEN dont les envoyés ont parcouru la terre pour arracher les hommes à la misère, à l'abrutissement et à la férocité, en leur enseignant l'agriculture, en leur donnant des lois, en leur apprenant à connaître et à servir Dieu, NON PAR LA FORCE DES ARMES [...], mais par la douce persuasion, les chants moraux, ET LA PUISSANCE DES HYMNES, en sorte qu'on les crut des Anges*'. *Essai sur le principe générateur*, p.385.

13. Maistre, *Considérations sur la France* in Glaudes (ed.), *Maistre: Œuvres*, p.213.

14. Maistre, *Considérations sur la France* in Glaudes (ed.), *Maistre: Œuvres*, p.219-20, 222.

those in Europe who explained the United States to be a feasible model for republican government. In a short paragraph, he rejected America as an example: 'On nous cite l'Amérique: je ne connais rien de si impatientant que les louanges décernées à cet enfant au maillot: laissez-le grandir'.[15] Though Maistre did not elaborate, he showed an impatience for positive views of the United States.

A selective reading of some of Maistre's comments on the United States allows the infant New Republic some chance for survival. Like many French observers of the new republic, Maistre found English traits in America. In doing so, he gave American political practice a firmer grounding. Select passages within the *Considérations sur la France* have Burkean qualities. Maistre argues that, in proclaiming independence, Americans were defending their historic rights as Englishmen. In a chapter entitled 'La république française peut-elle durer?', Maistre alluded to the French revolutionaries' attempt at 'la représentation *perfectionnée*'.[16] To Maistre, the French experiment at republicanism and popular sovereignty was perfectly radical (and unhistorical). In dismissing the United States as a viable example of a republic with representative government, Maistre de-radicalises America; America's practice of ancient political habits did not provide an example to prove the viability of 'ce système chimérique de délibération et de construction politique par des raisonnements antérieurs'.[17] America was rather English, and ordinary.

This impulse to see America as an extension of England coexists with other comments by Maistre that indicated a strong republican foundation in the United States. Maistre had made a similar argument a few years earlier (*Fragments sur la France*, 1794) where he argued that American revolutionaries had not been innovators. Richard Lebrun has pointed to an even more positive view of America as a refuge for freedom in a September 1775 work, the *Eloge de Victor-Amédée III*: 'La liberté, insultée en Europe, a pris son vol vers un autre hémisphère; elle plane sur les glaces du Canada, elle arme le paisible Pensylvanien; et du milieu de Philadelphie elle crie aux Anglais: pourquoi m'avez-vous outragée, vous qui vous vantez de n'être grands que par moi?'[18] As Charles Lombard explained of Maistre's views, 'Basic institutions in America remained intact and only the executive was changed. While the federal system had yet to be fully evaluated Maistre had to credit

15. Maistre, *Considérations sur la France* in Glaudes (ed.), *Maistre: Œuvres*, p.222.
16. Maistre, *Considérations sur la France* in Glaudes (ed.), *Maistre: Œuvres*, p.222.
17. Maistre, *Considérations sur la France* in Glaudes (ed.), *Maistre: Œuvres*, p.241.
18. As quoted in Triomphe, *Maistre: étude*, p.98. Events in Europe, post-1789, required a tougher view of the American republic. The United States could not become an archetype for the reforms suggested by European republicanism.

the Americans with far more restraint than their counterparts in France'.[19]

In giving American republican political practice a historical and less abstract foundation, Maistre portrays the fledgeling republic as less monarchical and more democratic in spirit than the Mother Country. Though Maistre noted that the time had not yet come to cite the United States as an example, he would provide a few illustrations of America's unique republican nature:

1. L'Amérique anglaise avait un Roi, mais ne le voyait pas: la splendeur de la monarchie lui était étrangère, et le souverain était pour elle comme une espèce de puissance surnaturelle, qui ne tombe pas sous les sens.
2. Elle possédait l'élément démocratique qui existe dans la constitution de la métropole.
3. Elle possédait de plus ceux qui furent portés chez elle par une foule de ses premiers colons nés au milieu des troubles religieux et politiques, et presque tous esprits républicains.
4. Avec ces éléments, et sur le plan des trois pouvoirs qu'ils tenaient de leurs ancêtres, les Américains ont bâti, et n'ont pas fait table rase, comme les Français.[20]

America, though republican, was conservative in its political practices. The United States was less experimental, less radical than the French attempt at republicanism. Whether Maistre portrayed America as English or republican, he consistently argued that the United States was a unique case with its own complexities, inapplicable as a model for France.

Maistre's comments foreshadowed the second chapter of Alexis de Tocqueville's *De la Démocratie en Amérique* (1835). Like Maistre, Tocqueville looked to early colonial history to find the character of the United States:

Examinez l'enfant jusque dans les bras de sa mère; voyez le monde extérieur se refléter pour la première fois sur le miroir encore obscur de son intelligence; contemplez les premiers exemples qui frappent ses regards; écoutez les premières paroles qui éveillent chez lui les puissances endormies de la pensée; assistez enfin aux premières luttes qu'il a à soutenir; et alors seulement vous comprendrez d'où viennent les préjugés, les habitudes et les passions qui vont dominer sa vie. L'homme est pour ainsi dire tout entier dans les langes de son berceau.[21]

19. Charles M. Lombard, *Joseph de Maistre* (Boston, MA, 1976), p.31.
20. Maistre, *Considérations sur la France* in Glaudes (ed.), *Maistre: Œuvres*, p.241.
21. Alexis de Tocqueville, *De la Démocratie en Amérique* (Paris, 1835), p.41-2.

Again, one sees the infant analogy. By Tocqueville's account, the American baby had grown into an adolescent harbinger of the Atlantic democratic revolution.

Both Maistre and Tocqueville believed that the mainstream of America's political heritage represented only a slice of that of Britain. In granting America a special republican bent, what Tocqueville described as propitious circumstances, Maistre distanced the United States further from French republicanism. To Tocqueville, America's democratic nature was providential, a harbinger for Europe; for Maistre, this democratic tendency made the United States an anomaly amongst nations. If America succeeded, it would be due to its own causes and was no real test of the durability of republicanism.

Having offered praise for America's moderation, Maistre then damned the new United States Constitution: 'Tout ce qu'il y a de véritablement nouveau dans leur constitution, tout ce qui résulte de la délibération commune, est la chose du monde la plus fragile; on ne saurait réunir plus de symptômes de faiblesse et de caducité'.[22] The last three decades of the eighteenth century was an era of constitution drafting, with the constitutions of even some of the American states having achieved some notoriety in Europe. Maistre was undoubtedly responding to this constitutional Americophilia, particularly the blatant political materialism of Thomas Paine. Paine bragged about the utility of a written constitution as a guide for Pennsylvanian legislators: 'Every member of the government had a copy; and nothing was more common, when any debate arose on the principle of a bill, or on the extent of any species of authority, than for the members to take the printed constitution out of their pocket, and read the chapter with which such matter in debate was connected'.[23] To Maistre, constitution drafting was no substitute for the wisdom of ages. He was intrigued by the unwritten nature of the English constitution:

> Si l'on s'avisait de faire une loi en Angleterre pour donner une existence constitutionnelle au Conseil privé, et pour régler ensuite et circonscrire rigoureusement ses privilèges et ses attributions, avec les précautions nécessaires pour limiter son influence et l'empêcher d'en abuser, on renverserait l'Etat. La véritable *constitution anglaise* est cet esprit public admirable, unique, infaillible, au-dessus de tout éloge, qui mène tout, qui conserve tout, qui sauve tout. – Ce qui est écrit n'est rien.[24]

America's recent Constitution and Bill of Rights, written and less mysterious, would not provide a similar foundation. The eighteenth century

---

22. Maistre, *Considérations sur la France* in Glaudes (ed.), *Maistre: Œuvres*, p.241.
23. Thomas Paine, *Rights of man* (Stilwell, K.S., 2007), p.94.
24. Maistre, *Essai sur le principe générateur* in Glaudes (ed.), *Maistre: Œuvres*, p.370, 371.

had gone too far in making America an example both in its savage and republican forms. Radicals were wrong to use a 'babe-in-arms' to rally against the established order of things.

Plans for a new federal capital on the Potomac River did not impress Maistre: 'Essentiellement il n'y a rien là qui passe les forces du pouvoir humain; on peut bien bâtir une ville: néanmoins il y a trop de délibér-ation, trop d'humanité dans cette affaire; et l'on pourrait gager mille contre un que la ville ne se bâtira pas, ou qu'elle ne s'appellera pas Washington, ou que le congrès n'y résidera pas'.[25] The proposed capital was a scheme, as was the entire nation.[26] Although at first glance Maistre's prediction seems ridiculous, there was truth to his calculation. The city failed to thrive in any meaningful sense or to rid itself of its nickname – 'city of magnificent distances' – for many decades. The lack of an American metropolis bothered foreign travellers, and many Americans, for at least another generation.[27]

Maistre failed to comment specifically on any important people of late eighteenth-century America. Franklin, Washington, Adams, Jefferson and the other American Founders – Maistre does not mention any of them by name. This omission of Washington seems especially significant considering Maistre's belief in the importance of eminent politicians in building durable government, usually by fiat through the reconciliation of a nation's laws to the reality of preordained societal nature. The United States had no lawgiver or creative genius to give the nation a durable government, no founding Father.[28] The North American repub-lic, like the indigenous tribes of America, was feeble. The United States might not pass the test of time.[29]

Maistre decried America's fragility: 'Ainsi les Etats-Unis d'Amérique ne seraient pas un *Etat* sans le *Congrès* qui les *unit*. Faites disparaître cette

---

25. Maistre, *Considérations sur la France* in Glaudes (ed.), *Maistre: Œuvres*, p.242.
26. Americans did respond to these criticisms of the District of Columbia, the most promi-nent rejoinder probably being David Bailie Warden's *A Chorographical and statistical description of the District of Columbia*, originally published in Paris in 1816.
27. As Richard Lebrun has noted, 'Maistre's prediction was not far off. Washington did become the political capital of the new nation; but unlike Paris or London, it never became a financial, cultural, or industrial capital'. Richard A. Lebrun, 'Introduction' to *Considerations on France*, trans. Richard A. Lebrun (Montreal and London, 1974), p.15. In his copy of the 1797 edition of the *Considérations*, Maistre made a very correct estimation of the District's future progress: 'Washington est une ville plutôt désignée que bâtie. Il lui faut encore cinquante ans pour signifier quelque chose'. Glaudes (ed.), *Maistre: Œuvres*, p.242 n.2, p.945.
28. See Darrin McMahon's article 'The genius of Maistre' in this volume.
29. Maistre's estimation of the uncertainty and fragility of the American experiment is reminiscent of the comments of my colleagues in Taiwan who point to the brevity of American history, a subject too short for study, and the thinness of American culture generally.

assemblée avec son président, l'unité disparaîtra en même temps, et vous n'aurez plus que treize états indépendants, en dépit de la langue et des lois communes'.[30] Though the United States had in fact grown to nineteen states, Maistre's point was clear: America had no organic unity. Crèvecoeur's image of a pluralistic, amalgamated people – 'melted into a new race of men, whose labours and posterity will one day cause great changes in the world' – becomes an incoherent, miscegenational nightmare.[31]

Maistre's comments on the lack of American unity remind of his diatribes against Protestants who, he laments, have 'malheureusement divisé l'Europe' where half of a continent had lost its religion.[32] Though Maistre does not seem to have commented specifically on the religious situation in America, one might compare his condemnation of the United States' lack of organic unity with that of later far-right French Catholic critics of America.[33]

Maistre was dismissive of the chances for American republicanism but did not paint the worst-case, doomsday scenarios as he had with the French Republic. It was not obvious where the Americans stood in what Maistre depicted as the fight to the death between Christianity and *philosophisme*. Though Maistre linked the Atlantic revolutions, he did not explicitly say that the connection was ideological. He did not deify America nor completely vilify her either.

Maistre's comments on America pale in comparison with the harsh terms he used to describe the French Republic: 'Dans quelle page de l'histoire trouve-t-on une aussi grande quantité de vices agissant à la fois sur le même théâtre? Quel assemblage épouvantable de bassesse et de cruauté! Quelle profonde immoralité! Quel oubli de toute pudeur!'[34] Maistre does not accuse Americans of being bloodthirsty Jacobins but just reckless in their fetish for putting their ideas to paper. Questions remained: would the American Revolution have a catastrophic ending? Would the New World become a new altar for the sacrifice of humanity? America's natives suffered because of the sins of an ancient father: would the political innovation of the Founding Fathers doom the United States to a similar fate of eternal misery?

Unlike most Francophone commentators, Maistre did not react to a specific American behavior, for example Jay's Treaty with Britain, which seemed to betray the 1778 Alliance with France. Maistre's criticisms of

---

30. Lovie and Chetail (ed.) *Du Pape*, p.335.
31. J. Hector St John de Crèvecoeur, *Letters from an American farmer*, ed. Susan Manning (Oxford, 1999), p.44.
32. Maistre, *Essai sur le principe générateur* in Glaudes (ed.), *Maistre: Œuvres*, p.378.
33. Philipe Roger, *The American enemy: the history of French Anti-Americanism* (Chicago, 2005).
34. Maistre, *Considérations sur la France* in Glaudes (ed.), *Maistre: Œuvres*, p.224.

the New World's inhabitants were essentialist, damning America's Indians just because they were Indians and descendant of an immoral chief, and critical of America's republicans just because they chose republicanism. Neither would be able to reform. Most importantly, both the New World's natives and republicans had to be wrong in order for Maistre's analysis of recent European history to be right.

In comparison with other Francophone writers, Maistre was by no means alone in depicting the United States in an unfavorable light. Directory era accounts of America were full of 'disappointments and doubts' regarding the New Republic, a 'very French wave of unflattering reports' that were, as an important French critic has noted, important predecessors to Jacksonian-era British accounts.[35] However, there was a qualitative difference in Maistre's denigration of the United States and British criticism.

The most damning British critics were not so denigrating in their assessment of the United States. Even extreme Tory observers such as Thomas Hamilton (*Men and manners in America* (1833)), who saw both class warfare and democratic mediocrity as threats to America's future, were not so damning. According to Tory critics, Americans were country bumpkins who, though fooled by faulty ideas of politics and lacking manners and culture, were still capable of building a great country. To Maistre, America's republicans had set themselves largely outside the mainstream of European civilisation.

If Maistre had not been so quick to doubt America's ability to exist as a republic, he, like most foreign commentators, might have elaborated on American lack of progress in the arts. In the January 1820 issue of the *Edinburgh review*, Sydney Smith asked: 'Who reads an American book?' An honest answer from a Scottish Whig perspective would have been 'no one [...] for now'.[36] It would be decades, perhaps centuries, before Americans could give their efforts to literature and the arts but America *would* advance along recognisable lines of progress. Maistre made no allowance for progress. A later English emigrant to the American West (Illinois) praised the absence of castles in the United States:

> Here are few public buildings worthy of notice. No kings going to open Parliament with gilded coaches and cream-coloured horses. [...] No old castles which beautify the rural scenes of the country. [...] No cathedrals or old Churches to ornament the cities as well as the counties of England. [...] America has none of these costly ornaments or beautiful monuments of

---

35. Roger, *American enemy*, p.37.
36. Sydney Smith, 'Statistical annals of the United States', *Edinburgh review* 33 (January 1820), p.79-80.

oppression. I thank God she has not; and hope she may be exempt from them.[37]

It is probable that Maistre doubted whether Americans could create beautiful castles had they wanted to. Whereas other critics believed that good things would come with material progress, Maistre's America might never mature from its infancy. America's youth becomes a negative. Rather than being void of societal and political ills as America's defenders in Europe claimed, young America was uninteresting and probably doomed.

Though it seems unlikely that Maistre influenced his American contemporaries, one might contrast Maistre with American conservative thinkers of his era.[38] Maistre's criticisms of the durability of the United States resembled contemporary conservative American opinion. Neither the universalism of the Declaration of Independence nor the deliberative mechanisms of the Constitution have a place in Maistre's schema. In the *Federalist papers* (no.11), American conservative leader Alexander Hamilton addressed the quarrel over American nature: 'Men admired as profound philosophers have, in direct terms, attributed to her inhabitants a physical superiority, and have gravely asserted that all animals, and with them the human species, degenerate in America – that even dogs cease to bark after having breathed awhile in our atmosphere'.[39] Little could Hamilton have anticipated Maistre's fierce moral criticisms of the New World and harsh dismissal of the Constitution.

Some aspects of Maistre's commentary would have appealed to American conservatives. If few Americans doubted the desirability of written constitutions, some of them had misgivings concerning the wisdom of creating a new capital from scratch and many more questioned whether the city would ever match Philadelphia, the premier American city. Orestes Brownson, a Catholic convert, led the American discovery of Maistre in the 1840s. The very impossibility of an American republic had been useful to Maistre in his polemics against the *philosophes*; by the mid-nineteenth century, the United States was self-assured enough for Brownson to cite Maistre's writings as a remedy to rampant individualism.[40]

---

37. Richard Flower, *Letters from Lexington and the Illinois* (London, 1819), p.92. In sharp contrast, John Ruskin refused to visit the United States because it lacked castles! Barry Rubin and Judith Colp Rubin, *Hating America: a history* (Oxford, 2004), p.54.
38. An ordinary search of the extensive databases of 'Early American imprints' (Readex) fails to turn up American references to Maistre during his lifetime.
39. *Federalist* no.11, 'The utility of the Union in respect to commercial relations and a navy'.
40. Orestes Brownson, Review of 'Essay on the generative principle of political constitutions', *Brownson's quarterly review* 1 (October 1847).

# Conclusion

Despite his extremely negative observations on America, Maistre was less concerned with constructing a coherent view of the New World than with combating the forces of revolution in the Old World. America was useful in contemporary polemics over the recent European past and future. Maistre's comments regarding indigenous Americans lacked specificity; his comments on the United States were out of date. For his information on the Americas, Maistre depended upon William Robertson's *History of the discovery and settlement of America*, a work that first appeared in 1777. Though Maistre was a vigorous, urbane reader, he did not bother to find the preeminent contemporary sources of information on the New World. Maistre's grand approach to America suited the continuing great debate over the New World in European intellectual life.[41]

Remarks on the impossibility of the proposed new capital and the appalling depiction of indigenous Americans demonstrate the colour and memorable nature of Maistre's writing but should not be isolated outside the substantive themes of his *œuvre*. The hellish landscapes of post-Reformation, post-French Revolution Europe were Maistre's main purview; the New World was only a useful topic in these larger battles. The supposed degeneracy of the original inhabitants of the Americas was a valuable weapon to attack Enlightenment fantasising about the state of nature; the young United States provided a convenient target for disabusing notions of popular sovereignty and republicanism. Cursing America was a means to challenge the republicans, the primitivists and the natural scientists. The Church represented the only civilising force in the New World. Maistre's comments are really about Europe, both in combating the legacy of the French Revolution and increasing the chances for a future rejuvenation of traditional European monarchy.[42]

Maistre's United States was malleable, sometimes moderate and English and sometimes innovative and self-destructive. Though Maistre found many examples in America, some of which appear contradictory, all of his illustrations were consistent with his larger worldview. Lessons pulled from the American example were helpful in polemics about European politics and science. It was Europe, not a 'babe-in-arms', which sustained Maistre's interest.

41. Maistre's employment of the New World to illustrate the follies of the Old had a long tradition. As historians of the quarrel over America remarked, 'With each passing year it became increasingly clear that those who took sides on the Problem of America were really using America as a kind of stalking horse for their own battles, campaigns, and crusades'. Commager and Giordanetti, *Was America a mistake?*, p.23.

42. Likewise, Tocqueville acknowledged after his visit to Jacksonian America that America was only the object of *Democracy in America*. His broader subject was the future of democratic government on both sides of the Atlantic.

# The negative of the Enlightenment, the positive of order and the impossible positivity of history

## JEAN-YVES PRANCHÈRE

If we reconsider or re-evaluate Maistre's work, it is because the meaning that it has for us is not independent of the movements of history.[1] This is the case with every great work: historical developments transform the perspectives that we take on the past, by prompting new questions that in turn, when we address the books of old masters, allow the responses – that these books have kept in reserve – to appear.

This situation is common, but in the case of Joseph de Maistre it takes on a particular acuteness by the fact that each of his published works, beginning with the *Considérations sur la France*, culminated in the adoption of a prophetic position that served him as a conclusion. Undoubtedly, prophetic desire is not the *centre* of *Les Soirées de Saint Pétersbourg* or of *Du Pape*. But it is in the *forefront*. Each of Maistre's works is enrolled in the tension of awaiting a great historical event called forth by the excess of the revolutionary event.[2] This tension, in its eschatological basis, is not the *theme* of Maistre's works, all linked to the restoration – against revolutionary confusion – of authority and of monarchical, ecclesial and divine order; all are linked, in other words, to bring about the fall of the revolutionary tension in order to re-establish the political détente that, according to Maistre, characterised the traditional, essentially pacific, order. Maistre's struggle against the Enlightenment and the Revolution is that of a radical conservatism, of which the *Essai sur le principe générateur des constitutions politiques* (1814) provides the ideal type by declaring that 'le mot de *réforme*, en lui-même et avant tout examen, sera toujours suspect à la sagesse'.[3] But for Maistre this conservatism is

1. This article was translated from French by Richard A. Lebrun.
2. The *Considérations sur la France* announces the restoration of the Christian monarchy; the conclusion of *Du Pape* prophesies the return of separated Christians to the bosom of the Catholic Church; and the last dialogue of *Les Soirées* warns that 'il faut nous tenir prêts pour un événement immense dans l'ordre divin, vers lequel nous marchons avec une vitesse accélérée qui doit frapper tous les observateurs'. In Glaudes (ed.), *Maistre: Œuvres*, p.762.
3. *Essai sur le principe générateur*, in Glaudes (ed.), *Maistre: Œuvres*, p.388. Soon after, Maistre praises the 'aversion machinale de tous les bons esprits pour les innovations'. The final piece of *Les Soirées* is in this same vein: 'contredisez sans cesse cet esprit de nouveauté et de changement, jusque dans les plus petites choses; laissez pendre sur vos murs les

no less registered in the tension, which overflows it, of the possibility of a divine rebuilding of the old order that God nevertheless commands to be defended.

It is easy, when we read Maistre, to observe the denial that history – which each one of his books repeats is 'la politique expérimentale'[4] – opposed the political predictions on which he had engaged and wagered his thought. The collapse of the French monarchy, the deployment of a powerful and stable American democracy whose capital has always been Washington,[5] the refusal of the Catholic Church to recognise itself in an essential bond with the royalist cause and the secularisation of European societies are so many massive historical facts that invalidate those analyses by which – from the *Considérations* to *Du Pape* – Maistre tried his best to persuade his reader that no great structured and prosperous society is possible outside the conditions of a monarchical sovereignty established on sacred foundations. However, it would be hasty to conclude simply that Maistrian thought falls, if not into insignificance, at least into the limbo of an irremediably dated past without a foothold in the present. Not that Maistre's thought, in its political choices, does not belong to the past to which it is bound; but this caducity of Maistre's political choices perhaps does not touch their theological-political heart.

From the *Considérations*, it appears in effect that the most visible prophecy, that of the triumph of the monarchy and the Church as the sole natural issue of the revolutionary crisis, is not the most profound prophecy. The announcement of the future monarchical restoration only makes sense in the light of the fundamental alternative enunciated by Maistre in these terms: 'tout vrai philosophe doit opter entre ces deux hypothèses: ou qu'il va se former une nouvelle religion, ou que le christianisme sera rajeuni de quelque manière extraordinaire'.[6] It is

---

tapisseries enfumées de vos aïeux; chargez vos tables de leur pesante argenterie'. *Les Soirées*, in Glaudes (ed.), *Maistre: Œuvres*, p.443.

4.   The expression appears for the first time in *De la Souveraineté du peuple*, bk.II, ch.2, p.186-87. 'L'histoire est la politique expérimentale, c'est-à-dire la seule bonne'. The formula is repeated in *Considérations sur la France* in Glaudes (ed.), *Maistre: Œuvres*, p.260; the *Lettres sur l'éducation publique en Russie* and the *Quatre chapitres sur la Russie* in *OC*, vol.8, p.267 and 294; the preface of the *Essai sur le principe générateur* in Glaudes (ed.), *Maistre: Œuvres*, p.363, and finally in Lovie and Chetail (ed.) *Du Pape*, bk.III, ch.2, p.232.

5.   We can recall the unfortunate wager in Chapter VIII of the *Considérations* with respect to the construction of the capital of the United States: 'l'on pourrait gager mille contre un que la ville ne se bâtira pas, ou qu'elle ne s'appellera pas *Washington*, ou que le congrès n'y résidera pas'. p.242. On Maistre's attitude to the fledgeling United States and its capital, see Joseph Eaton's article in this volume, 'This babe-in-arms: Joseph de Maistre's critique of America'.

6.   *Considérations sur la France* in Glaudes (ed.), *Maistre: Œuvres*, p.229.

the background of such an alternative that provides ambiguous relief to the announcement of a restoration of the Catholic monarchy.

Thus we see that, from one work to the other, Maistrian prophecy moves around: the hopes that the *Considérations* placed in the French Catholic monarchy alone are taken over in *Du Pape* by a much larger hope, that of an intensification of the monarchy of Catholicism itself, under the multiple form of an unambiguous affirmation of the monarchical essence of the Catholic principle, by an obliteration of Christian divisions under the pontifical authority, and by an assumption of temporal monarchies under the spiritual monarchy of the Pope who would give them their exact measure.[7] And this expectation of the end of schisms in turn takes, in the last dialogue of *Les Soirées*, a more unspecified form, less strictly constrained by the theological-political parallel of political and religious sovereignty. The unification of humanity which it seems must be the ultimate sense of the revolutionary crisis traces a strangely indistinct horizon, which troubles the purity of the Catholic lines drawn in *Du Pape* or the first ten dialogues of *Les Soirées*. For the end of schisms, it turns out, must be the end of this schism which is time itself,[8] and the entrance, if not into eternity at the end of time, for this point is not clear, at least into a new regime of temporality.

All prophecy, says the Senator in the eleventh dialogue of *Les Soirées*, is linked to this dimension by which we escape from time: 'l'homme est assujetti au temps, et néanmoins il est par nature étranger au temps'.[9] It follows that the essential burden of the prophecy is more in the separateness from time, in the break between the present and an impenetrable future, than in the capacity to render transparent in advance the nature of the announced events. Prophecy, the Senator emphasises, is inevitably confused because it confuses time. In the present, it is opaque.[10] Only the future event itself will be able to *show* what the prophecy could only *announce*, in a figurative fashion perhaps. This is how it happens not only with Biblical prophecies in respect to the Gospel, but with Biblical prophecies considered even outside their

---

7. On Maistre's idea of the primacy of spiritual authority and its origins in Rousseau, see Carolina Armenteros' article in this volume, 'Maistre's Rousseaus'.

8. In the eleventh dialogue of *Les Soirées*, the Senator explains that 'l'esprit prophétique est naturel à l'homme', because man 'n'est pas fait pour le temps' and 'le temps est *quelque chose de forcé qui ne demande qu'à finir*'. in Glaudes (ed.), *Maistre: Œuvres*, p.764.

9. *Les Soirées de Saint Pétersbourg* in Glaudes (ed.), *Maistre: Œuvres*, p.763.

10. 'Le prophète jouissant du privilège de sortir du temps, ses idées, n'étant plus distribuées dans la durée, se touchent en vertu de la simple analogie et se confondent, ce qui répand nécessairement une grande confusion dans ses discours. [...] Le Juif qui s'en tenait à l'écorce avait toute raison, *jusqu'à l'événement*, de croire au règne temporel du Messie; il se trompait néanmoins, comme on le vit depuis: mais savons-nous ce qui nous attend nous-mêmes?'. *Les Soirées de Saint Pétersbourg* in Glaudes (ed.), *Maistre: Œuvres*, p.763 and 768.

Christian outcome. The prophecy has such little right to claim to dispose of its own meaning that the prophet cannot even be sure of the happening of the event that he was inspired to prophecy: Jonas was not a false prophet even when God did not destroy Nineveh, contrary to what He had asked him to announce.

Here perhaps we touch on one of the causes of the fascination that Maistre exercises over us, even when we absolutely refuse to accept his praises of Russian despotism, the Spanish Inquisition, or the sacredness of the executioner and war. And perhaps we touch, by the same token, the principle of this strange ambiguity that has made certain interpreters persist in seeing in Maistre a paradoxically liberal thinker,[11] although all the texts protest against such a qualification; it is this same ambiguity that, in an inverse sense, makes it so difficult to get rid of the accusation of 'proto-fascism' launched against Maistre by Isaiah Berlin,[12] a manifestly unjust accusation in that it neglects Maistre's profound agreement with the Church of his time and the inscription of his thought in the tradition of Malebranchist rationalism, but which finds its credibility when we restrict ourselves to certain chapters in *De la Souveraineté du peuple* or to various works concerning Russia, where, in the flares of anger against the Enlightenment, we think we already see the glow of twentieth-century violence.

We ask ourselves if Maistre, by praising persecution and sacralising the violence of the state, announces the totalitarian mentality of the twentieth century or if, on the contrary, by critiquing the militarisation of life brought about by the revolutionary ideal of the rights of man,[13] he manifests a legitimate dread before the premises of totalitarianism, which he would have felt, without giving it its name or its precise

11. One will find in the very rich Barthelet (ed.), *Maistre: Dossiers H*, a certain number of texts that defend this philologically strange thesis. The question of Maistre's link to liberalism has been treated in a convincing way by Stéphane Rials, 'La Droite ou l'horreur de la volonté', in *Révolution et Contre-révolution au XIXᵉ siècle* (Paris, 1987), and by Gérard Gengembre in *La Contre-révolution ou l'histoire désespérante* (Paris, 1989), p.180ff. I am tempted to reference my own contribution to Barthelet (ed.), *Maistre: Dossiers H*.

12. The expression 'proto-fascism' is found in the third of the four conferences given by Isaiah Berlin in 1965 under the title *Two enemies of the Enlightenment* (see Berlin's unpublished text in *The Isaiah Berlin virtual library*, http://berlin.wolf.ox.ac.uk). See also 'Joseph de Maistre and the origins of fascism' in Berlin, *The Crooked timber of humanity*. Berlin's thesis, repeated by Enzo Traverso in *Le Totalitarisme* (Paris, 2001), has been critiqued by most of Maistre's interpreters.

13. It suffices to return, for the praise of persecutions, to the *Lettres sur l'Inquisition espagnole*. Maistre's worries about the militarisation of life were expressed frequently in his correspondence, but also in *Les Soirées*; the seventh dialogue looks back with regret to 'European war' before the Revolution: 'le soldat seul combattait le soldat. Jamais les nations n'étaient en guerre'. Glaudes (ed.), *Maistre: Œuvres* p.658.

contours, as the inevitable reverse side of democratic secularisation and the removal of sacred foundations, that is also to say the sacred *limits*, of sovereignty. It would certainly be possible to challenge these questions by denouncing the retrospective illusion that dooms the very usage of the notion of 'precursor' as an abusive usage.[14] And yet this does not suffice, since Maistre himself called for a judgement that takes into account not only his doctrine, but the prophetic function of his interventions. Now the meaning of a prophetic work, it seems, is in the effective event of which it is a figure: not only must the event certify the truth of the prophecy, but it must, in a certain way, well and truly capture its meaning.

We are not certain that Maistre would be refuted, in the first place, because we cannot forget that the doctrinaire, in so far as he is also a prophet, is to begin with a writer whose work has the sense of being a writing of the sublime, that is to say of what refuses representation;[15] then, because we are not certain of what he announces. If what he announces is the impossibility of an individualist society,[16] the impossibility of a society deprived of all founding transcendence, if he prophesies both the chance of a coming fusion of the human race and the danger that this will be ruined in barbarism, in the absence of all spiritual authority susceptible to limiting a scientific knowledge become purely technical, we cannot object that such anxieties have lost their meaning.

However it remains that we cannot take Maistre's work for a simple figure of a meaning that would escape the formulations that he gave it. The presence of prophecy in Maistre's work cannot be understood outside the thought of the order in which it is inserted and which can be called, by recapturing an expression from *Les Soirées*, the 'système de l'autorité'.[17] Undoubtedly, Maistre did not have a system, but his thought presents a systematic turn that opposes to the Enlightenment a defence of order seized under a triple aspect: political (monarchical), ecclesial (Catholic) and divine (providential, that is to say, historical). It is necessary to attempt to follow the lineaments of this system, if we want to detect how it can, in its very rigidity, welcome that which goes beyond it.

Maistre's first and last intuition, formulated in the *Considérations* and

---

14. On this subject, Georges Canguilhem's reflections – in *Etudes d'histoire et de philosophie des sciences* (Paris, 1989), p.21-22 – can easily be transposed from the history of science to the history of ideas.
15. Here we have to refer to Pierre Glaudes, 'Maistre et le sublime de la Révolution', *Revue des études maistriennes*, vol.14 (2004), p.183-200.
16. Maistre seems to have been the first author to use the word 'individualism' (in *OC*, vol. 14, p.286). On this point, see Alain Renaut, *L'Ere de l'individu* (Paris, 1989), p.70.
17. 'L'autorité [...] est la base de notre système'. *Les Soirées de Saint Pétersbourg* in Glaudes (ed.), *Maistre: Œuvres*, p.772.

reaffirmed in *Du Pape*, is that of the Satanism of the French Revolution.[18]
The radicalness of this position, whose equivalent would not be found in
either Bonald or the German Romantics, is undoubtedly that which
specifies Maistre among counter-revolutionary thinkers: the Revolution
is not simply illegitimate; it is not only criminal; it is the final form of
absolute evil, of this evil that the *Considérations* declares to be the 'schisme
de l'être', and by this token it opens a crisis in human history – a crisis
which Maistre foresees, in his most pessimistic moments, that could well
last 'cinq à six siècles'.[19]

This crisis had long been prepared. As soon as Maistre is seized by the
illumination that made the Revolution appear to him as an 'époque',[20] he
is led to see in it the natural end of the process of what we are inclined to
call, by using a perhaps inevitable term, though of opaque and unstable
meaning, 'modernity'. This word was not used by Maistre, who nevertheless declared that the revolutionary eighteenth century was only the
conclusion of premises posed by the sixteenth and seventeenth centuries.[21] However Maistre did not yet speak the language of anti-mod-
ernity exactly, although all the rudiments of this language were present
in his writings. Maistre denounces 'philosophisme'. The meaning of the
Revolution, according to the *Considérations*, is in the 'combat à outrance
du christianisme et du philosophisme'.[22] Philosophism designates the
intrusion of philosophy into areas where it has no business, and in
particular its pretention to organise social life by the means of philosophy alone – even Voltaire used this word in this pejorative sense.[23]

18. 'Il y a dans la révolution française un caractère *satanique* qui la distingue de tout ce qu'on a
    vu, et peut-être de tout ce qu'on verra'. *Considérations sur la France* in Glaudes (ed.), *Maistre:
    Œuvres*, p.226. '[L]a Révolution est *satanique* dans son essence' in Lovie and Chetail (ed.), *Du
    Pape*, p.23.
19. *OC*, vol.12, p.60.
20. Studies by Jean Rebotton and Jean-Louis Darcel have shown how Maistrian thought was
    born, in the period from 1793 to 1794, from an 'illumination' whose first content was
    expressed in the *Discours à Madame la marquise de Costa*, written during the summer of 1794:
    'longtemps nous n'avons point compris la révolution dont nous sommes les témoins;
    longtemps nous l'avons prise pour un *événement*. Nous étions dans l'erreur: c'est une *époque*;
    et malheur aux générations qui assistent aux époques du monde!' *OC*, vol.7, p.273.
21. 'Le XVIᵉ et le XVIIᵉ siècles pourraient être nommés les *prémisses* du XVIIIᵉ, qui ne fut en
    effet que la *conclusion* des deux précédents. [...] Le philosophisme ne pouvait s'élever que
    sur la vaste base de la réforme'. Lovie and Chetail (ed.), *Du Pape*, p.355.
22. 'La génération présente est témoin de l'un des plus grands spectacles qui jamais ait
    occupé l'oeil humain: c'est le combat à outrance du christianisme et du philosophisme. La
    lice est ouverte, les deux ennemis sont aux prises, et l'univers regarde'. *Considérations sur la
    France* in Glaudes (ed.), *Maistre: Œuvres*, p.229.
23. On Maistre's use of this word, see my 'Philosophisme' in Jean-Louis Darcel, Pierre Glaudes
    and Jean-Yves Pranchère, *Dictionnaire Joseph de Maistre* in Glaudes (ed.), *Maistre: Œuvres*.
    Chateaubriand devoted a note in his *Génie du christianisme* to passages from Voltaire, who
    denounced 'philosophisme' and the 'philosophes'.

However, under Maistre's pen, it is applied in the first place to an author like Voltaire; it applies to philosophy in the sense that the Enlightenment had given this word, as an effort of a thought without prejudices and of a reason enlightening itself. In *De la Souveraineté*, the polemic was aimed, not at philosophism, but at philosophy itself, denounced without distinction as a solvent force to be put out of harm's way.[24] In fact, it is difficult to trace a clear line of separation between philosophy and philosophism. The slogan 'penser par soi-même' seems to define both indifferently, as we see for example with Kant.[25]

'Think for yourself' is the formula of what Maistre at the end of his life will name individualism, where he will see the ultimate stage of the movement inaugurated by Protestantism. It is, in a certain sense, the very formula of Satanism to the extent that thinking for oneself means: thinking without God, thinking from the self rather than from God. This can also be expressed as thinking without authority, without the authority of a rule of universal truth, otherwise called Catholic. Luther, Calvin, Locke, Voltaire and Rousseau thus appear as the diverse heads of a single hydra, which Maistre summarily describes as 'haine de l'autorité'.[26] Each time, a single fundamental attitude is in play: a prideful rebellion against the necessity of bowing before a truth that precedes individuals and is deposed in an institution that safeguards it.

Protestantism draws a pretext from the text of the Bible to challenge the tradition of the Church, which is however the norm for the reading of the Biblical text, and to replace the interpretive authority of the Church founded by God with the single individual judgement, spontaneously led to project into the texts its arbitrary reading, deprived of the long duration and of the depth of the ecclesial reading.

Scientific empiricism, whose tutelary fathers are Bacon and Locke, takes the pretext of the performances of modern physical science, Galilean and then Newtonian, whose structure however it radically mistakes, to forget the limitation of this same science to phenomena

---

24. In the *Considérations* (X, sect.III), it is 'philosophisme' that is described as the 'dissolvant universel'. This title (which the *Réflexions sur le Protestantisme* will apply to Protestantism) was given in *De la Souveraineté du peuple*, I, 12, p.167, to 'raison individuelle' – identified a little later with philosophy ('la philosophie, c'est-à-dire la raison individuelle', I, 13, p.174). However he also restricts the accusation: 'qu'est-ce que la philosophie *dans le sens moderne*? C'est la substitution de la raison individuelle aux dogmes nationaux' (my emphasis). *De la Souveraineté du peuple*, I, 12, p.170.

25. In his *Critique of judgement* (sect.40), Kant lists the maxims 'think for yourself', and 'think without prejudices', among the maxims of 'common sense'. But in his *Pragmatic view of anthropology*, he gives it as one of the maxims of 'wisdom'. According to his article 'What is Enlightenment?' the 'motto of the Enlightenment' is '*Sapere aude!* Have courage to use your own understanding'.

26. *De la Souveraineté du peuple*, II, p.261.

alone. It then draws from it the conclusion of God's absence in nature and the impossibility of a rational foundation for faith: the absurd promotion of a blind rationality, paradoxically incapable of justifying the claims of science to truth, deprived as it is of the authority of the metaphysical reason that all science calls upon as its founding principle.

Finally, the Enlightenment aggravated the negation of authority to the point of undermining all social order: the critique of all revelation, even Scriptural, the relegation of all metaphysical truth to the rank of chimerical illusions, the demystification of all social distinctions and all political beliefs as simple conventions designed to mask the nudity of the natural man – all these operations, which are the work of the Enlightenment itself, could have no other result than the production of a new savagery, without any relation to the barbarism of primitive man, marking rather a deepening of sin.

Protestantism, continued by Gallicanism and Jansenism, the scientific empiricism of the seventeenth century and the militant Enlightenment of the eighteenth century are only the acceleration of a separation from God – what *Les Soirées* calls a 'théophobie' – which from the time of Voltaire takes the explicit form of an 'insurrection contre Dieu'. This insurrection had to find its end in the revolutionary regicide, whose meaning is that of a deicide.[27]

Refusing the Enlightenment, it seems, comes down to promoting obscurantism. The *Quatre chapitres sur la Russie* goes well and truly in that direction: Maistre there insists on the necessity of impeding the diffusion of knowledge among the popular classes. In a general way, all Maistre's politics is founded on a refusal of clarity: what is the most constitutional in a state is precisely that which does not allow itself to be put in full light of day. The *Essai sur le principe générateur* is organised around the idea that, to the impulsions of the revolutionaries of the Enlightenment, it is necessary to oppose obscurity, which alone permits the good functioning (and even the progress) of political institutions.[28] The shared opinions on which all states are based are not explicit opinions: civic ideals are not principles that can be fixed by written documents, but the certitudes inscribed in the obscurity of hearts, and which owe their power and their solidity only to that very obscurity that

27. On 'théophobie', see *Les Soirées*, p.147-8 (as well as the *Examen de la philosophie de Bacon*, *OC*, vol.6, p.262). On the meaning of the Enlightenment as an 'insurrection contre Dieu', see the *Essai sur le principe générateur*, LXI, in Glaudes (ed.), *Maistre: Œuvres*, p.399. For Maistre's triple critique of Protestantism, empiricism, and the Enlightenment, please refer to my *L'Autorité contre les Lumières. La philosophie de Joseph de Maistre* (Geneva, 2004), chap.5.

28. This is the thesis formulated from the outset by Maistre: 'ce qu'il y a précisément de plus fondamental et de plus essentiellement constitutionnel dans les lois d'une nation ne saurait être écrit'. *Essai sur le principe générateur* in Glaudes (ed.), *Maistre: Œuvres*, p.368.

protects them from critical examination and which itself must be protected.

This politics of obscurity is not, however, absolutely obscurantist. Without diminishing what is actually frightening in the advice that Maistre gave to the Tsar (but it must be underlined that this advice should not be separated from an attitude of hostility toward the Orthodox Church, and that it was also a question of proving to the tsar that an enlightened politics is impossible outside a return of Russia to the orb of Catholicism)[29] it is important to note that it is never accompanied by a condemnation of science and reason in principle. Science has its proper place, it is the honour of the human mind in its resemblance to God and, by this title, it must be practised and developed in virtue of a demand of piety: the *Examen de la philosophie de Bacon* accords an enormous importance to this theme from its explicit authorisation by Malebranche.[30]

It is also in Malebranche, the Cartesian philosopher of order, convinced of the infallibility of the Church,[31] that we will find the criteria of distinction between philosophy and philosophism. We know that Maistre was forever praising Malebranche and that it is not impossible to find the themes of Malebranche's rationalism behind many of the developments of the *Considérations* or *Les Soirées*. Malebranche retained from Descartes an essential lesson, which is that the I is based in God:[32] the certitude of self is only a certitude worthy of this name, a well-founded and stable knowledge, because it is discovered in itself, as its most proper intimacy which however goes beyond it, the certitude of a God whose infinity escapes from the 'mind' that nevertheless thinks it.[33]

29. Théodore Paléologue made this observation in his book *Sous l'oeil du grand inquisiteur* (Paris, 2004), p.238-39.
30. For example, we read there that there are 'peu de maximes à la fois plus fausses et plus dangereuses que celle qui tend à séparer la religion de la science. "L'esprit" a dit Malebranche, "devient plus pur, plus lumineux, plus fort et plus étendu à proportion que s'augmente l'union qu'il a avec Dieu, parce que c'est elle qui fait toute sa perfection"'. *Examen*, *OC*, vol.6, p.451-2. See Malebranche, Preface to *De la Recherche de la vérité* (1674-1675).
31. Let us recall that Malebranche thinks that 'l'amour de l'Ordre n'est pas seulement la principale des vertus morales, c'est l'unique vertu: c'est la vertu mère, fondamentale, universelle'. *Traité de morale* (1684), Part I, ch.2, art.9. *Les Soirées* does not go without citing this 'véritable oracle prononcé par l'illustre Malebranche: *l'infaillibilité est renfermée dans l'idée de toute société divine*'. *Les Soirées de Saint Pétersbourg* in Glaudes (ed.), *Maistre: Œuvres*, p.644. See Nicolas Malebranche, *De la Recherche de la vérité*, Bk.3, ch.2.
32. In Descartes' *Méditations métaphysiques*, the *cogito* only becomes real *knowledge* of self by the intermediary of the demonstration of God's existence that results immediately from it. See J.M. Beyssade, *La Philosophie première de Descartes* (Paris, 1979). Malebranche condenses the argumentation of the third *Méditation*: 'rien de fini ne peut représenter l'infini. Si on pense à Dieu, il faut qu'il soit'. Malebranche, *Entretiens sur la métaphysique*, II, 5. See also his *De la Recherche de la vérité*, IV, 11.
33. This movement of thought has been resumed in the twentieth century by Emmanuel

Consequently 'penser par soi-même' is out of the question if this means: think according to your own opinions. Philosophism perhaps defines itself in this way, but not the philosophy that is *'la science qui nous apprend la raison des choses'.*[34] And as Malebranche teaches, philosophy does not consist in thinking according to particular reason, but according to sovereign or universal reason, which carries within it the sign and the rule of divine transcendence. Maistre declares having had to prostrate himself in admiration the day that he read in Malebranche *'que Dieu est le lieu des esprits comme l'espace est le lieu des corps'.*[35] To think by oneself, in the Enlightenment sense, means precisely: no longer seeing things in God, no longer understanding that God is the place of minds.

It is therefore by the same movement that the so-called Enlighteners separate themselves from God (from the divine light) and from reason (from the natural light). We understand that Maistre does not use the word 'Lumières' to describe his philosophist enemy. This desire for clarity is in reality a refusal of chiaroscuro, which alone renders things visible; it is a refusal to see finite things in their finitude, on the basis of the divine infinite where they find their vanishing point. This is why Maistre takes the movement of the Enlightenment as a movement of pure negativity. Protestantism, scientific empiricism, the philosophy of the Enlightenment, are nothing other than what the very name of Protestantism indicates, and which adequately translates their common essence: the expression of a refusal, of a 'protestation contre toutes les vérités'.[36] Nothing positive is to be found in them.

The dogmatic content of Protestantism is nothing other than that of Catholicism; in so far as it preserves a Christian reality, Protestantism is only a mutilated Catholicism, amputated from the ecclesiology that

---

Lévinas. See Emmanuel Lévinas, 'L'Idée de l'infini', in *En découvrant l'existence avec Husserl et Heidegger* (Paris, 1982), p.171ff, and *Totalité et infini. Essai sur l'extériorité* (The Hague, 1980), p.18ff. Maistre had grasped perfectly that the Enlightenment's project of immanence was not Cartesian, but empiricist: 'j'avoue que je ne me permettrais point de tourner en ridicule une pensée de Descartes ou de Malebranche', he declared while adding that Bacon 'est leur opposé en tout'. (*Bacon, OC*, vol.6, p.131-2.)

34. 'Qu'est-ce donc que la philosophie? Si je ne me trompe, *c'est la science qui nous apprend la raison des choses*, et qui est plus profonde à mesure que nous apprenons plus de choses. La philosophie du dix-huitième siècle est donc parfaitement nulle (du moins pour le bien) puisqu'elle est purement négative, et qu'au lieu de nous apprendre quelque chose, elle n'est dirigée, de son propre aveu, qu'à détromper l'homme, à ce qu'elle dit, de tout ce qu'il croyait savoir, en ne lui laissant que la physique'. *Bacon, OC*, vol.6, p.455.

35. *Les Soirées de Saint-Pétersbourg*, in Glaudes (ed.), *Maistre: Œuvres*, p.732.

36. 'Il n'y a rien de si connu que la réponse de Bayle au cardinal de Polignac: *Je suis protestant dans toute la force du terme, car je proteste contre toutes les vérités*. Voilà le dogme qui est devenu universel. Il fallait seulement ajouter: *Et contre toute autorité*'. *Lettres sur l'éducation publique en Russie*, 4, *OC*, vol.8, p.214-15.

follows necessarily from Christian truths. Scientific empiricism has no scientific content – Maistre likes to recall that Bacon was hostile to Copernicus – it is nothing other than a counterfeit interpretation of the sciences that distorted the effective knowledge of physics into ignorance of God.

As for Enlightenment properly speaking, it was empty. When it announced truths, these were those of the great philosophical tradition of Plato, Descartes and Malebranche. What was really its own was only its incapacity to stand in the opening of this tradition to which it opposed a skeptical ignorance which, by falling into hate, absurdly transformed itself into a motive for aggression – as if ignorance was an argument against philosophical knowledge and the rigour of demonstrations of God. Intrinsically null, 'purement négative', intellectually it was only the height of nihilism.[37] Practically, the Enlightenment had only one power, that of producing disorder.

When attacking Enlightened subversion, Maistre displayed very coherent intellectual affects. Whether it is a question of protecting the political place of a paradoxically obscure fact, of maintaining the rights of onto-theological reason, of supporting the joint necessity of an ultimate state decision on law and an ultimate ecclesial decision on truth, the stakes are the same each time: to prevent human pride from flying into a rage and enclosing itself in the sphere of its own immanence.

However the paradox is that this struggle against the immanence of man to himself, concentrated in a struggle against the reduction of man to a single individual sphere, tends to promote the ideal of what risks being only another form of imprisonment in immanence, that is the immanence of society. This tendency, mastered in the books Maistre published, was given free rein in manuscripts such as *De la Souveraineté du peuple*, which preaches the crushing of the individual judgement to the profit of 'préjugés nationaux' and does not hesitate to give as a model of this crushing the fanaticism of the conquering troops of Islam. This tendency is also present in the *Réflexions sur le protestantisme*, which brandishes against Protestantism and democracy the principle of 'l'infaillibilité des chefs'.

These texts, from which Isaiah Berlin drew the core of his argumentation on Maistre's 'proto-fascism', cannot however be read as the formulation of a definitive position of his thought: they are certainly

37. We know that Maistre used the concept, referring to it as 'rienisme', which has exactly the same meaning. See, for example, *OC*, vol.8, p.28 and 291.

an expression of a deep tendency in Maistre's thought, but of a so-to-say impossible tendency, in as much as it is in contradiction with the positions that Maistre maintains elsewhere. Simply to affirm, in the manner of the *Réflexions sur le protestantisme*, the principle of the infallibility of leaders, this in effect renders Catholicism impossible at the very moment when one intends to formulate the principle: the infallibility of political leaders will inevitably enter into conflict with the infallibility of religious leaders. Maistre knows full well that this conflict is not a theoretical impossibility: while recognising in private that the Russian government could be 'politically correct' in expelling the Jesuits, he will never cease to preach tolerance in their favour, in the name of the principle that 'la vérité n'a pas d'empereur'.[38]

Here we touch on a serious difficulty, which will be the principle of the writing of *Du Pape*.[39] In considering Maistre's works before *Du Pape*, we observe in these works what we must name an incompatibility between the two great axes of criticism of the Enlightenment, an axis that we can call political, or theological-political, and an axis that we can call theological-philosophical. According to the theological-political axis, the Enlightenment is denounced as a corrosive social force, dangerous for the national homogeneity which the state must ensure by mixing the political and the religious; religion then merges with the 'raison nationale'.[40] But the concept of a 'religion nationale' is a concept nowhere to be found in Catholicism.[41] According to the axis of theological-philosophical reasoning, the justification of Catholicism lies precisely in its universality, in the double meaning of an assumption of the universal tradition of the human race by the universal tradition of the Church, and in its conformity to the universal truths of reason which

---

38. This formula is found in the *Lettre sur l'état du christianisme en Europe*, where a plea in favour of freedom of religion for the Catholic religion in Russia leads Maistre to declare that the principle of the absolute sovereignty of the tsar cannot 'être transporté dans la religion, qui se règle par d'autres lois', for '*la vérité n'a point d'empereur*'. *OC*, vol.8, p.511. Maistre had recognised in a letter in 1816 that in chasing out the Jesuits as enemies of the national religion, 'le gouvernement aurait raison *politiquement*'. *OC*, vol.14, p.9.

39. Concerning the reasons that led Maistre to support the Ultramontane thesis as developed in *Du Pape*, see Emile Perreau-Saussine's article in this volume, 'Why Maistre Became Ultramontane'.

40. 'Il faut qu'il y ait une religion de l'Etat comme une politique de l'Etat; ou, plutôt, il faut que les dogmes religieux et politiques mêlés et confondus forment ensemble une raison universelle ou nationale assez forte pour réprimer les aberrations de la raison individuelle'. *De la Souveraineté du peuple*, I, 10, p.147. *Les Soirées* – written it is true for the most part before *Du Pape* – repeats that 'celui qui parle ou écrit pour ôter un dogme national au peuple [...] doit être pendu comme voleur domestique'. *Les Soirées de Saint-Pétersbourg*, in Glaudes (ed.), *Maistre: Œuvres*, p.701.

41. On Maistre's concept of national religion, see also Carolina Armenteros' article 'Maistre's Rousseaus' in this volume.

lead of themselves to the Christian faith which completes them. To the closed particularism of political religions is opposed the universalism of spiritual loyalty to Christ and to the Sermon on the Mount, which for Maistre, despite all his praises of social and political violence, remains the touchstone of all morality.[42]

The question which is then posed is to know if the 'système de l'autorité' that Maistre opposes to the Enlightenment is really coherent and if the circles of order – political, ecclesial and divine circles – are really concentric. The defence of the traditional order against revolutionary disorder presents itself as the defense of a positivity against a negativity – whence the admiration that will be given to Maistre by the founder of positivism, Auguste Comte, who will pick up in an almost literal way Maistre's criticism of Protestantism and the purely negative philosophy of the eighteenth century.[43] But as for the 'retrograde' ideal that Maistre could treasure, Comte will not believe it could be an authentic example of the positive spirit, since it aimed at restoring a package that the very event of the Revolution demonstrated had lost any kind of social base. The fact that Maistre's defense of the positive order of the Catholic monarchy 'systematically' takes the opposite view of the Enlightenment can be worrisome: does not such a 'systematic' opposition also risk being an accumulation of disordered refusals, incapable of outlining the positive contours of a real system?

The positivity of the order defended by Maistre could in itself only be the negative of the negativity of the Enlightenment, a negative quite as nihilist as what it denies in an abstract way. Proof could be found in the decisionist tendencies that break through in several places in his work, for example in a passage in *Du Pape* where Carl Schmitt saw 'a reduction of the state to the moment of the decision, to a pure decision not based on reason and discussion and not justifying itself, that is, to an absolute decision created out of nothingness'.[44] Here we cannot avoid objecting that an order defined by the arbitrary decision of a sovereign power would with difficulty merit its title of order.

It must however be noticed that Carl Schmitt deforms and over-

---

42. Maistre considers the Sermon on the Mount to be 'l'un des morceaux de l'Ecriture sainte où le sceau divin est le plus saillant'. *OC*, vol.8, p.150. In *Du Pape*, the argument designed to convince the indifferent that pontifical infallibility is in the interest of all, even unbelievers, is formulated thus: 'Le *sermon sur la montagne* vous paraît-il un code passable de morale?'. Lovie and Chetail (ed.), *Du Pape*, p.116.
43. See Auguste Comte, *Cours de philosophie positive*, lesson 55, in *Physique sociale* (Paris, 1975), p.394-95.
44. Carl Schmitt, *Political theology: four chapters on the concept of sovereignty* (1922), trans. George Schwab (Chicago, IL, 2005), p.66.

interprets a text that does not say so much.[45] The reality is that Maistre's thought resists its own tendency – which tends to attenuate itself bit by bit as his work matures[46] – towards a pure decisionism which, as in the case of Schmitt, would define sovereignty by starting from a state of exception. Such a definition is foreign to Maistre: that one would come to 'croire *que celui qui commande est souverain*', he warns us, would justly be a 'très grand malheur' produced by that exceptional state that is the revolutionary situation. Maistre is legitimist: sovereignty, which is the authority of the law, is a legitimate power by the laws that found its exercise. To the revolutionary concept that identifies the sovereign as a 'commandant' or a war leader, Maistre opposes that 'tout souverain est un être ordonnateur et régulateur; il est né pour l'ordre, et ne comprend que l'ordre'.[47] Therefore it is not a question of defining sovereignty by exception; rather it is necessary to define it by the force of custom where it roots itself.

The parallel between temporal and spiritual sovereignty finds here its full justification. That the Pope be infallible as sovereign of the Church, in the same way as any political sovereign, as legislator, disposes of an irresistible authority, this rules out that the infallibility of the spiritual power and the irresistibility of the political power, as absolute as they are, be freed from any law.[48] There is no sovereignty without laws; but these laws are progressive laws, in constant historical development, which is why it is impossible to indicate once and for all in what they consist. The order of sovereignty is a historic order. This is obvious for political sovereignty. It is no less true for spiritual sovereignty: the

---

45. As Théodore Paléologue observed (*Sous l'oeil du grand inquisiteur*, p.34-5), Carl Schmitt falsifies Maistre's text by citing it in a truncated way. Maistre does not claim that the Pope can decide the faith arbitrarily, in a decision drawn from nothing – completely to the contrary, his decision must assume the whole tradition of the Church. However it is true that the whole sentence suggests a kind of indifference to the content of dogma. In another text, Maistre declares: 'S'il était permis d'établir des degrés d'importance parmi les choses d'institution divine, je placerais la hiérarchie avant le dogme'. *OC*, vol.8, p.141-2.

46. *De la Souveraineté du peuple* (1794-1795) and the *Réflexions sur le protestantisme* (1799) are much more decisionist than *Du Pape*. It is not a question of denying that a path leads from Maistre's defence of sovereignty to the conversion to dictatorship that would be realised in Donoso Cortés and of which Schmitt would claim the heritage. But it remains that Maistre did not take the step that leads to dictatorship. The path to dictatorship was not the inevitable destiny of Maistre's thought: in *Christianisme et démocratie* (New York, 1943), Maritain cites Maistre in support of Christian democracy.

47. On these two points, see *OC*, vol.13, p.93 and vol.11, p.517.

48. 'On peut dire également, sous deux points de vue différents, *que toute souveraineté est limitée*, et que *nulle souveraineté n'est limitée*. Elle est limitée en ce que nulle souveraineté ne peut tout; elle ne l'est pas, en ce que dans son cercle de légitimité, tracé par les lois fondamentales de chaque pays, elle est toujours et partout absolue, sans que personne ait le droit de lui dire qu'elle est injuste ou trompée'. Lovie and Chetail (ed.), *Du Pape*, p.136.

Church is subject to the 'loi universelle du *développement*' in virtue of which its dogmas are elaborated progressively.[49] It is in this long course of historical development that God reveals his intentions, that he indicates the places of political legitimacy at the same time that he allows the latent meanings of the evangelical message of which the Church is the depositary to become explicit.

The majority of theologians do not fail to object that this parallel limps: for Maistre cannot avoid recognising that the laws of the Church are much more written and more constraining than are political laws. Political laws are historically variable; they are not, like the dogmas of the Church, the development of an eternal truth that remains invariable in its transformations by which it makes explicit and reveals its latent contents. The mobile order of politics does not obey the same laws as the order of progress in the Church. As for the irresistibility of sovereign power, it is doubtful that it is homogenous with the infallibility of the spiritual power authorised by God: the sovereign decision can be reviewed and annulled by the sovereign, while the dogmatic decision is irreversible; the sovereign decision can be unjust and consequently obliges only a passive obedience (which is also a passive resistance),[50] while a dogmatic decision fixes a truth and obliges in faith.

Maistre knew this. In *Du Pape*, the parallel between the irresistibility of the sovereign and papal infallibility has no other function that to show the absurdity of criticism addressed to papal infallibility from outside as well as from inside Christianity. Unbelievers cannot be shocked that the Pope claims for his Church the general right of sovereignty; as for Christians, who believe that God himself founded the Church that manifests and continues in this sense His incarnation in Christ, they can logically not refuse to believe that God assures the infallibility of the leader of this Church who represents Him and who could not represent Him if he were not infallible.

Therefore it is normal that the parallel of the temporal and spiritual order limps; and it must do so, for the possible conflict between these

49. Thus as Maistre explains in his *Amica collatio* (1829, published in *Etudes*, October 1897, vol.73): 'le christianisme a été, comme toutes les grandes choses du monde, soumis à la loi universelle du *développement*. [...] On sait que durant trois bons siècles il resta des doutes dans l'Eglise sur l'éternité des peines et aussi sur la divinité du Saint-Esprit'.

50. It must be recalled that the texts in which Maistre defines all sovereignty as absolute and preaches – in terms of sometimes worrisome virulence – the irresistibility of the sovereign, do not have the value of an appeal to a blind identification with the orders of the sovereign whatever they may be. A note in *Du Pape* unambiguously explains the principle that 'pour aucune raison imaginable, il n'est permis de résister à l'autorité': 'quand je dis *aucune raison imaginable*, il va bien sans dire que j'exclus toujours le cas où le souverain commanderait le crime'. Lovie and Chetail (ed.), *Du Pape*, p.138.

two orders does not constitute an insoluble difficulty for the system of authority. Maistre does not deny that temporal sovereignty and spiritual sovereignty can enter into conflicts properly incapable of resolution, since each of the two sovereignties can claim its own absolute right. This conflict of sovereign rights does not however constitute an indication of a catastrophic contradiction by which the theological-political parallel of the Pope and of the sovereign would turn against itself. In principle, the temporal sovereignty and the spiritual sovereignty would not have to enter into contradiction since their spheres of exercise and their ends are heterogeneous: the prosperity and security of society on one side, eternal salvation of individuals on the other. However, in fact, these heterogeneous spheres have numerous points of overlap, especially in the radically religious alliance of the state and religion demanded by Maistre: the political action of the state inevitably includes a moral dimension. Now the political morality of the state, organised for care of the public good and the preservation at any price of sovereignty, can clash with the ecclesial morality of the salvation of souls.

In *Du Pape*, Maistre honestly recognised that this difficulty admitted of no absolute solution, at least in the absence of a Catholicity extending over the entire earth; it is only in a hypothetical way that he proposes recognising a papal power of political arbitration in inextricable situations. However it is not necessary that the problem of a possible overflowing of the temporal power outside its sphere receive an absolute solution; in the conditions of human finitude, it suffices that it not be absolutely insoluble. Irresolvable conflicts between the two orders of sovereignty are of the order of those rare possibilities that must be left in obscurity and invoked only in footnotes:[51] crisis and exception do not make a norm.

Maistre's ultimate response to the objections that one could draw from the logical necessity of choosing between the irresistibility of temporal sovereignty and papal infallibility is what we find in *Du Pape*: 'à ceux qui s'arrêtent aux faits particuliers, aux torts accidentels, aux erreurs de tel ou tel homme; qui s'appesantissent sur certaines phrases, qui découpent chaque ligne de l'histoire pour la considérer à part, il n'y a qu'une chose à dire: *Du point où il faut s'élever pour embrasser l'ensemble, on ne voit plus rien de ce que vous voyez*'.[52] In other words, it is the integration of the circle of

---

51. 'Fénelon a dit laconiquement, et dans un ouvrage qui n'était point destiné à la publicité: "L'Eglise peut excommunier le prince, et le prince peut faire mourir le pasteur. Chacun doit user de ce droit seulement à toute extrémité; mais c'est un vrai droit". Voilà l'incontestable vérité; mais qu'est-ce que *la dernière extrémité*? C'est ce qu'il est impossible de définir. Il faut donc convenir du principe, et se taire sur les règles d'application'. Lovie and Chetail (ed.), *Du Pape*, p.178.
52. Lovie and Chetail (ed.), *Du Pape*, p.142.

temporal sovereignty and the circle of papal sovereignty into the circle of divine Providence that guarantees their agreement or their concentricity.

However the principle of this agreement is itself obscure, quite as obscure as the origin of all political or religious legitimacy declared by time:[53] 'La souveraineté, de sa nature, ressemble au Nil: elle cache sa tête', we read in *Du Pape*; 'tout se réduit à ce que j'ai appelé *usurpation légitime*', Maistre comments in a letter, 'enfin, la Souveraineté s'assied, et sur son trône est écrit: *Je possède, parce que je possède*'.[54] The expression *usurpation légitime* indicates an assumed paradox: from a strictly philosophical point of view, this paradox does not pose a difficulty since it expresses what Maistre perceives as the only possible mode of action for the Eternal in historical time. The Eternal cannot continually break into the tissue of time to present itself in person – it had only done so twice, with Moses and in the person of Christ. So it is necessary that it act in secret in the present, and only clearly manifest its presence in the unfolding of time that reveals the power of the initial event.

God keeps himself hidden in the history that he animates and where he reveals himself clearly only after the event. The action of eternity in time takes a necessarily paradoxical form: that of the domination of the present by a past that is never itself present in person. The evangelical event itself was an obscure event, which had few witnesses.

However this situation has a formidable consequence: if the long course of history is what remains invisible in the short term of the present, where is legitimacy to be found in a time of crisis? There is no clear response to this question. Maistre himself never absolutely excluded the possibility that Napoleon might be the founder of a new legitimacy.[55] History, which is the positive criterion of legitimacy, is unfathomable to the view that wants to see in it, in the present, the

---

53. For the more optimistic aspects of Maistrian epistemology, see, in this volume, Philippe Barthelet's article, 'The Cambridge Platonists mirrored by Joseph de Maistre'.
54. Lovie and Chetail (ed.), *Du Pape*, p.152; *OC*, vol.13, p.124. Let us emphasise that the expression 'usurpation légitime', (which appears in a purely political context in the preface of the *Essai sur le principe générateur*) is applied here to the pontifical throne. *Du Pape* clearly recognises that European sovereignties have a troubled origin, including the French monarchy founded on an act of violence by Hugh Capet: 'dans ce moment même, avec toute notre philosophie, notre civilisation et nos beaux livres, il n'y a peut-être pas une puissance européenne en état de justifier toutes ses possessions devant Dieu et la raison'. Lovie and Chetail (ed.), *Du Pape*, p.144.
55. Even when declaring himself convinced that Napoleon's reign 'ne peut durer', Maistre writes in a letter of 1810: 'si je pouvais lui donner la mort par un seul acte de ma volonté, je m'en garderais bien. J'aurais peur de mêler mon ignorance humaine à des plans qui sont trop vastes pour qu'il soit permis au fils d'un homme et d'une femme de se jeter au travers'. *OC*, vol.11, p.447.

lineaments of the future order. Worse still, order is formed only in disorder, as the case of the English Constitution shows.[56]

In the impossibility of prophesying clearly the outcome of events, there remains only one thing to do: to remain attached to the old order, all the while knowing that this order is perhaps condemned and that God undoubtedly utilises the revolutionaries to separate and revise it. Thus it is that the *Considérations* explains that the counter-revolutionary undertaking must know that the French Revolution is the work of Providence. God is not on the side of the revolutionaries, whose work of destruction exhausts itself in itself; but He no less pursues in it his own proper ends across the revolutionary process, which can have no other meaning than to be the preparation of a divine revolution.[57]

On the nature of this divine revolution, Maistre remains extremely elliptical: here the prophetic power meets its limit. We know from his manuscripts that he did not exclude a Third Revelation, understood in the purest tradition of Joachim of Fiore as a manifestation of the Holy Spirit completing the Revelations that have already happened, those of the Father and of the Son.[58] The temptation is great to see in this a kind of picturesque detail of Maistre's thought, a curiosity that would remain foreign to the profound economy of the theodicy of *Les Soirées*. The eleventh dialogue of *Les Soirées*, where the prophecy of a Third Revelation crops up, is not far from giving us the impression of a tacked-on piece: the last response of the tenth dialogue seems to have given to the whole work its perfect conclusion, by justifying in a sentence the temporal government of Providence by the reversibility of merits. Why therefore this revival of the dialogue, where one could suspect a belated remorse

---

56. 'Les lois romaines, les lois ecclésiastiques, les lois féodales, les coutumes saxonnes, normandes et danoises; les privilèges, les préjugés et les prétentions de tous les ordres; les guerres, les révoltes, les révolutions, la conquête, les croisades; toutes les vertus, tous les vices, toutes les connaissances, toutes les erreurs, toutes les passions; tous ces éléments, [...] formant par leur mélange et par leur action réciproque des combinaisons multipliées par myriades de millions, ont produit enfin, après plusieurs siècles, l'unité la plus compliquée et le plus bel équilibre de forces politiques qu'on ait jamais vu'. *Essai sur le principe générateur* in Glaudes (ed.), *Maistre: Œuvres,* p.373.

57. See *OC*, vol.13, p.27, vol.14, p. 147-8. The *Considérations* already maintained that the 'political revolution' is only 'a secondary object in the [providential] grand plan'. p.211.

58. The Senator prophesies 'comme plus ou moins prochaine une troisième explosion de la toute-puissante bonté en faveur du genre humain'. (*Les Soirées*, in Glaudes (ed.), *Maistre: Œuvres*, p.767). In his correspondence, Maistre assumes this hope without reservation: 'le mal est tel qu'il annonce évidemment une explosion divine', he writes, for example, in a letter of 5 September 1818. *OC*, vol.14, p.148. The idea of the Third Revelation appears in a note copied in 1799 by Maistre from an unknown book. See Marc Froidefont, *Les Sources et les influences de la pensée religieuse de Joseph de Maistre* (unpublished Ph.D. thesis, Université de Chambéry, 2009), p.353.

that gives a false character of incompletion to what was in reality a completed text? Especially since the responsibility for the prophecy is left to the Senator, who does not belong to the Catholic Church: it is as if Maistre had wanted to indicate by this his reserve with respect to a discourse that he did not adopt, although he seemed to hold it in the first person in his correspondence.

However it could be that the incompletion introduced into *Les Soirées* by this eleventh dialogue is something other than the indication of a patchwork that the death of the author would have interrupted, and that it indicates on the contrary the most profound motive of Maistrian theodicy. The progress of the argument in *Les Soirées* takes us from a traditional theodicy – we could say Stoic – tied to a denial of evil in the world, to a fully Christian theodicy, which justifies the sufferings of the innocent through the salvation of the guilty that they assure, conforming to the meaning of the sacrifice of Christ. 'Lors donc que le coupable nous demandera *pourquoi l'innocence souffre dans ce monde*, nous ne manquons pas de réponses, comme vous l'avez vu, mais nous pouvons en choisir une plus directe et plus touchante peut-être que toutes les autres. – Nous pouvons répondre: *Elle souffre pour vous, si vous le voulez*'.[59]

Why did *Les Soirées* not stop at this statement by the Count that closes the tenth dialogue? It is precisely because the reversibility of merits cannot operate without the knowledge and gratitude of the guilty,[60] in other words, without Christianity being known and recognised by the whole world. The Senator's remark, that 'le grand Lama seul a plus de sujets spirituels que le pape', is the most serious objection to the theodicy of *Les Soirées*: it makes it appear that the truth of Christianity requires the globalisation of the world, which alone will offer it its true field of exercise. It is in this perspective that the French Revolution takes on its real meaning, that of a sign of acceleration of the movement begun in the sixteenth century towards the 'fusion du genre humain'.[61]

The transformation that Catholicism will experience in this fusion remains unforeseeable. Also it is not a question of drawing an argument from the Third Revelation to come for leaving the 'barque' of the Church, alone approved by God. In the same way that the revolutionary event did not authorise betraying loyalty to the attacked monarchy, the perspective of a rebuilding of the world by a coming of the Holy Spirit

59. *Les Soirées de Saint-Pétersbourg*, in Glaudes (ed.), *Maistre: Œuvres*, p.753.
60. On this point, see Yannis Constantinidès' article in this volume, 'Two great enemies of the Enlightenment: Joseph de Maistre and Schopenhauer'.
61. 'Il ne s'agit de rien moins que d'une fusion du genre humain', affirms a letter of 1818, 'l'univers marche vers une grande unité'. *OC*, vol.11, p.33.

must not overlook the fact that Christianity is completely under the care of the Catholic Church and its infallible sovereign.[62]

However one may still perceive an unexpected meaning in the fact that the prophetic last word was left to the Senator: instead of Maistre adopting a distance, he could be tacitly recognising the divine truth which awaits its hour.[63] The intolerance professed by Maistre finds itself put into context: the defence of the Catholic order, necessary and true as it may be, is not unaware that it has only a subordinate and provisional function, in the expectation of the divine intervention that will put an end to the divisions of Christians and reestablish the unity of the world. *Les Soirées'* incompleteness acquires symbolic value: it signifies that the providential order that Maistre defends is an unachieved order, still expecting its real meaning. It is perhaps from this that emerges the strange ambiguity of a thought in other respects so *fixed*.

62. Théodore Paléologue (*Sous l'oeil du grand inquisiteur*, p.50) notes that in Schmitt's vision any millennialist eschatology that would want to accelerate the end of the world is incompatible with the 'social order' founded on the 'principle of authority': one of the functions of the Church is precisely to slow down the course of the world towards its end. It is remarkable that in Joseph de Maistre we encounter a political theology which associates with his defence of order and authority the hope for an acceleration of the end of time. See the end of the second dialogue of *Les Soirées*.

63. In this respect Maistre's position would be much closer than Léon Bloy (1846-1917) himself thought to the eschatological expectation proposed in *Le Salut par les juifs*, where Bloy suggests that the Holy Spirit still holds on to the reserve of history, beyond the Catholic Church, from the side of the Jews who remain the depositaries of a secret of God still unknown to Christians. On the relationship of Bloy to Maistre, see Pierre Glaudes, 'Léon Bloy', in Darcel, Glaudes and Pranchère, *Dictionnaire Joseph de Maistre* and 'Léon Bloy et l'héritage maistrien', in Barthelet (ed.), *Maistre: Dossiers H*, p.776-88.

# II

# Makers and heirs of the Enlightenment

# The Cambridge Platonists mirrored by Joseph de Maistre

PHILIPPE BARTHELET

## An antidote

Joseph de Maistre had close ties with England.[1] When Savoy was invaded by the French revolutionary armies, Maistre was denounced before his King as a democrat, or in other words as a Jacobin, 'par la raison', as he said, 'que je parlois anglois et que je fesois venir des livres'.[2] According to the catalogue of his libraries established by Jean-Louis Darcel, prominent among these books[3] are the 1773 Leiden edition of the *Systema intellectuale hujus universi* by Ralph Cudworth, and the 1675 folio London edition of the *Opera theologica* of Henry More. Darcel comments on them accordingly: 'En l'absence de confidences explicites, on peut conjecturer que son anglophilie, révélée par le choix de ses livres, dénote un besoin d'antidote[4] idéologique et politique: choisir Newton, Cudworth, l'école des platoniciens de Cambridge, Burke enfin, c'était renier d'une certaine manière Bayle, Voltaire, Diderot et l'*Encyclopédie*, et même Montesquieu, l'idole des parlementaires et la référence de toutes leurs revendications.'[5]

Darcel might also have included Bacon. It was indeed with a mind set on reaction to what one has become accustomed to calling the 'philosophy of Enlightenment' that Joseph de Maistre first came across those one has become accustomed to calling 'the Cambridge Platonists'. The word 'reaction' appeared at the tip of Robert Triomphe's pen,[6] although ultimately it does not matter very much if it formed the basis for an ideological background or not; Robert Triomphe, following the analysis

---

1. Frederick Holdsworth, *Joseph de Maistre et l'Angleterre* (Paris, 1935).
2. Letter to Vignet des Etoles, 21 May 1793, in *Revue des études maistriennes* 10 (1987), p.27. See Henri de Maistre, *Joseph de Maistre* (Paris, 1990).
3. 'Joseph de Maistre et les livres 1769-1821', *Revue des études maistriennes* 9 (1985) (with Richard A. Lebrun).
4. Following a significant encounter, this word is used in the title of one of Henry More's works against Hobbes: *An Antidote against atheism, or an appeal to the natural faculties of the mind of man, whether there be not a God* (London, 1652).
5. Darcel, 'Joseph de Maistre et les livres', p.32-33.
6. Robert Triomphe, 'Travaux d'histoire éthico-politique' in *Maistre: étude*, p.470.

and conclusions of Ernst Cassirer[7] on this school of philosophy, argues 'qu'on en a sous-estimé à tort l'importance': 'l'école de Cambridge ouvre [...] une large avenue platonicienne au sein de l'empirisme du XVIIIe siècle anglais'.[8]

The word that has escaped us, *ideology*, is doubtless anachronistic; yet *ideomachy* would in fact be a better and more neutral term as we are talking about the intellectual combat of this time, that is to say a genuine form of combat: one merely needs to be reminded that Voltaire pretended to be a new St Michael – a rather inverted St Michael that is – when he completely gave himself to his mission to '*écraser l'infâme*', meaning the Church of Rome. If one looks at the Greek meaning, the word 'polemic' means 'fighting': 'Ecrits de combat' is the general title for the polemic works of Bernanos. One could, without any detriment or anachronism, also give this title to the complete works of Maistre. He drew the pen as one draws the sword, as he could not do the latter. It is enough to look at his portrayal by Sainte-Beuve: 'Il y a de la guerre dans son fait, du Voltaire encore. C'est la place reprise d'assaut sur Voltaire à la pointe de l'épée du gentilhomme...'.[9] A *gentilhomme* who, nevertheless, would never forget that he had been a magistrate, and who knew how to summon all the resources of the jurist to prepare a case[10] in favour of the fight he was undertaking.

We can conjecture with all likelihood that the interest Maistre had in the Cambridge Platonists was of a polemical nature. In addition to the pure metaphysical curiosity that prompted him all his life – a vast and insatiable curiosity as can be seen through the catalogues of his libraries[11] – likewise, contingent motives could have oriented him towards their works. He found their names attacked in the *Encyclopédie*,[12] and furthermore, for the same reasons that he might himself have been attacked in it; thus he recognised himself as their ally and went on the offensive by asking them for arguments to defend them and to defend himself against their common enemy. The central question of our thesis is to know what Joseph de Maistre asked the Cambridge Platonists or, in

---

7.  Ernst Cassirer, *Die platonische Renaissance in England und die Schule von Cambridge* (Leipzig, Berlin, 1932).
8.  Triomphe, *Maistre: étude*, p.472.
9.  Sainte-Beuve, 'Joseph de Maistre', in 'Portraits littéraires', *Œuvres* ('Bibliothèque de la Pléiade', Paris, 1960), vol.2, p.428.
10. See for example a title such as the *Examen de la philosophie de Bacon*.
11. See Darcel, 'Joseph de Maistre et les livres'.
12. See Triomphe, *Maistre: étude*, p.472: 'On comprend aussi que l'*Encyclopédie* n'oublie pas de dénoncer ses ennemis les platoniciens anglais, qui déshonorent la patrie de Locke; elle attaque Cudworth, Morus qui "passa successivement de l'aristotélisme au platonisme, du platonisme au scepticisme, du scepticisme au quiétisme et du quiétisme à la théosophie et à la cabale".

other words, what role he assigned to them in his polemics, or rather, siege warfare (what the ancients knew as poliorcetics) since, effectively, he considered the philosophy of his century as a stronghold worth recovering. This question, however, supposes a corollary: is talking about the 'Cambridge school' – as Robert Triomphe does in accordance with common thinking – anything more than a rhetorical convenience? In other words, does the collective name for the 'Cambridge Platonists' have a real meaning in the history of ideas? And finally – corollary of the corollary – which Plato does the Platonism of these 'Platonists' refer to? Which infers the ultimate implied question of our thesis: which Plato does Joseph de Maistre refer to?

## Against sensationalism

'Le célèbre Cudworth', as he calls him, appears twice in *Les Soirées de Saint-Pétersbourg* (1821). The first is right at the beginning of the second dialogue, where the crucial question is asked: namely whether, in accordance with Locke and his French disciple Condillac, ideas originate in the senses. Sensationalism is evidently the centrepiece of the fashionable philosophy that Joseph de Maistre assails. In the debate he opens – or rather in the suit he brings against Locke and his school – he cites a number of 'authorities', of well-respected authors who, from Pythagoras to Malebranche, have fought against this thesis. In this 'good company' he mentions Ralph Cudworth, with Plato, Cicero, Origen, St Augustine, Descartes, Pascal, Nicole, Bossuet, Fénelon, Leibniz and less illustrious authors like Father Lamy or Cardinal Melchior de Polignac. The principle of authority which he appeals to, in the name of the infirmity of human reason,[13] allows, and even imposes, the rhetorical process of this enumeration – of this 'name-dropping' as we would say in English. Maistrian innatism, which we call traditional, since it is one of the principal *topoi* of the tradition known as *philosophia perennis*, maintains that 'les sens n'ont rien de commun avec la vérité, que l'entendement seul peut atteindre'.[14] Sensationalism is based on a paralogism, a *petitio principii* that Joseph de Maistre easily brings to light: 'Toute doctrine rationnelle est fondée sur une connaissance antécédente, car l'homme ne peut rien apprendre que par ce qu'il sait'.[15] Knowledge by means of the senses presupposes the intellectual knowledge that must found it.

---

13. 'La raison humaine est manifestement convaincue d'impuissance pour conduire les hommes, car peu sont en état de bien raisonner, et nul ne l'est de bien raisonner sur tout; en sorte qu'en général il est bon, quoi qu'on en dise, de commencer par l'autorité'. Maistre, *Les Soirées de Saint-Pétersbourg* in Glaudes (ed.), *Maistre: Œuvres*, p.508.
14. Maistre, *Les Soirées de Saint-Pétersbourg*, in Glaudes (ed.), *Maistre: Œuvres*, p.629.
15. Maistre, *Les Soirées de Saint-Pétersbourg*, in Glaudes (ed.), *Maistre: Œuvres*, p.627.

And Joseph de Maistre appeals to Cudworth to illustrate his demonstration with an 'anecdote':

> J'ai lu que le célèbre *Cudworth*, disputant un jour avec un de ses amis sur l'origine des idées, lui dit: *Prenez, je vous prie, un livre dans ma bibliothèque, le premier qui se présentera sous votre main, et ouvrez-le au hasard*: l'ami tomba sur les *Offices* de Cicéron au commencement du premier livre: QUOIQUE depuis un an, etc. – *C'est assez*, reprit *Cudworth: dites-moi de grâce comment vous avez pu acquérir par les sens l'idée de* QUOIQUE. L'argument était excellent sous une forme très simple: l'homme ne peut parler, il ne peut articuler le moindre élément de sa pensée; il ne peut dire ET, sans réfuter Locke.[16]

Maistre's note about this development is very interesting from a literary point of view, given the intimate dramaturgy of *Les Soirées*: the author, who presents himself as the 'editor', hides behind his character, the Count. 'Cette anecdote, qui m'est inconnue [*sic*], est probablement racontée quelque part dans le grand ouvrage de Cudworth: *Systema intellectuale*, publié d'abord en anglais, et ensuite en latin, avec les notes de Laurent Mosheim [...]'. The *probably* is a charming expression of smartness. If there is one book that Joseph de Maistre read with great care and attention, excluding any flippancy and any *probability*, it was certainly Cudworth's *Systema intellectuale*. This book described as 'excellent [...] rare et pretieux', as indicated by the annotations picked up on by Darcel, who specifies that 'les deux encombrants volumes' by Cudworth/Mosheim belong to the few works 'qui avaient compté dans sa formation intellectuelle' and which he could save from ransacking when leaving Chambéry occupied by the French on 22 September 1792.

The 'good company', in which Joseph de Maistre places Cudworth and to which he refers, means simply the company of metaphysicians worthy of the name, philosophers who do not renounce the primacy of ontology. It is very significant that the first of those he cites are among the most illustrious of the ancient philosophers: Pythagoras, Plato; then Cicero, author of *De Natura deorum*, to whom he subsequently adds Origen, 'the sublime theologian' for whom he had never ceased to manifest a profound delight, even though the Church had condemned his doctrines – or more precisely the system presumably derived from them.[17] After that, and only after that, came St Augustine: one may be surprised that the first real Christian thinker that he names, father and doctor of the Church, only comes in fifth place; there is, in this, clearly a chronological

---

16. Maistre, *Les Soirées de Saint-Pétersbourg*, in Glaudes (ed.), *Maistre: Œuvres*, p.627.
17. Maistre, *Les Soirées de Saint-Pétersbourg*, in Glaudes (ed.), *Maistre: Œuvres*, p.835. On Maistre's Origenism, see, in this volume, Aimee Barbeau's article 'The Savoyard philosopher: deist or Neoplatonist?' and Elcio Verçosa-Filho's article 'The pedagogical nature of Maistre's thought'.

reason. Yet this succession according to the times is in itself only a sign of a deeper unity, of the absence of a discontinuity in what appeared to be, in the eyes of Joseph de Maistre and following his formula, 'total Christianity' ('le christianisme total').[18] The almost instinctive anxiety never to separate divine revelation from natural truths – even less oppose them – is definitely one of the main points of convergence between Joseph de Maistre and the 'Cambridge Platonists': if there are families of spirits, in a quasi-physiological sense, then this is a major point they have in common.

## '*Res illuminata, illuminans*'

Benjamin Whichcote, who presided over the destiny of King's College, is traditionally regarded as being the founder of the 'Cambridge school', according to the denomination of Cassirer, and it appears that Joseph de Maistre never knew of his work. This renowned preacher defended a 'reasonable Christianity', which should not be understood as the same as nineteenth-century concordism – brushing Christian divinity under the carpet so that it agrees with modern rationalism – but instead, as the recognition of the true identity of natural light and supernatural light, the former coming from the latter. Whichcote distinguished between two types of truths: those which are directly revealed by God and by His word and those, which connect with the first, that are 'of first inscription' and 'conatural' with the human mind. Natural truths and revealed truths differ uniquely 'in way of descent to us'.[19] This theory of knowledge has its theological foundation in the Book of Proverbs, XX, 27: '*Lucerna Domini spiraculum hominis/quæ investigat omnia secreta ventris*'.[20] In one of his famous *Aphorisms*, Whichcote defines reason according to this dual aspect: 'lighted by God and lighting us to God, *res illuminata, illuminans*';[21] a characteristic feature of the 'Cambridge school' is the preoccupation of founding a theory of knowledge which makes ethics and even politics possible:[22] this is precisely the meaning of 'eternal and immutable morality' that Cudworth was looking for.[23]

---

18. *Eclaircissement sur les sacrifices*, in Glaudes (ed.), *Maistre: Œuvres*, p.830, note C.
19. Benjamin Whichcote, *The Works of the learned Benjamin Whichcote* (Aberdeen, J. Chalmers for A. Thompson, 1751), vol.3, p.20.
20. 'The spirit of man is the lamp of the Lord, searching all his innermost parts'.
21. *Aphorism* 916. This definition of reason as 'an illuminated, illuminating thing' inevitably makes one think of, in its Latin form, the *res cogitans* of Descartes, but the difference here is that the past participle precedes and commands the present participle: this is because having been illuminated by God, reason can then illuminate man.
22. See Cudworth, *Traité de morale/Traité du libre-arbitre*, ed. and trans. J.-L. Breteau ('Fondements de la politique', Paris, 1995).
23. *Treatise concerning eternal and immutable morality* (London, J. & J. Knapton, 1731).

Preserving human freedom is the real motive for Cudworth's refutation of determinism, of what he calls *fatalism* in all forms,[24] be it theological (Gomarian Calvinism, since the suspicion of Arminianism had not ceased to be attached to Whichcote as to his successors) or philosophical, meaning more precisely atheist (and even more than Gassendi, it was Hobbes this time who was targeted). The refutation of Hobbes is one of the constant theories of the 'Cambridge school', which is common between Cudworth and his friend Henry More, who reproached Hobbes with an expression which is almost *Maistrian* in advance, its 'prettie perversness of wit'.[25] As far as Joseph de Maistre was concerned, he could not separate Hobbes from Locke, simultaneously condemning them both.[26]

For them Hobbesian atheism was the extreme consequence of a determinism in which God ended up being excluded, and with him, human freedom – political atomism demanding not just chance tyranny, but a system of it. Even if they grant Descartes the divine excellence of his principles, their final rejection of Cartesianism had no other meaning. The correspondence that More (Morus, according to the usage of the time) exchanged with Descartes is famous:[27] initial indulgence in his theist rationalism ended up giving way to the accusation of *nullibism*, according to the word Henry More coined for the occasion; it was a reproach for not leaving God any place in his system.[28] On this point, Joseph de Maistre moves away from More unambiguously. Because of his Malebranchism[29] he maintains Descartes, whom he called 'le grand restaurateur de la philosophie',[30] in the 'good company' of the metaphysicians to whom he appeals: it is remarkable that, when he quotes him, he (almost) never fails to praise him.[31]

---

24. In the preface to *The True intellectual system of the universe*, Cudworth talks about his project to write a 'discourse *Against the fatall necessity* of all *actions and events*'.

25. Henry More, *The Immortality of the soul, so fare forth as it is demonstrable from the knowledge of nature and the light of reason*, Book II, Chap.3, sect.11, p.74 in *A collection of several philosophical writings of Dr Henry More* (London, James Flesher, 1662): 'So that it is manifest, that though there be some prettie perversness of wit in the contriving of this Argument, yet there is no solidity at all at the bottome'. The 'Argument' is Hobbes' Proposition: 'Every sufficient Cause is a necessary cause' that More calls before 'a pitifull piece of Sophistry'.

26. *Essai sur le principe générateur*, in Glaudes (ed.), *Maistre: Œuvres*, p.368.

27. Descartes, *Correspondance avec Arnauld et Morus*, ed. G. Lewis (Paris, 1953).

28. More, *Enchiridion metaphysicum sive de rebus incorporeis succincta et luculenta Dissertatio* (London, G. Morden, 1671).

29. On Maistre and Malebranche, see Richard Lebrun, 'Joseph de Maistre et Malebranche', in *Revue des études maistriennes* 11 (1990), p.127-37, republished in Barthelet (ed.), *Maistre: Dossiers H*, p.290-97.

30. Maistre, *Mémoire au duc de Brunswick*, in Rebotton (ed.), *Ecrits maçonniques de Joseph de Maistre et de quelques-uns de ses amis franc-maçons*, (Geneva, 1983), p.116.

31. See Jean-Yves Pranchère, 'Descartes', in *Dictionnaire Joseph de Maistre* in Glaudes (ed.),

## Towards a 'transcendental Christianity'

One of the French commentators of Henry More did not hesitate to write that, for the 'Cambridge school', the passage between the first and the second generation, that is from Benjamin Whichcote to Ralph Cudworth and Henry More, had witnessed the displacement of the 'vital centre' of the school from Emmanuel College to Christ's College and 's'est traduit par le passage d'un christianisme "raisonnable" à une théosophie luxuriante'.[32] It is not without great care that we employ the word 'theosophy', which requires, at the very least, a minimal amount of philosophical disinfection. For us it serves as the handy homonym of 'Illuminism', in the sense that Joseph de Maistre referred to this word in the eleventh dialogue of *Les Soirées*, and that he accepted because it is founded upon the intuition of 'transcendental Christianity'[33] ('christianisme transcendental') or, as he remarked elsewhere, of 'true philosophy' ('véritable philosophie').[34] In the same way that there is no discontinuity between ancient philosophy, that of Pythagoras and Plato, and Christian doctrine, there is no break between Creation and its principle, but on the contrary an infinite gradation. (We take the liberty to mention an author, Edgar Allan Poe, who could be called *Maistrian* without even knowing it, and in particular his *Colloquy of Monos and Una*: Baudelaire found something of himself in both writers, and his theory of 'correspondences' does not have any other origin.)

It is in the *Eclaircissement sur les sacrifices* (1821) that Joseph de Maistre draws out this at once mystical and physical solidarity of the parts of the universe, and in particular of man with the world, of which he is not only the usufructuary – 'master and possessor' in the Cartesian sense – but in a way the cocreator, through *onomaturgy*,[35] the power of nomination that God left to Adam.[36] So-called 'polytheism' is nothing other than the recognition of the details of this divine gradation, God's action presupposing that of his messengers, or angels, his obedient servants,[37] and that of men who sacrifice themselves to God's design on Earth. When

---

*Maistre: Œuvres*, p.1156-7. On this point Joseph de Maistre imitates More, who always distinguished carefully his opposition to Cartesianism from the admiration that he professed for its author. We know his famous letter of 1648, when he wrote to Descartes: 'All the great leaders of Philosophy who ever existed or who may exist, are pygmies in comparison with your transcendent genius'.

32. S. Hutin, *Henry More, Essai sur les doctrines philosophiques chez les platoniciens de Cambridge* ('Studien und Materialen zur Geschichte der Philosophie', Hildesheim, 1966).

33. *Les Soirées de Saint-Pétersbourg*, in Glaudes (ed.), *Maistre: Œuvres*, p.770.

34. Maistre, *Examen de la philosophie de Bacon* in *OC*, vol.6, p.152.

35. Maistre, *Les Soirées de Saint-Pétersbourg* in Glaudes (ed.), *Maistre: Œuvres*, p.505.

36. *Genesis*, II, 19.

37. Alain de Lille, a twelfth-century Platonist sometimes presented in this respect as a

Joseph de Maistre wrote in his *Théorie chrétienne des sacrifices*[38] that 'il est bien vrai que les nations et les villes ont des *patrons*, et qu'en général *Jupiter* exécute une infinité de choses dans ce monde par le ministère des *génies*', he calls More as witness, or rather as an authority on the matter: 'De même que les anciens païens eurent leur propres divinités tutélaires des royaumes, des provinces et des cités (par lesquelles la stabilité de l'empire fut assurée), de même l'Eglise romaine a ses divinités tutélaires, les saints, etc'.[39] Thus More does not hesitate to assimilate the holy apostles Peter and Paul to Romulus and Remus. This assimilation of the gods of paganism with God, the Virgin and the saints of Christianity, whom they prefigure in some way, is familiar to him.[40] And Joseph de Maistre will doubtless remember it when he writes, in his conclusion to *Du Pape*, his famous hypotyposis of the Roman Pantheon dedicated to all the saints by the Sovereign Pontiff, 'TOUS LES SAINTS à la place de TOUS LES DIEUX!'.[41] Cudworth is also quoted in the *Eclaircissement sur les sacrifices*: on the major point of the 'vertu expiatrice utile à l'homme', on 'l'effusion de sang', or rather it is a quotation that he uses from Strabo that Maistre quotes through him – on blood as the 'âme des victimes', the part reserved to the gods in sacrifice.[42] Joseph de Maistre contrasts this conception with the 'idées envenimées' put forward by Hume in his 'vilaine *Histoire naturelle de la religion*', and associates it with the 'théories hébraïques suivant lesquelles l'effusion de sang constitue l'essence du sacrifice'.[43]

The fact that Joseph de Maistre found himself agreeing with Cudworth on such key points is hardly surprising given that this was an author he looked to and used carefully since his youth. We have seen that the two quarto volumes of the latter's 'excellent book, rare and precious' (*The True intellectual system of the universe*) were among those books that the

precursor of the 'Cambridge school', summarises this theology of the organization of the cosmos as God's city through a tripartite formula: 'Deus imperat, angelus operat, homo obtemperat'.

38. *Eclaircissement sur les sacrifices* in Glaudes (ed.), *Maistre: Œuvres*, p.831-32.

39. Henry More, *Synopsis prophetica sive compendiosus prospectus in sacrarum scriptuarum Vaticinia de Antichristo venturo*, in *Opera theologica* (London, Johan Martyn & Gualteri Kettilby, 1675), lib. I, cap. XVII, p.665. Cited in *J. Maistre: Œuvres*, ed. Glaudes, p.1103. One will note in the original the list of examples that More gives: 'ut *S. Georgium* pro *Anglia*, *S. Andræam* pro *Scotia*, *S. Patricium* pro *Hibernia*, (...) *S. Michaëlem* pro *Gallia*, (...) *S. Dionysium* pro *Lutetia Parisiorum*, (...) *S. Petrum & S. Paulum*, vice *Romuli & Remi*, pro *Roma*'.

40. See *Synopsis*, p.667: 'Cujus egregium quidem Exemplum est Beatæ *Virgini* omnibusque sanctis *Panthei* consecratio, quod a Pagani dedicatum erat *Cybelæ omnibusque Diis*'.

41. Lovie and Chetail (ed.), *Du Pape*, p.361.

42. Strabo, *Geographica*, Lib. XV, quoted in Cudworth, *De vera notione cœnæ Domini*, I, p.vii and in Maistre, *Eclaircissement sur les sacrifices* in Glaudes (ed.), *Maistre: Œuvres*, p.826, note A.

43. Maistre, *Eclaircissement sur les sacrifices* in Glaudes (ed.), *Maistre: Œuvres*, p.826.

former chose to save from his library as he fled Chambéry when it was about to fall into the hands of revolutionary armies. Furthermore, his first Masonic writings bear witness to his assiduous dealings with Cudworth's main work and the comments of his editor and Latin translator, Laurent Mosheim, 'homme sage et d'une érudition profonde'.[44] Chapter IV in particular, the longest of the *System*, has *Maistrian* elements even before the adjective existed: Cudworth employs them to demonstrate that all men have an innate notion of a unique God,[45] that Paganism implies monotheism, and that monotheism is the last, albeit secret word of any transcendent religion.[46] Cudworth even speculates on the belief in 'a certain Trinity', common to Plato and Pythagoras, and already 'pre-Christian';[47] he even evokes the myth of Thespesius and his 'three geniuses, sitting in the form of a triangle' according to the treatise of Plutarch which Joseph de Maistre would comment on and translate later (*Sur les Délais de la justice divine*). Robert Triomphe, who quotes Cudworth according to Cassirer – 'No effect is greater than its cause... the spirit is older than the world' – does not miss the occasion to be ironic when not only talking about the cosmological, but also the political consequences that Joseph de Maistre, with his 'instinctive logic', had to draw from such a theory of emanation: 'les vrais principes tombent sur le peuple de haut en bas, "comme la pluie"'.[48] Apart from irony, we find here, *in nuce* if we dare say so, the *Maistrian* theory of sovereignty.

## 'More than humane'

The Platonism of the Cambridge Platonists, or, as one could also easily say, their Pythagorism, is for them almost the expression of a natural philosophy[49] of humanity, a humanity that defines itself merely by an original revelation that is concomitant to its creation. This is why More defines Plato's philosophy as 'more than humane'.[50] But which Plato are

---

44. Maistre, *Mémoire au duc de Brunswick* in Rebotton (ed.), *Ecrits maçonniques*, p.92 and 97.
45. 'Notionem Dei [...] natura omnibus innatam' (trans. Mosheim). We find in More similar considerations about the secret monotheism of the ancient pagans, e.g. in his *Modesta inquisitio in mysterium iniquitatis Synopsis*, p.470: 'Num inter multos illos Deos quod coluerunt, unum solum colebant tanquam summum, quem *Latini* Jovem, *Græci* Δια appellabant, qui *Pater Deorum* existimabatur'.
46. A thesis that Simone Weil takes up.
47. In the sense that Simone Weil would describe 'pre-Christian intuitions'.
48. Triomphe, *Maistre: étude*, p.471.
49. 'Natural' here is not the opposite of supernatural, but on the contrary integrates or supposes it in the same way as Chesterton: 'Only the supernatural has taken a sane view of Nature' (*Orthodoxy* (New York, 1908), ch.VII).
50. 'The School of Plato, whose Philosophy to this very day I look upon to be *more than humane*...' *An explanation of the grand mystery of Godliness* (London 1660), p.vi.

we talking about? One will note that we are mainly talking about the author of the *Phaedreus*, *Phaedo* and *Timaeus*:[51] the same remark – the same restriction – is valid for medieval Platonists.[52] On the other hand, whether the Platonists are familiar with Greek or not, the custom of the day is to quote Plato from the Latin translations by Marsilio Ficino. In short – and here we are measuring to what extent the 'Platonism' of the "Cambridge school" is composite in appearance – not only does it not ignore Iamblichus and Plotinus, it also mixes multiple sources: the *Corpus Hermeticum* and the Kabbalah, to which both Cudworth and More refer – Cudworth being a Hebraist and professor of Hebrew at Clare Hall – without forgetting the theosophists of the Renaissance, who are also philosophers and poets.[53] All this highlights an intellectual landscape that, although diverse, was nonetheless homogeneous, and that Joseph de Maistre spontaneously recognised as his native country.[54] One should not forget the air that we inhale in this country: that is, according to the precious remark that Douglas Hedley kindly made to us, the epistemological optimism that, as an informed admirer of Newton, Joseph de Maistre shared with the Cambridge philosophers.[55] His Platonism is contained entirely in the famous passage of *Les Soirées*, which one could say summarises his great work: 'La philosophie de Platon, qui est la préface humaine de l'Evangile'.[56] For him one need say no more, especially given that the affirmation is stronger and more precise than Pascal's 'Platon pour disposer au christianisme', which it seems to echo. Not only that, but the affirmation of *Les Soirées* goes hand in hand with the more definitive condemnation of Bacon – Maistre's best enemy – the master of Empiricism and, because of it, the hero of the *Encyclopédie*; Bacon, 'qui n'a rien oublié [it is the first part of the sentence] pour nous dégoûter de la philosophie de Platon...'. The enemies of Comte de Maistre would find it difficult to contest his coherence.

---

51. The notion of the 'plastic mediator' that Cudworth uses, to which Joseph de Maistre alludes, inscribes itself in the posterity of *Timaeus*. See Pierre Janet, *Essai sur le médiateur plastique de Cudworth* (Paris, 1860).
52. Peter Dronke, *Fabula. Exploration into the uses of myth in medieval Platonism*, 'Mittellateinische Studien und Texte', IX (Leiden, Cologne, 1985) and, for example, about a twelfth-century author, Marie-Thérèse d'Alverny. See *Alain de Lille. Textes inédits* ('Etudes de philosophie médiévale', Paris, 1965).
53. Among the authors whose metaphysical orientation influenced Henry More, Serge Hutin in *Henry More* mentions Edmund Spenser's *Faerie Queene*.
54. On Maistre's Platonism, see Douglas Hedley's article 'Enigmatic images of an invisible world: sacrifice, suffering and theodicy in Joseph de Maistre' in this volume.
55. On Maistre's idea of the epistemologically inaccessible, see, conversely, Jean-Yves Pranchère's article in this volume, 'The negative of the Enlightenment, the positive of order, and the impossible positivity of history'.
56. Maistre, *Les Soirées de Saint-Pétersbourg*, in Glaudes (ed.), *Maistre: Œuvres*, p.588.

If one wanted to parody a famous question, one with which Maistre amused himself, one could say that he asks our Cambridge authors: how can one be a Platonist? One can be a Platonist, they replied – each one in his own way and much earlier than is commonly agreed: it is to this key point that we would like to return later[57] – and their response presumably helped him, in turn, to answer the only question which was definitively important to him: how can one be Joseph de Maistre?

---

57. We would like to show that the 'cours complet d'illuminisme' which forms the eleventh dialogue of *Les Soirées* dates back much further in Joseph de Maistre's intellectual biography than is generally admitted (Martinism, Martinesism, Freemasonry) and that one must look for these roots in our author's early dealings with the Cambridge Platonists.

# Maistre's Rousseaus

CAROLINA ARMENTEROS

Since the 1970s the suspicion has grown ever stronger that Jean-Jacques Rousseau was not exactly the nemesis that Joseph de Maistre defamed. The criticism was too earnest, profuse and reflective to intimate anything but a close intellectual rapport. The fact that Maistre first formulated his political thought in two long essays that were detailed refutations of Rousseau has suggested that he formed himself intellectually on the Genevan's philosophy.[1] The emergence of Rousseau as a founder of the Counter-Enlightenment has further revealed that he and Maistre actually fought as close allies in the onslaught against *philosophie*.[2] The evidence is by now overwhelming that Maistre owed an immense debt to Rousseau that he masked with reproaches or passed over in silence. But he was not being consciously hypocritical: there were probably few things he would have disliked more than to realise the extent of Rousseau's influence on him.

We now know that Maistre's idea of the legislator, his argument that religion is indispensable to politics, his critique of science, his exaltation of national reason over individual varieties and his psychological rendition of natural law all derived from Rousseau.[3] We know also that it was by reworking Rousseau that Maistre helped to establish moral statistics and expressed the historicism that informed his entire thought.[4] We know, finally, that long before the Revolution he harboured sympathy for Rousseau, sharing with him psychological traits and attitudes that transmuted, after the Terror, into a deep intellectual engagement.[5] This paper builds on this knowledge to draw a portrait of Rousseau as Maistre transformed and appropriated him throughout his writing career.

Maistre's reading notes of 1770-1809 show that, since his adolescence or young adulthood, he was deeply preoccupied with Rousseau, that this preoccupation was largely religious in tenor, and that it remained so

1. Armenteros, 'Parabolas and the fate of nations', p.230-52.
2. See Garrard, *Counter-Enlightenments* and Garrard, 'Rousseau, Maistre, and the Counter-Enlightenment', p.97-120.
3. Pranchère, *L'Autorité contre les lumières*, p.199-226.
4. Armenteros, 'From human nature to normal humanity', p.107-30.
5. Richard Lebrun, 'Joseph de Maistre and Rousseau', *SVEC* 1972:88, p.881-98.

after the French Revolution.[6] This evidence opens up new perspectives on the Maistre-Rousseau relationship. Research on the subject has so far focused on *De l'Etat de nature* and *De la Souveraineté du peuple*, the essays that Maistre wrote on Rousseau in 1794-1796 when he first became active as a polemicist. Line-by-line critiques of Rousseau's *Discours sur les origines et les fondements de l'inégalité parmi les hommes* (1754) and *Du Contrat social* (1762), respectively, these pieces are usually assumed to contain the bulk of Maistre's Rousseauism. Yet they were only springboards for a reworking of Rousseau's philosophy that was orderly and spanned Maistre's writing life. Abhorring philosophical systems and preferring to express himself in memorable and sporadic pieces rather than in logically exhaustive treatises, Maistre is often portrayed as an occasion-alist thinker who disliked systematic philosophy as advocated by the *Encyclopédistes*. His own thought, however, contained the same potential for total explanation that he deplored in his enemies,[7] and it was Rousseau, more than any other thinker, who lent to it its aggregate quality.

Jean-Jacques Rousseau inhabited Maistre's thought in three main personas – as the educational writer, as the critic of revelation, and as the theorist of conscience and freedom. Retrieving Maistre's attitudes to these personas enables new insights into his theories of liberty, absolut-ism, civil religion, sacrifice and education. Concomitantly, *Du Pape* (1819) emerges as a watershed in Maistre's thought that separates the political vision of the 1794-1796 essays from his final Ultramontanism.

Reconstructing Maistre's Rousseaus is significant also for the study of Rousseau's Francophone posterity during the revolutionary era (1789-1848). Reproached by liberals for what they saw as his oppressive views, Rousseau influenced the early conservatives most directly and system-atically during these years. He forged the political thought of Louis de Bonald (1754-1840) as he did that of Maistre;[8] while the writings of Félicité de Lamennais (1782-1854) were suffused with his sociology. Like the left, the Counter-Revolution blamed Rousseau for revolutionary violence and had no intention to celebrate him; yet its representatives were his most thorough transmitters. Half-consciously, they fashioned uses for him that remained standard themes in French thought for over a century, especially as the Maistrian synthesis filtered through the work of Claude-Henri de Saint-Simon (1760-1825) and his heirs to be reborn in

---

6.  As the articles in Part III of this volume demonstrate, the religious question was central to Maistre's engagement with the Enlightenment.
7.  On Maistre's condemnation of the Enlightenment desire to usurp God's knowledge, see Darrin McMahon's article, 'Maistre's genius', in this volume.
8.  On Bonald's debt to Rousseau, see Gérard Gengembre, *La Contre-révolution ou l'histoire désespérante* (2nd edn. Paris, 1989).

socialist and positivist philosophy. This paper sketches the features of the Rousseaus that Maistre appropriated and criticised with a view to tracing the outlines of the Rousseauian tradition that he silently co-founded and represented.

## Rousseau the critic of revelation

Maistre's disapproval began long before the Revolution, when he read *Emile, ou De l'Education* in the 1770s. Intimating things to come, and harmonising with the Catholic Church's reception of the book, the young Joseph objected to the way Rousseau addressed and discussed God:

> Toutes les fois que nous parlons à Dieu, ou de Dieu, il faut créer, pour ainsi dire, un langage nouveau: il faut que nos discours respirent l'humilité et l'Anéantissement, qu'il soient simples, dénués de tout ornement recherché [...] il faut bien se garder de vouloir avoir de l'Esprit, car ce n'est que par Orgueil qu'on court après l'Esprit, et ce sot orgueil doit se taire, quand nous prions Dieu ou que nous parlons de lui.[9]

Twenty years before the Revolution, when he was still a teenager or in his early twenties, Maistre's mind was made up on the relationship between religion and the philosophy of the eighteenth century. Adopting already the tone of impatience that would characterise his counter-revolutionary publications, he argued that Rousseau, like the *philosophes*, discoursed on divine matters with a spirit of pride that was his sole innovation:

> 'ô que ce Rousseau à de grande idée de la Divinité'! ils se laissent éblouïr par ce Vernis Philosophique, et ne font pas attention que Cette Epigramme prétendue sublime n'est qu'une repetition de ce que le Ministre de St Pierre avoit appris à Rousseau quand il étoit encore Marmot. Toute la Différence qu'il y a, c'est que Le Ministre s'expliquoit simplement et en homme Sage, au Lieu que les expressions de Rousseau sont complettement ridicules, car il n'y a rien de plus pitoyable que de vouloir avoir de L'esprit en parlant à Dieu.[10]

Maistre's spite and irritation in these notes is surprising because his prerevolutionary notebooks and writings are generally completely devoid of angry feelings. The only persona they convey is 'l'homme Sage' that Maistre believed all public men should incarnate. In this respect, the notes on Rousseau are texts apart, showing the uncanny ability that the Genevan possessed, from the beginning, to agitate Maistre. The notes likewise illustrate how the French Revolution changed the latter, especially in his attitudes to public writing. It was then, when righteously

---

9.  Maistre, *Extraits F*, in *Archives de Joseph de Maistre et de sa famille*, CD-ROM du fonds de Maistre, Archives départementales de la Savoie, 1996, 2J15, p.313.
10. Maistre, *Extraits F*, p.313.

revealing one's interiority – or successfully pretending to do so – was consecrated as the political act *par excellence*, that he decided to make his inner emotions public: to publish in the same tones that he wrote his private, critical notes.

But if his public rhetoric changed, his ideas did not. Maistre did not have to await the Terror to make up his mind on Jean-Jacques. Nor, in a sense, did he have to await the Terror to make up his mind on the Terror. By the time Maistre was in university, the Enlightenment had already cast the Apple of Discord that would split France down the middle in 1791 among supporters and opponents of the Civil Constitution of the Clergy, prompting the royal family to flee to Varennes.[11] The difference between this apple and the one that Eris brought to Thetis' wedding was that the words engraved upon the former read: '*To the best religion.*'

Young Maistre thus chided *Emile* for its attitude to revelation:

> Certes je ne reviens pas de mon étonnement quant j'entends M. Rousseau avouer qu'il ya quelque chose de divin dans l'Evangile; et se plaîner un moment après 'que ce meme Evangile est plein de choses qui repugnent à la raison, et qu'il est impossible à tout homme sense de concevoir d'admettre'. Quoi! Dieu aura assez haï les misérables humains pour leur presenter dans le meme livre des Vérités Sublimes, et des Mensonges affreux; il aura permis qu'on nous prêchat une Religion où le faux est toujours à côté du vrai, et nous aura laissé le soin d'en faire la Distinction, à Nous qu'il a créés foibles, insensés, ignorans! Il nous aura Condamnés à chercher continuellement...[12]

Rousseau contradicted himself whenever he sought to make reason lord it over revelation, and none of his texts demonstrated this better than the *Lettre à Christophe de Beaumont* (1763) – which, tellingly, Maistre referenced under the title *Lettre à l'Archevêque*. A plea to replace revealed religion with natural religion, the *Lettre* protested that the message of revelation, having been imparted in the remote past, was suspect for having been transmitted to contemporary times through intermediaries. The argument, of course, was laden with a heavy polemical charge, echoing the controversies over revelation and the nature of miracles that had traversed the French eighteenth century from the vogue for Spinoza during the Regency to the quarrel over the *convulsionnaires* of Saint-Médard during 1730-1752.[13] Maistre was deeply struck by its claims. As

---

11. See Van Kley, *The Religious origins of the French Revolution.*
12. Maistre, *Extraits F*, p.316.
13. On Spinoza's theological reception in France and the miracles controversy, see Burson, *The Rise and fall of theological Enlightenment*, Chapters 2 and 5. On the *convulsionnaires*, see Catherine Maire, *Les Convulsionnaires de Saint-Médard: miracles, convulsions et prophéties à Paris au XVII<sup>e</sup> siècle* (Paris, 1985) and *De la Cause de Dieu à la cause de la nation: le jansénisme au dix-huitième siècle* (Paris, 1998), as well as Monique Cottret, *Jansénisme et Lumières, pour un autre XVIII<sup>e</sup> siècle* (Paris, 1998).

he objected in 1809, Rousseau's *Lettre*, though professing reason, abounded in contradictions. It stated, for instance, that miracles are God's special way of communicating revelation to the people, who in their simplicity are the ones most affected by them; yet several pages later, it asked how God could have chosen to employ means so contrary to his purpose.[14] When writing about religion, in fact, Rousseau was driven by prejudice rather than reason. Thus when, in the *Lettres écrites de la montagne* (1763-1764), he proclaimed that he would never wish to witness a miracle, because he was afraid of going mad, Maistre replied: 'Voilà un homme qui a pris son parti et qui justifie bien ce qui a été dit: *Quand même ils verroient des miracles ils ne les croiroient pas*' (the Qur'an, Sura 6, verse 25).[15]

To make matters worse – and sabotaging the Enlightenment's own aims – Rousseau's scepticism about revelation accompanied a sort of hyper-authoritarianism that belittled the role of reason, especially female reason, in religious discovery. Because women could not judge for themselves, proclaimed *Emile*'s Book V, in religious matters they had to submit to their fathers, their husbands and the Church. '[I]l ne voit pas', Maistre lamented, 'que cette raison est décisive pour les 99 centièmes du genre humain'.[16] Women and men alike needed authority in religion. But Rousseau's prescriptions to women denied them the chance of exploring divine truth on their own and therefore of understanding, as much as possible, the rulings of authority. 'Toute fille doit avoir la religion de sa mère, et toute femme celle de son mari', wrote Rousseau. 'Et si par hazard le Mari n'étoit pas de la religion de la Belle-mère?' asked Maistre, 'et si le Père n'étoit pas de celle de sa femme? – Rousseau a oublié de traiter ces grandes questions'.[17] This was not exactly true: for Rousseau, if a husband's religion differed from that of his mother-in-law, his wife had to convert; but for Maistre this was unconscionable, insofar as it subordinated religious truth, and the individual's right to preserve and access it, to the imperatives of social cohesion. It required, à la Mandeville, creating a perfect society at the expense of saving souls. Rousseau's insistence on rational religion cohabited impossibly with a social absolutism that banished reason from religious self-determination, with potentially dismal results for the individual.

Perhaps provoked by *Emile*, Maistre wrote two works encouraging women to examine religious truth rationally, even when such examination threatened their social and familial environment: the *Lettre à une dame protestante sur la nature et les effets du schisme* (composed in 1797) and

14. Maistre, *Religion E*, in *Archives de Joseph de Maistre et de sa famille*, 2J21, p.392.
15. Maistre, *Religion E*, p.392.
16. Maistre, *Religion E*, p.393.
17. Maistre, *Religion E*, p.393.

the *Lettre à une dame russe sur la maxime qu'un honnête homme ne change jamais de religion* (composed in 1810). He also personally converted Russian noblewomen to Catholicism, a religion that was never that of their husbands, reaching such zeal in this endeavour that he was ultimately expelled from Russia because of its stellar success.

In addition to attacking reason, Rousseau's religious rationalism rejected Providence and made divine exceptions impossible. *Emile* stated: 'C'est l'ordre inaltérable de la nature qui montre mieux l'être suprême: s'il arrivait beaucoup d'exceptions, je ne saurois plus qu'en penser'. Maistre reacted with irate sarcasm:

> On n'a jamais vu d'exception plus superficielle et plus misérable contre la Révélation. *L'ordre inaltérable* prouve bien l'existence, la puissance et la sagesse infinie de la divinité; mais sa *volonté* à l'égard de l'homme ne peut se prouver que par *l'exception.* – Lui-même a dit *"Ô si Dieu eut daigné me dispenser de tout ce travail et me parler lui-même... à moi J.J. Rousseau!"* [*Lettre à l'archevéque*] eh! quelle plus grande *exception* aux règles inaltérables qu'un Dieu qui se manifesterait visiblement à Monsieur Jean-Jacques Rousseau.[18]

Exceptionalism was close to Maistre's heart because it created historical theoretical space for a personal and political God who, implicated in the lives of individuals and chosen groups, enabled all the departures from the rule that the rule itself makes possible, and that constitute the content of history, that exercise on remainders. Thankfully, elsewhere in his works Rousseau was less annoying, because he did not insist on consistency. Indeed Rousseau's excellence at paradox rendered him dear to 'l'homme des paradoxes', as Maistre has been called,[19] his accomplice against Enlightenment. The oxymorons of philosophy showed the limits of critical and *a priori* reason, playfully unmasking its errors and its excesses, while forcing through, ever ironically, the sight of another, higher reason that could both confirm and exceed its attainments.[20]

Divinely willed exceptions were also the stuff of revelation and prophecy, another source of Maistre's complaints about Rousseau in the notebooks. *Emile* objected that Scripture was written in unknown languages, and that if God deigned to speak to humans, then interpreters were unneeded. '[I]l faut donc', Maistre wrote in exasperation,

> que Dieu se présente en personne à chaque homme et parle à chacun sa langue: français à Rousseau, hollandais à Spinoza, etc. Ces Messieurs sont bien exigeans. Mais ce n'est pas tout – 'Le langage humain n'est pas assez clair. Dieu lui-même, s'il daignait nous parler dans nos langues ne nous dirait

18. Maistre, *Religion E*, p.395.
19. Pierre Glaudes, 'Paradoxe', in *Dictionnaire Joseph de Maistre*, in Glaudes (ed.), *Maistre: Œuvres*, p.1243.
20. On Maistre's valorisation of intuition over reason, see Yannis Constantinidès' article in this volume, 'Two enemies of the Enlightenment: Joseph de Maistre and Schopenhauer'.

rien sur quoi l'on ne put disputer' [*Lettre à l'archevêque*] – De sorte que si Dieu, *sans interprète* étoit venu parler français à Rousseau, le Genevois auroit répondu je vous demande pardon; mais celà n'est pas clair!!![21]

Rousseau's way of thinking led to a radical scepticism that suspected not only prophecy, revelation and miracles, but also all knowledge human and divine, and all capacity for its clear transmission – one of his many divergences from the *philosophes*. To address this problem, Maistre followed Nicolas-Sylvestre Bergier (1718-1790), who had used Hume's *Essay upon miracles* (1701) to interpret supernatural events naturalistically as exceptional applications of natural laws. According to Bergier, if the miraculous was an exceptional instance of the natural, doubting miracles meant distrusting all knowledge and natural manifestations themselves. Maistre adopted this logic to suggest that Rousseau's rejection of miracles implied a radical and self-defeating scepticism. '[A]insi', he wrote, 'il ne faut croire ni Dieu, ni les hommes, ni les livres, ni la parole, ni la raison – mais il faut cependant raisonner tant qu'on peut'.[22] The absurdity made it possible to discard Rousseau's religious ideas on the same naturalistic grounds that he himself had put forward to criticise religion.

But Maistre was not content to show the epistemological inconsistencies of Rousseau's argument. He strove to prove also that the divine exceptions Jean-Jacques condemned as irrational were entirely consistent with a rational account of nature. This was the aim of *Les Soirées de Saint-Pétersbourg*, which elaborated an extensive and rational defence of the divine exceptions that its author cherished, and that Rousseau suspected – miracles, prophecies and prayer.

Ultimately, Maistre levelled the same judgement against Rousseau's thought that he did against the radical Enlightenment: that it had exchanged the humility of wise understanding for the pride of criticism. The difference was that Rousseau was in part redeemable. Hence the struggle, the tension, the ambiguity in Maistre's unwilling yet irresistible penchant toward him, well captured in a passage from *De la Souveraineté du peuple*:

Tel est le caractère de Rousseau: il rencontre souvent des vérités particulières, et les exprime mieux que personne; mais ces vérités sont stériles entres ses mains; presque toujours il conclut mal, parce que son orgueil l'éloigne constamment des routes battues par le bon sens pour le jeter dans la singularité. Personne ne taille mieux que lui les matériaux, et personne ne bâtit plus mal. Tout est bon dans ses ouvrages, excepté ses systèmes.[23]

21. Maistre, *Religion E*, p.395.
22. Maistre, *Religion E*, p.396.
23. Maistre in Darcel (ed.), *De la Souveraineté du peuple*, p.118.

## Rousseau the theorist of conscience and freedom

One might think that Maistre focused so much on religious issues when reading Rousseau because he was himself a deeply pious person. But that would be to miss the central, if often obscured, position that religion occupied in Rousseau's philosophy, and that interested keenly his early conservative interpreters.

All of Rousseau's sociology may be conceived as a response to the burning question introduced into European philosophy by the wars of religion: how to reorganise society and contain the passions so as to integrate polities without religious institutions. The *philosophes'* answer was to replace religious dogma with natural reason. Rousseau's was to identify true religion with divine feeling by resuscitating the Christian idea of conscience. 'Conscience! conscience!' exclaimed the Savoyard vicar in Book IV of *Emile*, 'instinct divin, immortelle et céleste voix; guide assuré d'un être ignorant et borné, mais intelligent et libre; juge infaillible du bien et du mal, qui rends l'homme semblable à Dieu, c'est toi qui fais l'excellence de sa nature et la moralité de ses actions'.[24]

The fascination and the repulsion that Rousseau inspired in his counter-revolutionary readers hinged on the way that he restored conscience to the forefront of philosophy. Conscience replaced the reason that had usurped religion's functions, suggesting that God – rendered psychologically as the intuition of the good – still produced and apprehended society. Even more, divine conscience knocked down the ancient iron wall that Augustine had built between the City of God and the City of the World. No longer merely an intimate link between humanity and God, conscience became the organiser of the world. Concomitantly, the civil religion of *Du Contrat social* began to do what the radical Enlightenment claimed religion could do no longer: it saved and constituted polities and societies.

Yet Rousseau's suggestion that the state should be an object of religious worship was anathema to the Counter-revolution for being a form of idolatry; while his dislike of institutions as the sites of civilisation's corruption was incompatible with Catholicism, whose Church was the supreme institution, the preserver of a revelation that, scattered through society, ensured individual freedom by breaking the passions' chains. To dim Rousseau's vision, Maistre used Rousseau originally against Rousseau, ascribing to the institutions Rousseau abhorred the same moral qualities that Rousseau attributed to the society of the general will. Abstract society disappeared and was replaced by a myriad

---

24. Rousseau, *Emile, ou De l'éducation*, ed. François and Pierre Richard (Paris, 1964), p.354-5.

particular societies – institutions, nations, families, indeed any kind of social group, even those temporarily formed like military battalions.[25] The world became filled with autonomous 'personnes morales' who, thanks to their dual particular and social status, could generate history and be described in detail. Maistrian historicism and sociology thus arose from the attempt to destroy the unmediated relationship that Rousseau posited between the individual and the state, and between the individual and society absolutely conceived. With God become immanent and society enchanted, man free of social ties – that trope of Protestant philosophy – was safely blotted out. Unsubtly, Maistre joined Voltaire and the *philosophes* in censuring Rousseau's idea of natural man: 'il y a peut-être aussi loin de la caverne à la cabane, que de la cabane à la colonne Corinthienne, et comme tout est *artificiel* dans l'homme en sa qualité d'être intelligent et perfectible, il s'ensuit qu'en lui ôtant tout ce qui tient à l'*art*, on lui ôte tout'.[26]

The set of claims so far described constituted Maistre's first response to Rousseau and was complete by the late 1790s. Two decades later in St Petersburg, however, the Sardinian minister returned to the charge with a fuller answer. Against Rousseau's prescription that the state and religion be one, *Du Pape* (1819) indicated that all of European history could be read as the acting out of Jesus' commandment 'Give unto Caesar what is Caesar's, and unto God what is God's' (Matthew 22:21). As separate entities, Church and state in Europe had been allies and enemies like nowhere else in the world, keeping each other constantly in check, and generating a Montesquieuian kind of freedom – with a twist – whose theoretical fortunes marked a turn in Maistrian thought.

In 1794-1796, Maistre had agreed with Rousseau that Church and state should meld to form a civil religion. 'De l'âme nationale', Chapter 10 of *De la Souveraineté du peuple*, stated: 'Il faut qu'il y ait une religion de l'Etat comme une politique de l'Etat; ou, plutôt, il faut que les dogmes religieux et politiques mêlés et confondus forment ensemble une *raison universelle* ou *nationale* assez forte pour réprimer les aberrations de la raison individuelle qui est, de sa nature, l'ennemie mortelle de toute association quelconque, parce qu'elle ne produit que des opinions divergentes'.[27] Like the civil religion of *Du Contrat social*, this state religion exercised its empire strictly over opinion, as the *Considérations sur la France* (1797) confirmed when remembering the role of the clergy in the *ancien régime*:

25. *Les Soirées de Saint-Pétersbourg* argues that the moral qualities of armies can be more important than their number and change the outcome of battles. See *Les Soirées de Saint-Pétersbourg* in Glaudes (ed.), *Maistre: Œuvres*, p.663.
26. Maistre, *De l'Etat de nature* in Constantinidès (ed.), *Contre Rousseau*, p.29.
27. Maistre in Darcel (ed.), *De la Souveraineté du peuple*, p.147.

tandis que le sacerdoce était en France une des trois colonnes qui soutenaient le trône, et qu'il jouait dans les comices de la nation, dans les tribunaux, dans le ministère, dans les ambassades, un rôle si important, on n'apercevait pas ou l'on apercevait peu son influence dans l'administration civile; et lors même qu'un prêtre était premier ministre, on n'avait point en France un *gouvernement de prêtres*.

Toutes les influences étaient fort bien balancées, et tout le monde était à sa place. Sous ce point de vue, c'est l'Angleterre qui ressemblait le plus à la France. Si jamais elle bannit de sa langue politique ces mots: *Church and state*, son gouvernement périra comme celui de sa rivale.[28]

By 1819, the Church-as-opinion-maker had withdrawn from Maistre's thought to leave room for the Church-as-sovereign-government. But the government in question was purely spiritual: there was no '*gouvernement de prêtres*', no ecclesiastical temporal power, in *Du Pape* any more than in the *Considérations*. Certainly, *Du Pape* acknowledged that the Church's empire over opinion had resulted in a real political power, that is, in the papal prerogative to excommunicate monarchs and dispense subjects from obedience. Yet *Du Pape* also pointed out that, rather than foster tyranny, as the *philosophes* claimed, the constant tension between Church and state had resulted in a unique culture and politics of freedom. By imparting a Christian education apart from the state, the clergy had spread virtues consistent with liberty, teaching people that one does not always have to comply, at least inwardly, with the masters of this world. And by binding monarchs with a spiritual law, it had prevented them from holding their peoples in the despotic grip of the Orient, where law and the sovereign will were one.

This did not mean, however, that Maistre ever advocated a return to the Middle Ages. *Du Pape* was a profoundly revolutionary text by its author's own definition. The *Considérations* identified Counter-Revolution as the art of waiting for Providence to speak.[29] The same pamphlet also defined Revolution (and its nemesis Anti-Revolution) as the result of the ability of an unfettered human reason to accelerate and multiply political action. Historically, Revolution had been, despite – or rather because of – its rationalistic pretensions, profoundly irrational, a destructive and illusory force that knew not what it did: 'Il n'y a [...] point de souveraineté en France; tout est factice, tout est violent, tout annonce qu'un tel ordre de choses ne peut durer'.[30] The irony was that this most condemnable of epochs was salvific because it was providentially

---

28. Maistre, *Considérations sur la France*, in Glaudes (ed.), *Maistre: Œuvres*, p.243.
29. Philippe Barthelet, 'Joseph de Maistre entre Révolution et contraire de la Révolution', paper presented at *Actualité de Joseph de Maistre*, colloquium held at the University of the Human Sciences, Moscow, 20 June 2009.
30. Maistre, *Considérations sur la France*, in Glaudes (ed.), *Maistre: Œuvres*, p.238.

decreed. Its role was to govern tyrannically over the critical ages of history, the times when catastrophe educated mankind.[31] 'Sans doute la Providence n'a pas besoin de punir dans le temps pour justicier ses voies; mais à cette époque elle se met à notre portée, et punit comme un tribunal humain'.[32]

Revolution cleansed and regenerated whenever it forced reason to serve faith and bring Providence down to our level. It practised the kind of salutary compulsion that *Du Pape* itself sought to achieve, refashioning religion as an instrument of political reorganisation, as the key to a post-revolutionary European order devoid of social, political and military violence. In Maistre's account, a Church-led revolution had given birth to Europe on the day that a pope forsook Italy's formal obeisance to neglectful Byzantium and crowned Charlemagne as emperor.[33] Europe, that is, had arisen from an ecclesiastical revolt. Its future had therefore to be assured not so much by eradicating revolts, as by ensuring that they were as peaceful as the first. What shocked Maistre the lawyer and magistrate about the French Revolution was not that it had deposed a monarch or executed people; but that that monarch and those people had been innocent, and that they had been put to death without fair procedure. To prevent such state crimes from recurring along with their violent consequences, the Pope should exercise powers of arbitration and deposition when a nation, no longer able to endure oppression by a mad or unjust sovereign, is on the brink of rebellion. Ecclesiastical intervention is invaluable on such occasions, because revolutions can become collaborative rather than destructive when they are arbitrated by a foreign and impartial power that commands widespread moral authority.[34] To enter modernity, in other words, the Church must become a revolutionary queller of revolutions whose political powers are confined to critical times to those *exceptions* that reveal the divine will.

There is thus little resemblance between the political role of the medieval Church, constantly wielding excommunication over the heads of sovereigns, and the political role of the modern Church, whose purpose is to enact political change non-violently, and whose temporal role depends not on the power to excommunicate – now a strictly spiritual matter – but on the capacity to arbitrate. Compared with its medieval predecessor, the modern Church has a temporal power that is at once severely diminished and greatly magnified: diminished, because

---

31. On the idea of divine education in Maistre's thought, see Elcio Verçosa Filho's article in this volume, 'The pedagogical nature of Maistre's thought'.
32. Maistre, *Considérations sur la France*, in Glaudes (ed.), *Maistre: Œuvres*, p.206.
33. Lovie and Chetail (ed.), *Du Pape*, p.150.
34. Lovie and Chetail (ed.), *Du Pape*, p.137.

it comes into play only intermittently and at the request of a people; magnified, because it is now strictly political in character.

The modern, revolutionary Church is the historical force that manufactures *Les Soirées'* utopia at the end of time, that dream of socialists, traditionalists, positivists and integralist Catholics in the nineteenth century; an age when bloodless and legal revolts will proceed not only in Europe, but everywhere, since all the world will have converted; indeed when they will be superfluous, because all monarchs and all peoples will have learned Christian freedom, and political violence will no longer exist.

It was all a complex response to Rousseau's sociology of religion, a certification that, although religion was socially necessary, it could neither unite with the state, nor reside solely within it. As a matter of fact, Maistre never advocated allying throne and altar in the manner that is commonly supposed.[35] Nor did he seek to politicise religion at the price of freedom. Far from it: for him, religion separate from the state yet politically empowered was the *guarantee* of both modern freedom – in the sense of freedom from state interference[36] – and ancient freedom, in the sense of freedom from the passions.

Reconsidering Maistre's much-vaunted absolutism in the light of these new insights, it emerges that in his early days as a public writer he drew on the political thought of Jean Bodin (1529-96),[37] only to abandon the path trodden by it later. In the essays on Rousseau of 1794-1796, the king still holds all powers in his hands; he is still ultimately unpunishable, and no bounds exist to his actions except those of a customary opinion he can choose to ignore. On the subject of sovereign power, the early Maistre posited a republic which was one and indivisible, and in this sense he was at least in partial harmony with both Rousseau and Bodin. A year later, however, the *Considérations* cited the *Développement des principes fondamentaux de la monarchie française* (1795), a work by *émigré* magistrates of the *parlements* that presented the *ancien régime* as a moderate constitutional monarchy.[38] Embarrassing Maistre in the wake of Louis XVIII's reactionary Declaration of Verona, this reference signalled the errant magistrate's sympathy for limited government, and foreshadowed his later break with absolutism.

Maistre's last years found him strongly if quietly sceptical of sovereign

---

35. See Richard Lebrun, *Throne and altar*.
36. Maistre did not understand modern freedom as civic participation, although he may have conceived of freedom as absence from dependence. Further research would be required on the subject. On the three political concepts of liberty, see Quentin Skinner, *Liberty before liberalism* (Cambridge, 1998).
37. See, for instance, Pranchère, *L'Autorité contre les lumières*, p.210, 217, 220, 268.
38. Lebrun, 'Joseph de Maistre as pamphleteer', p.19-46.

power.[39] A deep distrust of kings permeates *Du Pape* discreetly, supported by a political theory that limits royal prerogative not so much with a quelled opinion, as was the case in the early modern order for which Bodin wrote *Les Six livres de la République* (1576); but through a revolutionary Church that, compelled to enter history and legally empowered to direct nations' politics at times, holds the reins of history. Enlightenment philosophy from Kant to Ferguson had declared that it was impossible to know when too much is too much, and rebellion is legitimate.[40] Maistre does not presume to argue otherwise; but he proposes that the modern Church is, firstly, the barometer that measures how much pressure a nation can bear, and secondly, a neutral establishment capable of channeling discussion and ensuring that grievances are voiced, vented and resolved. The modern Church is a forum, in other words, for the expression of the general will. Yet where Rousseau's general will is free to harm the very people from whom it emanates – a nation's liberty, Jean-Jacques maintains, quite anti-Platonically, is consummated by its right to self-damage – *Du Pape*'s Church ensures that the general will serves the common interest as rationally as possible.

The late Maistre thus emerges in a thoroughly unfamiliar and – given his reputation – rather shocking light: as an anti-absolutist wishing to incorporate popular opinion into the political process, and as a social planner who specified how to make revolutions and depose monarchs irenically.

## Rousseau the pedagogue

Rousseau theorised socialisation as a process of breaking and denaturing individuals. Natural man existed only for himself, but social man had to live for others. Achieving this transformation required re-routing the passions so that they could serve moral rather than physical needs, and transforming the individual from a self-sufficient whole into the dependent part of a larger whole.[41] Socialisation, in this optic, was inherently violent, and sociability naturally compulsive. Although reason could identify the good, and bring men to love it, it was itself powerless to reorient the passions toward social ends. *That* was achieved only environmentally, by imparting the capacity for self-sacrifice. The idea pervades Rousseau's fiction. *Emile* (1762) and *Julie, ou La nouvelle Héloïse* (1761) – *romans à thèse* whose philosophical influence far exceeded that of

39. I would like to thank here Jean-Yves Pranchère for his extremely enlightening conversation on Maistrian absolutism.
40. Fania Oz-Salzberger, *Translating the Enlightenment: Scottish civic discourse in eighteenth-century Germany* (Oxford, 1995), p.251.
41. Bertram, *Rousseau and the social contract*, p.142.

Rousseau's other texts[42] – portray heroes and heroines who are adepts of submission fond of performing socially useful self-sacrifice. During their courtship, for example, Emile and Sophie

> se voient parfaits, ils s'aiment, ils s'entretiennent avec enthousiasme de ce qui donne un prix à la vertu. Les sacrifices qu'ils lui font la leur rendent chère. Dans des transports qu'il faut vaincre, ils versent quelquefois ensemble des larmes plus pures que la rosée du ciel, et ces douces larmes font l'enchantement de leur vie: ils sont dans le plus charmant délire qu'aient jamais éprouvé des âmes humaines. Les privations mêmes ajoutent à leur bonheur et les honorent à leurs propres yeux de leurs sacrifices. Hommes sensuels, corps sans âme, ils connaîtront un jour vos plaisirs, et regretteront toute leur vie l'heureux temps où ils se les sont refusés![43]

Julie is also a manager of privation, an Epicurean who abstains from coffee in order to enjoy it more when she drinks it.[44] But Rousseau does not aim solely to encourage Stoicism in the service of delight. Self-denial is generally essential because of the inner violence of the human condition. The Rousseauian self is continually torn between passional and spiritual tendencies, between base instincts and the sentiments that elevate the soul toward knowledge of the good.[45] Vanquishing the bodily passions requires sacrifice; and channelling them socially demands submission. The political writings do not advertise this, but the novels illustrate it. The emotional torment that the characters of *Julie*, especially the two lovers, endure for each other's sake offers a magnified view of the emotional price of utopia – a price that its Legislator and Christ figure, Julie, finally pays with her life. The centrality of self-sacrifice to Rousseau's social philosophy suggests that the intimate relationships of his novels prefigure and realise the political relationship he models between state and citizen, so that Emile's wedding promise to submit to Sophie, for instance, symbolises the citizen's signing of the social contract.[46]

The Savoyard vicar explains to his young pupil that bad men organise the world around themselves, while good men submit to the surrounding order:

> Il y a quelque ordre moral partout où il y a sentiment et intelligence. La

42. Richard Lebrun, Review of Jean-Jacques Rousseau, *Julie, or the new Heloise: letters of two lovers who live in a small town at the foot of the Alps* (Hanover and London, 1997), H-France Reviews, http://www.h-net.org/reviews/showrev.php?id = 2270e (August 1998), last accessed 20 July 2010.
43. Rousseau, *Emile*, p.542.
44. Rousseau, *Julie, ou La Nouvelle Héloïse*, 2 vol. (Paris, 1958), vol.2, p.178.
45. Rousseau, *Emile*, p.337.
46. Elizabeth Wingrove, 'Sexual performance as political performance in the *Lettre à M. D'Alembert sur les spectacles*', *Political theory* 23, 4 (1995), p.594-95.

différence est que le bon s'ordonne par rapport au tout, et que le méchant ordonne le tout par rapport à lui. [...] Alors [le bon] est ordonné par rapport au centre commun, qui est Dieu, et par rapport à tous les cercles concentriques, qui sont les créatures.[47]

A good education must therefore mould sentiment and intelligence to 's'ordonne[r] par rapport au tout' and repress the passions sacrificially. This was a strategy basic to Christian education – which, like Rousseau, posited a self divided – but unknown among the *Encyclopédistes*, all of whom put forward a unitary humanity rendered whole by understanding. Maistre's *Eclaircissement sur les sacrifices* (1821), the first treatise in the sociology of violence, also theorised a fragmented and conflicted self. The difference was that, Neoplatonic and ancient,[48] compartmentalised into spirit, soul and body,[49] this self was more precisely mapped than Rousseau's, a far less contoured, more Augustinian site for the play of conflicting feelings whose social consequences were exceedingly vague.[50] The self of the *Eclaircissement* was better poised to be a historical agent; while its brand of sacrifice could angelise humanity[51] – an aim far from the mind of Jean-Jacques, who expected no moral progress from history, and whose Emile was meant to be no saint. The *Eclaircissement* also argued, with unprecedented concreteness, that society is integrated when individuals willingly submit to the spirit, and that social violence arises from the disordered reign of the passions.[52] The idea was hugely popular. Lamennais, who was intellectually formed by Rousseau and Maistre, summarised it well (though missing Maistre's historicist overtones) when he wrote that '[l]es actes commandés par la loi morale ont pour caractère essentiel commun le sacrifice. Tout devoir est un dévouement, la subordination de soi à autrui, dont la raison se trouve dans la subordination nécessaire à Dieu'.[53] Sacrifice derived from being

---

47. Rousseau, *Emile*, p.356.
48. On Maistre's Neoplatonism, see Aimee Barbeau and Elcio Verçosa-Filho's articles in this volume, 'The Savoyard philosopher: deist or Neoplatonist?' and 'The pedagogical nature of Maistre's thought', respectively.
49. On Maistre's model of the soul, see the *Eclaircissement sur les sacrifices*, in Glaudes (ed.), *Maistre: Œuvres*, p.807.
50. Carolina Armenteros, 'Revolutionary violence and the end of history: the divided self in Francophone thought, 1762-1914', in *Historicising the French Revolution*, ed. Carolina Armenteros, Tim Blanning, Isabel DiVanna and Dawn Dodds (Newcastle, 2008), p.7.
51. On Maistre's idea of sacrifice, see, in this volume, Yannis Constantinidès' article, 'Two great enemies of the Enlightenment: Joseph de Maistre and Schopenhauer' and Douglas Hedley's article, 'Enigmatic images of an invisible world: sacrifice, suffering and theodicy in Joseph de Maistre'.
52. Maistre, *Eclaircissement sur les sacrifices*, in Glaudes (ed.), *Maistre: Œuvres*, p.803-39.
53. Lamennais, *De la Société première et de ses lois, Œuvres complètes*, 21 vol. (Reprint, Geneva, 1981), vol.18, p.194.

itself: 'l'idée antique selon laquelle la Création étoit représentée comme une sorte d'anéantissement et de sacrifice de l'Etre infini' was very probably right.[54]

Maistre and Rousseau also parted over perfectibility. Though both agreed that human nature is the impulse to self-perfection, they diverged on how perfectibility works across time. Rousseau was an 'enemy of the future',[55] a thinker who believed that perfectibility leads only to moral corruption and the conquest of nature. This is why the society of *Du Contrat social* is possible only among innocent peoples, newly born, whose limpid souls can be manipulated with ease by the Legislator. By contrast, Maistre drew much closer to the Enlightenment mainstream in believing that humanity can progress morally and almost endlessly by accumulating social experience through time. He welcomed civilisation. But where the *philosophes* saw experience and reason as the fruits and vehicles of moral progress, Maistre believed that experience could not aid advance unless it was accompanied by the desire to be saved.[56]

If society's altars demanded sacrifice, the passions had to be quieted. On this point Maistre rejoined Rousseau, although the two differed on the means to be employed. Like the Legislator of *Du Contrat social*, Emile's tutor restrained the passions through carefully staged arrangements designed to educe prescribed feelings from his pupil. Maistre's teachers, on the contrary, moulded characters by discipline and example. Recalling how he was made to recite his lessons daily as a child, Maistre wrote that he had been 'élevé dans toute la sévérité ancienne, abîmé dès le berceau dans les études sérieuses'.[57] The language of spoiling ('abîmé') recalls Rousseau's denaturation, the fragmentation of natural man into a rifted social being. Maistre put it bluntly in his notebooks: 'La puissance une fois domptée demeure toujours dans cet état [...] c'est ainsi qu'un enfant morigéné pour un gâteau apprend à s'abstenir dans la suite d'une femme ou d'une Terre'.[58]

Despite all these similarities, Maistre chided *Emile* as the culmination of a philosophy incapable of allaying suffering. Discussing Herder's reaction to Voltaire's poem on Lisbon, the Count of *Les Soirées* notes:

> Les éléments s'assemblent, les éléments se désunissent; *c'est une loi nécessaire de la nature:* qu'y a-t-il donc là d'étonnant ou qui puisse motiver une plainte? [...]

54. Lamennais, *Esquisse d'une philosophie*, in *OC*, vol.8, p.112.
55. On Rousseau's attitude to the future, see George Armstrong Kelly, 'Rousseau, Kant, and history', *Journal of the history of ideas* 29, 3 (1968), p.347-64.
56. For a fuller discussion of this theme, see, in this volume, Yannis Constantinidès' article, 'Two great enemies of the Enlightenment: Joseph de Maistre and Schopenhauer'.
57. Maistre, Letter to Comte de Marcellus, 13 March 1820, *OC*, vol.14, p.208.
58. Maistre, *Archives de Joseph de Maistre et de sa famille*, 2J21, p.120.

N'est-ce pas, Messieurs, que voilà une belle consolation [...]? Mais la philosophie n'en sait pas davantage. Depuis Epictète jusqu'à l'*évêque de Weimar*, et jusqu'à la fin des siècles, ce sera sa manière invariable et *sa loi nécessaire*. Elle ne connaît pas l'huile de la consolation. Elle dessèche, elle racornit le coeur, et lorsqu'elle a endurci un homme, elle croit avoir fait un sage.

The observation applies also to *Emile*, as Maistre explains in a footnote:

Jean-Jacques a justifié cette observation, lorsqu'à la suite de son vain pathos de morale et de vertu, il a fini par nous dire: 'L'homme sage et supérieur à tous les revers est celui qui ne voit dans tous ses malheurs que les coups de l'aveugle nécessité'. [...] Toujours l'homme *endurci* à la place de l'homme *résigné*! Voilà tout ce qu'ont su nous prêcher ces précepteurs du genre humain. Emile, retiens bien cette leçon de ton maître: ne pense point à Dieu avant vingt ans, et tu seras à cet âge une charmante créature![59]

*Emile*'s readers may find it odd that a book whose professed originality rested on developing sentiment at the expense of dry reason should be accused of dessicating the heart. Yet Maistre believed that this was the case both because *Emile*'s religious education was tardy, and because his theology was minimalist. In depriving religion of mystery and dogma, Rousseau's religion divested the heart of love objects and shrank it. When it came to developing emotion, leading the self out of itself and depositing it in something greater than itself, Maistre was more Rousseauist than Rousseau;[60] and he blamed *Emile* for undermining its own ends.

Nor could Maistre have approved of Rousseau's tendency, discerned too by Edmund Burke, to glorify narcissism. The virtue of Rousseau's lovers, rewarded by self-regard, would have seemed dubious to any serious Christian moralist and reader of the masters of Port-Royal. In the passage quoted above, Emile and Sophie rise in their own esteem as they contemplate their sacrifices. Nothing similar in Maistrian thought: the child who gives up cake learns to do so simply because the health of his body and soul and the order of the world requires it, not because he will think better of himself as a result. The contrary implied what Christian thinkers from Paul to Nicole had warned was the most dangerous, because least perceptible, source of corruption – the pride that is born of the awareness of one's virtue.[61]

A further disadvantage of an education based wholly on rational

---

59. Maistre, *Les Soirées de Saint-Pétersbourg*, in Glaudes (ed.), *Maistre: Œuvres*, p.563-64.
60. Maistre modelled the process of learning as the soul's movement of love for objects of knowledge. See the *Examen de la philosophie de Bacon*, in *OC*, vol.6, p.305.
61. See Dale Van Kley, 'Pierre Nicole, Jansenism, and the morality of enlightened self-interest', in *Anticipations of the Enlightenment in England, France and Germany*, ed. Alan C. Kors and Paul J. Korshim (Philadelphia, PA, 1987), p.69-85.

appeal was its ultimate dependence on manipulation. In the eighteenth
century, the word 'manipulation' was not used to describe human
relations, but the concept it denotes is present in Rousseau's works.
*Emile*'s tutor and the Legislator of *Du Contrat social* both excel at creating
situations that bring their pupils/peoples to follow, of their own accord,
the course of action pre-arranged for them – all the while believing that
they are doing what they please. These are situations of 'consensual
nonconsensuality' whereby individuals desire the circumstances of their
own domination.[62] But what happens when the manipulator leaves? *Du
Contrat social* falls silent about life in the society of the general will after
the departure of the quasi-divine Legislator. Nor do we know much
about Clarens' fate after the death of its Legislator figure Julie.[63] More
than one sign, however, suggests that the utopia will not survive her.[64]
The impression is reinforced by *Emile et Sophie, ou Les solitaires* (1780),
*Emile*'s unfinished sequel, where Rousseau explores the dangers of an
education founded entirely on the stimulation of reason by external
agents. In this fragmentary novel, Emile's life breaks down after his tutor
leaves, and he recaptures peace only in the nostalgic solitude that
succeeds a relentless series of calamities.

Free of manipulation, Maistre's own pedagogy works through
example, habit and authority instead. The goal is, firstly, never to
dehumanise people by making them the objects of another's hidden
and designed control; and, secondly, to make of virtue not a piecemeal,
rational response to circumstance – since reason may sometimes fail if it
has to consider every moral situation in turn – but of will and habit
ingrained. Only so can one choose virtue invariably and without waver-
ing. Which is not to say that virtue requires thoughtlessness. Quite the
contrary: in his educational writings Maistre defends the classical curriculum and the study of the humanities over the sciences because he
believes that education should above all impart the capacity for moral
reflection. In the schools of old, he reminisces,

> Le professeur choisissait un sujet tiré tantôt de la religion, tantôt de la
> morale, ou même de la Fable, et le proposait à ses élèves. Il disait, par
> exemple: *Midas obtint des dieux la grâce que tout ce qu'il toucherait se changeât en or:
> amplifiez, Messieurs, les inconvénients de cette folle demande.* Tout jeune homme les
> voyait bien en masse, mais chacun y mettait le degré d'imagination dont il

62. Elizabeth Wingrove, *Rousseau's republican romance* (Princeton, NJ, 2000).
63. On Julie as a Machiavellian character, see Emanuele Saccarelli, 'The Machiavellian
    Rousseau: gender and family relations in the *Discourse on the origin of inequality*', *Political
    theory* 37, 4 (2009), p.482-510.
64. Melissa Matthes, '*Nouvelle Héloïse* and the supplement of sexual difference', in *The Rape of
    Lucretia and the founding of republics: readings in Livy, Machiavelli and Rousseau* (University Park,
    PA, 2000), p.129.

était pourvu, et il s'accoutumait à voir un objet sous toutes les faces possibles. Toutes ces *amplifications* étant faites et mises sous les yeux du professeur, il montrait à ses disciples avec quelle grâce et quelle fécondité Ovide a traité ce sujet, et c'était une nouvelle leçon.[65]

Ovid's story so eloquently told would move the young pupils given their own, recent attempt to recount it. It would teach them to love beauty and develop their moral reason. It would elevate their souls and feed their minds at once.

Rousseau's overt attitude to reading literature could not be more opposed to this – although his full opinion, as so frequently happens, was more complex than at first appears. Emile does not read works of fiction. In fact, Emile reads hardly at all, only Homer's *Iliad* and some works by objective historians. As the most ancient work of classical literature, the *Iliad* is the least dishonoured by civilisation; and as one based on real events, it is less fiction than history, a poem that develops the imagination without corrupting it. The objective historians who refrain from judgment, for their part, allow their readers to reach their own conclusions.[66] They are the obverses of Ovid, that seductive protagonist of eighteenth-century schoolbooks: *his* story is educational less because of the events it relates, than because of the eternal voice that recounts them.

Of course the fact that *Emile* itself – like *Julie* – was a novel, did not exactly lend credit to its creator's warnings against fiction. Rousseau was aware of this and defended himself in the first preface to *Julie*, writing that '[i]l faut des spectacles dans les grandes villes, et des romans aux peuples corrompus'; that '[c]e livre n'est point fait pour circuler dans le monde, et convient à très peu de lecteurs'; that no girl should read it, since 'jamais fille chaste n'a lu de romans'.[67] These caveats contrasted strangely with the book's instant and massive success, especially among women; but their concern with moral degeneration by fiction was real. Excepting the *Iliad*, Fénelon's *Télémaque*[68] and his own novels, Rousseau did not advocate reading literature of any kind.[69] His entire pedagogy strove to encourage the individual to interact directly with the world and nature, driving him to form his own, uninfluenced opinions, preventing his mind from being filled with unnecessary facts, and privileging the practical arts over intellectual exercise.

65. Maistre, *Cinq lettres,* in *OC,* vol.8, p.176-77.
66. *Emile,* Book IV.
67. Rousseau, *Julie,* p.vi.
68. This, along with a book on arithmetic – useful in teaching her how to keep household accounts – is Sophie's sole reading in Book V.
69. On the reading that Rousseau reserves for his ideal pupils, see Barbara Negroni, 'La bibliothèque d'Emile et de Sophie: la fonction des livres dans la pédagogie de Rousseau', *Dix-huitième siècle* 19 (1987), p.379-90.

Maistre too complained about the Encyclopedist drive to orient education around the assimilation of facts. He wrote one of his pedagogical works against the *Prospectus disciplinarum* of Ignatius Fessler (1756-1839), a renegade Hungarian monk who enjoyed great influence in Russia, and who proposed to give the Nevsky seminarians at St Petersburg an encyclopedic education aimed at the mastery of dozens of disciplines.[70] Maistre believed that this plan would promote mental sterility and confusion by stuffing students' heads with an immensity of information. And he thought that the Nevsky educators should remember with Aristotle that the true aim of education is learning how to learn. Under the *ancien régime*, teachers had encouraged, but not exacted, memorisation of the classics.[71] What they *had* demanded was abundant reflection and eloquent writing on ethical and rhetorical paragons. Accordingly, they had privileged the study of what we would now call the humanities over that of the sciences. Having stood the test of time, the classics were eternally able to nourish the mind and soul; and failure to read them could leave both in a state of desolation. Voltaire exemplified this.[72] Although Maistre always disliked him, he was unpleasantly surprised when browsing through his library in Russia:

> en parcourant les livres rassemblés par un homme, on connaît en peu de temps ce qu'il sait et ce qu'il aime. C'est sous ce point de vue que la bibliothèque de Voltaire est particulièrement curieuse. On ne revient pas de son étonnement en considérant l'extrême médiocrité des ouvrages qui suffirent jadis au *patriarche* de Ferney. On y chercherait en vain ce qu'on appelle les *grands* livres et les éditions recherchées, surtout des classiques. Le tout ensemble donne une idée d'une bibliothèque formée pour amuser les soirées d'un campagnard. [...] La collection entière est une démonstration que Voltaire fut étranger à toute espèce de connaissances approfondies, mais surtout à la littérature classique.[73]

The reference to the evenings of a 'campagnard' recalls the second preface to *Julie*, the 'Entretien sur les romans', where Rousseau explains that his own work is not like fashionable books, which 'pourraient servir à la fois d'amusement, d'instruction, de consolation au campagnard, malheureux seulement parce qu'il pense l'être', but which 'ne semblent

---

70. The *Observations sur le* Prospectus disciplinarum *ou plan d'étude proposé pour le Séminaire de Newsky par le Professeur Fessler*, in *OC*, vol.8, p.233-65.

71. Maistre, *Cinq lettres*, p.176.

72. On Maistre and Voltaire, see also, in this volume, Douglas Hedley's article, 'Enigmatic images of an invisible world: sacrifice, suffering and theodicy in Joseph de Maistre'.

73. Maistre, 'La Bibliothèque de Voltaire', in Barthelet (ed.), *Maistre: Dossiers H*, p.261. The original passage is from Maistre, *Les Soirées de Saint-Pétersbourg*, in Glaudes (ed.), *Maistre: Œuvres*, p.573n.

faits [...] que pour le rebuter de son état'.[74] Unlike these productions *Julie* is targeted primarily at 'campagnards', whose simplicity its author prizes.

By contrast, and though originally a provincial himself, Maistre compared Voltaire to a country person in order to suggest someone who was not intellectually serious. The analogy was negative because city people were most likely to read the classics and thus be morally inspired. Where for Rousseau the literary imagination was dangerous and best made to defer to reality, for Maistre it was the indispensable forge of morally insightful individuals. Hence the central pedagogical role the latter ascribed to literature – down to the dramatic plays of Vittorio Alfieri (1749-1803), a contemporary poet whose plays were rife with republican sympathies and Enlightened opinions, but whose verse was morally illustrative and provided models of eloquence.[75]

Maistre and Rousseau were both participating in a debate on the relationship between morality and fiction, and on the role of the imagination in the formation of character, that had traversed French thought at least since the *Traité de l'éducation des filles* (1687) of François de Fénelon (1651-1715). Germaine de Staël (1766-1817) had made a notable recent contribution to it in her *Essai sur les fictions* (1795), which rejected marvellous and allegorical fiction, philosophical and historical novels, in favour of moral tales realistically depicting the great panoply of human characters and social conditions. Staël's aim – which she may have discussed with Maistre during the conversations the two held at Coppet around the time of the *Essai*'s publication[76] – was to find a genre where fiction and moral philosophy could complement each other. As Maistre saw it, however, the classics could still stimulate reflection ideally, so that moral education depended less on devising new genres, than on knowing how to read existing ones. In the post-revolutionary world, the most urgent task was to make sure that 'amplifying' on literary texts continued to precede scientific fact-crunching. Indeed as early as 1791 Maistre was already mourning, with Rousseau, the rise of the sciences and the flight of early education from the domestic sphere:

> Au lieu de laisser mûrir le caractère sous le toit paternel, au lieu de le comprimer dans la solitude pour lui donner du ressort, ils ont répandu l'enfance au dehors: ils ont voulu faire des savants avant de faire des hommes [...] ils ont présenté la morale comme une *thèse*, et non comme un *code*.
> [...]
> Le bon sens, éclairé par la vertu, suffit pour donner une excellente éducation

---

74. Rousseau, *Julie*, p.xiv.
75. On Maistre's opinion of Alfieri, see Maistre to Adèle de Maistre, 7 January 1807, *OC*, vol.10, p.295-96.
76. For Maistre's account of these conversations, see *OC*, vol.9, p.443-44.

> [...] nous confondons deux éducations absolument différentes: l'éducation
> morale et l'éducation scientifique. La première seule est nécessaire [...] On ne
> peut nier, sans doute, l'importance secondaire et les difficultés de la seconde;
> mais lorsque le décorateur entre dans un hôtel, l'architecte s'est retiré.[77]

Training the heart must come first, as Rousseau maintained, and during
childhood, this requires some retirement. None, however, should be as
severe as Emile's, an orphan who before adolescence has no human
contact with anyone besides his nanny and his tutor. The withdrawal
Maistre advocates – and that Rousseau too recommends in cases less
optimal than his fictional pupil's – is within the family, the social
microcosm that develops children's feelings before releasing them into
'le grand monde', that cruel educator of minds. Here Maistre and
Rousseau are perfectly agreed.

Maistre wrote several opuscules on education in St Petersburg in 1810
– the *Observations sur le Prospectus disciplinarum*, the *Cinq lettres sur
l'éducation publique en Russie* and the *Mémoire sur la liberté de l'enseignement
public*. 1810 was the year that Alexander I's Kantian minister, Mikhail
Speransky (1772-1839), set out to replace the classical curriculum with a
science-based one inspired by the radical Enlightenment. A detractor of
these reforms, Maistre responded to them by attacking 'la science', a
term by which he meant alternately the natural sciences and specialised
knowledge of any kind. In the *Cinq lettres*, he counselled against studying
the former throughout the six years of pre-university education. Physics
could be studied in the seventh year, but as an optional subject.[78] It came
last because the sciences are inherently subversive subjects that implant
in the heart feelings of omniscience and pride, so that students must be
solidly grounded in virtue before confronting them.[79] It was a very
Rousseauian attitude. Emile's own training in the sciences had been
exceedingly sparse, imparting to him only those aspects of them he could
execute himself. Thus he knew nothing of medicine except hygiene,
because hygiene is the only practical part of medicine. '[E]ncore',
Rousseau added, 'l'hygiène est-elle moins une science qu'une vertu'.[80]
True science, or at least that worth knowing, flowed less from technical
knowledge than from moral attitudes.

Maistre and Rousseau diverged, however, around the practicality/
intellectualism and solitude/socialisation dualities. Following Fénelon's
counsel that girls acquire only applicable knowledge, Rousseau made

---

77. Maistre, *Discours à Madame la marquise de Costa sur la vie et la mort de son fils Alexis-Louis-Eugène de Costa, OC,* vol.7, p.236.
78. Maistre, *Cinq lettres,* p.178.
79. Maistre, *Cinq lettres,* p.165.
80. Rousseau, *Emile,* p.31.

sure that Emile and Sophie were pragmatists. Maistre lacked such qualms. His pedagogy gave objects of knowledge to the soul to enable it to grow in love,[81] convinced that even impractical things are worth knowing – or, more accurately, that there need be no such thing as impractical knowledge, since once the soul learns to love knowledge, it can expand in beneficence.

Not that Maistre was a trusting Platonist who assumed that knowing the good yields right action.[82] Virtue for him was a habit acquired through incessant effort and adequate socialisation in relative retirement. Rousseau isolated Emile and kept him friendless to preserve his innocence. More moderate, Maistre wrote to the Marquise de Costa that '[é]loigner l'enfant des mauvais exemples, c'est-à-dire du grand monde, ramener doucement sa volonté lorsqu'elle s'écarte du pôle, et surtout bien agir devant lui'[83] were the essentials of a good education. But though these essentials might require domesticity, they never required solitude. Objecting to Fessler's *Prospectus*, Maistre reminisced on the practices of the *ancien régime*'s *collèges* to argue that a good education requires constant, if carefully arranged, socialisation:

> Le jour, les élèves n'étaient jamais seuls. Le travail même se faisait dans une salle de réunion, sous les yeux des supérieurs; et la loi stricte du silence donnait tous les avantages de la solitude, séparés de ses inconvénients. La nuit, les élèves dormaient chacun dans une chambre séparée, pour éviter toute espèce de communication; et chaque porte vitrée, ou à claire-voie, ouvrait sur un dortoir commun, éclairé aux deux extrémités. Un homme de confiance s'y promenait jusqu'à l'heure du lever, et veillait cette jeunesse comme on veille un malade.

A footnote adds: 'Je relèverai ici en passant une distraction de l'auteur du plan.[84] Au chap. VIᵉ, il met au nombre des corrections la *clôture isolée, sans aucun moyen d'occupation*. Il n'est pas possible de se tromper plus visiblement et plus dangereusement. Le jeune homme ne doit jamais habiter seul avec son imagination; et la plus mauvaise compagnie pour lui, c'est lui-même'.[85] Emile's tutor had discerned the same danger, prudently controlling the length of the child's sleep. Maistre and Rousseau knew that the imagination could degrade minds, as Fénelon maintained, and Staël worried in certain cases; but only when it was undirected and left to its own devices. Well socialised, guided by good

---

81. On the role of love in Maistrian epistemology, see *OC*, VI, p.305.
82. For an account of Maistre's Platonism, see Philippe Barthelet's paper in this volume, 'The Cambridge Platonists mirrored by Joseph de Maistre'.
83. Maistre, *Discours à Madame la marquise de Costa*, p.236.
84. A reference to Fessler and his *Prospectus*.
85. Maistre, *Cinq lettres*, p.191-92.

teachers and – Maistre insisted – great writers like Ovid, it was the faculty that enabled the love of beauty, the appreciation of virtue, and the rational discovery of good.

## Maistre's Rousseaus and their posterity

Rousseau's legacy to Maistrian thought is exceedingly varied, yet all the multiplicity acquires order once one considers that religion and, more specifically, the theme of the subtitle of *Les Soirées* – 'le gouvernement temporel de la Providence' – was the crux of the intellectual relationship between the two thinkers. As Maistre's notebooks reveal, he and Rousseau first diverged over revelation and God's immanence. Rousseau's denial of prophecy, miracles, prayer – all beliefs essential to Catholicism – challenged divine voluntarism and the anomalous knowledge it makes possible. Rousseau's God, moreover, was personal yet transcendent, reposing within conscience but abandoning nature to be ruled by laws. This was a God who could be in the world only in a derivative sense, as the consciences He inhabited deposited themselves in the state. Though originally Christian, He was incompatible with Catholicism, whose Church, clergy and saints, all visibly manifested in the world, were loci of direct contact between the divine and the secular, and whose political and religious institutions were divinely ordained, not humanly designed. So while for Maistre Rousseau was right that institutions were moral and could be known by reason, his intimation that God was absent from some of them and had arrived late in the rest was unthinkable. To dispel the nightmare, Maistre particularised Rousseau's society, mapped the self precisely, and developed, in *Les Soirées*, a historicism based on the idea of divinely willed exceptions.

Maistre's Rousseaus were three, each distinguished from the others by the philosophical function he exercised, and by Maistre's attitude to him. The first Rousseau was the pious smuggler, the theorist of conscience who let Christian metaphysics enter surreptitiously into the world of naturalist description that deist reason had claimed as its exclusive domain. He was a helpful and admired figure, and he survived, hushed and disguised, at the heart of the Counter-Revolution. Not so his alter egos: less interested in delaying God's departure, *they* formed Maistrian thought by antithesis. One of them, the critic of revelation, appeared as the herald of disillusionment who banished God from the homes that had so long been his, replacing his libertarian reign with a human tyranny devoid of limits. He had a pedagogical equivalent in the third Rousseau, a revolutionary who campaigned for solitude and whose philosophy taught the value of despair. Maistre fought these last two phantoms throughout his writing life with all the strength of his intellect.

Maistre's Rousseaus kept a low profile throughout the first half of the French nineteenth century, but the pious smuggler and the critic of revelation had a fertile posterity. They lurked behind Saint-Simon's *Nouveau christianisme* (1825), which echoed *Du Pape* by examining the interplay between Church and state throughout European history, prescribing that the temporal and spiritual powers of industrial society be renovated by being ever more carefully distinguished and defined. It was the argument that made Saint-Simon's heirs read Maistre enthusiastically. Building fervently on *Du Pape*, Auguste Comte,[86] the Saint-Simonians,[87] Philippe Buchez and the Buchezians[88] all looked forward to a new society directed by spiritual and temporal entities at once separate and collaborative. Eventually, all of them also maintained that the spiritual power should enjoy moral, social and political priority over the temporal. *Du Contrat social* had proposed this tacitly; but it was Maistre who concretised Rousseau sufficiently to enable the philosophy of history that bound traditionalists, socialists and positivists to emerge together.

As for the counter-revolutionaries, they made uses of Rousseau's philosophy that they were not anxious to advertise. Religion having been expelled from the state and civil society, it had to be put back in by force and reinvented as a social, political and psychological tool. Lamennais and his companions at *L'Avenir* did this more fervently than anyone. They executed what Maistre would have dubbed an Anti-Revolution, that is, the design to overthrow the Revolution by employing its own means.[89] Instead of waiting 'angelically' for evil to exhaust itself as the Counter-Revolution recommended. Maistre decried the Anti-Revolution as a perfidious shadow of the 'satanic' object it sought to destroy. But having learned from Rousseau that religion is the cement of polities, he tried to pour it as generously as he could into the widening cracks within post-revolutionary European society – perhaps without realising fully the implications of his choice.[90]

---

86. On Comte's conception of the spiritual and temporal powers, see Mary Pickering, *Auguste Comte: an intellectual biography*, 3 vol. (Cambridge, 1993-2009).

87. On the Saint-Simonians' religion, see Serge Zenkine, 'L'Utopie religieuse des saint-simoniens: le sémiotique et le sacré', in *Etudes saint-simoniennes*, ed. Philippe Régnier ('Littératures et idéologies', 2002), p.33-60.

88. On Buchez's religion, see Michael Reardon, 'The reconciliation of Christianity with progress: Philippe Buchez', *The review of politics* 23, 4 (1971), p.512-37 and François-André Isambert, *Politique, religion et science de l'homme chez Philippe Buchez (1796-1865)* (Paris, 1967).

89. Antoine Compagnon, *Les Antimodernes. De Joseph de Maistre à Roland Barthes* (Paris, 2005), p.28-9.

90. Although he does seem to have adumbrated them anxiously. '*Mon livre ne fera que du mal*', he wrote to his daughter Constance regarding *Du Pape* in a moment of despondency. Quoted in Jacques Lovie, 'Constance de Maistre: Eléments pour une biographie', *Revue des études maistriennes* 4 (1978), p.164.

# Two great enemies of the Enlightenment:
# Joseph de Maistre and Schopenhauer

YANNIS CONSTANTINIDÈS

Joseph de Maistre was completing in sorrow his writing of *Les Soirées de Saint-Pétersbourg* when the young Schopenhauer published, in 1818, to general indifference, his masterwork, *The World as will and idea*.[1] Although fond of French works, which he read without difficulty since he had lived in Le Havre during his adolescence, Schopenhauer nowhere in his writings (posthumous works included) mentions the famous counter-revolutionary. In his library we find only Xavier de Maistre's *Voyage autour de ma chambre* (1794). No doubt, however, he would have recognised in him a precursor if he had read him, since they have in common a ferocious rejection of rationalist optimism and of the generous ideals of the Enlightenment. So it is not so much a question here of any influence, even indirect, of Maistre on Schopenhauer, than of drawing the outlines of an elective affinity, largely ignored in the secondary literature.

To my knowledge, there exists only one article,[2] already quite old, which attempts this undoubtedly risky parallel between two thinkers who at first glance seem so disparate in every respect. How in effect can we establish a convincing link between the great Ultramontane Catholic and the 'grumpy Buddhist' and atheist? The first has only disdain for 'philosophism' and treats Kant bluntly and with a certain casualness while the second only rejects the university philosophy of his time, on the contrary showing an unlimited admiration for the author of the *Critique of pure reason* (1781). However, despite the fundamental differences between their thoughts, they share a common vision of life.

It is indeed striking to see to what extent Maistre and Schopenhauer

1.   This article was translated from French by Richard A. Lebrun. The title of the article is of course an ironic wink at the well-known text by Isaiah Berlin, 'Two Enemies of the Enlightenment' (Hamann and Maistre). Rather than defending the Enlightenment against obscurantist thinkers, the purpose here is to highlight the critique of the Enlightenment's own obscurantism. I would like to thank Carolina Armenteros, François Félix, Richard Lebrun and Jean-Yves Pranchère for their critical comments.

2.   Fernand Caussy, 'Joseph de Maistre et Schopenhauer', *L'Ermitage*, July-December 1906, p.24-42. Some brief indications on the relationship between Schopenhauer and Maistre will also be found in some notes in Emile Dermenghem's work, *Joseph de Maistre mystique* (Paris, 1923).

are closely related as regards the heart of the matter: a tragic conception
of the world undoubtedly, but which all the same allows a glimpse of
salvation. The critique of the naïve optimism of the Enlightenment in the
case of both these dream breakers is based on the evidence of the tragic
character of an existence deprived of all freedom, the individual being
only a plaything – of Providence for the one and of the will to live (*Wille
zum Leben*) for the other. Certainly, Schopenhauer believes in neither
Providence nor original sin, but that does not keep him from considering man as a 'guilty innocent', predestined to be a wicked egoist. Where
Maistre takes it out on the Rousseauian fiction of the natural goodness of
man, Schopenhauer makes his own the Hobbesian vision of the state of
nature as a war of all against all. The conclusive 'all is bad' of the Count[3]
finds an echo in the gibes that the Frankfurt philosopher addresses to
Leibniz's 'best of all possible worlds'.[4] This extremely black picture too
often overshadows the belief of the two authors in a final reversibility:
even as the 'satanic' Revolution is for Maistre a kind of ruse by Providence, which only allows humanity to sink into sin in order to permit
grace, Schopenhauer's Will ends up suppressing itself by clearly becoming conscious of its nature.

This idea of a universal restoration of all things, in the sense that
Origen understood it (*apocatastasis pantôn*), forbids their being con-
veniently classified as reactionary thinkers or 'prophets of the past'. If
they are really *anti-moderns*,[5] this is not because of the rejection of all
possibility of human perfectibility, but only of the illusion characteristic
of the Enlightenment of an emancipation of man by his own forces.
Humanity as a whole *is* morally progressing in the course of time
although it gives the false impression of regressing continually. There
is thus a tortuous dialectic that for both leads to the final Redemption:
the total unchaining of evil is the condition of its exhaustion. The
individual, be he exceptional, counts for nothing in the realisation of
this last justice, divine for Maistre, immanent for Schopenhauer, who

---

3.    Maistre, *Considérations sur la France*, ch.3, in Glaudes (ed.), *Maistre: Œuvres*, p.218: 'Il n'y a que
      violence dans l'univers; mais nous sommes gâtés par la philosophie moderne, qui a dit que
      *tout est bien*, tandis que le mal a tout souillé, et que, dans un sens très vrai, *tout est mal*,
      puisque rien n'est à sa place. La note tonique du système de notre création ayant baissé,
      toutes les autres ont baissé proportionnellement, suivant les règles de l'harmonie. *Tous les
      êtres gémissent* et tendent, avec effort et douleur, vers un autre ordre de choses'.
4.    Arthur Schopenhauer, *The World as will and idea*, bk.4, sect.59. See also Supplements to
      bk.4, ch.46: 'And to this world, to this scene of tormented and agonised beings, who only
      continue to exist by devouring each other [...] to this world it has been sought to apply the
      system of optimism, and demonstrate to us that it is the best of all possible worlds. The
      absurdity is glaring'. Trans. R. B. Haldane and J. Kemp (London, 1883, tenth printing,
      1957), vol.3, p.392.
5.    See Compagnon, *Les Antimodernes*.

does not however hesitate to make his own the Christian eschatological vocabulary in the fourth part of *The World*. The genius ceases to be an unconscious instrument of Providence or the Will, contrary to the common mortal, but his extreme lucidity scarcely permits him to recognise the invisible hand everywhere in the work.

Maistre and Schopenhauer's opposition to the ideals of the Enlightenment is thus clearly of Gnostic inspiration:[6] this world is *radically* bad, but there is at the same time the dream or the matching piece of an ideal 'world' (Schopenhauer identifies it with the Buddhists' nirvana), whose epiphany is dogmatically judged certain. The blind confidence of the Enlightenment in the critical power of reason gives way to the irresistible force of a quasi-mystic illumination. This, in passing, is what explains the apocalyptic tone often employed by Maistre as by Schopenhauer, which seems to discredit them as philosophers. It is that the ultimate truth remains hidden for the greatest number; it is necessary to begin by disillusioning people if one really wants them to see straight. Despite the famous *Sapere aude*, the rationalism of the Enlightenment does not dare reflect on the essence of existence. The boldness of knowing stops before this 'gnose', which only reveals itself to those who go beyond reason.

These enemies of the Enlightenment cannot however be rightly accused of irrationalism: it is simply a question for Maistre and for Schopenhauer of becoming conscious of the limits of reason, whose role is important but subordinate to intuition. They should not therefore be classified as *Counter-Enlightenment* thinkers since the Enlightenment's thirst for emancipation is challenged less than its bad orientation. Their aim is paradoxically to fulfill the programme the Enlightenment has not succeeded in realising: to struggle effectively against voluntary alienation so as to have humanity finally leave the state of minority in which it takes pleasure even while it strongly denies it.

Before considering alternately their harsh criticism of the rationalist optimism of modernity and the eschatological horizon of their thoughts, let us begin with some idiosyncratic considerations that will give flesh to this parallel. Far from being negligible, the *little facts*, as Nietzsche calls them, often help to understand great doctrines. What is striking, first of all, is the community of destiny of these two unclassifiable thinkers, who were deliberately behind their time. One could thus say of Schopenhauer that he was more a man of the eighteenth than of the nineteenth century.

---

6.   This of course does not mean that Maistre is an orthodox Gnostic. As Jean-Louis Soltner rightly observes, he was influenced by many systems of thought, and in particular Origen's Gnosticism: 'Où situer Maistre parmi ces systèmes? [...] Il est surtout proche d'Origène et de sa gnose chrétienne, interprétation spirituelle des écritures, ainsi que de sa vision cosmogonique très large'. 'Le Christianisme de Joseph de Maistre', in Barthelet (ed.), *Maistre*: Dossiers H, p.485-86.

He could even be portrayed as a romantic hero, just like Maistre.[7] Challemel-Lacour's famous description of him as a disabused wise old man is very eloquent in this respect.[8] Very critical towards triumphant scientism, Schopenhauer very much interested himself in unexplained phenomena: animal magnetism, turning tables, manifestations of spirits, etc.[9] He thought, like Maistre, for a time seduced by Illuminism, that the invisible matters more than the visible.[10] Moreover they both understood genius as an inspired being, an exception to the order of nature[11].

Let us add to this general framework the common experience of solitude and the bitterness of not being recognised for their just worth. With this slight difference: Schopenhauer never doubted that the future would end by proving him right. This is why he welcomed with a certain irony ('The Nile has reached Cairo') in his last years the first signs of the consecration of his thought. Maistre, for his part, had not even had the right to this consolation. His unshakeable faith in himself did not however render Schopenhauer particularly serene: his intimate notes show us that he was always anxious, to the point of a delirium of persecution.[12] The Savoyard count's faith undoubtedly preserved him from such intimate distress, but his correspondence all the same reveals some accents of despair, at which he prefers to smile out of a sense of decency, faced with the really long delays of divine justice.

They were both probably too conscious of their mission of awakening others to experience peace of mind themselves. Besides, anyone who goes against the current and poses as a moral censor can obviously provoke only the hostility or rejection of his contemporaries. Without the help of a fundamental intuition, one could not go as far as assume the uncomfortable position of a mocked or ignored Cassandra, if not by a vain bravado. In Maistre's case, it was his understanding of the Revolution as an 'epoch' and not as a simple historical event. One can say without exaggeration that his whole work follows from this 'illumination', that he formulated for the first time in the *Discours à Madame*

7.   See in this volume Douglas Hedley's paper, 'Enigmatic images of an invisible world: sacrifice, suffering, and theodicy in Joseph de Maistre'.
8.   Paul-Armand Challemel-Lacour, 'Un Bouddhiste contemporain en Allemagne. Arthur Schopenhauer,' in *Etudes et réflexions d'un pessimiste* (Paris, 1901), p.241-323.
9.   See especially the surprising 'Essay on spirit seeing and everything connected therewith', *Parerga and paralipomena*, trans. E. F. J. Payne, 2 vol. (Oxford, 1974), vol.1, ch.5, p.225-309.
10.  See *Les Soirées*, 5th dialogue: 'J'ai lu des millions de plaisanteries sur l'ignorance des anciens *qui voyaient des esprits partout*: il me semble que nous sommes beaucoup plus sots, nous qui n'en voyons nulle part'. Glaudes (ed.), *Maistre: Œuvres*, p.579.
11.  See in this volume Darrin McMahon's paper, 'The genius of Maistre'.
12.  See *About myself*, in *Manuscript remains*, trans. E. F. J. Payne, 4 vol. (Oxford, 1988–90), vol.4, p.483-520.

*la marquise de Costa* (1794). Schopenhauer in the same way constantly presents his 'unique thought', that is to say that the world is in its essence a merciless will to live, as the result of a true revelation. Moreover, he considered that his mission on earth was fulfilled with the publication of his *opus magnum, The World as will and idea.*

Despite the difference in content, these are unquestionably experiences of awakening, from which the truth appears in a single blow, without mediation of any kind. Perhaps this explains the haughtiness and absence of indulgence in the criticisms that they address to their adversaries as well as to human weaknesses. The certainty of possessing the truth seems to give them a kind of right to excess as well as guarding them in advance against the accusation of intellectual dishonesty. That Maistre was very unjust towards Rousseau and Kant, and Schopenhauer excessively severe with respect to the 'three sophists' (Fichte, Hegel and Schelling) – is not in doubt, but what better way to soothe the bitterness of being seen as outmoded than to use every available means, without the least restraint? After all, moderation suits only those who laboriously seek the truth and not those who have already found it and who are furious to see it trampled underfoot. Maistre's extravagances (eulogy of the executioner, etc.) are in this respect as famous as those of Schopenhauer, who went as far as composing a treatise detailing the different tricks that were permitted to gain influence over one's adversary in a discussion![13]

In this way their writings let a real jubilation show through in polemics, which contrasts with their flaunted pessimism. Relentlessness in discrediting a mortal enemy (Protestantism, for example, for Maistre, and university philosophy for Schopenhauer) is thus served by a caustic humour that diverts the reader in default of always convincing him. Malcontent minds will definitely judge this agonistic mood scarcely philosophic, but in reality there is in it the price of radicality, half-measures being precisely the usual flaw of rationalism according to Schopenhauer.

Certainly, the author of *The World*, unlike Maistre, did not directly or specifically criticise the Enlightenment, but he is the first philosopher to witness the decay of absolute reason and the failure of the vague desires for the emancipation of humanity. Reason for him is a docile instrument of the Will and only ends by freeing itself because, finally enlightened about its very nature, the Will renounces the blind tyranny that it exercises by suppressing itself. Schopenhauer is as fascinated by this major enemy of the human race, which he compares to the vital force of

---

13. *Eristische dialektik* (in *Manuscript remains*, vol.3), a posthumous work better known as *The Art of controversy* or *The Art of always being right.*

Bichat and Cabanis, as Maistre is by the Revolution. Surely what they both needed was such an arch-rival. This undoubtedly explains the extreme character of their critique of the rationalistic optimism of the Enlightenment: sometimes it is necessary to shout if one wants to make even the hard of hearing listen, as Nietzsche will subsequently say.

We have already mentioned the apocalyptic tone that our two authors willingly adopt. It is that they feel invested with a double mission of unveiling the true nature of things and indicating the possible horizon of salvation. Rationalistic optimism appears then as not only puerile, but absolutely scandalous. Maistre of course condemns the project of helping man to emancipate himself as a negation of original sin as well as grace. That is precisely 'le double et invariable caractère du philosophisme moderne, l'ignorance et l'effronterie'.[14] Moreover, ignorance of the truth necessarily leads to impudence, as Schopenhauer observes in his virulent critique of the 'philosophic farce' that the Hegelian theodicy represents to his eyes.[15] The chapter of the *Parerga and paralipomena* criticising university philosophy denounces more generally the eagerness of modern sophists to make themselves advocates of the *good* God to the point of peremptorily judging reality perfect and even rational. Schopenhauer, like Maistre, believes that philosophy and theology must remain distinct, philosophy having for its object not God, but the world.

Certainly, Schopenhauer defined himself as a philosopher while Maistre generally declined this label. Although he did not call himself a theologian either, the latter insisted on the danger of philosophy, 'c'est-à-dire la raison individuelle', venturing into the moral world.[16] It is admitted there as long as it stays in a subordinate position, but it appears to him 'détestable'[17] when it claims to legislate in those matters that are foreign to it. Even if he refuses categorically that philosophy be submitted to religion, Schopenhauer also considers that reason, being a simple instrument, in no case should be elevated to the rank of the source from which all virtue flows.[18] In starting from very different premises, he thus rejoins Maistre in his less solidly supported but suggestive critique of Kant's practical reason.[19] Even 'pure' reason, being

---

14. *Les Soirées* in Glaudes (ed.), *Maistre: Œuvres*, 2nd dialogue, p.509.
15. See *On philosophy at the universities*, in *Parerga and paralipomena*, vol.1, ch.3, p.137-97.
16. See Darcel (ed.), *De la Souveraineté du peuple*, bk.I, ch.13, p.174.
17. Darcel (ed.), *De la Souveraineté du peuple*, p.175.
18. See *Prize essay on the basis of morals*, sect.6, in *The Two fundamental problems of ethics*, trans. C. Janaway (Cambridge, 2009), p.150-51.
19. See 'Sur la Philosophie de Kant (Notes de lecture), Analyse du livre de M. Villers intitulé Philosophie de Kant ou Principes fondamentaux de la philosophie transcendantale, traduit de l anglais de l'Edinburgh Review, tome I, janvier 1803, no. 3, pp. 352 ff, ed. Yves Madouas, in Barthelet (ed.), *Maistre*: Dossiers H , p.223-48 (especially p.239-41).

fallen, does not have access to the truths of intuition, which spring from a mysterious 'sens religieux'.[20] As for Schopenhauer, he postulates the existence of 'man's need of metaphysics',[21] which is not satisfied by physical explanations of reality. Notwithstanding their differences, most religions aim to satisfy this diffused but universal need to give a metaphysical meaning to death, sorrow, and moral evil.

It is for this reason that Schopenhauer is so wound up with respect to the materialism of his time, as flatly optimistic at base as its rival, absolute idealism. In reducing nature to a blind play of chemical forces, 'boy hairdressers'[22] like Büchner or Moleschott attack the very root of the irreducible metaphysical need, which they seek in some way to extirpate from the human heart. The *disenchantment* of the world is certainly something to achieve for Schopenhauer, but scientific materialism only inverts the idealist position without going past it. In its relentlessness to banish every transcendent principle, it shows itself as superficial as its enemy brother since it forgets equally to take into consideration the 'intimate core of nature', the obscure will to live. Yet, this reminds us more of the bad principle of the Gnostics than of the good finality of the rationalists. Even if Schopenhauer's Will is a blind force which does not really have the intention to harm, the truth is that the world is bad, radically bad.[23] Idealists as well as materialists marvel similarly at the order and the apparent beauty of the world, ruled according to them by divine or natural laws. It is therefore not that surprising that materialism ends by pledging allegiance to the traditional moral principles after having denied to religions any transcendent ground.

Schopenhauer does not have words hard enough to blast the irresponsibility of optimists of all colours, who repeat in choir the *panta kala lian* ('all is good') of Genesis:

> *optimism*, when it is not merely the thoughtless talk of such as harbour nothing but words under their low foreheads, appears not merely as absurd, but also as a really *wicked* way of thinking, as a bitter mockery of the unspeakable suffering of humanity. Let no one think that Christianity is

---

20. See *Les Soirées* in Glaudes (ed.), *Maistre: Œuvres*, 9th dialogue, p.711. On this point, see Dermenghem, 'L'Intuition', *Maistre mystique*, ch.2, second part.
21. 'On man's need of metaphysics', *The World*, vol.2, Supplements to bk.1, ch.17, p.359.
22. See his letter to Frauenstädt dated 29 June 1855 in *Gesammelte Briefe*, ed. Arthur Hübscher (Bonn, 1987), p.364-66.
23. See for instance this passage from the *Aphorisms on the wisdom of life*: 'generally speaking, the whole world lieth in wickedness, as was said long ago. Savages eat one another and civilised folk deceive one another; and this is what is called the way of the world'. *Parerga and paralipomena*, vol.1, ch.6, p.455.

favourable to optimism; for, on the contrary, in the Gospels world and evil are used as almost synonymous.[24]

Schopenhauer always judges scandalous and so to speak impious the optimism of the Old Testament. But if one sets aside his anti-Semitism or rather anti-Judaism, one will notice that he here renews, as atheist as he may be, the tragic vision of the world conveyed by Christianity and obviously by Maistre as well.

It is the modest veil thrown over original sin that indeed permits the defusing of the charge of despair that the Christian religion carries within itself. In thus choosing to conceal the first cause of moral evil, one can easily underestimate its effects. It is for this reason that the author of *Les Soirées* always makes it a duty to recall 'la grande loi de la destruction violente des êtres vivants', a consequence of the corruption of the world by original sin. There is no room for a more subtle portrait of life where the good and bad aspects would balance each other: 'La terre entière, continuellement imbibée de sang, n'est qu'un autel immense où tout ce qui vit doit être immolé sans fin, sans mesure, sans relâche, jusqu'à la consommation des choses, jusqu'à la mort de la mort'.[25]

What is particularly striking from our point of view in the famous passage from *Les Soirées* that outlines this great law with some strange delight, is that it applies to the whole of the kingdom of life, from plants to man, by following a gradation in cruelty. The similarity with the description that Schopenhauer gives of the will to live, already present in the mineral realm and more and more active insofar as it 'objectifies itself', is noteworthy. Moreover, Maistre speaks of 'une force *à la fois cachée et palpable*',[26] which prefigures exactly Schopenhauer's idea according to which we only know the Will by its indirect manifestations, its essence being for ever inaccessible to us. We must however decipher it by the marks it leaves behind to gain full consciousness of its underground action.

This is why Maistre and Schopenhauer constantly apply themselves to unveiling the principle of evil, which often advances masked. One could even say that its supreme ruse consists in convincing rationalists that it does not exist or that its role is subordinate to that of the good.[27] The

---

24. *The World*, vol.1, bk.4, sect.59, p.420.
25. *Les Soirées* in Glaudes (ed.), *Maistre: Œuvres*, 7th dialogue, p.661. This is at the conclusion of the Senator's long development on the 'loi générale qui pèse sur l'univers' (p.659) and which commands all living things to kill.
26. *Les Soirées* in Glaudes (ed.), *Maistre: Œuvres*, p.659 (emphasis added). The whole sentence reads as follows: 'Une force à la fois cachée et palpable se montre continuellement occupée à mettre à découvert le principe de la vie par des moyens violents'.
27. Here one thinks of Spinoza, for whom evil is only a bad encounter, and of Leibniz, who refuses to see it as diabolical.

dramatisation to which our iconoclasts willingly resort to thus has a didactic as well as a polemic virtue: it aims at brutally awakening, at putting an end to the dogmatic sleep of reason through the constant reminder of the nightmare of life.

This better explains the sarcasms that they addressed respectively to the infinite perfectibility attributed to Rousseau and to the alleged moral progress of humanity as conceived by Kant. Against the Rousseauian belief in a natural goodness of man, Maistre innovates in terms of theology by imagining an original sin of the second order.[28] 'L'homme est mauvais, horriblement mauvais',[29] the Count states, in sharp contrast with Rousseau's optimism. The paradoxical theme of the *bad* savage[30] seems precisely destined to deny the very possibility of natural innocence, nature necessarily carrying the stigmata of original sin. This is why Maistre considers the savage as the last rather than the first man, and even as the most debased being, while the true primitive, so to speak, on the contrary is placed at the origin and summit of civilisation. This mysterious first man, promised a fine future, certainly refers to humanity's condition in Eden before the Fall, to that Golden Age on which Maistre scarcely lingered, unlike the thinkers of the Primordial Tradition, René Guénon for instance, that he largely inspired. That was undoubtedly the real state of nature, irreversibly lost.

If he thus agrees with Rousseau in judging impossible a return to the state of nature, Maistre equally discourages any dream of improving humanity except by divine grace.[31] To the Enlightenment's utopian will of an historic accomplishment of mankind, he opposes the obviousness of an involution, of a growing natural and especially moral degradation. This anthropological pessimism is shared by Schopenhauer, who rejects Kant's eschatological vision of the progressive moral achievement of humanity. On the contrary, he agrees with Gobineau, who sees in man 'l'animal méchant par excellence':

> he is right, for man is the only animal who causes pain to others with no other object than wanting to do so. Other animals never do this except to satisfy their hunger or in the heat of conflict. [...] No animal tortures merely

---

28. See *Les Soirées* in Glaudes (ed.), *Maistre: Œuvres*, 2nd dialogue, p.485: 'il y a telle prévarication ou telle suite de prévarications qui peuvent dégrader absolument l'homme. C'est un *péché originel* du second ordre, mais qui nous représente, quoique imparfaitement, le premier'.

29. *Les Soirées* in Glaudes (ed.), *Maistre: Œuvres*, p.489.

30. See the afterword (entitled 'Le mauvais sauvage') to my edition of *Contre Rousseau (De l'état de nature)* by Joseph de Maistre (Paris, 2008), p.81-9.

31. In *Les Soirées*, the Senator thus announces 'une troisième explosion de la toute-puissante bonté en faveur du genre humain' (11th dialogue, p.767). This stunner would be the Coming of the third and last Reign, that of the Holy Spirit.

for the sake of torturing, but man does and this constitutes the *devilish* character that is far worse than the merely animal.[32]

Radical evil is in this sense the most complete expression of the will to live, which is the source and driving force of all bad passions: envy, wickedness, cruelty and the crafty joy (*Schadenfreude*), which Schopenhauer describes as 'diabolic'.[33] Civilisation for him is only a thin veneer or a cage which hardly contains the beast that lies within us. This is why he thinks, in accordance with his Hobbesian reading of the state of nature, that man needs a muzzle to keep him out of harm's way.

For one like Schopenhauer who claims that the human character is immutable,[34] historical progress can only appear as a gratifying illusion. 'The motto of history in general', he writes, 'should run: *Eadem, sed aliter*'.[35] Nothing new then under the sun; modernity has no reason to pride itself on its alleged moral superiority over more remote epochs. The same first cause, the will to live, produces the same disastrous effects as long as it has not been suppressed. Since envy, wickedness and cruelty are *involuntary* expressions of this avid thirst to live, the human will is unable to overcome them. As with Maistre, a providential outcome is required to break this eminently vicious circle, this 'wheel of Ixion' of the Will. Just as Providence uses the satanic Revolution as a roundabout way to achieve Redemption, it is the Will finally becoming aware of its diabolic character, in the person of this providential man that the saint is, that precipitates its end according to Schopenhauer.

Certainly, the German 'Buddhist' rejected the Christian doctrine of original sin, but he nevertheless went along with the ideas of guilt and redemption. Man in effect is *condemned* to exist and he cannot repent of being born, that is to say oppose himself to the will to live, until the scales fall from his eyes. A 'guilty innocent', he is above all guilty of still playing the fool's game of the Will, which seeks only to perpetuate itself. Final redemption is a simple matter of *conversion*: a changing of sign of the Will, which negates itself in us as will to live.[36] Man is therefore no more the author of his salvation than of his loss. He cannot strictly speaking be held responsible for radical evil, which is due to his very nature as a being of will for Schopenhauer and as a sinner for Maistre. It is then necessary to put into perspective the extreme judgments brought by the latter on

32. 'On ethics', *Parerga and paralipomena*, vol.2, ch.8, sect.114, p.118-9.
33. See *Prize essay*, sect.14, p.194.
34. In this he differs from Maistre, who believes in the historical perfectibility of human nature. See Armenteros, 'From human nature to normal humanity', p.121-5. See also her contribution to the present volume, 'Maistre's Rousseaus'.
35. ['the same things happen again and again, only differently']. 'On history', *The World*, vol.3, Supplements to bk.3, ch.38, p.226.
36. See the last section of *The World* (bk.4, sect.71).

vicious humanity. If man oscillates between greatness and misery, if he constantly hesitates between acting the angel and acting the beast, it is because he is a 'centaure monstrueux', 'le résultat de quelque forfait inconnu, de quelque mélange détestable qui [l']a *vicié* jusque dans son essence la plus intime'.[37] What is certain anyway is that he has never been innocent and that he can only be saved by a divine intervention.

Let us now consider the tortuous dialectic that led both Maistre and Schopenhauer to this most unexpected outcome: salvation. A true miracle was needed to unravel the skein of evil and to resolve the intimate contradiction that man is. This ultimate twist however fails to convince the reader: one cannot help finding these odd prophets more inspired in fulmination than in announcement, as if they were fundamentally susceptible to the deleterious charm of vice.

In any case, the conventional label of pessimism can hardly apply to thoughts that contain such a clear soteriological dimension. Readers always focus on the complacent descriptions that both give of the horror of existence and of the degradation of man, without paying the same attention, far from it, to the happy end that they promise. It is true that Maistre and Schopenhauer display treasures of imagination to paint everything black, their first goal being to awaken easy dreamers by force. But they sketch equally, with a certainly less assured line, the contours of the ideal future, that of the redemption of humanity, which presupposes the end of time for Maistre and the destruction of the world (as Will) for Schopenhauer.

The Count bases his quite optimistic prophecy on a very personal interpretation of the Christian dogma of the reversibility of merits.[38] Bearing perhaps in mind Voltaire's well-known objections to Leibniz's theodicy, he does not hesitate to highlight moral evil instead of lightening it as did the latter. It is no longer the innocent victim who complains about seeming divine injustice, but strangely the culprit himself who asks 'pourquoi l'innocence souffre dans le monde'.[39] To make such an appeal to the good will of the guilty can appear quite naïve, but it is not so much

---

37. *Les Soirées* in Glaudes (ed.), *Maistre: Œuvres*, 2nd dialogue, p.487 (emphasis added). Without totally clearing man of vice, this passage, which sounds strangely Pascalian, compares it to an organic illness. Besides, quoting the saying of Hippocrates, 'l'homme entier n'est qu'une maladie', Maistre comments in a note: 'Cela est vrai dans tous les sens'.

38. See the helpful article about reversibility in the *Dictionnaire Joseph de Maistre* in *Maistre: Œuvres*, p.1268-9. Pierre Glaudes there observes that 'dans la lecture qu'en donne Maistre, le dogme de la réversibilité conduit à une sorte de sacralisation du mal, dont il fait l'instrument privilégié de la Volonté divine dans le commerce qu'elle entretient avec les hommes depuis la Chute'. p.1269.

39. *Les Soirées* in Glaudes (ed.), *Maistre: Œuvres*, 10th dialogue, p.753. The reply is also surprising: 'elle souffre pour vous, si vous le voulez'.

a question here of repentance as of becoming conscious of the essential solidarity between good and evil, the victim and the executioner. If one remembers that for Maistre no human being is really innocent, one understands that the redemption of the executioner, and therefore of humanity in its entirety, can only happen through the recognition of a community of destiny resembling a *communio peccatorum*.

Let us note in passing that Baudelaire's *Heautontimoroumenos* poem is much closer to Maistre's thought than René Girard's scapegoat theory, which however is largely inspired by it. In refusing the idea of expiation,[40] the latter removes from the Maistrian doctrine of reversibility all its paradoxical force. The victim, chosen a bit by chance, is sacrificed on the altar of the general interest to re-establish a social rather than a cosmic equilibrium. The sacrifice of Christ, the only innocent who really expiates the sins of others, is supposed to overcome the 'logic' of violence precisely by putting an end to the arbitrariness of compensations. René Girard's thought thus culminates in an altogether trite dialectic compared to that of Maistre: the truth (about violence) is destined to abolish violence; Jesus, in giving his life for the salvation of humanity, deprives the human sacrifices of their social legitimacy.

For the author of the *Eclaircissement sur les sacrifices*, the truth, far from being the mortal enemy of violence, is revealed and reinforced by it. The sacrifice of the Man-God is the proof *par excellence* of the reversibility of merits, that is of the necessity for innocents to suffer also for the salvation of the guilty. These will only be saved however if they accept this sacrifice, because they are corrupt enough to reject God's grace. The redemption of humanity, be it duly Christianised, can then only be achieved through bloodshed. There is therefore no reason to oppose, as René Girard does, pagan societies, eager for bloody sacrifices, and an idealised Christian community that would succeed in overcoming endemic social violence. The universal practice of sacrifice testifies rather to its miraculous effectiveness in terms of salvation, even if the pagan cults only prefigure the definitive truth revealed by Christianity.[41]

---

40. See *La Violence et le sacré* (Paris, 1972), p.17: 'Il n'y a rien à "expier". La société cherche à détourner vers une victime relativement indifférente, une victime "sacrifiable", une violence qui risque de frapper ses propres membres, ceux qu'elle entend à tout prix protéger'.

41. See 'Théorie chrétienne des sacrifices', *Eclaircissement*, ch.3. Maistre responds in advance to René Girard in the following passage from this chapter: 'Comment donc ne pas croire que le paganisme n'a pu se tromper sur une idée aussi universelle et aussi fondamentale que celle des sacrifices, c'est-à-dire *de la rédemption par le sang*? Le genre humain ne pouvait deviner le sang dont il avait besoin. Quel homme livré à lui-même pouvait soupçonner l'immensité de la Chute, et l'immensité de l'amour réparateur? Cependant tout peuple, en confessant plus ou moins clairement cette Chute, confessait aussi le besoin et la nature du remède'. Glaudes (ed.), *Maistre: Œuvres*, p.832-33.

The Girardian theory is in fact underlain by the hardly Christian idea of a moral progress of humanity while Maistre adopts the more orthodox view of a world submitted to the perpetual struggle between good and evil principles:

> Le christianisme nous montre bien une autre balance. D'un côté tous les crimes, de l'autre toutes les satisfactions; de ce côté les bonnes œuvres de tous les hommes, le sang des martyrs, les sacrifices et les larmes de l'innocence s'accumulant sans relâche pour faire équilibre au mal qui, depuis l'origine des choses, verse dans l'autre bassin ses flots empoisonnés. Il faut qu'à la fin le côté du salut l'emporte, et pour accélérer cette œuvre universelle, dont l'attente *fait gémir tous les êtres* (Rom. 8:22), il suffit que l'homme veuille. Non seulement il jouit de ses propres mérites, mais les satisfactions étrangères lui sont imputées par la justice éternelle, pourvu qu'il l'ait voulu et qu'il se soit rendu digne de cette *réversibilité*.[42]

In order to upset this equilibrium of Terror, if we can wink at the providential role played by the French Revolution according to Maistre, grace alone does not suffice. An act of will is equally required, the 'horribly wicked' man having to accept wholeheartedly the sacrifice of the just in order to be saved. Now, the human will has been 'broken' by original sin.[43] The margin of freedom of the individual consequently seems quite reduced, considering that Providence determines the course of history.[44] In the economy of the universe, what always tips the scales in favour of salvation is the recognition of the reversibility of merits: love thus finally overcomes hate by sacrificing itself for it. If Maistre speaks in the passage above of '*accelerating* this universal work', it is because the great delays in divine justice, which often lead to doubt about its existence, are precisely due to the obstinacy of the guilty to refuse the divine grace. This is assuredly the best illustration of the famous 'péché originel du second ordre'.

In simple terms, freedom consists in understanding one's role in creation, in ceasing to be a docile, but blind, instrument of Providence. We must do what it expects from us knowingly rather than unwillingly. Even a 'genius of evil' like Robespierre or a usurper like Napoleon serves the mysterious designs of Providence and we must be careful, Maistre tells us, not to stand in its way. In contrast to the Hegelian cunning of reason, the ruse of Providence is difficult to unmask; faith in it must therefore be absolute and unconditional. For example blatant injustice

---

42. *Les Soirées* in Glaudes (ed.), *Maistre: Œuvres*, 10th dialogue, p.751-52.
43. *Les Soirées* in Glaudes (ed.), *Maistre: Œuvres*, 2nd dialogue, p.487-88: 'Il ne sait ce qu'il veut; il veut ce qu'il ne veut pas; il ne veut pas ce qu'il veut; il *voudrait vouloir*'.
44. On the difficult reconciliation of freedom of the will and 'providentialist historicism', see Jean-Yves Pranchère, 'L'Historicisme généralisé', in *L'Autorité contre les Lumières* (Geneva, 2004), ch.6, sect.6, p.376-88.

must be accepted, since the triumph of evil is only temporary and can even be seen as the forerunner of salvation, just as the reign of the Anti-Christ precedes and announces the Last Judgement and the re-establishment of all things. The French Revolution has thus succeeded in making a *tabula rasa* of the past, paving the way for the divine revolution that Maistre prophesied in particular at the end of *Les Soirées*[45] and in the conclusion of *Du Pape*: '[...] tout annonce que l'Europe touche à une révolution mémorable, dont celle que nous avons vue ne fut que le terrible et indispensable préliminaire'.[46]

It would be mistaken to interpret this counter-revolution as a simple return to the Edenic state,[47] because universal history would then have been just a parenthesis; it is rather about attaining a *second innocence*, human nature being finally purified after having been long vitiated. What makes the Maistrian theodicy interesting is indeed the positive role it gives to evil. Without the spur of evil, the supreme good would fail to happen and the universal restoration of all things would be a total miracle: Providence would change tack, so to speak, and would suddenly and without any reason renounce using diabolical means to accomplish its designs. And yet, the excess of evil would be absurd rather than scandalous if it were not the goad of superabundant good. Maistre thus escapes the legitimate criticisms that can be made of Leibniz's more accommodating theodicy, which seeks at all costs to exonerate God from responsibility for evil. Rather than explaining the unequal distribution of evil in the world by means of pre-established harmony, Maistre insists on the cosmic disorder entailed by the political and social revolution, which he sees as a necessary precondition for the fusion of the human race announced by the Book of Revelation. Therefore one *has* to go through the depths of the night to catch a glimpse of the dawn; there exists no simpler and less costly way. Maistrian Providence may appear a bit perverse, but in reality it can only triumph over evil by letting it have an entirely free field for a time.

We find exactly the same dialectic in Schopenhauer, with the Will playing the double role of the Revolution and Providence since he rejects all transcendence. There is here some sort of *self-revelation*, the Will removing its veils one by one to finally appear such as it really is and

---

45. See *Les Soirées* in Glaudes (ed.), *Maistre: Œuvres*, 11th dialogue, p.762: '[...] il faut nous tenir prêts pour un événement immense dans l'ordre divin, vers lequel nous marchons avec une vitesse accélérée qui doit frapper tous les observateurs. Il n'y a plus de religion sur terre: le genre humain ne peut demeurer dans cet état. Des oracles redoutables annoncent d'ailleurs que *les temps sont arrivés*'.

46. Lovie and Chetail (ed.), *Du Pape*, p.344.

47. See, for example, Dermenghem, 'L'Eschatologie maistrienne', *Maistre mystique*, 4th part, ch.33, p. 320-38.

suppress itself. This slow suicide can be interpreted as passive eutha-nasia,[48] the Will dying of starvation after having fully displayed its power. Schopenhauer obviously sees himself as the prophet of this belated self-sacrifice,[49] which allows the merciless will to live to redeem itself. It immolates itself, just like Christ, but to expiate its own sins, of which it was unconscious as long as it sought to perpetuate itself. The intercession of the Man-God, who symbolises and personifies the negation of the will to live,[50] is therefore, strictly speaking, unnecessary: '[...] the only way of salvation is, that the will shall manifest itself *unrestrictedly*, in order that in this individual manifestation it may come to apprehend its own nature'.[51]

Certainly, geniuses and saints *accelerate* this crucial awareness of the diabolic character of the Will, but they do so first as beings of will, since it is the will to live that struggles in them against itself. Indeed, to say that they freely break the yoke of the Will, while the majority of humanity largely satisfies itself by being its docile instrument, would not be quite true. Here Schopenhauer is as ambiguous as Maistre: the freedom of the will is undoubtedly a gratifying illusion for him. At the beginning of the *Prize essay on the freedom of the will*, one finds this passage which is very close to that of *Les Soirées* on human indecisiveness:[52]

> given that we are enquiring about the freedom of *willing* itself, this question would accordingly frame itself thus: 'Can you also *will* what you will!'-which comes out as if willing depended on yet another willing lying behind it. And supposing this question was answered in the affirmative, the second would immediately arise: 'Can you also will what you will to will?' and in this way the matter would be pushed up higher into infinity, in that we would always be thinking of *one* instance of willing as dependent upon an earlier or deeper-lying one, and by this route striving in vain finally to reach one that we had to regard as dependent on nothing at all, and had to assume.[53]

But Schopenhauer admits all the same the possibility of freeing oneself from the Will, insomuch as the knowledge of its essence acts on it as a sedative.[54] Freedom then is another name for grace, as understood by Christian theology. The would-be atheist mentions Malebranche's well-known sentence, 'la liberté est un mystère', before adding that his ethics

---

48. As opposed to violent suicide, which is still an affirmation of the will to live since it aims at shortening suffering. See *The World*, vol.1, bk.4, sect.69, p.514-20.
49. See *The World*, vol.1, bk.4, sect.71, p.530: 'it is an entire and certain gospel; only knowledge remains, the will has vanished'.
50. See *The World*, vol.1, bk.4, sect.70, p.520.
51. See *The World*, vol.1, bk.4, sect.69, p.518.
52. Quoted in note 43.
53. See *The Two fundamental problems of ethics*, p.34.
54. See *The World*, vol.1, bk.4, sect.70, p. 521.

of abnegation 'fully agrees with the Christian dogmas properly so called, and indeed, as regards its essence, was contained and present in them'.[55]

One cannot even say of the Will itself that it acts freely, since it only expresses its essence. It 'wills' nothing consciously, even if it sometimes uses very subtle means to achieve its unending self-perpetuation. For example, love for Schopenhauer is only a refined disguise for the instinct of reproduction.[56] Although he challenges any idea of finality, the author of *The World* unexpectedly attributes to the Will something like a hidden wisdom that permits it to use trickery and illusion. This is undoubtedly Schopenhauer's system's main weakness: the Will, which explains everything, moves in mysterious ways. It is therefore very similar to Providence, even though it embodies the bad principle.

It goes without saying that Schopenhauer cannot, unlike Maistre,[57] invoke faith in support of his doctrine of the Will. That does not keep him, as we have seen, from making his own the Christian notions of salvation and redemption. Even the doctrine of reversibility of merits finds an echo in his work. Not to mention that he also uses the metaphor of the balance to describe the immanent justice that somehow manages to compensate for all evil:

> Now if, as we have done, we have kept in mind human *depravity* and feel inclined to be horrified thereat, we must at once cast a glance at the *misery* of human existence, and again at the former when we are shocked by the latter. We shall then find that they balance each other and shall become aware of eternal justice, by noticing that the world itself is the tribunal of humanity, and by coming to understand why everything that lives must atone for its existence first in living and then in dying. Thus the *malum poenae* [the evil of punishment] tallies with the *malum culpae* [the evil of guilt]. From the same point of view, there also disappears the indignation at the intellectual incapacity of the masses which in life so often disgusts us.[58]

Indeed, how could one someday break the vicious circle of the will to live if nothing was to make up for human depravity? Punishment is therefore not only about returning evil for evil but also the means of regeneration. For Schopenhauer, most persons wrongly believe that the goal of life is

---

55. *The World*, vol.1, bk.4, sect.70, p.526. He had already made this clear a little above: 'That in recent times Christianity has forgotten its true significance, and degenerated into dull optimism, does not concern us here'.

56. See 'The metaphysics of the love of the sexes', *The World*, vol.3, Supplements to bk.4, ch.44, , p.336-75.

57. See *Les Soirées* in Glaudes (ed.), *Maistre: Œuvres*, 10th dialogue, p.751: 'Mais en nous essayant sur ce grand sujet [la réversibilité], nous nous sommes bien gardés de croire que ce mystère qui explique tout eût besoin lui-même d'être expliqué. C'est un fait, c'est une croyance aussi naturelle à l'homme que la vue ou la respiration; et cette croyance jette le plus grand jour sur les voies de la Providence dans le gouvernement du monde moral'.

58. 'On ethics', *Parerga and paralipomena*, vol.2, ch.8, sect.114, p.218-19.

happiness, whereas suffering is the true destiny of human existence. Failing a profound reflection on the essence of life, they remain prisoners of the illusion woven by the Will, which never fulfills the naïve aspirations it arouses. In taking upon himself the suffering that others flee, the Awakened liberates them from the vital illusion and shows them the way of salvation.[59] It is in this sense, inspired by Buddhism, that knowledge leads to redemption. Certainly, this is not literally innocence sacrificing itself for the salvation of the guilty, as with Maistre, but Schopenhauer all the same insists on the discreet and constant presence of the good principle at the heart of a world devoted to evil:

> the human world is where morally depravity and baseness, intellectually incapacity and stupidity, prevail to a fearful extent. Nevertheless, there appear in it, although only very sporadically yet always astonishing us afresh, phenomena of honesty, kindness, and even nobility, as also of great intellect, the thinking mind, and even genius. These never go out entirely, but glitter at us like isolated points that shine out of the great mass of darkness. We must take them as a pledge that in this *Samsara* there lies hidden a good and redeeming principle which can break through and inspire and release the whole.[60]

Even if Schopenhauer here mentions *samsara*, the dark side of *nirvana*, the terms he otherwise uses are obviously more Christian than Buddhist. In this surprising portrayal of 'eternal justice', which of course brings to mind Maistre's divine justice, the geniuses and the saints seem *predestined* to save humanity. Their freedom is in effect limited to the accomplishment of the reign of grace. Their remarkable sense of self-sacrifice permits them only to escape the tyranny of the principle of individuation, which is exemplary of the triumph of the will to live, and to reveal the vanity of egoism,[61] that condemns us to an existence of suffering.

Schopenhauer's ethics of salvation, whose Christian inspiration is obvious, follows thus from his metaphysics of the Will. Altruism, compassion and charity providentially appear to compensate for egoism, envy and cruelty. Already, the fact that such virtues remain in a world so incurably bad is a deep mystery,[62] just like freedom. We must anyhow go

---

59. See *The World*, vol.3, Supplements to bk.4, ch.49, p.462: 'Suffering is, in fact, the purifying process through which alone, in most cases, the man is sanctified, i.e., is led back from the path of error of the will to live'.
60. 'On ethics,' *Parerga and paralipomena*, vol.2, ch.8, sect.114, p.218-19.
61. See *Prize essay*, sect.14, p.190: 'Egoism is colossal: it towers above the world. For if the choice were given to any individual between his own destruction and that of the world, I do not need to say where it would land for the great majority'.
62. Schopenhauer presents compassion (*Mitleid*), which is for him the very basis of morality, as 'the great mystery of ethics, its primitive phenomenon and the boundary stone beyond which only metaphysical speculation can dare to step'. *Prize essay*, sect.16, p.201.

through an *active depersonalisation* to suppress our ego,[63] and deliver ourselves from a world that in great part is the product of our representations so that one day these virtues can prevail over their rivals.

Then everything is consummated. The world is abolished at the same time as the Will and only nothingness remains – nothingness understood in the sense of the Buddhist *nirvana*. It is always useful to quote the last lines of *The World* to refute common interpretations of Schopenhauer's thought as nihilistic: 'Rather do we freely acknowledge that what remains after the entire abolition of will is for all those who are still full of will certainly nothing; but, conversely, to those in whom the will has turned and denied itself, this our world, which is so real, with all its suns and milky ways – is nothing'.[64] This horizon of hope reminds us of the divine retribution of which Maistre dreams with Plutarch. Undoubtedly it took the 'rienisme'[65] of the Enlightenment to spark off the Count's millenarianism.

In conclusion, can one still say that these two eccentric and excessive thinkers were behind their time? To that, Schopenhauer would respond that one does well to stand back, when he sees his epoch going backwards. 'Le temps est *quelque chose de forcé qui ne demande qu'à finir*', Maistre had already said at the end of *Les Soirées*.[66]

---

63. Maistre offers a fine illustration of this in a letter to his daughter Constance: 'Je n'aime pas *moi*, je ne crois pas *moi*, je me moque de *moi*. Il n'y a de vie, de jouissance, d'espérance que dans *toi*. Il y a longtemps que j'ai écrit dans mon livre de maximes: *l'unique antidote contre l'égoïsme, c'est le tuïsme*'. *OC*, vol.14, p.101-102.
64. *The World*, vol.1, bk.4, sect.71, p.532. This crucial passage also proves that Schopenhauer is wrongly accused of having mistaken Buddhism for nihilism.
65. See Pranchère, 'Le Complot nihiliste', *L'Autorité contre les Lumières*, 3rd part, ch.V, sect.2, p.303-10.
66. *Les Soirées* in Glaudes (ed.), *Maistre: Œuvres*, p.764.

# III

# Maistrian afterlives of the theological Enlightenment

# Enigmatic images of an invisible world: sacrifice, suffering and theodicy in Joseph de Maistre

## DOUGLAS HEDLEY

Owen Bradley, in his learned work *A Modern Maistre: the social and political thought of Joseph de Maistre* (1999), notes that the Savoyard Count's critique of Enlightenment highlights a remarkable awareness of the fundamental ambivalence of human action. Thus Maistre can be retrieved in the postmodern milieu as an improbable precursor to Freud or Foucault. Bradley seeks 'to make of Maistre the ambiguous, equivocal, undecidable figure I believe he ought to be for modern thought rather than a monster plain and simple'.[1] Rather than revealing a morbid obsession with violence, Maistre presents ritual sacrifice as a spiritualising process that reduces the violence required to sustain social order.[2] As Bradley has argued most eloquently, Maistre's thought depends upon the *mot clé* 'sacrifice'. Judicial punishment and war are domains where ritualised violence upholds the social order through representing the legitimate power of the sovereign. Notwithstanding the interpretation of Berlin, Bradley claims that Maistre 'was among the first to thematise how power is based not merely on coercion but also, and even more fundamentally, on the symbolic, on custom, representation, and belief'.[3] The real question is order and disorder within a larger logic of history. How can we understand justice, wickedness, mercy and forgiveness as part of a providential and law-governed process of expiation and redemption?

This is a brilliant restatement of Maistre's prodigious intellectual legacy as a critic of the Enlightenment. Indeed, Maistre is warning of the danger of underestimating man's potential for violence. But I am unsure that this makes the Savoyard Count into a modern. One might just as readily compare Maistre with Euripides. Euripides in his *Bacchae*, writing during the Peloponnesian war, reveals the violent and destructive dimension of their world to the Athenians of the Athenian Enlightenment; the Savoyard Count can show how the French Enlightenment is

---

1. Bradley, *A Modern Maistre*, p.xviii.
2. On the idea of sacrifice in Maistrian thought, see, in this volume, Carolina Armenteros' article, 'Maistre's Rousseaus' and Yannis Constantinidès article, 'Two great enemies of the Enlightenment: Joseph de Maistre and Schopenhauer'.
3. Bradley, *A Modern Maistre*, p.90–91.

equally blind to its own destructive potential. I think that Bradley's is a brilliant and illuminating reading of Joseph de Maistre; but it does not go quite far enough.

I wish to emphasise not so much the modern as the Romantic Maistre. Maistre is very much a philosopher of tradition, opposed to the Cartesian doubt or the principle of individual judgement. Like Vico, Maistre is a trenchant critic of the paradoxical barbarism of Enlightenment and the hidden Providence of tradition. Maistre sees decadence as the fruit of Baconian science, scepticism and the erosion of the religious foundations of society.

## The double perspective of Romanticism

I believe that Romanticism is a key juncture in Western thought because it brings together an interest in the cultural specificity of human life, the importance of tradition. Consider Maistre's famous lines:

> La constitution de 1795, tout comme ses aînées, est faite pour l'*homme*. Or, il n'y point d'homme dans le monde. J'ai vu, dans ma vie des Français, des Italiens, des Russes, etc., je sais meme, grâce à Montesquieu, *qu'on peut être Persan*: mais quant à l'*homme*, je déclare ne l'avoir rencontré de ma vie, s'il existe, c'est bien à mon insu.[4]

Maistre reveals a deep aversion to abstractions. But he combines this interest in history, language and culture with a strong sense of the transcendent. Maistre's great work on the French Revolution, his *Considérations sur la France*, begins with the supreme transcendent cause: God. And his attack upon the French Revolution is precisely an attack upon its Faustian ambitions. Maistre's view of the Revolution as satanic is based upon his critique of its failure to respect natural human limits.

The Romantic period was the age of a revival of Neoplatonism, first in England (Thomas Taylor), then in Germany (Friedrich Creuzer), and then in France (Victor Cousin). Maistre's own version of Neoplatonism is particularly derivative, based largely on Christian sources. The Neoplatonists generally have little interest in history or facts of culture. Plotinus, for example, shows little awareness of the fact that Plato and Aristotle inhabited very different intellectual worlds to third-century Alexandria or Rome. Nor does he seem to possess a sense of Plato struggling with problems in different phases of his writing. A writer like Maistre shares with Vico the combination of both a strong sense of transcendence while stressing particularity, history and contingency. Thus I think that Pranchère is quite wrong to say: 'It is incontestable that Maistre absolutises the relative by affirming that the will of God is

---

4.  Maistre, *Considérations sur la France*, in Glaudes (ed.), *Maistre: Œuvres*, p.235.

"perfectly declared by the facts" and known above all by history'.[5] This is to overlook the subtle dialectic of the eternal and the contingent in Maistre. Far from absolutising the relative, Maistre combines the transcendent with the particular, the eternal with the historical. This characteristically Romantic combination, so evident in Maistre, is a very intriguing and important development in Occidental thought. Both of these aspects of Romantic thought form the basis of an attack upon metaphysical naturalism.[6] This is the theory that all knowledge is derived from the natural sciences, especially physics. Maistre's attack on Bacon and Locke is motivated by their canonical role for the *philosophes*. Is culture, for example religion, the conventional shape of universal natural instincts? That is to say, is culture a level of life that rests neatly upon biological structures? If so, then a biological account of 'religion' is feasible. However, perhaps human culture is not the conventional shape of passions that are universal in human nature. This is the position of Hume or Voltaire. According to Maistre the distinctively human passions are shaped by cultural traditions and history. This, I think, is a subtle and intriguing criticism of naturalism in ethics. Man is made by society, by institutions and rituals and, as such, human nature is irreducible to the stimulus-response model of the crude naturalists and barely explicable by the more sophisticated versions of naturalistic theory. Closely allied to this doctrine is Maistre's resolute innatism. We do not dwell in the same world as brute animals with an extra layer of culture or language added. The human world is radically different: through innate ideas mankind can interpret the visible world as the isthmus between the temporal and the divine – and thus view the images of the Platonic 'cave' as signs of a higher world.

There is a tradition in French thought that sees religion in primarily social terms. The *locus classicus* is Durkheim's *Les Formes élémentaires de la vie religieuse* (1912). But Durkheim's idea that religion is 'society divinised' is the exact opposite of Maistre's view of society as the product of Providence, that is, Divine action. One is the theory of an agnostic who wishes to explain the nature of religion; the other is the doctrine of a stalwart theist who wants to see structures of society as embodying a sacred dimension.

Bradley speaks of the 'lay tone, the altogether worldly approach to ritual and to theodicy, from both of which alike the figure of the

---

5.  Jean-Yves Pranchère, 'The persistence of Maistrian thought' in Lebrun (ed.), *Maistre: life thought and influence*, p.290-325, p.314.
6.  Here the contrast is with methodological naturalism – the position that experimental science proceeds by excluding any non-'natural' considerations while remaining agnostic about the ultimate constituents of the universe.

Christian deity virtually disappears'.[7] Here, I think, Bradley is conflating two rather different elements. There is, of course, the tone of the salon. The structure and style of Maistre's pen is imbued with the wit and elegance of the drawing room rather than the scholastic asperities of the medieval university. We sense the urbanity and wit he shares with Hume and Voltaire. The Count writes in a similar mode to the 'moderns', but his philosophy is with the 'ancients'. I think that 'worldly' is quite misleading. Metaphysical and theological is more appropriate.

Voltaire believed that the Christian God was morally inferior to the God of deism. In his 1722 poem *Epître à Uranie* Voltaire notoriously claimed that God can only be offended by injustice and that humanity is judged by its virtues and *not* by sacrifices. Yet Voltaire did not relinquish entirely the idea of sacrifice. A celebrated writer since his youth and feted as an adult by the European literary elite, including the Francophile Frederick the Great of Prussia, Voltaire was eminently capable of self-dramatisation. He eloquently presented his own life, indeed with some justification, as a persecuted existence: in flight or exile or fearing jail for his thought. His lines in the *Dictionnaire philosophique* about the sacrificial role of intellectuals is telling:

> Les gens de lettres qui ont rendu le plus de services au petit nombre d'êtres pensants répandus dans le monde, sont les lettrés isolés, les vrais savants renfermés dans leur cabinet, qui n'ont ni argumenté sur les bancs des universités, ni dit les choses à moitié dans les académies; et ceux-là ont presque tous été persécutés. Notre misérable espèce est tellement faite, que ceux qui marchent dans le chemin battu jettent toujours des pierres à ceux qui enseignent un chemin nouveau. [...] Descartes est obligé de quitter sa patrie, Gassendi est calomnié, Arnauld traîne ses jours dans l'exil; tout philosophe est traité comme les prophètes chez les Juifs. Qui croirait que dans le XVIIIe siècle un philosophe [Hélvetius] ait été traîné devant les tribunaux séculiers, et traité d'impie par les tribunaux d'arguments, pour avoir dit que les hommes ne pourraient exercer les arts s'ils n'avaient pas de mains? Je ne désespère pas qu'on ne condamne bientôt aux galères le premier qui aura l'insolence de dire qu'un homme ne penserait pas s'il était sans tête: 'Car, lui dira un bachelier, l'âme est un esprit pur, la tête n'est que la matière; Dieu peut placer l'âme dans le talon, aussi bien que dans le cerveau; partant je vous dénonce comme un impie'. [...] Le plus grand malheur d'un homme de lettres n'est peut-être pas d'être l'objet de la jalousie de ses confrères, la victime de la cabale, le mépris des puissants du monde; c'est d'être jugé par des sots. Les sots vont loin quelquefois, surtout quand le fanatisme se joint à l'ineptie, et à l'ineptie l'esprit de vengeance. Le grand malheur encore d'un homme de lettres est ordinairement de ne tenir à rien. Un bourgeois achète un petit office, et le voilà soutenu par ses confrères. Si on lui fait une injustice, il trouve aussitôt des défenseurs.

---

7.   Bradley, *A Modern Maistre*, p.190.

L'homme de lettres est sans secours; il ressemble aux poissons volants: s'il s'élève un peu, les oiseaux le dévorent; s'il plonge, les poissons le mangent. Tout homme public paye tribut à la malignité; mais il est payé en derniers et en honneurs.[8]

In *Les Soirées* we find a remarkably trenchant rebuttal of Voltaire, a thinker that the learned Count dismisses as a pernicious mountebank.[9] In particular, Voltaire's presentation of the persecuted hommes de lettres and noble sacrifices must have struck Maistre as an intolerable pretension. Voltaire in his grand house at Ferney, the most famous writer in Europe, receiving visitors and admirers, surrounded by servants and friends, doubtless looked to Maistre as a strange candidate for the martyr's mantle. Especially for Maistre, who lived the sad life of an exile and a cruel separation from his family and home. The trenchant and paradoxical theological and metaphysical genius of Maistre is consciously pitted against the subtle and indefatigable talent of the consummate publicist, Voltaire. One can sense both Maistre's resentment of, and feeling of superiority towards, the literary icon of Enlightenment.

The main issue addressed by Maistre is that of *le bonheur des méchants* and *le malheur des justes*. Bradley claims:

> The justification to man of the ways of the world was one of Maistre's central preoccupations, motivated I would argue not so much by a mystical fascination with Providence for its own sake as by the attempt to refute what he understood as a revival of the Gnostic depiction of man's world as radically unjust and unjustifiable, in need of total renovation.[10]

Terms like 'mystical' are potentially misleading. Firstly Maistre, like Milton, wishes to 'justify the ways of God to men', emphatically *not* the ways of the world! And his sources are often explicitly 'mystical': from Origen to the Cambridge Platonists, Saint Martin and Fénelon. The great Ultramontane defender of Catholic authority is happy to appeal to heretical and Protestant thinkers that share in a common mystical tradition in which salvation consists in 'likeness to God'.

Further, I think we should be cautious about Bradley's claim that Maistre's idea of Providence was barely traditional: 'While like every providentialist he does insist that the world obeys final causes that tend toward the good, neither God nor his personal intentions appear anywhere in Maistre's argument'.[11] Yet in *Les Soirées* we have an explicit

---

8. Voltaire, 'Lettres', *Dictionnaire philosophique*. I owe this reference to Caspar Hirschi of Clare Hall, Cambridge.
9. For Maistre's opinion of Voltaire's library in *Les Soirées*, see, in this volume, Carolina Armenteros' article, 'Maistre's Rousseaus'.
10. Bradley, *A Modern Maistre*, p.167.
11. Bradley, *A Modern Maistre*, p.170.

reference to the incarnation: 'L'Homme-Dieu (Man-God), the Godman called us to be his friends.' This, I think, is explicitly Christian. A philosophy deeply sympathetic to Christianity, Kant's, speaks of the 'Holy One of the Gospel', but even he shrinks before the explicitly Calcedonian 'Godman'. A deist or atheist, quite apart from a Jew or a Muslim would not have written thus. 'Whatever topic one treats one always speaks of her' says Maistre; but not because it is a bland topic. I think that Bradley is failing to stress the full force of the theological dimension in Maistre's work, especially *Les Soirées*.

## Maistre's heterodoxy?

Bradley refers to the heterodox character of Maistre's Catholic Neoplatonism.[12] Joseph de Maistre is writing prior to *Aeterni patris* of 1879. With this document Thomas Aquinas became the official philosopher of Roman Catholicism, and a rather narrow interpretation of the angelic doctor came to prevail. Maistre cites Aquinas enthusiastically yet he is not a Thomist but a Christian Platonist. Indeed, *Aeterni patris* was motivated not just by the fear of atheism but by the Romantic Neoplatonism that formed the backbone of much nineteenth-century Catholic theology. By the standard of mid-twentieth century textbook Thomism Maistre is heterodox, but so is Nicholas of Cusa, Malebranche, that is to say, the Platonic strand. I think we should be cautious about placing too much emphasis upon the 'heterodox' Maistre, if only for fear of crass anachronism.

Bradley becomes rather sidetracked by a debate about Gnosticism. 'Gnosticism' has been much discussed in figures like Jonas and Voegelin. However, I do not really think that Maistre sees the philosophy of the Enlightenment as tainted by Gnosticism. For him it is empiricism and naturalism that constitute the problem. And philosophy is, as Maistre tells us in a wonderful and characteristically pungent passage, like counterfeit money. A few rogues produce it, and then it passes through the hands of many honest men: 'Mais les fausses opinions ressemblent à la fausse monnaie qui est frappée d'abord par de grands coupables, et dépensée ensuite par d'honnêtes gens, qui perpétuent le crime sans savoir ce qu'ils font'.[13] Among the false tenets circulated by the *philosophes* is an unwarranted and dangerous optimism about human nature. Maistre avers:

> Il n'y a que violence dans l'univers; mais nous sommes gâtés par la
> philosophie moderne, qui a dit que tout est bien, tandis que le mal a tout

---

12. Bradley, *A Modern Maistre*, p.172.
13. Maistre, *Les Soirées de Saint-Pétersbourg*, in Glaudes (ed.), *Maistre: Œuvres*, p.464.

souillé, et que, dans un sens très vrai, tout est mal, puisque rien n'est à sa place. La note tonique du système de notre création ayant baissé, toutes les autres ont baissé proportionnellement, suivant les règles de l'harmonie. Tous les êtres gémissent et tendent, avec effort et douleur, vers un autre ordre de choses.[14]

One solution to the problem of evil was to deny the existence of a providential Deity and to seek remedy for ills in cultural reform: the abolition of Church, monarch and aristocracy. Voltaire presented Christianity as not just false but immoral. Voltaire, through his *Candide*, is the thinker most associated with the critique of theodicy. His *Traité sur la tolérance à l'occasion de la mort de Jean Calas* of 1763 is a critique of iniquity perpetrated in the name of religion, inspired by the persecution and execution of the French Protestant Jean Calas by the Toulouse magistrature, the last man to be executed on the wheel in France on the trumped-up charge of murdering his son (in all likelihood it was a suicide). Voltaire's moving and scathing critique of the cruelty inflicted upon Calas became celebrated throughout Europe and thirty-nine of Voltaire's works were placed upon the index. One gains a sense of the more intransigent and polemical side of Maistre's nature in his remarks about the doubtful innocence of Calas. Yet it is perhaps helpful to view Maistre's metaphysics of punishment in the context of the controversy raised by Voltaire.

Punishment is a knotty philosophical problem. Most theories are either retributive or consequentialist. Punishment is justified either because it redresses an intrinsic wrong or because it has favourable results for society at large (for example: protection from violence, theft or dishonesty). Many liberal thinkers maintain that the 'just desert' retributive punishment is either atavistic (revenge) or illusory (because metaphysically impossible). Since Foucault, many have claimed that punishment merely reflects the desire to exert power over others. Both the ultra-liberal and the Foucault positions rest upon the anti-Platonic view that there are no objective values. For both the liberals and Foucault, punishment is just a human institution, not a natural fact – and it could theoretically be dispensed with. For Maistre, punishment is not an arbitrary fact about human society but reflects a spiritual law. I think that this Platonic dimension of Maistre's thought can be seen in his emphasis upon the mirroring of eternal justice upon earth, however obliquely. The executioner represents order amidst disorder. For all the horror of his acts, they are not – *pace* Foucault – the expression of brute power.

14. Maistre, *Considérations sur la France*, in Glaudes (ed.), *Maistre: Œuvres*, p.218, and *Les Soirées de Saint-Pétersbourg*, in Glaudes (ed.), *Maistre: Œuvres*, p.709.

Let us consider the notorious executioner passage. It is remarkable in its imaginative engagement with the person of the executioner, as well as his ambivalent status in society: 'Il est fait comme nous extérieurement, il naît comme nous, mais c'est un être extraordinaire; et pour qu'il existe dans la famille humaine, il faut un décret particulier, un FIAT de la puissance créatrice'.[15] What does Maistre imply with the allusion to the 'Fiat Lux' of the Vulgate? In the creation story of Genesis, God creates heaven and earth and light and darkness, and the light is good. Maistre suggests that the executioner is an organ of Divine justice: 'Il y a donc dans le cercle temporel une loi divine et visible pour la punition du crime, et cette loi, aussi stable que la société qu'elle fait subsister, est exécutée invariablement depuis l'origine de choses; le mal étant sur la terre, il agit constamment; et par une conséquence nécessaire il doit être constamment réprimé par le châtiment'.[16]

Rather than being akin to the *bellum omnium contra omnes* of Hobbes, Maistre's perspective is quite the opposite: resolutely providentialist. For Hobbes sovereignty is grounded in the pressing need to combat the chaotic violence of man's natural state. For Maistre, the existence of society at all presupposes the victory of *justice*, however imperfectly realised, over sheer power. The institution of capital punishment is a shadow of the eternal and immutable divine law which lies at the basis of human association and society. Whereas the God of Hobbes is at best a *Deus absconditus*, for the Platonic Maistre God is the transcendent source of earthly and temporal justice and order. In the words of Dante: 'La gloria di colui che tutto move/per l'universo penetra e risplende/in una parte più e meno altrove'.[17] Maistre avers, 'tenons nos yeux fixés sur ce monde invisible qui expliquera tout'.[18]

Voyez ce qu'il est dans l'opinion des hommes, et comprenez, si vous pouvez, comment il peut ignorer cette opinion ou l'affronter! A peine l'autorité a-t-elle pris possession, que les autres habitations reculent jusqu'à ce qu'elles ne voient pas la sienne. C'est au milieu de cette solitude et de cette espèce de vide formé autour de lui qu'il vit seul avec sa femelle et ses petits qui lui font connaître la voix de l'homme: sans eux, il n'en connaîtrait que les gémissements.

Est-ce un homme? Oui. Dieu le reçoit dans ses temples et lui permet de prier. Il n'est pas criminel: cependant aucune langue ne consent à dire, par exemple, qu'il est vertueux, qu'il est honnête homme, qu'il est estimable,

15. Maistre, *Les Soirées de Saint-Pétersbourg*, in Glaudes (ed.), *Maistre: Œuvres*, p.470.
16. Maistre, *Les Soirées de Saint-Pétersbourg*, in Glaudes (ed.), *Maistre: Œuvres*, p.471.
17. 'The glory of Him who moves all things penetrates the universe and shines in one part more and in another less'. Dante's *The Divine comedy*, 3 Paradiso (Oxford 1939), p.19.
18. Maistre, *Les Soirées de Saint-Pétersbourg*, in Glaudes (ed.), *Maistre: Œuvres*, p.661.

etc. Nul éloge moral ne peut lui convenir; car tous supposent des rapports avec les hommes et il n'en a point...[19]

Maistre is speculating about the *anomalous* status of the executioner. He stands without relation to other creatures. Moral categories collapse: necessary for the well-being of the state, he is regarded with a mixture of anxiety and awe by his fellows. Yet this uncanny figure is presented from a very human perspective. Maistre depicts the literally dreadful loneliness of the executioner's role. The executioner is an organ of justice and yet isolated from human contact, only his own family 'acquaint him with the human voice'. In this short passage, sometimes cited by critics as evidence for Maistre's sadism, we find a remarkable empathy for the human being performing this grim and yet necessary task.

Maistre uses the thought-experiment of an extra-terrestrial visiting the world presented with the two kinds of men allowed to kill: the soldier and the executioner. Given that the former kills honest and good men and the latter kills criminals, the visitor will doubtless be surprised to discover the esteem exhibited for the warrior and the ignominy of the executioner.[20] And Voltaire hovers in the background, especially his famous bon mot: 'Il est défendu de tuer; tout meurtrier est puni, à moins qu'il n'ait tué en grande compagnie, et au son des trompettes'. It is important to note Maistre's careful and subtle attunement to the Enlightenment critics. Maistre's strategy is often to deploy the criticisms of such figures as Voltaire against their own theories. Of course, Voltaire is correct to think there is something puzzling about murder being forbidden in one case and exalted in another! But this, Maistre avers, reveals a deeper metaphysical fact about humanity, rather than our hypocrisy. Warfare and punishment are indexes of mankind's duality: man as 'the monstrous centaur'.

Maistre uses the example of war to attack materialistic theories of human behaviour such as 'God is always on the side of the big battalions'. On the contrary, here laws of physical force are often quite impotent: 'C'est l'imagination qui gagne et qui perd les batailles'.[21] In such passages Maistre is attacking the crude mechanical anthropology employed by prominent *philosophes* like La Mettrie or D'Alembert. The violence of warfare is grounded in man's spiritual nature and resists mechanical explanation.

But Maistre is fascinated by the ethical ambivalence of warfare and its relation to society. Doubtless the Count would have regarded many of the wars of the twentieth century as an instance of a brutality unrestrained by

19. Maistre, *Les Soirées de Saint-Pétersbourg*, in Glaudes (ed.), *Maistre: Œuvres*, p.471.
20. Maistre, *Les Soirées de Saint-Pétersbourg*, in Glaudes (ed.), *Maistre: Œuvres*, p.650.
21. Maistre, *Les Soirées de Saint-Pétersbourg*, in Glaudes (ed.), *Maistre: Œuvres*, p.665.

'traditional' decency. Perhaps the primary shock of Maistre's meditations upon war is the product of our contemporary anaesthetic civilisation. Maistre is scandalous to the contemporary mind because of the remarkable capacity of a highly developed technological society not merely to prevent pain for its own members, but also to hide suffering. One does not have to be an adherent of Foucault to see the craving for comfort and security as part of an attempt to administrate life and eradicate the unsightly and troubling: avoiding confrontation with the old and the sick. For democratic politicians understandably worried about votes, the dead and the wounded of wars are rendered, as far as possible, invisible.

Consider the paradoxical claim that 'war is divine'. It is typical of his penchant for misleading rhetoric. In fact, Maistre refers again to the 'horrible enigma', that is the anomalous status of war: 'Rien n'est plus contraire à sa nature, et rien ne lui répugne moins: il fait avec enthousiasme ce qu'il a en horreur'.[22] Yet in Maistre's account of war much is quite true. Post-Napoleonic warfare had become more brutal than warfare under the *ancien régime*. The political order of the early modern period prior to the French Revolution was largely dynastic-sacred rather than national-secular. The Ottomans were not 'Turks'; the Prussian court spoke French during the age of Goethe; the Emperor of the Germans sat in Vienna or Prague. The Holy Roman Empire, neither Holy nor Roman perhaps, nevertheless expresses the residual feudal ideals of the old European order. It was doubtless an imperfect order, but order it was.

The wars of religion in the seventeenth century created devastation in Europe. Writers like Grotius tried to develop an influential secular justification of the political order, one that moved from transcendental or sacerdotal reasons to issues of human need and justice. The Enlightenment in Europe was distinguished by this shift from religious to secular legitimisation. Grotius was a Christian, but he was motivated by the brutality and disruption of the European wars of religion.

One of the great ironies of the twentieth century was that prominent 'secular' national totalitarian states were crueller than the empires of the *ancien régime*:

> L'esprit divin qui s'était particulièrement reposé sur l'Europe adoucissait jusqu'aux fléaux de la justice éternelle, et la guerre européenne marquera toujours dans les annales de l'univers. On se tuait, sans doute, on brûlait, on ravageait, on commettait même si vous voulez mille et mille crime inutiles, mais cependant on commençait la guerre au mois de mai; on la terminait au mois de décembre; on dormait sous la toile; le soldat seul combattait le

---

22. Maistre, *Les Soirées de Saint-Pétersbourg*, in Glaudes (ed.), *Maistre: Œuvres*, p.660.

soldat. Jamais les nations n'étaient en guerre et tout ce qui est faible était sacré à travers les scènes lugubres de ce fléau dévastateur.[23]

Note first that Maistre is not glamourising warfare. He speaks clearly of war as 'this devastating plague' and the functions of the soldier are terrible. His point is rather that war too reflects a 'great law of the spiritual world'.

Carolina Armenteros notes that the modern period is seen by Maistre as veering between the relative calm of the seventeenth century and the turbulence of the eighteenth century.[24] The violence of the eighteenth century can be seen to correspond to the loosening of bonds that reduced and controlled the violent dimension of human nature:

> [L]es saintes lois de l'humanité foulées aux pieds; le sang innocent couvrant les échafauds qui couvraient la France; des hommes frisant et poudrant des têtes sanglantes, et la bouche même des femmes souillée de sang humain. Voilà l'homme *naturel*! ce n'est pas qu'il porte en lui-même les germes inextinguibles de la vérité et de la vertu: les droits de sa naissance sont imprescriptibles; mais sans une fécondation divine, ces germes n'éclaireront jamais, ou ne produiront que des êtres équivoques et malsains.[25]

The critics of Christianity were correct to note that the Church colluded in great injustice, absurd privilege and authoritarianism, but at least it provided an ethical structure and culture for Western civilisation that, contra Machiavelli and Hobbes, was at odds with any politics based on *arbitrary power*. Maistre predicted that modern Utopias would generate terrible tyranny. Burke and Maistre appealed to the terror of the French Revolution as a harbinger of future horrors and as a vindication of their conservatism. But Burke was not a theologian. Maistre was more sensitive to any arbitrary dimension in Christian theology, especially in its ultra Augustinian forms. Augustine's doctrines of double predestination and the damnation of unbaptised infants would have been hard to accommodate in a thinker like Maistre, a thinker so committed to the idea of Christianity as a guardian against the arbitrary violence of the state. Thus I suspect that the attraction of Origen resided in the latter's resolute attachment to the goodness of God. The espousal of a God of inscrutable will, the Augustine so important for Luther and Calvin as well as Jansenism, is problematic for a thinker like Maistre. Origen is the Church Father who is dedicated to freedom.[26] Yet signifi-

23. Maistre, *Les Soirées de Saint-Pétersbourg*, in Glaudes (ed.), *Maistre: Œuvres*, p.658.
24. Carolina Armenteros, 'Revolutionary violence and the end of history', p.19.
25. Maistre, *Eclaircissement sur les sacrifices*, in Glaudes (ed.), *Maistre: Œuvres*, p.824.
26. See T. Kobusch's classic essay, 'Die philosophische Bedeutung des Kirchenvaters Origenes', in *Theologische quartalschrift* (1980), p.9-31.

cantly, for Origen the Christian view of the world is that of a place of
warfare as well as a festival and celebration of the Divine.[27] Only in the
midst of conflict and violence can virtue, as man's true nature, emerge.
The world and history is thus the arena of human freedom within the
parameters of Divine Providence.[28]

## Suffering and substitution

The motor of Maistre's theology of evil is his theistic metaphysics. If
'mystical' is shorthand for 'irrational', I would claim that there is nothing
mystical about the problem of theodicy. It has interested serious philosophers since Plato. Indeed, if the fact of evil disproves the theistic idea of
God, that is momentous.

> Tout esprit droit est convaincu par intuition que le mal ne saurait venir d'un
> être tout-puissant. Ce fut ce sentiment infaillible qui enseigna jadis au bon
> sens romain de réunir, comme par un lien nécessaire, les deux titres augustes
> de TRES BON et TRES GRAND. Cette magnifique expression quoique née
> dans le sein du paganisme a paru si juste, qu'elle a passé dans votre langue
> religieuse, si délicate et si exclusive. Je vous dirai même en passant qu'il m'est
> arrivé plus d'une fois de songer que l'inscription antique, IOVI OPTIMO
> Maximo, pourrait se placer tout entière sur le fronton de vos temples latins;
> car qu'est-ce que IOV-I, sinon IOVAH.[29]

How can a God who is good and all-powerful allow evil, or if God exists,
why do we experience evil? Let us extend the classic problem as
formulated by the Senator to include knowledge. How can evil exist if
God is good, omnipotent and omniscient? Consider the following argument:

1. God is good, omnipotent and omniscient.
2. If God is omniscient, he knows about all evil.
3. If God is omnipotent, God can remove all evil.
4. If God is good, he will desire the removal of evil.
5. Evil exists.
6. If evil exists, God does not know about it, cannot remove it or does
   not wish to.
7. Therefore God does not exist.

So expressed, this argument is valid but not necessarily sound. Are all

---

27. Eberhard Schockenhoff, *Zum Fest der Freiheit. Theologie des Christlichen Handelns bei Origenes*
    (Mainz, 1999), esp. p.258ff.
28. I would therefore reject as mistaken the view that Maistre is 'deistic', except possibly from
    the perspective of a very extreme Augustinianism. For the contrary view, see, in this
    volume, Aimee Barbeau's article, 'The Savoyard philosopher: deist or Neoplatonist?'
29. Maistre, *Les Soirées de Saint-Pétersbourg*, in Glaudes (ed.), *Maistre: Œuvres*, p.466.

the premises correct? Any deductive argument is *valid* when, given true premises, the truth of the conclusion is guaranteed. A deductive argument, however, can only be deemed *sound* if and only if its structure is valid, and its premises are *indeed* correct.

Maistre starts by turning the traditional problem around. He uses evil as an argument for divine existence. Maistre's position may be summarised thus:

1. Evil exists.
2. Without an intuition of Goodness, we could have no sense of evil: cosmic disorder presupposes order.
3. We have a sense of our own interior discord as a source of evil, indeed as the primary source of evil in the world.
4. The existence of evil illuminates both God's existence and His nature. If the world consisted wholly and uniquely of goodness and righteousness there would be no need for God since the world itself would be divine. God exists because evil exists and this means in particular that through freedom mankind is thrust back to the reality of God.
5. God cannot force men to love Him. But he can provide a world in which the love of God (subjective and objective genitive!) can be realised through prayer and sacrifice. In particular, innocent suffering represents the expiation of the guilt of sinners by the just.

In *Les Soirées* Maistre avoids two unattractive solutions to the problem of theodicy. One is the *overarching harmony* model. On such an account, it is argued that the quantity of goods in the world outweighs the number of evils. Dostoyevsky seems to bite here: ('I reject that higher harmony. It's not worth one little tear from one single little tortured child...').[30] The difficulty resides in any quantitative justification of the existence of evil. Such theories seem to minimise the reality of suffering in the world; and indeed can even be seen to provide a *ratio essendi* for suffering. No one could accuse Maistre of minimising the extent and intensity of suffering in the world. It becomes integrated into the drama of redemption.

Another response to the problem of evil is the opposite extreme: the praxis model. This manoeuvre consists in dismissing the theoretical question and attempting to overcome evil through a Christ-like life. The Christian should take up the cross and ignore theoretical justification. Yet such a position depends upon a Christocentric positivism, in which Christ is the unique revelation of the suffering of God. Such an approach to theodicy just begs the question. If the God of theism is problematic on account of the problem of evil, the status of a Christian

---

30. Fyodor Dostoyevsky, *Crime and punishment*, trans. David McDuff (Harmondsworth, 1991), p.307.

God in a world of egregious ills seems at least as unsettling for any notion of Providence. Moreover, any practice must depend upon a satisfactory theory and the radical irrationality of the world does *prima facie* support the atheist case.

One of the most powerful challenges to theodicy comes from David Hume's brilliant *Dialogues concerning natural religion* of 1779. Hume argues that *either* the theologian claims too much for the argument from design and then we cannot avoid the problem of evil, *or* he claims ignorance of divine purpose and avoids the problem of evil – but with the unfortunate consequence of conceding to the agnostic the futility of philosophical theology. If God is posited *radically* beyond human comprehension, he cannot be worshipped. There must be some link between the transcendent and human experience. Indeed, Maistre brilliantly avoids Hume's theological fork. Maistre is anti-apophatic: he argues against an undue stress upon the unknowability of the Divine. He writes that philosophy warns us that God is not like us, but that it is religion which makes us like unto God. The God-man called us to be his friends:

> Une des choses que la philosophie ne cesse de nous répéter, c'est qu'il faut nous garder de faire Dieu semblable à nous. J'accepte l'avis, pourvu qu'elle accepte à son tour celui de la religion, de nous rendre semblables à Dieu. La justice divine peut être contemplée et étudiée dans la nôtre bien plus que nous ne le croyons. Ne savons-nous pas que nous avons été créés à l'image de Dieu; et ne nous a-t-il pas été ordonné de travailler à nous rendre parfaits comme lui.[31]

Indeed, the principle of correspondence between the material and the spiritual worlds is a recurring theme of Maistre's metaphysics:

> Nous sommes tous attachés au trône de l'Etre suprême par une chaîne souple, qui nous retient sans nous asservir.
> Ce qu'il y a de plus admirable dans l'ordre universel des choses, c'est l'action des êtres libres sous la main divine. Librement esclaves, ils opèrent tout à la fois volontairement et nécessairement: ils font réellement ce qu'ils veulent, mais sans pouvoir déranger les plans généraux. Chacun de ces êtres occupe le centre d'une sphère d'activité, dont le diamètre varie au gré de l'éternel géomètre, qui sait étendre, restreindre, arrêter ou diriger la volonté, sans altérer sa nature.[32]

The image of the *aurea catena homeri* (see *Iliad* VIII, 18) and that of the divine geometer are typically Neoplatonic motifs and both are integral to Maistre's tenet of correspondences between the spiritual and material levels of existence.[33] 'Correspondences' exist on manifold levels. Life

31.  Maistre, *Les Soirées de Saint-Pétersbourg*, in Glaudes (ed.), *Maistre: Œuvres*, p.552-53.
32.  Maistre, *Considérations sur la France*, in Glaudes (ed.), *Maistre: Œuvres*, p.199.
33.  On Maistre's Neoplatonism, see, in this volume, Aimee Barbeau, 'The Savoyard

properly ordered means that reason controls the passions, just as a king ruled his subjects, the parent ruled the child, and the sun governed the planets. However chaos present in one realm is mirrored in other realms. Shakespeare's *King Lear*, for example, reveals the horror of chaos pervading family, state and mind: the madness of Lear mirrors the terrors of nature (the raging storm). Lear compares his insanity to 'a tempest in my mind'.

Maistre's apologetic tactic starts from the human side: the experience of evil. Rather than produce a theodicy in the sense of a reason for God or a defence in the sense of Leibniz, Maistre endeavours to turn the argument of the sceptic on its head. Evil becomes an integral aspect of his theological vision. Hence he expends much effort attacking materialism, especially Locke.[34] (Locke was not, in fact, a materialist, but he was perceived in such terms by the French Enlightenment.)[35]

> J'entends bien que ces mots ne doivent point être pris à la lettre; mais toujours ils nous montrent ce que nous sommes, puisque la moindre ressemblance avec le souverain être est un titre de gloire qu'aucun esprit ne peut concevoir. La ressemblance n'ayant rien en commun avec l'égalité, nous ne faisons qu'user de nos droits en nous glorifiant de cette ressemblance. Lui-même s'est déclaré notre père et l'ami de nos âmes. L'homme-Dieu nous a appelés ses amis, ses enfants et même ses frères; et ses apôtres n'ont cessé de nous répéter le précepte d'être semblables à lui. Il n'y a donc pas le moindre doute sur cette auguste ressemblance; mais l'homme s'est trompé doublement sur Dieu; tantôt il l'a fait semblable a l'homme en lui prêtant nos passions; tantôt au contraire, il s'est trompé d'une manière plus humiliante pour sa nature en refusant d'y reconnaitre les traits divins de son modèle. Si l'homme sait découvrir et contempler ces traits, il ne se trompera point en jugeant Dieu d'après sa créature chérie. Il suffit d'en juger d'après toutes les vertus, c'est-à-dire d'après toutes les perfections contraires à nos passions; perfections dont tout homme se sent susceptible, et que nous sommes forcés d'admirer au fond de notre coeur, lors même qu'elles nous sont étrangères.[36]

Let us first distinguish between three kinds of evil:

1. Natural evil. That is earthquakes, famines, droughts: events that are usually not due to direct human agency.
2. Moral evil. Here one might think of serial killers, genocide.

---

philosopher: deist or Neoplatonist?' and Elcio Verçosa Filho, 'The pedagogical nature of Maistre's thought'. On Maistre's Plato, see Philippe Barthelet, 'The Cambridge Platonists mirrored by Joseph de Maistre', also in this volume.

34. J. Yolton, *Locke and French materialism* (Oxford, 1991).
35. On the radical Enlightenment's construction of a materialist Locke, see the 'Introduction' to this volume.
36. Maistre, *Les Soirées de Saint-Pétersbourg*, in Glaudes (ed.), *Maistre: Œuvres*, p.552-53.

3.  Metaphysical evil. This is the most moot sense of evil. It is mytho-
    logically expressed in various forms. In the Christian Scriptures, it is
    personified or embodied in Satan.

At the heart of Christianity is a deep ambivalence about the source of
evil. Ultimately it is grounded in free will, and yet it is the product of a
Fall beyond the moral orbit of a particular agent. Maistre reflects this
Christian ambivalence in seeing moral evil as the root of natural evil: 'S'il
n'y avait point de mal moral sur la terre, il n'y aurait point de mal
physique'.[37] Yet this moral evil is not an accidental disposition to wrong
doing but a deeply entrenched structural inclination to evil ground in
the division or dividedness of the human soul. The cosmos is the arena
for a painful return to God through submission of the will on the model
of Christ's suffering love. War and disease are part of the *via purgativa* to
be endured by a sinful humanity. But this does not mean that Maistre has
a crude understanding of pain and suffering as due deserts for man's
sinfulness. That would be inconsistent with the poignant and tender
description of the pious girl suffering from cancer at the end of the third
*Soirée*. Maistre's vision is gloomy rather than cruel.

The idea of sacrifice is inalienable in Christian thought because of the
idea of the Fall: the special sense of the imperfection of the world.
Redemption in Christian terms, unlike both Judaism and Islam, requires
much more than a renegotiation of the relation between God and man,
but a radical liberation from the fallen state. John Henry Newman
observes that those 'who know nothing of the wounds of the soul' will
not seek deliverance.[38]

Sacrifice is important for Christian ethics because it discloses a level of
reality otherwise obscured in quotidian human society. Sin is a state of
dispersion, of being torn asunder like Isis or Pentheus. And the violence
of man's fallen state reflects this dispersion. The visible world is a portion
of that transcendent spiritual domain from whence the former is
derived. As human beings, our vocation is a harmonious communion
with this intelligible universe that is the mind of God. Prayer and
sacrifice are forms of communion with God. Christian Platonism starts
from the soul, the unique individuality ignored by materialism, an
individual who must experience life in apocalyptic terms as the struggle
between good and evil.[39] Sacrifice is the expiation of the vicious duality
in the human being:

37.  Maistre, *Les Soirées de Saint-Pétersbourg*, in Glaudes (ed.), *Maistre: Œuvres*, p.473.
38.  John Henry Newman, *An Essay in aid of a grammar of assent*, edited with an introduction and
       notes by I. T. Ker (Reprint, Oxford, 1998), p.321.
39.  Armenteros, 'Revolutionary violence and the end of history'.

[L'homme] *gravite* [...] vers les régions de la lumière. Nul castor, nulle hirondelle, nulle abeille n'en veulent savoir plus que leurs devanciers. Tous les êtres sont tranquilles à la place qu'ils occupent. Tous sont dégradés, mais ils l'ignorent; l'homme seul en a le sentiment, et ce sentiment est tout à la fois la preuve de sa grandeur et de sa misère, de ses droits sublimes et de son incroyable dégradation. Dans l'état où il est réduit, il n'a pas même le triste bonheur de s'ignorer: il faut qu'il se contemple sans cesse, et il ne peut se contempler sans rougir; sa grandeur même l'humilie, puisque les lumières qui l'élèvent jusqu'à l'ange ne servent qu'à lui montrer dans lui des penchants abominables qui le dégradent jusqu'à la brute. Il cherche dans le fond de son être quelque partie saine sans pouvoir la trouver: le mal a tout souillé, *et l'homme entier n'est qu'une maladie.* Assemblage inconcevable de deux puissances différentes et incompatibles, centaure monstrueux, il sent qu'il est le résultat de quelque forfait inconnu, de quelque mélange détestable qui a vicié l'homme jusque dans son essence la plus intime.[40]

Maistre is insistent that, however this tenet may seem to the *philosophes*, the doctrine of an original sin has its counterpart in the pagans. He refers explicitly to Plato's dialogue the *Phaedrus*:

Platon nous dit *qu'en se contemplant lui-même, il ne sait s'il voit un monstre plus double, plus mauvais que Typhon, ou bien plutôt un être moral, doux et bienfaisant, qui participe de la nature divine.* Il ajoute que l'homme, ainsi tiraillé en sens contraires, ne peut faire le bien et vivre heureux *sans réduire en servitude cette puissance de l'âme, où réside le mal, et sans remettre en liberté celle qui est le séjour et l'organe de la vertu.* C'est précisément la doctrine chrétienne, et l'on ne saurait confesser plus clairement le péché originel.[41]

There is a long tradition of identifying redemption with Isis picking up the dismembered parts of Osiris.[42] Plutarch, the Middle Platonist and one of Maistre's favourite authors, writes in the following manner:

Therefore the effort to arrive at the Truth, and especially the Truth about the gods, is a longing for the divine. For the search for truth requires for its study and investigation the consideration of sacred subjects, and it is a work more hallowed than any form of holy living or temple service; and not least of all, it is well-pleasing to that goddess whom you worship, a goddess exceptionally wise and a lover of wisdom, to whom, as her name at least seems to indicate, knowledge and understanding are in the highest degree appropriate. For Isis is a Greek word, and so also is Typhon, her enemy, who is conceited, as his name implies, because of his ignorance and self-deception. He tears to pieces and scatters to the winds the sacred writings, which the goddess collects and puts together and gives into the keeping of those that are initiated into the holy rites, since this consecration, by a strict regimen and by abstinence from many kinds of food and from the lusts of

---

40. Maistre, *Les Soirées de Saint-Pétersbourg*, in Glaudes (ed.), *Maistre: Œuvres*, p.487.
41. Maistre, *Les Soirées de Saint-Pétersbourg*, in Glaudes (ed.), *Maistre: Œuvres*, p.489.
42. Michael Lieb, *Milton and the culture of violence* (London, 1994).

the flesh, curtails licentiousness and the love of pleasure, and induces a habit of patient submission to the stern and rigorous services in shrines, an end and aim of which is the knowledge of Him who is the First, the Lord of All, the Ideal One. Him does the goddess urge us to seek, since He is near her and with her in close communion. The name of her shrine also clearly promises knowledge and comprehension of reality; for it is named Iselon, to indicate that we shall comprehend reality if in a reasonable and devout frame of mind we pass within the portals of her shrines.[43]

The imagery reinforces the Neoplatonic metaphysics of the Fall from primal unity and the return of all being to its transcendent Source. The (Platonic) metaphysics of unity plays a central role in Maistre's theory of sacrifice and reversibility. It is because of the arcane kinship of mankind that the fragmentary state of the current world can be transformed through Providence into the ultimate point of reconciliation where God will become all in all.

> Truth indeed came once into the world with her divine Master, and was a perfect shape most glorious to look on: but when he ascended, and his Apostles after him were laid asleep, then straight arose a wicked race of deceivers, who, as that story goes of the *Ægyptian Typhon* with his conspirators, how they dealt with the good *Osiris*, took the virgin Truth, hewd her lovely form into a thousand peeces, and scatter'd them to the four winds. From that time ever since, the sad friends of Truth, such as durst appear, imitating the careful search that *Isis* made for the mangl'd body of *Osiris*, went up and down gathering up limb by limb, still as they could find them. We have not yet found them all, Lords and Commons, nor ever shall doe, till her Master's second comming; he shall bring together every joynt and member, and shall mould them into an immortall feature of loveliness and perfection. Suffer not these licensing prohibitions to stand at every place of opportunity forbidding and disturbing them that continue seeking, that continue to do our obsequies to the torn body of our martyr'd Saint.[44]

Maistre's vision of the disordered soul is deeply Origenistic.[45] And when Maistre says that disorder presupposes order: 'Ils parlent de désordre dans l'univers; mais qu'est-ce que le désordre',[46] he is producing a similar argument. I suggest Maistre gets the right balance between the theoretical and the hermeneutical or existential dimension of the problem. His is a vision of the return of the cosmos to God. God is drawing the

---

43. Plutarch, 'Isis and Osiris', 351-52, in Plutarch, *Moralia,* trans. and ed. Frank Cole Babbitt, 15 vol. ('Loeb classical library', Cambridge, MA and London, 2003, first publ. 1936), vol. 5, p.8-11.

44. John Milton, *Areopagitica, a speech of Mr John Milton for the liberty if vnlicens'd printing, to the parliament of England* (London, 1644), p.29.

45. On Maistre's Origenism, see, in this volume, Elcio Verçosa-Filho's article 'The pedagogical nature of Maistre's thought'.

46. Maistre, *Les Soirées de Saint-Pétersbourg,* in Glaudes (ed.), *Maistre: Œuvres,* p.698.

universe towards him.[47] Hence Joseph de Maistre is starting from the human side, from the experience of evil. Rather than produce a theodicy in the sense of a reason for God or a rationalistic defence in the manner of Leibniz.

Notwithstanding the macabre note of 'régénération dans le sang', the key concepts of Maistre are those of the restitution of creation and theosis. He presents a theodicy in his account of the world as a process of purification and communion in which prayer and sacrifice play a central role: 'La terre entière, continuellement imbibée de sang, n'est qu'un autel immense où tout ce qui vit doit être immolé sans fin, sans mesure, sans relâche, jusqu'à la consommation des choses, jusqu'à la mort de la mort'.[48] Here we find the Pauline sense of how the 'whole creation groans and travails in pain'. The world seems to present a spectacle of infinite conflict, waste and ravaged atrophy. This is indeed incompatible with the naked perfection of the world. But does it mean that the world is just a see-saw of brute and cruel force in the sense of Schopenhauer's *Wille*? Clearly not.[49] 'Y a-t-il quelque chose de plus certain que cette proposition: tout a été fait par et pour l'intelligence', Maistre exclaims? [50] The proposition that everything has been made by and for intelligence is rationalist, not irrationalist. Schopenhauer's metaphysical pessimism would represent a kind of position that all Platonists from Origen to Maistre would identify as disappointed hedonism parading as a bogus realism. The fundamental question goes back to Plato's Republic. Is the Good, or goal of ethics, pleasure or a principle of goodness that radically transcends human inclinations and immediate interests?

From Maistre's Christian perspective, in which the supremacy of love ('la *loi d'amour*') is the core tenet, we can see – albeit dimly – that the apparent wasteland is part of a larger process of love, a process of struggle in which love is revealed as self-sacrifice.[51] Here we have the note of *Christus consummator*, the one who is the omega point of the cosmos (in Teilhard's terms). There is a correspondence between physical, moral and spiritual. Evil is not a hindrance to divine design and purpose but makes it clearer: it shows the necessity of expiation and substitution. The most profound evil is the obscuring of the divine presence.

Let us not forget that Christianity views evil as overcome through

---

47. Rather like the Omega Point of Teilhard de Chardin.
48. Maistre, *Les Soirées de Saint-Pétersbourg*, in Glaudes (ed.), *Maistre: Œuvres*, p.661.
49. For a study of the similarities between Maistre and Schopenhauer's thought, see, in this volume, Yannis Constantinidès, 'Two great enemies of the Enlightenment: Joseph de Maistre and Schopenhauer'.
50. Maistre, *Les Soirées de Saint-Pétersbourg*, in Glaudes (ed.), *Maistre: Œuvres*, p.836.
51. Maistre, *Les Soirées de Saint-Pétersbourg*, in Glaudes (ed.), *Maistre: Œuvres*, p.823.

transformation rather than separation. The cross is an image of the man-God suffering and transforming evil and violence into peace and harmony. The key to evil is thus not separation but absorption and change. There are doubtless enormous problems in the attempt to articulate an adequate theoretical framework: both with the highly problematic Anselmian move that God needs a sacrificial object or victim to appease his wrath and the position that God is the subject of the sacrifice – he is sacrificing himself in the quasi-cabbalistic sense of a self-contraction or limitation, for example in German Idealism where God is the infinite who sacrifices himself for the finite and finite beings must sacrifice themselves to reveal the infinite. No one can seriously deny problems for Christian theology arising from discontent since the Enlightenment with the doctrine of penal substitution. But these difficulties should not obscure the philosophical basis for seeing the idea of sacrifice as an immensely important part of an adequate anthropology, and the basis for a critique of a narrow reductionism.

## Maistre from Dante to Dostoyevsky

Maistre, I suggest, should not be viewed as a specifically modern figure, but as a Christian thinker in the great tradition of Christian metaphysics. Dante, no stranger to conflict and grim violence in real politics, employed the idea of sacrifice in a very prominent manner. Dante is a poet of exile. The biblical motif of exodus pervades his *Commedia*. He is a poet who has been through the fiery furnace of the loss of his place of birth and his most intense worldly love. Canto V of the *Inferno* with Paolo and Francesca is a meditation on love, disordered love and love lost. Canto VI with his debate with Ciacca is the adumbration of the ground of his exile for the paradigmatic earthly city of the *Commedia*, Florence. Dante is the Florentine in exile. The brutal civil war in Florence ending in 1266 between the Guelphs and Ghibellines resulted in the victory of the Guelphs. And there was subsequently the later repetition of such battles between the White and Black Guelphs referred to by Ciacca: the period of the 1290s and the violence that erupted in 1300. One might consider also the meeting in *Inferno* X between Dante and Farinata, the great Ghibelline warlord. Suffering and salvation, exile and atonement are linked not just through happenstance but integrally, on the model of crucifixion and resurrection. Maistre's insistence upon suffering and sacrifice draws upon a deep Christian tradition as well as his provocative and idiosyncratic manner.

Yet Maistre also exerted considerable influence upon the nineteenth century. He stayed in Russia for fourteen years and had considerable personal influence amidst the court. He was esteemed by the Slavophiles.

Franz von Baader (1765-1841), who saw Russia and the Orthodox religion as a bulwark against Western rationalism and materialism, was a great admirer of Maistre. He wrote one of the first essays on Maistre's thought and was appreciative. His close friend, Dostoyevsky, one of the greatest literary figures to emerge out of the Slavophile world, was referred to as a Russian Joseph de Maistre.[52]

> The blood that's on everyone's hands [...] that flows and has always flowed through the world like a waterfall, that is poured like champagne and for the sake of which men are crowned in the Capitol and then called the benefactors of mankind. It is, in fact, worth noting that the majority of those benefactors and guiding spirits of mankind were particularly fearsome bloodletters.[53]

The Maistrian element in Dostoyevsky extends beyond the rhetoric of blood. The whole of *Crime and punishment* (1866), for example, is about the freedom that consists in self-renunciation and the salvation that emerges from the recognition of guilt and evil. The physical crime of Raskolnikov corresponds to the spiritual crime that is grounded in his self-assertion, and his banishment to Siberia mirrors the profounder fact of his exile from God. It is the figure of Sonya who says: 'You must accept suffering and redeem yourself by it'. The novel revolves around this law of the spirit – that positivistic science cannot, *per definitionem*, grasp. The law is the principle of atonement and redemption. Here we should recall both the joy and the Light. Light is a very important image for the Platonic tradition: one need only think of the Cave in Plato's *Republic* or of enlightenment in *The Seventh letter*. The philosophy of Plotinus has often been described as a metaphysics of light.

One might consider the beautiful surroundings of the 'Introduction' to the first *Soirée*, which starts with the light of the splendid Northern European summer:

> Rien n'est plus rare, mais rien n'est plus enchanteur qu'une belle nuit d'été à Saint-Pétersbourg, soit que la longueur de l'hiver et la rareté de ces nuits leur donnent, en les rendant plus désirables, un charme particulier; soit que réellement, comme je le crois, elles soient plus douces et plus calmes que dans les plus beaux climats.[54]

Maistre says in his typically tender manner:

> Si le ciel, dans sa bonté, me réservait un de ces moments si rares dans la vie où le coeur est inondé de joie par quelque bonheur extraordinaire et

52. Vera Miltchyna, 'Joseph de Maistre in Russia', in Lebrun (ed.), *Maistre: life thought and influence*, p.263.
53. Dostoyevsky, *Crime and punishment*, p.312.
54. Maistre, *Les Soirées de Saint-Pétersbourg*, in Glaudes (ed.), *Maistre: Œuvres*, p.455.

inattendu; si une femme, des enfants, des frères séparés de moi depuis longtemps, et sans espoir de réunion, devaient tout à coup tomber dans mes bras, je voudrais, oui, je voudrais que ce fût dans une de ces belles nuits sur les rives de la Néva, en présence de ces Russes hospitaliers.[55]

It is a *soirée*. Maistre refers explicitly to the Platonic *Symposium* with its association with wine and conviviality.[56] Remember that for Maistre mankind '*gravitates*... to regions of light'. But then we are plunged into the abyss of the Fallen world. The vision is akin to that of Dante or Dostoyevsky. The complacency of worldly hopes and ambitions must be broken. Here philosophy and theology converge. It was Plato who defined philosophy as the practice of death, and through his formative experience of the *Pénitents noirs*, Maistre knew the dimension of the *memento mori* of Christian theology. I would also like to note the special role of the psalms. These have always appealed to Christian mystics, and they play a core role in *Les Soirées*, especially the notorious seventh dialogue.

Sacrifice is ambivalent in the sense that it represents both a non-reducible cultural and a transcendent dimension to human experience. As such, it provides a double bulwark against the naturalist. For the naturalist can neither provide a satisfactory reduction of the irreducible hermeneutical dimension of sacrifice, its role in our stories about ourselves. Nor can the naturalist do justice to the sense of the transcendent in the making sacred of sacrifice. Thus we should exercise caution when Bradley says that Maistre's approach to the question of sacrifice was 'veritably sociological'.[57] We have to keep both dimensions of Maistre's thought in mind: especially in relation to sacrifice. The transcendent dimension is very important. Sacrifice is not just a principle of social cohesion, but an index of the transcendent converging with the immanent, revelation with human culture. Bradley is quite right to see Joseph de Maistre's work as a precursor of the nineteenth-century science of religion and the intense discussion of science. But we should pause before drawing too strong a conclusion. After all, Augustine was veritably psychological but remained a theologian. I think the same is true of Maistre's 'sociology'.[58]

55. Maistre, *Les Soirées de Saint-Pétersbourg*, in Glaudes (ed.), *Maistre: Œuvres*, p.457.
56. Bradley, *A Modern Maistre*, p.6.
57. Bradley, *A Modern Maistre*, p.35.
58. I am very grateful to Carolina Armenteros, Richard Lebrun and the late and much missed Emile Perreau-Saussine for their suggestions and assistance.

# Why Maistre became Ultramontane

EMILE PERREAU-SAUSSINE

I would like to answer a question, which, despite its importance, has not been sufficiently considered: why did Joseph de Maistre become Ultramontane?[1] Why did he reject the great Gallic tradition that he initially greeted? Why abandon such a powerful strand of thought? Indeed, why precipitate its fall?

## i. From the revolution of 1682 to the revolution of 1789

Maistre saw an analogy between the 'revolution of 1682' and the 'revolution of 1789'. To his eyes Gallicanism is 'the pit of the abyss' from which came the eighteenth century, a prejudice 'destructive of the religious system and political religion'. The Gallicanism of the *ancien régime* thus appeared as the first stage of the Revolution. In 1682, the Assembly of the Clergy had adopted a 'Déclaration du Clergé de France sur la puissance ecclésiastique' whose first article stated: 'les papes n'ont reçu de Dieu qu'un pouvoir spirituel. Les rois et les princes ne sont soumis dans les choses temporelles à aucune puissance ecclésiastique; ils ne peuvent donc pas être déposés en vertu du pouvoir des chefs de l'Eglise et leurs sujets ne peuvent pas être déliés du serment de fidélité.' No ecclesiastical authority (pope, bishop or council) had any direct or indirect power over the temporal, could depose a prince, or release a prince's subjects from the submission that they owed him. This was the doctrine of the French monarchy, *political* Gallicanism: the king of France held his realm from God alone, and had no temporal superior. Subject of the pope as a Catholic, the monarch was not subject to him as 'sovereign'. While this doctrine was condemned by the Holy See, it did not present any difficulty in the eyes of French Catholics. Certain articles of the Declaration of 1682 were the object of sharp disagreement, but not the first – at least not in France, where Bellarmine's theory of indirect power was willingly criticised. In the eyes of Gallicans, the Pope could not go beyond purely spiritual matters, and the scope of his action could not exceed the limits of this domain.[2] The clergy, and even the Jesuits, although in principle

---

1. This article was translated from French by Richard A. Lebrun.
2. Victor Martin, *Le Gallicanisme politique et le clergé de France* (Picard, 1929), p.25-40.

attached to the rights of the papacy, were in agreement on the principle
of the autonomy of the monarchy in temporal matters.[3]

With the benefit of hindsight, this autonomy of the temporal seems to
announce the end of the confessional state during the Revolution – the
moment when full membership of the political body no longer depended
on the Catholic religion, when the French were no longer, *at the same time*,
subjects of the prince and sons of the Church, when the crime of heresy
was abolished and when canon law became foreign to the state.

For Lamennais, Louis XIV solemnly proclaimed the separation between religious society and civil society:

> en 1682, des évêques serviles proclamèrent comme un dogme de la religion,
> ce qui n'avait été jusque là qu'une lâche flatterie des cours judiciaires [le
> gallicanisme politique], savoir, que la souveraineté chez les peuples chrétiens
> est indépendante du Christ et de sa loi. [...] de sorte que, dans l'ordre
> temporel, c'est à dire en tout ce qui regarde l'exercice propre de la
> souveraineté, les souverains n'ont aucun juge, ni temporel, sans quoi ils ne
> seraient pas souverains, ni spirituels, sans quoi ils ne seraient pas
> indépendants, comme souverains, de la puissance ecclésiastique ou spiritu-
> elle.

Lamennais related these themes directly to the question of liberalism
(the word, in its modern sense, had just been invented): 'le libéralisme
refuse de reconnaître la loi divine, aussi bien que l'autorité par qui seule
on peut la connaître certainement, et le gallicanisme affranchit de l'une
et de l'autre le souverain, en tant que souverain'.[4] In the same vein, the
Ultramontane author of a *Histoire critique du catholicisme libéral jusqu'au
pontificat de Léon XIII*, Monseigneur Justin Louis Pierre Fèvre (1829-1907),
systematically relates liberalism to Gallicanism. Having learnedly
explained that 'le libéralisme existe, comme idée, depuis la révolte de
Lucifer', and that 'le libéralisme est, par lui-même, un péché mortel', he
traces the 'origines hétérodoxes du libéralisme' to Philip the Fair, the
hero of political Gallicanism, and insists on the continuity between the
absolutist (Gallican) era and the liberal era. 'On oppose volontiers ces
deux ères l'une à l'autre', he writes, 'et il y a, en effet, dans leur
organisation, une opposition absolue; mais, dans leur principe, il y a
*identité*'.[5]

In his *Histoire de l'idée laïque en France au XIX^e siècle* (1929), Georges Weill
notes that with Protestant evangelism, deism and free thought,

---

3.  Martin, *Le Gallicanisme politique*, p.314-22; P. Blet, 'Jésuites gallicans au XVII^e siècle?',
    *Archivicum historicum Societatis Jesu*, vol.29, 1960, p.55-84.
4.  Lamennais, *Des Progrès de la révolution et de la guerre contre l'Eglise* (Paris, 1829), p.47, p.49-50,
    p.56-57.
5.  Mgr Justin Fèvre, *Histoire critique du catholicisme libéral jusqu'au pontificat de Léon XIII* (Saint-
    Dizier, 1897), p.6, 8, and 5. See also p.58-80.

Gallicanism is one of the four sources of the secular idea. Bossuet, who is often represented as the most medieval or the most obscurantist of classical thinkers, is the author of formulas that with hindsight appear as singularly liberal. In his justification of Article 1 of the Declaration of 1682, he affirms that 'D'un côté, l'Eglise et la vraie religion peuvent subsister parfaitement et solidement sans être unies à la puissance temporelle; d'un autre côté, la puissance temporelle et le gouvernement politique peuvent aussi subsister et être dans un état parfait sans la vraie Eglise et la vraie religion.'[6] Submissive as a Christian, the monarch knows that he must not be so as a sovereign. That Bossuet's expressions had something liberal before their time, is obvious to Maistre. Like Lamennais, Fèvre and Weill, Maistre detects a real direct continuity between Gallicanism and liberalism – a continuity that he deplores with the utmost energy.

For Maistre, the great error of Gallicanism is that it attempted to distinguish clearly between a 'temporal' sphere and a 'spiritual' sphere. Far from appreciating the political utility of the distinction, he is sensitive to what appears to him to be its specious character. In his eyes, authority in the last analysis always goes back to the divine, and relations between authorities go back to more or less sacred hierarchies of orders. With Maistre, apologetics is never entirely separable from social realism. Being a 'good Christian' and being a 'loyal subject' go together. As he explains in the *Considérations sur la France* that he opposed to the Revolution, 'toutes les institutions imaginables reposent sur une idée religieuse, ou ne font que passer. Elles sont fortes et durables à mesure qu'elles sont *divinisées*, s'il est permis de s'exprimer ainsi'.[7] [...] 'La politique et la religion se fondent ensemble: on distingue à peine le législateur du prêtre; et ses institutions politiques consistent principalement en cérémonies et vacations religieuses'.[8] Politics and religion exchange attributes with each other. The end of the confessional state appears impossible, for that amounts to separating what it is not even possible to distinguish clearly: religion and politics. Maistre's distrust of Gallicanism is consubstantial with his political theology. For Gallicanism, by affirming the autonomy of the temporal sphere, goes hand in hand with a critique of political theology. For the same reason, Maistre disputes democracy, Gallicanism and what will soon be called liberalism, which supposes the existence of a natural framework irreducible to the religious framework of the supernatural.

6. Bossuet, *Défense de la déclaration de l'assemblée du clergé de France de 1682* (Amsterdam, Compagnie des Libraires, 1745), bk.I, sect.II, ch.32.
7. Maistre, *Considérations sur la France* in Glaudes (ed.), *Maistre: Œuvres*, p.226.
8. Maistre, *Considérations sur la France* in Glaudes (ed.), *Maistre: Œuvres*, p.233-34.

For Maistre, the revolutionary state is not indifferent or incompetent in religious matters. Since human and social reality is at bottom religious, the affirmation of the neutrality of the state in religious matters can only be a lie that masks anti-Catholic religious bias. Maistre oscillates between four explanations that have in common the same religious character: divine punishment, Satan, atheism and Protestant heresy.

The Revolution is described as a chastisement for the sins of France and Europe. '[J]amais la Divinité ne s'était montrée d'une manière si claire dans aucun événement humain. Si elle emploie les instruments les plus vils, c'est qu'elle punit pour régénérer'.[9] However the suggestion that the Revolution is a result of God's intervention does not exclude the possibility that the Revolution is also the work of the devil. 'Il y a dans la révolution française un caractère satanique qui la distingue de tout ce qu'on a vu, et peut-être de tout ce qu'on verra'.[10] Or that it is the work of atheists. For his part, Maistre thinks that 'l'athéisme, dans notre siècle, s'est uni à un principe éminemment actif, l'esprit révolutionnaire'.[11] The counter-revolutionaries were inclined to insist on the more or less underground role of men of letters, intellectuals, Freemasons and other people of the same type.

Maistre proposes another interpretation, that of a Protestant plot. The Revolutionary state is not a state without a confession; it is a state newly confessionalised by a heresy: the Reformation whose exaltation of free examination created the basis of liberalism. In his *Réflexions sur le protestantisme dans ses rapports avec la souveraineté* (1798), Maistre denounces the Reformation as a heresy at once religious and civil: neither authority nor sovereignty is any longer respected; individual reason is in rebellion. For Maistre 'lorsque l'autorité commande, il n'y a que trois partis à prendre: l'obéissance, la représentation, et la révolte, qui se nomme *hérésie* dans l'ordre spirituel, et *révolution* dans l'ordre temporel'.[12] Protestantism shares with the Revolution a refusal of constituted authorities. Maistre thinks of democracy and the Reformation as two closely linked errors. The Protestant idea of free examination appears to him as the theological presupposition of the Declaration of the Rights of 1789. Protestant individualism and the de-legitimisation of the clergy go hand in hand with the de-legitimisation of the monarchy. Maistre condemns the Protestant primacy of private judgement and the liberal primacy of individual consent as the matrix of modern individualism.

The counter-revolutionaries are not the only ones to think this way.

---

9. Maistre, *Considérations sur la France* in Glaudes (ed.), *Maistre: Œuvres*, p.202.
10. Maistre, *Considérations sur la France* in Glaudes (ed.), *Maistre: Œuvres*, p.226.
11. Maistre, *De l'Eglise gallicane*, in Maistre, *OC*, vol.3, p.83, n.1.
12. Lovie and Chetail (ed.), *Du Pape*, p.79. See Michèle Sacquin, *Entre Bossuet et Maurras. L'Antiprotestantisme en France de 1814 à 1870* (Paris, 1998), p.302-15.

Edgar Quinet, who devoted his life to the defence of the Revolution and to denouncing the misdemeanours of Ultramontanism, agrees with Maistre on the political meaning of Protestantism. Like Maistre, Quinet sees in Gallicanism the prelude to the Revolution.

> Une seule chose servait de limite à la monarchie de Louis XIV; c'était l'autorité de l'Eglise qui planait sur le roi. Cette ombre éloignée devient insupportable; le demi-dieu de Versailles ne peut tolérer d'être primé par l'autorité du demi-dieu du Vatican. Le clergé de France, par la déclaration de 1682, affranchit le monarque de ce reste de dépendance spirituelle. L'Etat politique est ouvertement délié de l'Etat religieux; on brise le nœud gordien, le trône se sépare de l'autel; il s'estime assez puissant pour ne s'appuyer que sur lui-même. Tout le monde pense, ce jour-là, à Versailles, que la monarchie absolue, débarrassée du contrôle de Rome, n'a plus rien à redouter; et, au contraire, il se trouve que ce prétendu affranchissement est la ruine de cette royauté sans limites; et les libertés de l'Eglise gallicane, proclamées au profit de Louis XIV, deviennent, dans le fond, le premier acte de la Révolution française. [...] La monarchie absolue de Louis XIV avait pour condition la monarchie absolue du catholicisme romain. Ces deux choses sont inséparables. Vouloir s'affranchir de Rome, c'était en réalité, pour Louis XIV et ses successeurs, se dépouiller de leur principe et détruire leur fondement.

Quinet congratulates himself on the 'separation of the spiritual and the temporal, which is the basis of the Gallican Church', but this does not seem to him to be compatible with Catholicism; this separation appears to him rather as Protestant in nature.[13] Quinet agrees with Maistre in seeing in Catholicism an essentially Ultramontane doctrine, the kind of doctrine that an absolutist king (Louis XIV) necessarily needed to support his power. The Declaration of 1682 appeared to him therefore, as it did to Maistre, as the 'premier acte de la Révolution'.

Quinet's historical summary, *La Révolution*, appeared in 1865, under Napoleon III, at a time when the republicans had the feeling that they had failed to achieve their ideal regime. Quinet maintained that at bottom the French Revolution had been too exclusively limited to the political field. It should have gone hand in hand with a Reformation which would have completed its work, anchoring its political principles in religious arrangements. Oddly, Quinet came to reproach the Revolutionaries for their timidity: 'Luther eût ri de ce qui fit trembler Robespierre et Danton'.[14] It would have been necessary, besides the

13. Edgar Quinet, *Le Christianisme et la Révolution française*, in *Œuvres complètes* (Paris, 1857), vol.3, p.206 and 207.
14. Quinet, *La Révolution* (Verboeckhoven, 1865), vol.2, p.147 (XVI.4). See François Furet, *La Gauche et la révolution au milieu du XIXᵉ siècle. Edgar Quinet et la question du Jacobinisme (1865-1870)* (Paris, 1986), and Claude Lefort, 'Edgar Quinet: La Révolution manquée', in *Essai sur le politique* (Paris, 1986), p.140-61.

Revolution, to convert the French to Protestantism. When it comes down to it, Quinet almost came to deplore that the Revolution had not added a war of religion to the Terror, and had not extended the Vendée war to all of France. For Quinet, political revolutions and religious revolutions have to be coordinated, and it is France's misfortune that it had not succeeded in doing so, unlike Holland, England or the United States.

Quinet and Maistre both think that the Gallican separation of the temporal and the spiritual foreshadowed the Revolution, while thinking at the same time that the separation was something artificial and exaggerated. Their parallel theses give rise to two closely linked questions. First: how did the Gallican doctors justify in their own eyes the separation of the temporal and the spiritual? Second: why did this separation not raise any fundamental difficulty for Catholics before the French Revolution, even though it became more and more difficult to accept after the Revolution?

For a long time, Gallicanism found numerous defenders because the temporal power liked to think it was eminently Catholic. The temporal power kept its distance from Rome, but not from the true religion. The *political* separation of the temporal and the spiritual was justifiable, for the temporal was not foreign to the spiritual. This is what changed with the Revolution. The end of the confessional state dissociated the temporal from the spiritual much more than did classical Gallicanism. The classical justifications of Gallicanism seemed to collapse.

## ii. The submission of the state to confessional constraints

In the era of absolutism, French Catholics tended to consider that they had no need of Roman threats or censures to behave in a Christian manner. This is the impression that is given especially in the work of Bossuet, who was led both to draw up the Declaration of 1682 and to justify it in a large work condemned by the Holy See, the *Defensio declarationis*. For Bossuet, 'l'Eglise gallicane a porté les évêques les plus doctes, les plus saints, les plus célèbres qui aient jamais été'.[15] In his *Politique tirée de l'Ecriture sainte*, Bossuet sought the essentials of his inspiration in the Book of Kings, to the detriment of the majority of the other books of the Old Testament and, especially, of the New Testament. He did not dwell excessively on the political meaning of Genesis, the Exodus, the Exile, the Crucifixion or the Apocalypse. Bossuet related the absolute monarchy of Louis XIV to the monarchy of David and Solomon, because he had the feeling that the history of France had something in common with that of an established people,

---

15. Bossuet, *Politique tirée de l'Ecriture sainte*, (1709), VII, vi, 14ème prop.

with that of a chosen nation. France being the eldest daughter of the Church, it has a fundamental place in the divine plan: its history is filled with the manifest action of God. The connection between Louis XIV and the kings of Israel does not involve an anachronism but an Old Testament certitude of divine election, which justifies the autonomy of the nation state on a theological plan.[16] One may imagine that a chosen nation benefits from guarantees that prevent it from making errors at the most fundamental level. Sustained directly by God, and based on His decisive choices, such a nation is assured of doing good.

The comparison of the king of France with King David had been used at the time of Philip the Fair to affirm the sovereignty of the king. It was to assert their indisputable authority that, from the fifteenth century, the kings of France called themselves 'Very Christian'. The thesis of the *divine right of kings* had not been conceived to justify the omnipotence of the ecclesiastical hierarchy and the Pope. This was a thesis defended especially by public lawyers, a thesis that served to subordinate the Church to the state. The thesis of the divine right of kings conferred a sacredness on the temporal power, thus permitting it to rival the spiritual power. Crowned in the Cathedral of Rheims, that is to say chosen by God himself, Louis XIV did not fear the divine right of the Pope, to which he opposed his own divine right.[17] The new David did not feel the need to bow deeply before the successor of Peter. In the end, 'le trône royal n'est pas le trône d'un homme, mais le trône de Dieu même'.[18] What theologian, what bishop would have the impertinence to contest the authority of such a throne?

A theoretician of absolutism, Bossuet elaborates the theology that came to crown the state in its maturity. His work presents, if not the canonical version of the theology of the state, at least one of its privileged expressions. Bossuet, who belonged to a family of high magistrates that had been honoured for its loyalty to the crown, offered the political theology of the state come to full consciousness of itself. The Church accommodated itself to absolutism because it did not really have any other choices, but also because the primacy of politics was counterbalanced by the state's membership in the Church. 'Un Etat

---

16. Joseph R. Strayer, 'France, the holy land, the chosen people and the most Christian king', in *Action and conviction in early modern Europe: essays in honor of E. H. Harbison*, ed. Theodore K. Rabb and Jerrold E. Seigel (Princeton, NJ, 1969), p.3-16; Colette Beaune, *Naissance de la nation de France* (Paris, 1985), p.75-229.

17. Joseph Lecler, 'Le Roi de France "Fils aîné de l'Eglise"', *Etudes*, 5 and 20 January 1933, p.21-36; Jacques Krynen, *L'Empire du Roi. Idées et croyances politiques en France (XIIIᵉ-XVᵉ siècle)* (Paris, 1933), p.339-414; John Neville Figgis, *The Divine right of kings* (Cambridge, 1896).

18. Bossuet, *Politique tirée de l'Ecriture sainte*, III, 2. See Aimé-George Martimort, *Le Gallicanisme de Bossuet* (Paris, 1953).

chrétien est lui-même une portion de l'Eglise universelle répandue partout, et en y entrant, cet Etat a contracté l'engagement d'obéir à ses lois constitutionnelles, qui existaient indépendamment de son admission.'[19] Even an author like Bossuet, who sometimes seems so complacent with respect to absolutism, also insists on the moral limits of absolutism. The *Politique tirée de l'écriture sainte* had been written when Bossuet was occupied with the education of Louis XIV's son. His book demonstrates above all his care to inculcate in the future monarch a sense of the moral limits of his action. His *Politique* belongs to the genre of the 'mirror of princes', which it renewed in an anti-Machiavellian spirit, inveighing against immorality in politics.[20] One never finds under his pen any equivalent to '*salus populi suprema lex esto*'. Bossuet justified the state, but not reason of state. By showing that it is possible to draw a politics from Scripture, he sought to establish, on the one hand, that Christianity is not as apolitical as the author of *The Prince* suggests, and on the other hand that a good politics is a Christian politics.

At the end of the dedication of his *Politique*, he noisily announces that 'those who believe that piety is a weakening of politics are confused'. He thus suggests, against Machiavelli, that the prince does not need to 'enter evil'. Absolute monarchy does not leave monarchs the right to do everything that they wish ('*ab legibus soluta*'): they remain bound by fundamental laws. Bossuet distinguishes clearly between absolute power and arbitrary power.[21] Absolute, paternal and sacred, royal authority remains submissive to reason and revelation.

The most famous jurist of the century of Louis XIV, Jean Domat, underlines the importance of revelation in his *Traité des lois*, which opens on a striking thesis: 'les premiers principes des lois ont été inconnus aux païens':

19. Jabineau, Maultrot, *Mémoire à consulter et consultation sur la compétence de la puissance temporelle, relativement à l'érection et suppression des sièges épiscopaux* (Paris, Desaint, 1790), p.4. See Malebranche, *Traité de morale* (1684), II, ix, §vii: 'comme l'Église et l'Etat sont composés des mêmes personnes, qui sont en même temps Chrétiens et citoyens, enfants de l'Église et sujets du Prince, il n'est pas possible que ces deux puissances, qui se doivent mutuellement respecter, et qui doivent être absolues et indépendantes dans l'exécution de leur charge, exercent leur juridiction, et exécutent l'ordre de leur maître commun, si elles ne sont parfaitement d'accord'.

20. Innocent Gentillet, *Discours d'état sur les moyens de bien gouverner* (Geneva, 1576); François de Gravelle, *Politiques royales* (Lyon, J. Périer, 1596). See Robert Bireley, *The Counter-Reformation prince: anti-Machiavellianism or Catholic statecraft in early modern Europe* (Chapel Hill, 1990). Bossuet's library contained Machiavelli's *Œuvres complètes* as well as two copies of *The Prince*.

21. Bossuet, *Politique tirée de l'Ecriture sainte*, IV, i, VIII, ii. This is a classic distinction among theoreticians of absolutism, such as Bodin or Loyseau, for example. See Denis Richet, *La France moderne: l'esprit des institutions* (Paris, 1973), p.37-54.

Les Romains qui entre toutes les nations, ont le plus cultivé les lois civiles, et qui en ont fait un si grand nombre de très justes, s'étaient donné, comme les autres peuples, la licence d'ôter la vie et à leurs esclaves, et à leurs propres enfants. Comme si la puissance que donne la qualité de père et celle de maître pouvait dispenser des lois de l'humanité.[22]

Domat insists on the role of reason and on the rootedness of laws in human nature, and he recalls that the Romans had made 'un si grand nombre' of 'très justes' laws. But he underlines no less that, thanks to the 'lumières de la religion', men can do better. Christianity imposes supplementary and salutary restraints.

As a historian of canon law writes, 'it was in the nature of theocratic law to confer its strength on the king, but it was also in the nature of this law to impose strict limits on him'.[23] The divine right on which kings leaned, often for strictly political reasons, remained a *divine* right, which carried a Christian symbolism and therefore specific demands. The divine right of kings did not release the monarch from his Christian obligations. On the contrary, it made his superiority in the temporal depend on a divine mark. His superiority had as its counterpart moral and spiritual demands. The sovereignty of the king was only justified by his membership in the Church.

'*Non est potestas nisi a Deo*' we read in St Paul. 'There is no authority that does not come from God'. The strong phrases of the Epistle to the Romans have generally been understood as justifying a duty of obedience to the civil authorities, but this obedience remains to a certain point subordinate to respect for natural and divine laws by the civil authorities. In considering the royal office as an ecclesiastical office, the jurists, theologians or publicists raised the prince above the people and the nobles, but they constrained him within a Christian horizon. Bossuet did not exalt the liberties of the Gallican Church in order to put that very Church in the hands of a state inclined to instrumentalise it cynically. Neither had Richelieu been the Machiavellian without scruples that has sometimes been depicted: if he utilised religion to consolidate the authority of the state, it was without ever losing sight of the interests of the religion to which he was profoundly attached.[24] For Richelieu as for Bossuet, Gallicanism could not go as far as schism, the prospect of which horrified them both: the political logic of independence could not

22. Domat, *Traité des lois*, (Caen, Centre de philosophie politique et juridique, 1989), 1.
23. Walter Ullmann, *Principles of government and politics in the Middle Ages* (London, 1961), p.139.
24. William F. Church, *Richelieu and reason of state* (Princeton, NJ, 1972); P. Blet, 'La Religion du Cardinal', in Antoine Adam, Maurice Andrieux, Pierre Blet, Georges Bordonove, Philippe Erlanger, Georges Mongrédien, Roland Mousnier, Victor-L. Tapié, *Richelieu* (Paris, 1972), p.163-79; Jörg Wollenberg, *Richelieu: Staatsräson und Kircheninteresse: zur Legitimation der Politik des Kardinalpremier* (Bielefeld, 1977).

in any way justify the transformation of Gallicanism into the equivalent
of Anglicanism.

Certainly, the kings of France have not often been saints, and tensions
between the civil authorities and the ecclesiastical authorities have not
been lacking. In a complex interplay, royal Gallicanism, parliamentary
Gallicanism, episcopal Gallicanism and Ultramontanism have sometimes
been opposed, sometimes allied, in a variety of different combinations.
The blows have often been brutal. But there were rules. The practice of
Gallicanism rested on a subtle equilibrium. The bishops obtained from
the popes more than the legists granted, and for the king more than the
Roman theologians were prepared to give.[25] If the pope was displeased
with the king, he refused to fill vacant sees. If the king was displeased with
the pope, Roman decrees and bulls were subject to an indefinite quar-
antine at the border (a bull had force only when registered by the
Parlement and 'received' by the episcopate). The papacy tried above all
to avoid the Gallican Church becoming autocephalous, and practised a
politics that joined severe warnings with flexibility and patience. As for
the kings of France, they had nothing much to gain from a schism, for
they had already obtained much from the Concordat of Bologna of 1516.
The Gallican Church pushed independence from Rome as far as it could,
but, wanting to be at once national and Catholic, it could not go so far as
to sacrifice the Catholic component to the national component. The
conflicts unfolded with, for a background, the desire not to go as far as a
rupture.[26] The religious and civil powers were too intertwined not to
sense, despite their incessant quarrels, the imperious need to take care of
each other. The most vigorous pope could not deprive Catholicism of the
largest, most vigorous and most knowledgeable Church of the time.

In his *Défense de la déclaration de l'assemblée du clergé de France de 1682*,
Bossuet was constrained by the logic of the first article to separate
religion and politics: 'la religion n'étant point établie pour troubler les
empires, elle les laisse dans la situation où le droit des gens de chaque
nation particulière les a placés'.[27]

Bossuet maintained that even a pagan monarch can be perfectly
legitimate. But is this what he really thought? Is he not, more fundamentally, attached to the first article because he remains convinced that
God will want to preserve the French monarchy in the bosom of
Catholicism? In his missive of March 1682, in which the nuncio explained
to the Holy See that the four articles had been adopted, he remarks with

25. Victor Martin, *Le Gallicanisme politique et le clergé de France*, p.268-70. Victor Martin, *Les Origines du gallicanisme* (Paris, 1939), vol.1, p.209-39.
26. P. Blet, *Les Assemblées du clergé et Louis XIV de 1670 à 1693* (Rome, 1972).
27. Bossuet, *Défense de la déclaration de l'assemblée du clergé de France de 1682*, bk.I, sect. II, ch.14.

respect to the subject of the first article: 'je pense qu'on ne trouvera pas un Français dans l'état actuel des choses qui ne le tienne pour vrai. Toutefois, si, ce qu'à Dieu ne plaise, il venait un roi hérétique, alors beaucoup de ceux-là même qui confessent maintenant cette opinion sur l'indépendance temporelle commenceraient aussitôt à professer avec beaucoup de constance l'opinion contraire.'[28] The Catholics of France recognised in law the autonomy of the king in the temporal, but in fact they reserved to themselves the right of contesting the legitimacy of a prince who would fall into heresy and who would persecute Catholics. The 'independence of the temporal' protected the king against the pope much more than it isolated politics from religion.

The theological-political economy of absolutism was berated by the Revolutionaries, who considered that the distinction between absolute power and arbitrary power did not suffice. For the constituents, the better way of limiting the state was not by its confessional character, but by putting into place a legislative power open to controlling the executive power and by a demand for representativeness. The Constituent Assembly, which led the French Revolution in its first phase, progressively withdrew absolute power from the king. Rather than a monarch by divine right, it made him a constitutional monarch. Article 2 of the *Déclaration des droits de l'homme et du citoyen* affirmed that 'le principe de toute souveraineté réside essentiellement dans la nation'. The architecture of the *ancien régime* was thus profoundly questioned. The monarch no longer held his power from God, but from the nation and its representatives.

This transformation raised numerous questions. If the Church recognised the legitimacy of the state that granted it a privileged status, what were its reasons for recognising a state that did not grant it this status? When Caesar was a good Catholic chosen by God, it was possible to separate 'God and Caesar', but when Caesar was no longer faithful in principle? Why would believers obey a state that was no longer bound by divine law and by revelation? What would frame the state when it was no longer framed by a religion? What ends would it pursue when it no longer pursued those it received from the Church? If 'le principe de toute souveraineté réside essentiellement dans la nation', would the judgment of the nation necessarily be wiser than that of the Church which reminded monarchs what God expected of them?

The deconfessionalisation of the state is often presented as a step in the development of 'modernity', as a liberation from obscure and infertile times. The idea of Progress and the advent of individual autonomy is

---

28. Quoted by André Latreille, 'Les Nonces apostoliques en France et l'Eglise gallicane sous Innocent XI', *Revue d'histoire de l'Eglise de France*, 1959, vol.41, p.226.

seen as going in tandem with what is called the 'secularisation' of the public sphere. However, considerations of this type are somewhat one-sided. For we forget too quickly that revelation imposed constraints on the confessional state that protected its citizens' security.[29] By insistently recalling the content of the evangelic message, the Church checks, hinders and thwarts iniquitous designs and policies that lack the most elementary demands of justice. I have noted this above: despite his absolutism, Bossuet opposed arbitrariness and was anti-Machiavellian. Certainly, Christianity did not prevent either injustice or despotism. But it offered a moral framework and a background of fundamental laws which a Christian state could not, in so far as it was one, free itself from either easily or completely. This point has become especially familiar to us since the advent of totalitarian and atheistic regimes, whose barbarism and anti-Christianity were inseparable. The secularisation of the state opened to it a field of unlimited action.

Seized by the importance of the changes that had been provoked by the Revolutionaries, Maistre thought that it was no longer possible to remain attached to Gallicanism, neither in its political version, nor in its religious version. So he went to seek in Rome the constraints and the moral direction that an apparently de-Christianised state could no longer guarantee. Maistre expressed his surprise in the face of what appeared to him as the recklessness of the men of 1789: 'Je prends la liberté de dire à mon siècle qu'il y a contradiction manifeste entre son enthousiasme constitutionnel et son déchaînement contre les Papes'.[30] Liberals argue that sovereignty must be limited and absolute power distrusted, that power must be divided, and the inalienable rights of man opposed to states. At the same time, they seek to move the Church, and especially the Holy See, away from power. Does the best way of limiting the state not consist in leaving the limitations to the Church? Maistre does not propose to confide the interests of humanity to the pope, but at the least he proposes to confide them to a co-sovereignty of Rome and kings.

Maistre quite willingly agrees that the state must be limited; the liberals are undoubtedly right on this. But as a source of those limits why turn to the people who are so fickle? Why not turn to the Holy See, which is more worthy of confidence? 'S'il fallait absolument en venir à poser des bornes légales à la puissance souveraine, j'opinerais de tout mon cœur pour que les intérêts de l'humanité fussent confiés au

---

29. On Maistre's discernment of the danger of releasing the state from the ties of Christian morality, see Carolina Armenteros' article in this volume, 'Maistre's Rousseaus'.
30. Maistre in Lovie and Chetail (ed.), *Du Pape*, bk.2, ch.4, p.138.

Souverain Pontife.'[31] A right of veto by the pope on the action of sovereigns would be more appropriate. It is more prudent to ask the pope to release subjects from their oaths of loyalty than to authorise them to release themselves, unless one wants to support anarchy. Maistre bases his suggestion on a historical observation: 'trompés par les criailleries philosophiques, nous croyons que les Papes passaient leur temps à déposer les rois',[32] but this is not the case. Maistre writes that 'si la France d'aujourd'hui, pliant sous une autorité divine, avait reçu son excellent roi des mains du Souverain Pontife, croit-on qu'elle ne fût pas dans ce moment un peu plus contente d'elle-même et des autres?'[33] The representatives of the Holy See must be admitted to great international congresses. The pope must get back his right of arbitration in international relations.

For Maistre, the revolutionary desire to make a clean sweep of the past is an unhealthy way to get rid of the customs that frame public life. In his *Considérations sur la France* (1797), he denounces the rationalism of the Enlightenment, which detaches practical reason from all particular contexts, as if it were desirable or even possible to free oneself from religious and national traditions. By abolishing privileges, by transforming the laws and the political regime, the French have not thrown off their yokes, but have instead thrown away the very things that guaranteed their security. Those who established the republic had done so 'sans savoir ce qu'ils faisaient'.[34]

In his *Considérations sur la France*, Maistre eulogised 'l'ancienne constitution française' and insisted on a certain 'élement théocratique' proper to the French monarchy. Maistre appears to enrol himself in the school of Bossuet, insofar as he sees in France a chosen nation, albeit one that has been chosen to be punished for the sins of Europe. The suffering of the French, in being subjected to political misfortunes and to persecution, attests to the exceptional interest that an incensed God has in them. However, this way of being exceptional carried in germ an overturning of the classical order. As long as the Church of France had 'les évêques les plus doctes, les plus saints, les plus célèbres qui aient jamais été', as Bossuet wrote, it could claim its autonomy with respect to the Holy See. From the moment when France's punishment became exemplary, the justifications for national independence became less convincing.

31. Maistre in Lovie and Chetail (ed.), *Du Pape*, bk.2, ch.4, p.138.
32. Maistre in Lovie and Chetail (ed.), *Du Pape*, bk.2, ch.5, p.141.
33. Maistre in Lovie and Chetail (ed.), *Du Pape*, bk.2, ch.10, p.188-89.
34. Maistre, *Considérations sur la France* in Glaudes (ed.), *Maistre: Œuvres*, ch.1, p.201.

# The Savoyard philosopher: deist or Neoplatonist?

## AIMEE E. BARBEAU

## Introduction

In his well-known essay, 'Joseph de Maistre and the origins of fascism', Isaiah Berlin states that the 'personality and outlook of Joseph de Maistre are not normally considered to be puzzling or problematic'.[1] The typical portrait of Maistre stands in monolithic black and white, casting him as '*plus royaliste que le roi, plus catholique que le Pape*' and the 'symbol of reactionary opposition to the spirit of modern civilisation'.[2] However, a closer examination of Maistre's thought, particularly undertaken in recent scholarship, reveals contradictory claims and points to a more complex portrait of his thought. He is claimed as both the 'founding father [...] of the far right in France' and as an 'economic liberal, and moderate conservative'; called both the 'prophet of the past' and an 'ultra-modern, born not so much after as before his time'; deemed both the first exponent of the 'militant anti-rational Fascism of modern times' and 'an outspoken critic of what was to become fascism'.[3] An intractable opponent of the empiricism of Locke and Bacon, Maistre also finds himself acknowledged by Comte and Maurras as the precursor of positivism, which appropriated empirical scientific methods to form the social sciences.[4] His hatred of Voltaire and all the *philosophes* is evident. But he has also been characterised 'as the last and ablest abstract rationalist of the whole Voltairean Age of Reason'.[5] He expresses

1. Berlin, *The Crooked timber of humanity*, p.91.
2. Graeme Garrard, 'Joseph de Maistre's civilization and its discontents', *Journal of the history of ideas* 57, 3 (1966), p.429; Richard Lebrun, 'Joseph de Maistre, Cassandra of science', *French historical studies* 6 (1969), p.214.
3. Peter Davies, *The Extreme right in France, 1789 to the present: from De Maistre to Le Pen* (London, 2002), p.15; Camcastle, *The More moderate side*, p. xvi; John C. Murray, 'The political thought of Joseph de Maistre', *The review of politics* 11, 1 (1949), p.80; Isaiah Berlin, 'Introduction', in Lebrun (ed.) *Considerations on France*, p.xiii; Berlin, *The Crooked timber*, p.150; Alberto Spektorowski, 'Maistre, Donoso Cortés, and the legacy of Catholic authoritarianism', *Journal of the history of ideas* 63, 2 (2002), p.302; Bradley, *A Modern Maistre*, p.xvii.
4. Watt, 'Locked in', p.129-32; Lebrun, 'Joseph de Maistre, Cassandra of science', p.221-26; Jack Hayward, *After the French Revolution: six critics of democracy and nationalism* (New York, 1991), p.62-63.
5. Jack Lively, 'Introduction', in *The Works of Joseph de Maistre* (New York, 1965), p.8-9; Peter

fundamental disagreement with Rousseau, prompting some to suggest that he 'detested the romantic spirit'. However, others peg him as 'an incorrigible romanticist', or at least 'an important forerunner of the Romantic period'.[6] He is both 'the supremely splenetic apologist of uncompromising and all-consuming reaction' and 'the voice of moderation in his day'.[7] The tenor of his thought is 'red in tooth and claw', yet a more careful analysis intimates that 'he was a theorist and not an advocate of violence'.[8]

More specifically, Maistre's religious thought has elicited puzzlement from and disagreement among scholars. While at first blush he appears to be a staunch defender of the faith, 'call[ing] for a return to orthodox Catholicism', many find it problematic to view him as a traditional Catholic.[9] Bradley observes the 'strange spectacle' of Maistre's 'heterodoxy, his marginality to received doctrine and his ambivalence toward royal power'.[10] The Catholic theologian John Courtney Murray avers that 'Maistre's treatment of religion may have been good sociology and good statesmanship, but it was far from being good theology'.[11] Similarly, Jean-Louis Soltner also observes that Maistre was no theologian and laments that his brilliant mind unfortunately did not follow the more thoroughly orthodox theology of Aquinas.[12] Others have also observed Maistre's divergences from the great scholastic theologian – an odd feature for a thinker who is ostensibly simply trying to defend the Catholic tradition.[13] Faguet goes even further, suggesting that 'Maistre is really utterly irreligious, or at least un-Christian, at heart'.[14] The sheer variety of opinions on the matter suggests that Maistre's religious

Viereck, *Conservative thinkers: from John Adams to Winston Churchill* (New Brunswick, NJ, 2006), p.43-54.

6.  Berlin, *The Crooked timber*, p.93; Roger Henry Soltau, *French political thought in the nineteenth century* (New York, 1959), p.24; C. Lombard, *Joseph de Maistre*, p.127.
7.  Berlin, *The Crooked timber*, p.viii; Hayward, *After the French Revolution*, p.44.
8.  Berlin, *The Crooked timber*, p.xvii; Bradley, *A Modern Maistre*, p.231; Ivan Strenski, *Contesting sacrifice: religion, nationalism, and social thought in France* (Chicago, IL, 2002), p.40-41. On Maistre's theory of violence, see, in this volume, Douglas Hedley's article 'Enigmatic images of an invisible world: sacrifice, suffering and theodicy in Joseph de Maistre', and Caroline Armenteros' article 'Maistre's Rousseaus'.
9.  Lombard, *Joseph de Maistre*, p.127.
10. Bradley, *A Modern Maistre*, p.231.
11. Murray, 'The political thought of Joseph de Maistre', p.77.
12. Jean-Louis Soltner, 'Le Christianisme de Joseph de Maistre', *Revue des études maistriennes* 5-6 (1980), p.97-110.
13. See Berlin, *The Crooked timber*, p.109-10; Spektorowski, 'Maistre', p.290; Elisha Griefer, 'Joseph de Maistre and the reaction against the eighteenth century', *The American political science review* 55, 3 (1961), p.595; Richard A. Lebrun, *Joseph de Maistre: an intellectual militant* (Kingston & Montreal, 1988), p.93-96; Pranchère, 'The persistence of Maistrian thought', p.300-05.
14. Quoted in Soltau, *French political thought*, p.21.

thought is more complex than often thought. Further, as it lies at the heart of his social and political theorising, Maistre's theology deserves closer analysis.

More recent scholarship, which has sought to do just that, has established Maistre's indebtedness to the Christian Neoplatonist tradition. Elcio Verçosa Filho asserts that Maistre's theology of providential punishment is best understood within the Greek *paideia* tradition, which Maistre received through the Christian Neoplatonist thinker, Origen.[15] Philippe Barthelet similarly establishes Maistre's debt to a more proximate source of Neoplatonism, the Cambridge Platonists.[16] This paper will build on these insights, but also qualify them, pointing out respects in which Maistre draws on, but also differs from, the tradition of Christian Neoplatonism exemplified by Origen. As I will argue, this is because Maistre's appropriation of Origen occurs in the context of his engagement with the religious thought of the Enlightenment. Maistre was well acquainted with the Enlightenment and even initially endorsed the very French Revolution that he would become so famous for decrying. Not actually a Frenchman, Maistre was nurtured in the more politically liberal environment of Savoy,[17] where his young adulthood was ostensibly characterised by all the ideologies that he would later renounce, including Gallicanism and Freemasonry, and by an attraction to the Enlightenment, liberal reform and anti-absolutism.[18] In his biography, Lebrun avers that Maistre 'was attracted to the company of intelligent, open-hearted, "liberal" young colleagues, to the exciting intellectual ferment of the Enlightenment, and to the exotic lure of "illuminist" Freemasonry'. Lebrun suggests that 'he could have gone either way in the crisis of Revolution', but in the end, he chose the Catholicism and monarchism of his family and the Jesuit training of his childhood.[19]

This training made Maistre well-suited to attack the Enlightenment tradition, but, as I shall show, it also intimates his debt to that tradition. Further I will argue that Maistre's engagement with Enlightenment thought prompted and shaped his appropriation of Origen's Christian

15. See the article by Elcio Verçosa Filho, 'The pedagogical nature of Maistre's thought' in this volume.
16. See the article by Philippe Barthelet, 'The Cambridge Platonists mirrored by Joseph de Maistre' in this volume.
17. Savoy was more liberal in some respects (e.g. legal codes), though not in others (it was a classic example of Enlightened despotism).
18. Jacques Godechot, *The Counter-Revolution: doctrine and action, 1789-1804*, trans. Salvator Attansio (New York, 1971), p.85 and 86-8; Berlin, *The Crooked timber*, p.105; Davies, *Extreme right in France*, p.30; Lebrun, *Maistre: intellectual militant*, p.94; Garrard, 'Joseph de Maitre's civilization and its discontents', p.437.
19. Lebrun, *Maistre: intellectual militant*, p.94.

Neoplatonism. While Maistre's encounter with the Enlightenment began in his youth and remained a point of engagement, his interest in Origen grew over the course of his life. In many respects, the Origenist tradition allowed Maistre to address and grapple with the Enlightenment tradition at key points. Thus, Maistre's reading and incorporation of Origen bear in mind the interests and concerns of his Enlightenment audience. Further, I will argue that in the end, Maistre's debt to the Enlightenment is not inconsistent with his appropriation of Christian Neoplatonism. Specifically, with respect to Providence, soteriology and the relationship between Church and state, Maistre adapts Origen's theology to address the political concerns of the Enlightenment. To put it differently, Maistre's politisation of Origen's theology indicates his engagement with the Enlightenment on its own terms.

## Maistre's 'immanentised' Providence

One of the most striking features of Joseph de Maistre's thought presents itself in his almost ubiquitous references to Providence. An instrument that he utilises to criticise the French Revolution and the Enlightenment, Providence acts everywhere in Maistre's writings, restoring order in the midst of human chaos, standing as the unassailable authority, and the ultimate explanation which requires no other. It operates both within the physical, material order and, more importantly for Maistre, also in the social and political world of human action. As a result, some scholars have called his history an essentially '"theological interpretation" of events', which 'takes it as self-evident that divine Providence commands the lives of nations and of individuals'.[20] At first blush, Maistre's 'over-reliance on Providence' seems to demonstrate his distance from the Enlightenment and to locate him squarely within the Catholic tradition: 'in really believing in the government of all things by Providence', Maistre often finds himself placed among theocrats like Louis de Bonald and Saint-Martin, who desired 'a fundamentally religious society, under the guidance of God'.[21]

However, many Enlightenment thinkers also used the language of Providence, though in a distinctively deistic way. Contrary to stereotypes of the Enlightenment, its thinkers held a complex range of views on the subject of religion, and most did not advocate complete disbelief in God. However, the religious thought of the Enlightenment was typified by a

---

20. Davies, *Extreme right in France*, p.31; George Steiner, 'Aspects of counter-revolution', in *The Permanent revolution: the French Revolution and its legacy, 1789-1989*, ed. Geoffrey Best (London, 1988), p.144.
21. Davies, *Extreme right in France*, p.33. Lebrun, *Throne and altar*, p.27. Hayward, *After the French Revolution*, p.51; Godechot, *Counter-Revolution*, p.84.

deep distrust of traditional religion and the 'superstition' it engendered. Thinkers like Rousseau, Hobbes and Locke preferred a religion known through natural and individual means alone – apart from revelation or the authority of the magisterium. Thus, deism is typically contrasted with both atheism and orthodox belief and 'holds that knowledge of God comes through reason rather than revelation, and that after God created the world, God has had no further involvement in it'.[22] Frequently, deistic religion, while dethroning the place of special revelation, authority and Scripture, accords a high place to the witness of nature, both of the inward soul and the physical universe. However, within deism, accounts of nature are not uniform. Perhaps the most common is the empiricist, Newtonian view of a mechanistic, orderly universe, created by a distant Providence.[23] Another approach, invoked by the Romantics, views nature/Providence as a dynamic principle that both orders and animates the world and speaks in the inner recesses of the heart. Importantly, Charles Taylor has identified this Romantic view of nature with the influence of Renaissance Neoplatonism. Thus, one can detect at least two strands of deism: an empiricist one and a Neoplatonist-inspired one.[24] Of course, neither empiricism nor Neoplatonism necessarily implies deism as opposed to Christian orthodoxy. What distinguishes the deistic version is an emphasis on autonomous human reason, a scepticism of established ecclesiastical authority, and the emphasis on nature at the expense of grace.[25] While in some respects, Maistre's account of Providence bears resemblance to both strands of deism, and most particularly, the second Neoplatonist/Romantic strand of deism (exemplified in this account by Rousseau), he finds them to be not entirely adequate, particularly with respect to accounting for evil. It is at these points that he invokes Origen's 'Neoplatonist Christianity'.

Though Maistre's providentialism ostensibly indicates a 'narrow', totally committed Catholicism',[26] the language he uses to describe divine government suggests something more subtle. Maistre was quite aware of

---

22. Donald J. McKim, *Westminster dictionary of theological terms* (Louisville, KY, 1996), p.73.
23. John Locke laid a foundation for the movement with his *Reasonableness of Christianity*. Matthew Tindal's *Christianity as old as Creation* is considered the seminal work of English deism, and in France, deism is represented by Voltaire's *Dictionnare philosophique* and Rousseau's 'Profession de foi du vicaire Savoyard' in *Emile*. C. J. Betts, *Early deism in France: from the so-called "déistes" of Lyon [1564] to Voltaire's "Lettres philosophiques" [1734]* (Boston, MA, 1984), p.3; F. L. Cross and E. A. Livingstone, eds., *The Oxford dictionary of the Christian Church*, 3rd ed. (Oxford 1997), p. 465; Ray Porter, *The Enlightenment*, 2nd ed. (Houndmills, Hampshire and New York, 2001), p.29-37.
24. Charles Taylor, *Sources of the self: the making of modern identity* (Cambridge, 1989), p.251, 416-17.
25. Taylor, *Sources of the self*, p.251.
26. Charlotte Touzalin Muret, *French royalist doctrines since the Revolution* (New York, 1993), p.15.

the power of words. He understood their power to harm and dissimulate, asserting that '[l]es mots engendrent presque toutes les erreurs', but he also recognised their necessity.[27] As the Count observes in *Les Soirées*, 'avoir éteint le flambeau de l'analogie' is 'avoir renoncé au raisonnement'.[28] Thus, Maistre's frequent use of language that draws on mechanistic Enlightenment accounts of nature and its laws is significant. Most obviously, his analogies for providential order frequently involve scientific and mechanical images. For instance, he finds individuals to be moved by Providence like 'le bois et les cordages employés par un machiniste'. In establishing the religious orders, Providence 'choisit quelques hommes, et les isole du monde pour en faire des *conducteurs*'.[29] Maistre's providential laws of society resemble 'l'harmonie proprement dite, *dans le clavier général*', and they are also 'aussi certain[es], aussi palpable[s] que le magnétisme, et plus aussi générale[s] que la gravitation universelle dans le monde physique'.[30] The philosopher who is aware of this order will find language to be a 'véritable baromètre' of social health, and those who do not perceive this providential design 'tourner[ont] éternellement autour du principe, comme la courbe de Bernouilli, sans jamais le toucher'.[31] Throughout Maistre's works, a variety of scientific terms and ideas are utilised to convey theological notions of providential government.

One oft-used mechanistic image is that of the watch. For instance, at the beginning of the *Considérations sur la France* (1797), Maistre uses it as an image of divine sovereignty and human free will working together: 'Si l'on imagine une montre dont tous les ressorts varieraient continuellement de force, de poids, de dimension, de forme et de position, on se formera quelque idée de l'action des êtres libres qui viennent se ranger dans l'ordre général'. For Maistre, this image captures how '[n]ous sommes tous attachés au trône de l'Etre suprême par une chaîne souple, qui nous retient sans nous asservir' so that '[l]ibrement esclaves, [...] ils [les êtres libres] font réellement ce qu'ils veulent, mais sans pouvoir déranger les plans généraux'.[32] In *Les Soirées*, the Count uses the image of the watch twice to emphasise the providential design apparent in the physical, moral and social worlds: 'Un garde-temps, perdu dans les forêts d'Amérique et trouvé par un sauvage, lui démontre

---

27. Maistre, *Considérations sur la France* in Glaudes (ed.), *Maistre: Œuvres*, p.258.
28. *Les Soirées de Saint-Pétersbourg*, in *Joseph de Maistre: Œuvres*, p.504.
29. *Considérations sur la France* in Glaudes (ed.), *Maistre: Œuvres*, p.256 and 218.
30. *Essai sur le principe générateur*, p.389, and *Les Soirées*, p.603. Both in Glaudes (ed.), *Maistre: Œuvres*.
31. *Essai sur le principe générateur*, p.398; *Les Soirées de Saint-Pétersbourg*, p.618. Both in Glaudes (ed.), *Maistre: Œuvres*.
32. *Considérations sur la France* in Glaudes (ed.), *Maistre: Œuvres*, p.199.

la main et l'intelligence d'un ouvrier'.[33] Though the savage may not fully understand the purpose of the watch, he can perceive symmetry at work and can infer an intelligence behind it. As the Count rhetorically asks early in the dialogues, 'L'âme d'un horloger n'est-elle pas renfermée dans le tambour de cette pendule, où le grand ressort est chargé, pour ainsi dire, des commissions d'une intelligence?'[34]

Interestingly, this image of the watch is a common trope of deism. William Paley, in his version of the teleological argument, compares the intelligible order of the universe to that of a watch. He argues that from the sheer existence of a watch, with its complicated structure obviously designed for the purpose of keeping time, 'the inference [...] is inevitable, that the watch must have had a maker'.[35] Analogously, the evident design of the universe begs the existence of a creator God. Also, Maistre's much-despised enemy, Rousseau, uses a similar analogy in his deistic 'Profession de foi du vicaire Savoyard': he may not know the purpose of the universe, but like 'un homme qui verrait pour la première fois une montre ouverte', and is 'sûr que tous ces rouages ne marchent ainsi de concert que pour une fin commune' and 'admire l'ouvrier dans le détail de son ouvrage'.[36] In both Paley and Rousseau, the watch image expresses deism in two respects: first, the individual apprehends the existence of God without the need for special revelation, and second, the watch (and by analogy, the universe) is whole of itself. God is only needed as the maker at the beginning; afterwards, the universe runs largely without his intervention. Maistre borrows this image of the mechanistic watch, but subtly adapts it. Like Paley and Rousseau, Maistre's theology, here and elsewhere, stands primarily without special revelation.[37] He frequently seems to limit himself to Christian doctrines that can be established by the lights of nature. However, while Paley and Rousseau both express the image of the watch similarly, the larger context of their works demonstrates that they mean different things by 'nature'. Paley's nature stands in the empiricist tradition and is known through the human senses and scientific reasoning. Rousseau's nature, though an ordered, created world, is also apprehended through the inward conscience, which unites humans to both nature and the deity. Closer to Rousseau, Maistre's image reinforces divine involvement in human affairs and the close relationship between Providence and nature. As Carolina Armenteros notes, Maistre formally advocated God's transcendence, but '[t]aking sides

33. *Les Soirées de Saint-Pétersbourg* in Glaudes (ed.), *Maistre: Œuvres*, p.697-98.
34. *Les Soirées de Saint-Pétersbourg* in Glaudes (ed.), *Maistre: Œuvres*, p.580.
35. William Paley, *Natural theology* (Boston, MA, 1860), p.6.
36. Rousseau, *Emile*, p.332.
37. Lively, 'Introduction', p.15.

definitively for immanence or transcendence was [...] unnecessary for [his] purposes', because he identified the divinity with nature.[38] Maistre perceives a 'force, qui opère dans nous, agit de même dans tous les animaux depuis l'éléphant jusqu'au ciron, et dans toutes les plantes depuis le cèdre jusqu'à la mousse'. And this force, or 'being' as he also calls it. executes 'la volonté de l'intelligence infinie' so that 'en les [les principes de la nature] nommant on la [la divinité] nomme'.[39] Here Maistre seems to edge strikingly close to pantheistic notions of God wherein the divinity and nature are one, but he can also be interpreted as advocating a Neoplatonism in which divine principles animate nature. In either case, however, nature and divinity become isomorphic.

Thus, interpreting Maistre's language of a mechanistic though divine nature require the context of Maistre's broader views of science. Frequently, Maistre does in fact refer to 'la loi éternelle' that governs both the moral and physical universe.[40] As Owen Bradley has noted, 'voluntarism, human or divine, is consistently downplayed', as 'the idea of Providence approximates the simple regularity of nature upon which science itself relies'.[41] Further, the epistemological basis for knowing this law seems to be entirely empirical: 'l'expérience, qui décide toutes les questions en politique comme en physique', thus, 'l'histoire, [...] qui est la politique expérimentale'.[42] Moreover, along with his Enlightenment colleagues, Maistre avers that the basic laws of society can be apprehended with similar certainty to those of the physical realm. More than once he suggests that '[s]i l'on avait des observations morales, comme on a des observations météréologiques', the laws governing the moral world could be uncovered.[43] Similarly, he ascertains political knowledge from the other sciences: from physics he finds that 'la force de la fermentation est en raison des masses fermentantes'; from mechanics, he discovers that 'les théories trompent, si l'on ne prend en considération les différentes qualités des matériaux qui forment les machines'; and from Newton's second law, he gathers that 'la réaction [doit] être égale à l'action'.[44] However, in spite of his frequent recourse to the language of empirical

38. Armenteros, 'From human nature to normal humanity', p.114.

39. Joseph de Maistre, *De l'Etat de nature*, in Constantinidès (ed.), *Contre Rousseau*, p.21.

40. *Les Soirées de Saint-Pétersbourg* in Glaudes (ed.), *Maistre: Œuvres*, p.590; *Considérations sur la France* in Glaudes (ed.), *Maistre: Œuvres*, p.211.

41. Bradley, *A Modern Maistre*, p.177-78.

42. *Considérations sur la France*, p.275; *Essai sur le principe générateur*, p.363. Both in Glaudes (ed.), *Maistre: Œuvres*.

43. *Les Soirées de Saint-Pétersbourg*, p.538; *Considérations sur la France*, p.216. Both in Glaudes (ed.), *Maistre: Œuvres*.

44. *Considérations sur la France* in Glaudes (ed.), *Maistre: Œuvres*, p.269, 255, 209, 18, 78, 96-97.

natural laws and science, Maistre explicitly disavows the mechanistic Enlightenment views he seems to advance. In *Les Soirées*, the Senator and the Count agree that 'la tentation la plus perfide qui puisse se présenter à l'esprit humain' is 'de croire aux lois invariables de la nature'. He explains his view of science, asserting that 'Il n'y a donc aucune loi sensible qui n'ait *derrière elle* [...] une loi spirituelle dont la première n'est que l'expression visible'.[45] Here, Maistre subscribes to the classic Neoplatonist view wherein exploration of the physical world corresponds to apprehending the metaphysical principles that govern both the material and the spiritual worlds.

Further, Maistre opposes mechanistic deism on the grounds that it 'nous mènerait droit au fatalisme et ferait de l'homme une statue'.[46] It seems a bit curious for Maistre, who consistently denies the agency of those involved in the French Revolution, to be obstinately defending human free will. However, these two principles of free will and eternal laws can be reconciled in Maistre's thought by recalling his Origenist Neoplatonism. Like Maistre, Origen sought to refute the determinism, not of naturalism or deism, but of Gnosticism.[47] Moreover, Providence was similarly a dominating concept for Origen.[48] Echoing the patristic Neoplatonist, Maistre affirms that the will can only be truly free when it acts in concert with the divine order of creation. Thus, 'lorsque l'homme travaille pour rétablir l'ordre, il s'associe avec l'auteur de l'ordre, il est favorisé par la *nature*, c'est-à-dire, par l'ensemble des causes secondes, qui sont les ministres de la Divinité. Son action a quelque chose de divin'. In this passage, Maistre distinguishes God from his order in nature, and he clarifies how humanity can both exercise free will and be an instrument of Providence. When humanity works with the divine order, its actions take on the divine character and 'tou[s] [...] efforts seront Positifs'. Conversely, the human will is 'impuissant' when acting on its own.[49] Human dignity demands that the individual not stoop to 'agir [...] comme un instrument aveugle de la Providence [...] mais comme un ministre intelligent, libre, et soumis'.[50] Origen also presents this choice: 'this freedom of will incited each one either to progress by imitation of God, or reduced him to failure through negligence'. However, Origen, like Maistre, understands Providence as taking into account the variations of

45. *Les Soirées de Saint-Pétersbourg* in Glaudes (ed.), *Maistre: Œuvres*, p.737.
46. *Les Soirées de Saint-Pétersbourg* in Glaudes (ed.), *Maistre: Œuvres*, p.558, 559.
47. Rowan A. Greer, 'Introduction', *Origen* (Mahwah, NJ, 1979), p. 12-13.
48. *The Westminster handbook to Origen*, ed. John Anthony McGuckin (Louisville, KY, 2004), p.181-82.
49. *Considérations sur la France* in Glaudes (ed.), *Maistre: Œuvres*, p.259-60.
50. *Les Soirées de Saint-Pétersbourg* in Glaudes (ed.), *Maistre: Œuvres*, p.477-78.

the individual wills in crafting the whole.[51] As a result of this Neoplatonic view, Maistre can aver, 'je ne vois point ces règles immuables, et cette chaîne inflexible des événements [...] Je ne vois au contraire dans la nature que des ressorts souples, tels qu'ils doivent être pour se prêter autant qu'il est nécessaire à l'action des êtres libres, qui se combine fréquemment sur la terre avec les lois matérielles de la nature'.[52] Thus, Maistre's view of Providence is more dynamic than the empiricist deistic notion of the 'absentee landlord' and his immutable nature laws.[53] He works hard to accord his notions of Providence to the dynamic actions of human free will – both good and evil.

Maistre not only disavows the empiricist deism of the mechanistic universe, but, as I shall show more fully in the next section, his Providence also differs from Rousseau's more 'Romantic'[54] Providence.[55] Rousseau, like Maistre, makes room for human freedom in his notion of Providence: Providence 'l'a fait libre [l'homme] afin qu'il fît non le mal, mais le bien par choix. Elle l'a mis en état de faire ce choix en usant bien des facultés dont elle l'a doué; mais elle a tellement borné ses forces, que l'abus de la liberté qu'elle lui laisse ne peut troubler l'ordre général'.[56] Maistre follows Rousseau, making this point repeatedly in the *Considérations* and also in *Les Soirées*.[57] However, importantly, Maistre's discussion of Providence occurs in response to (what is for him) an egregious evil – the French Revolution. A common criticism of deistic notions of Providence, and one picked up by Hume in the *Dialogues concerning natural religion* (1779), is that such concepts have a hard time grappling with the problem of evil.[58] Rousseau's notion of a benign deity, known through the natural impulses of the heart and through nature, has a difficult time addressing the severe evil that faces Maistre. In Rousseau's response to Voltaire's poems on the earthquake disaster in Lisbon, he expresses an 'optimisme qui [...] me console pourtant dans les mêmes douleurs que

---

51. *De principiis*, 2.9.6. in *The Writings of Origen* (Edinburgh, 1895), trans. Frederick Crombie.
52. *Les Soirées de Saint-Pétersbourg* in Glaudes (ed.), *Maistre: Œuvres*, p.562-63.
53. See Alister E. McGrath, *Nature*, in *A Scientific theology* (Grand Rapids, MI, 2002), vol.1, p.184.
54. Obviously, referring to Rousseau as a 'Romantic' is anachronistic. That said, he does stand as a progenitor of Romanticism and a source of Platonism for the Romantics in the nineteenth century. I use the term here for lack of a better one to distinguish Rousseau's views from empiricist deism. See David Lay Williams, *Rousseau's Platonic enlightenment* (University Park, PA 2007) for a discussion of Rousseau's Platonic influences.
55. On Rousseau's influence on Maistre, see Carolina Armenteros' article 'Maistre's Rousseaus' in this volume.
56. Rousseau, *Emile*, p.341.
57. See *Considérations sur la France*, p.3-8 and 84-5; *Les Soirées de Saint-Pétersbourg*, p.146. Both in Glaudes (ed.), *Maistre: Œuvres*.
58. Richard A. Rosengarten, *Henry Fielding and the narration of Providence: divine design and the incursions of evil* (New York and London, 2000), p.48-49; see David Hume, *Dialogues concerning natural religion*, (1779), ch.9 and 10.

vous me peignez come insupportables'.[59] For Rousseau, generally, '*Le tout est bien, ou tout est bien pour le tout*'.[60] For Maistre, it must have been apparent that applying this sort of argument to the terror of the French Revolution seems weak at best. Hence, he develops a more robust notion of providential pedagogy that brings correction even through pain. As I will discuss in the next section, he does this by drawing on Origenist thought. Because of the French Revolution, Maistre feels more acutely than Rousseau the need to account for the incredible evils that humans can bring on themselves.

In spite of these distinctions with Rousseau and the mechanistic (or Newtonian) notions of Providence, Maistre's engagement with the Enlightenment tradition fundamentally shaped his use of Providence by dictating its temporal focus. The Providence of Enlightenment thinkers, like Rousseau, sought to address the terrestrial questions of politics and history. Conversely, Origen's Providence operated on a cosmic framework and involved both the pre-existence of souls and the afterlife, while Maistre's is often an 'immanentised' and historicised Providence. Nowhere is this clearer than in his discussions of Providence and politics. For Maistre, the 'monde politique' is 'organisé, dirigé, animé par cette même sagesse qui brille dans le monde physique'.[61] However, human attempts, such as the French Revolution, are often at cross-purposes with nature. For Maistre, such human creations will decompose in the end, and the natural divine order will re-emerge. As a result, the divine order can be known in history, which Maistre calls 'la politique expérimentale'.[62] As Armenteros has noted, Maistre 'functionalize[d] nature as a set of social and historical principles that execute' the divine will.[63] If corrupt forms of government disappear as a result of the workings of natural laws, then 'tout gouvernement est bon lorsqu'il est établi et qu'il subsiste depuis longtemps'.[64] Pranchère observes that this radical historicism of Providence, and consequently of justice, results in a traditionalism 'which holds inherited custom for the will of God', a positivism, which asserts 'what is, is good', and a relativism, 'which denies the existence of a universal norm'.[65] Thus, Providence is not rigid, but rather, 'flexible' and 'supple', invoking the law of averages and statistical distribution: 'the normal is destined to survive' and thus, it is the divine

59. Rousseau, Letter to Voltaire, 18 August 1756, in *Correspondance complète de Rousseau*, ed. R. A. Leigh, 52 vol. (Geneva, Madison, WI, Banbury, Oxford, 1965-1989), vol.4 (1967), p.38.
60. Rousseau, Letter to Voltaire, p.45.
61. *Considérations sur la France* in Glaudes (ed.), *Maistre: Œuvres*, p.259.
62. *Considérations sur la France* in Glaudes (ed.), *Maistre: Œuvres*, p.275.
63. Armenteros, 'Human nature to normal humanity', p.114.
64. Maistre in Lovie and Chetail (ed.), *Du Pape*, p.181.
65. Pranchère, 'The persistence of Maistrian thought', p.305.

will.[66] Armenteros notes that for Maistre, Providence casts and recasts the circumstances, and only the combinations 'morally made to develop through time were able to interact successfully with divine chance' and persist.[67]

Here, a comparison between Maistre's notion of Providence (drawing on both Origen's Christian Platonism and Enlightenment deism) and that of Augustine, as a preeminent providentialist thinker of the West, is instructive. Like Maistre, Augustine understands Providence to be the source of all, but he acknowledges that 'to examine the secrets of men's hearts and [...] the varying merits of human kingdoms – this would be a heavy task for us men, a task indeed far beyond our powers'.[68] Augustine's Providence is a person, whose purposes, though inexplicable from the human viewpoint, ultimately find expression, not in this world, but in the next. His Providence gives structure to history through promise and fulfillment, but the fulfillment often belies the perception of humans and is an otherworldly in-breaking beyond the structure of nature. Maistre's Providence finds not only that in the end, God will be all in all, but also that in the meantime, the divine law will on average win out. On Maistre's account, history can be the test of what is providential. Maistre's immanent Providence allows him to predict the return of the French monarchy, while conversely Augustine's permits only spiritual hope, but not necessarily the restoration of the Roman Empire.

Clearly, though Maistre's frequent references to Providence suggest a strong tie to the Catholic tradition, I have shown his debt to the providentialism current among Enlightenment thinkers. He draws on the language of science and mechanics; he compares the rule of Providence to nature laws discernible without special revelation; and he circumscribes his discussion of Providence to the temporal. At the very beginning of *Les Soirées*, the Chevalier, the pupil who is to be dissuaded from falling under the spell of the Enlightenment, restricts the discussion of Providence to the this-worldly. Both the Count and the Senator agree to this stipulation. Neither Augustine nor Origen define Providence in these terms, but rather, for both, the eschatological dimension is prominent. However, I have also suggested a few subtle

66. Bradley, *A Modern Maistre*, p.179; Armenteros, 'Parabolas and the fate of nations', p.250.
67. Armenteros argues that Maistre provides a theoretical foundation for the use of statistics in the social sciences. See Armenteros, 'Parabolas and the fate of nations', p.251. She suggests that Maistre 'set[s] the stage for the taming of chance by proposing chance's subordination to some underlying, deterministic order of happenings'. Armenteros, 'Human nature to normal humanity', p.116.
68. Augustine, *Concerning the City of God against the pagans*, trans. Henry Bettenson (London, 2003), p.215.

ways in which he differs from both the mechanistic Providence of Tyndal and Newton, as well as the more flexible schema of Rousseau. Though he places a high value on history, this history is both open to and occluded by empirical observation: the spiritual principles which lie at the back of nature and its workings in history are only fully discerned by the prophetic mind.[69] Most importantly, Maistre felt the gravity of the problem of evil. While any conception of Providence has to account for the existence of evil, the religious assumptions of the Enlightenment – a wholly natural theology, an emphasis on the present life and a conflation of natural laws and divine Providence – make the existence of evil harder to explain. Interestingly, in *Les Soirées*, his book devoted to explicating Providence, Maistre trots out the mechanistic and Rousseauian accounts of Providence in turn, in the first and fifth dialogues respectively. However, as I shall discuss more in the next section, the climax of his discussion of Providence does not occur until dialogues nine, ten and eleven, where he moves beyond an Enlighten-ment theodicy to Origen's theodicy and discusses how the innocent suffer for the guilty. Therein, he finds, lies redemption and renewal.

## Maistre's political soteriology

Perhaps unsurprisingly, Maistre's providentialism relates closely to his understandings of free will, sin and salvation. Maistre finds Origen a helpful antidote to a perceived Enlightenment naïvety about the gravity of sin and its effects. Specifically, he incorporates Origen's concepts of secondary sins, providential pedagogy and the power of innocent blood. As Verçosa Filho has observed, placing Maistre in this Neoplatonist tradition helps explain some of his more striking beliefs, particularly with respect to sacrifice.[70] Though this is true, Maistre's appropriation of Origen also demonstrates his Enlightenment concerns. Specifically, · Maistre applies Origenist theology to address the political and social questions that occupied many Enlightenment thinkers.

For Maistre, like Origen, evil is a result of free will: 'le mal physique n'a pu entrer dans l'univers que par la faute des créatures libres'.[71] Essen-tially, '[t]out mal [est] un châtiment' for some crime. Importantly, following Origen, Maistre believes not only in original sin, but also in 'prévarications originelles du second ordre'. To put it differently, human beings continue to retain the capacity to fall further away from God

69. See the article by Jean-Yves Pranchère 'The negativity of the Enlightenment, the positivity of order and the impossible positivity of history' in this volume.
70. See the articles in this volume by Elcio Verçosa Filho, 'The pedagogical nature of Maistre's thought', and Douglas Hedley, 'Enigmatic images of an invisible world'.
71. *Les Soirées de Saint-Pétersbourg* in Glaudes (ed.), *Maistre: Œuvres*, p.466-67.

through their evil wills. Similarly, humans also have the ability to work with Providence and move towards God. As one scholar says of Origen's view: 'The world is a dynamic arena of pedagogic soteriology as souls may, through the exercise of their free choice, advance spiritually or fall farther away'.[72] This emphasis on free will prompted Jerome to anachronistically associate Origen with Pelagianism. As with Origen, Maistre's account of evil leans heavily in favour of the continued importance of free will.[73] As Maistre puts it,

> [t]out mal étant un châtiment, il s'ensuit que nul mal ne saurait être considéré comme nécessaire; et nul mal n'étant nécessaire, il s'ensuit que tout mal peut être prévenu ou par la suppression du crime [...] ou par la prière qui a la force de prévenir le châtiment ou de la mitiger. L'empire du mal physique pouvant donc encore être restreint indéfiniment par ce moyen surnaturel.[74]

This dynamic anthropology is perhaps not so different from Rousseau's description of the plasticity of human nature.[75] For Maistre, Origen and Rousseau, the corruption of human nature remains more tractable than it is for someone like Augustine or Calvin. The Augustinian tradition places much greater emphasis on the first fall, which then deprived humans of their ability to return to God. To put it differently, Maistre, in particular, differs from the Augustinian tradition in not having a major role for divine grace, over and above the work of nature. While for Augustine, original sin places all of humanity in a state of powerlessness that can only be overcome through grace, Maistre and Origen understand human beings to be prone to sin, yet capable of moving towards the good.

The notion of 'original sins of the second order', which Maistre derives from Origen, allows Maistre to present human sinfulness in terms palatable to the empirical sensibilities of his age. Origen, and others in the Eastern tradition, place less emphasis on the first sin of Adam and Eve and its imputed guilt on all humankind. Rather, Origen's dynamic view of sin and human guilt involves fewer theological assertions and is

---

72. *Les Soirées de Saint-Pétersbourg* in Glaudes (ed.), *Maistre: Œuvres*, p.484, 486; see *De principiis*, 1.7.2, 2.9, 2.11.1, 1.6.2. Origen states: 'For the Creator gave, as an indulgence to the understandings created by Him, the power of free and voluntary action, by which the good that was in them might become their own, being preserved by the exertion of their own will; but slothfulness, and a dislike of labour in preserving what is good, and an aversion to and a neglect of better things, furnished the beginning of a departure from goodness'. *De principiis*, 2.9.2, vol.1.

73. McGuckin (ed.), *The Westminster handbook to Origen*, p.114-17.

74. *Les Soirées de Saint-Pétersbourg* in Glaudes (ed.), *Maistre: Œuvres*, p.484.

75. Graeme Garrard, 'Rousseau, Maistre, and the Counter-enlightenment', p.105. See also Caroline Armenteros' article in this volume, 'Maistre's Rousseaus'.

more amenable to empirical proof. In drawing on this tradition, Maistre approximates theories of evil propounded by some Enlightenment philosophers including Locke and Rousseau. They all equivocate on having 'all Adam's posterity doomed to eternal infinite punishment, for the transgression of Adam', and rather, they acknowledge a version of original sin based on experience, rather than revelation.[76] For Locke, '[i]f any of the posterity of Adam were just, they shall not lose the reward of it, eternal life and bliss, by being his mortal issue'. Even so, Locke acknowledges that 'death must have seized upon all mankind, because all had sinned'.[77] Similarly, Maistre's Origenist tendencies allow him to set aside the 'original sin' of Adam and Eve, saying, 'what does it matter?' and explicitly sidestep 'the theological question of imputation', as does Locke.[78] Rousseau understands from personal experience that humans exhibit evil and are the cause of its existence in the universe, not God. In a passage remarkably reminiscent of Romans 7, Rousseau acknowledges, 'je veux et je ne veux pas, je me sens à la fois esclave et libre; je vois le bien, je l'aime, et je fais le mal'.[79] Reminiscent of Rousseau and Paul, Maistre asserts that 'il veut ce qu'il ne veut pas; il ne veut pas ce qu'il veut [...] Il voit dans lui quelque chose qui n'est pas lui'.[80] Thus, Maistre appeals to his Enlightenment audience by downplaying metaphysical theological doctrines like grace or original sin, but emphasising the empirical existence of evil. He even consciously utilises the terms 'crime' and 'criminel' which 'appartiennent à toutes les langages', rather than the words 'péché' and 'pécheur', which are distinctly Christian.[81]

Importantly, Maistre departs from Origen in emphasising sin – or crime – as a political problem, and one that requires a political solution. On the whole, while Origen is concerned about the progress of the soul from its pre-existing unity with God through a fall into a human body and its redemption back into God, Maistre is more focused on how sin is a social and political disorder. Further, while Origen understands sin to be 'transmitted less by generation than by bad teaching and example', Maistre not only believes in 'original transgressions of the second order', but he also emphasises how these sins can 'perpétuer ainsi plus ou moins

76. John Locke, 'The reasonableness of Christianity', in *Readings in the history of Christian theology*, ed. William C. Placher (Philadelphia, PA, 1988), p.83.
77. Locke, 'The reasonableness of Christianity', p.84.
78. Maistre, *Les Soirées de Saint-Pétersbourg* in Glaudes (ed.), *Maistre: Œuvres*, p.482-83.
79. Rousseau, *Emile*, p.337. In Romans 7:18-20, Paul states, 'For I know that nothing good dwells within me, that is, in my flesh. I can will what is right, but I cannot do it. For I do not do the good I want, but the evil I do not want is what I do. Now if I do what I do not want, it is no longer I that do it, but sin which dwells within me' (RSV).
80. *Les Soirées de Saint-Pétersbourg* in Glaudes (ed.), *Maistre: Œuvres*, p.488.
81. *Les Soirées de Saint-Pétersbourg* in Glaudes (ed.), *Maistre: Œuvres*, p.668.

dans leur descendance les vices comme les maladies'.[82] This is not to say that Maistre emphasised communal notions of sin, while Origen's view was more individualist. In fact, Maistre draws on Origen's belief that human sin impacts both the individual and the community. The distinction is rather that Origen's views emphasise the metaphysical and eschatological, while Maistre, like his Enlightenment colleagues, focuses more on the political and temporal aspects. This is clear in Maistre's account of civilisation and sin, which focuses on the advance and decline of whole peoples. This project of understanding sin as political was something Rousseau also attempted, though Maistre explicitly refutes Rousseau's account. *Contra* Rousseau, Maistre asserts with Hesiod and the Greek myths that the original state of man was that of civilisation. It is only through sins that civilisation falls into savagery. For Maistre, this savagery should not be confused with 'l'état naturel et primitif de l'homme', which is 'l'état de civilisation et de science'.[83] Savagery results rather from second-order sins, which degrade a people. Savagery should also not be conflated with barbarism, which is 'une espèce de moyenne proportionnelle entre l'homme civilisé et le sauvage'.[84] Savagery refers to a people fallen from civilisation, and barbarism refers to one who is growing into civilisation. Interestingly, Maistre finds that any religion can civilise a barbarian nation, though only Christianity can perform that redemptive task for a savage people. Thus, Maistre both applauds the work of the Catholic missionaries among the Native Americans, and he censures them for supposing such peoples to be their equals: he avers that '[i]l n'y a que trop de vérité dans ce premier movement des Européens qui refusèrent [...] de reconnaître leur semblables dans les hommes dégradés qui peuplaient le nouveau monde'.[85] Maistre utilises Origen's dynamic views on sin to not only advance an empirical proof for original sin, but also to address the progress of societies, a common theme of Enlightenment philosophers – not only Rousseau, but also others like David Hume, Adam Smith and Montesquieu.

Just as Maistre situates the concept of evil and sin in the context of societal development, he also understands providential salvation within the context of political and social concerns. Again, Maistre relies on Origen for insight into human nature and into Providence's pedagogical work, but he subtly turns these notions to questions of politics. As

82. McGuckin (ed.), *The Westminster handbook to Origen*, p.116; *Les Soirées de Saint-Pétersbourg* in Glaudes (ed.), *Maistre: Œuvres*, p.486.
83. *Les Soirées de Saint-Pétersbourg* in Glaudes (ed.), *Maistre: Œuvres*, p.494.
84. *Les Soirées de Saint-Pétersbourg* in Glaudes (ed.), *Maistre: Œuvres*, p.496.
85. *Les Soirées de Saint-Pétersbourg*, p.495; *Essai sur le principe générateur*, p.384-5. Both in Glaudes (ed.), *Maistre: Œuvres*.

already noted, Maistre's Origenist emphasis on free will also allows him to construct an anthropology which sees humanity as capable of both extreme depravity but also of redemption. He understands 'deux mouvements diamétralement opposés dans un sujet simple'.[86] Thus, the human being is 'a monstrous centaur', both brute and angel.[87] Though positing a complex view of the human being is typical of the Christian tradition, Maistre here is drawing more specifically on Origen's dualist understanding of two souls – one intelligent and the other fleshly, which 'réside dans le sang'. Maistre admits, 'Je n'ignore pas que la doctrine des *deux âmes fut condamnée dans les temps anciens; mais je ne sais si elle le fut par un tribunal compétent; d'ailleurs il suffit de s'entendre*'. Thus, he gestures towards an understanding of human beings as consisting of two principles: 'intelligence' and 'principe sensible', though sensation is not strictly material, but rather consists of a 'principe vital'. Moreover, 'c'est sur la *puissance animale*, sur la *vie*, sur *l'âme* [...] que tombe la malédiction avouée par tout l'univers'. Thus, humanity is 'coupable par son *principe* sensible, par sa chair, par sa vie, l'anathème tombait sur le sang'.[88]

This association between guilt and human physicality relates to Maistre's notions of providential pedagogy. Because culpability rests in materiality, the body undergoes the brunt of the divine educative process and in turn aids in the purification of the soul. Again, Maistre draws on Origen, who also understood the physical condition to be an aspect of Providence's pedagogical work. It was meant to instruct and purify the soul.[89] Maistre finds that 'c'est aussi une opinion aussi ancienne que le monde, *que le ciel irrité* contre la chair et le sang, *ne pouvait être apaisé que par le sang*'. From this, Maistre develops his notion of substitution, by which 'l'innocent pouvait payer pour le coupable'.[90] While religion throughout history demonstrates the importance of sacrifice – both animal and human – Christianity proffers the quintessential sacrifice, that of Christ. Following Origen, however, Maistre not only recognises Christ's ultimate blood sacrifice for the salvation of the universe, but he also refers to 'rédemptions particulières', by which other innocent victims participate in and contribute to cosmic redemption.[91] Such lesser sacrifices represent the complement of secondary original sins. Just as human beings have the freedom to sin and degrade themselves further, they can also choose to imitate Christ and provide an expiation for sin: '[l]es deux

86. Maistre, *Eclaircissement sur les sacrifices*, in Glaudes (ed.), *Maistre: Œuvres*, p.808.
87. Maistre, *Les Soirées de Saint-Pétersbourg* in Glaudes (ed.), *Maistre: Œuvres*, p.484-86. Before Maistre, this image was evoked by Pascal.
88. *Eclaircissement sur les sacrifices*, in Glaudes (ed.), *Maistre: Œuvres*, p.810-11.
89. McGuckin (ed.), *The Westminster handbook to Origen*, p.56; Origen, *De principiis*, 2.8.5.
90. *Eclaircissement sur les sacrifices*, in Glaudes (ed.), *Maistre: Œuvres*, p.812-13.
91. *Eclaircissement sur les sacrifices*, in Glaudes (ed.), *Maistre: Œuvres*, p.836.

rédemptions ne diffèrent donc point en nature, mais seulement en excellence et en résultats'.[92]

Importantly, while both Origen and Maistre concur on this notion of secondary sacrifices, for Origen this is predominantly associated with Christian martyrdom.[93] In the *Eclaircissement*, Maistre even quotes Origen referring to the sacrifice of the martyrs.[94] Conversely, for Maistre, the primary examples he gives of sacrifice are political, namely capital punishment and war. Maistre explains how in the ancient world the sacrifice most often offered was 'la vie d'un coupable ou d'un ennemi'.[95] This 'loi divine et visible pour la punition du crime' continues to hold, thus rendering '[c]apital punishment... as an instance of sacrificial violence'[96] and this law... 'est exécutée invariablement depuis l'origne des choses'.[97] Moreover, it operates through a very human person – the executioner, an 'agent incompréhensible' without whom 'l'ordre fait place au chaos; les trônes s'abîment et la société disparaît'.[98] Maistre even goes so far as to equate the human sacrifices of ancient priesthoods and the workings of the Inquisition with 'les juges modernes qui les envoient à la mort en vertu d'une loi'.[99] This doctrine of sacrifice explains Maistre's response to the possibility of the miscarriage of justice: he suggests that while some criminals will escape and a few will be wrongfully punished, on average, justice will be served. As punishment is redemptive rather than retributive, the salient point remains that blood will be shed in accordance with the divine order, and what is less important is that the guilty individual receive due penalty. Thus, ironically, while for Origen, martyrdom is the primary example of redemptive sacrifice, for Maistre, execution serves a salvific purpose. For Origen the martyr's sacrifice stands in defiance of the political order and has an eschatological dimension – the martyr dies for a faith that transcends the this-worldly. The martyr's willingness to give up life for the sake of faith implies the limits of the temporal, political world. In contrast, Maistre's conception of execution as sacrifice reinforces the pre-eminence of political order and the need to conserve it.

---

92. *Eclaircissement sur les sacrifices*, in Glaudes (ed.), *Maistre: Œuvres*, p.837.
93. McGuckin (ed.), *The Westminster handbook to Origen*, p. 148; in Origen, *Exhortation to martyrdom*, ch.50.
94. *Eclaircisssement sur les sacrifices*, in Glaudes (ed.), *Maistre: Œuvres*, p.836.
95. *Eclaircisssement sur les sacrifices*, in Glaudes (ed.), *Maistre: Œuvres*, p.814.
96. Bradley, *A Modern Maistre*, p.74.
97. *Les Soirées de Saint-Pétersbourg* in Glaudes (ed.), *Maistre: Œuvres*, p.471; see Jesse Goldhammer, *The Headless republic: sacrificial violence in modern French thought* (Ithaca, NY, 2005), p.72
98. *Les Soirées de Saint-Pétersbourg* in Glaudes (ed.), *Maistre: Œuvres*, p.471.
99. *Eclaircissement sur les sacrifices*, in Glaudes (ed.), *Maistre: Œuvres*, p.827; see also Maistre's defense of the Spanish Inquisition in his *Lettres sur l'Inquisition espagnole*.

However, for Maistre, the law of punitive regeneration operates not only on the order of individual human beings through executions, but also on that of entire peoples and even that of the universe. For Maistre, war serves this purpose, thus, it is 'donc divine en elle-même, puisque c'est une loi du monde'.[100] With 'la *terre* qui crie et demande du sang', man, normally 'un être moral et miséricordieux', is overcome 'd'une fureur *divine*' and engages in a slaughter that is wholly 'contraire à sa nature'.[101] Hence the proliferation of war, which is 'l'état habituel du genre humain'.[102] Again, martial violence is not about ensuring that the guilty receive their just deserts, but about re-achieving overall harmony and balance. Society, and humankind as a whole, is guilty; blood is required, and the propitiatory sacrifice of the criminal, the soldier, the innocent victim all accrue to the benefit of society. Civilisation 'ne peut être retrempée que dans le sang' – and not only civilisation, but the entire universal order.[103] In a vivid passage, Maistre extends the law of sacrificial regeneration beyond the bounds of humanity:

> Dans le vaste domaine de la nature vivante, il règne une violence manifeste, une espèce de rage prescrite qui arme tous les êtres *in mutual funera* [...] Ainsi s'accomplit sans cesse, depuis le ciron jusqu'à l'homme, la grande loi de la destruction violente des êtres vivants. La terre entière, continuellement imbibée de sang, n'est qu'un autel immense où tout ce qui vit doit être immolé sans fin, sans mesure, sans relâche, jusqu'à la consommation des choses, jusqu'à l'éxtinction du mal, jusqu'à la mort de la mort.[104]

The cosmic vision described here demonstrates Maistre's debt to Origen's notion of *apocatastasis*, or the redemption and reunification of all things in the end. Maistre, like Origen, understands that within the purview of Providence even 'la destruction violente' has a redemptive role.[105] Thus, Maistre understands 'violence to be ultimately inescapable', but seeks to sublimate it as an instrument of the divine economy, which will restore all things in the end.[106]

In describing this cosmic dénouement, Maistre comes closest to expressing an eschatological vision. Yet, on the whole, Maistre's soteriology strongly emphasises the political and temporal aspects of the providential economy. Here again, one finds Maistre's concerns closer to those of various Enlightenment thinkers, such as Rousseau and

100. *Les Soirées de Saint-Pétersbourg* in Glaudes (ed.), *Maistre: Œuvres*, p.661.
101. *Les Soirées de Saint-Pétersbourg* in Glaudes (ed.), *Maistre: Œuvres*, p.660.
102. *Considérations sur la France* in Glaudes (ed.), *Maistre: Œuvres*, p.213.
103. *Considérations sur la France*, p.216; *Les Soirées*, p.729. Both in Glaudes (ed.), *Maistre: Œuvres*.
104. *Les Soirées de Saint-Pétersbourg* in Glaudes (ed.), *Maistre: Œuvres*, p.659-61.
105. *Considérations sur la France* in Glaudes (ed.), *Maistre: Œuvres*, p.212.
106. Owen Bradley, 'Maistre's theory of sacrifice', in Lebrun (ed.), *Maistre: life thought and influence*, p.82-83.

Hobbes, than those of Origen's Neoplatonism. For Origen, the sacrifice
of the martyr and the pacifism of the Christian point to the values that
transcend politics. Conversely, Maistre, like Hobbes and Rousseau, concerns himself with how civilisation is renewed, how polities are best
organised, and how human nature is best dealt with. Of course, Maistre's
recognition of the enduring nature of violence in politics remains
something quite antithetical to most political proposals of the Enlightenment. While many hope for the progress of commerce to forever
exorcise the martial spirit from human nature, Maistre recognises this as
naïvety. Thus, he remains both close to and distant from his Enlightenment colleagues – close in advancing an empirical account of human
fallenness and proposing a political soteriology, yet distant in finding
war, execution, and sacrifice to be the divine remedy.

## Maistre's divine unity

Maistre's political soteriology goes beyond his discussions of execution
and war. He also develops a theory of political regimes. Of course, here
Maistre's political solution differs from that of his Enlightenment colleagues: for instance, Rousseau finds the general will to be the answer to
the corruption of human nature; for Hobbes, it is a Leviathan, and for
Maistre, a hereditary monarchy with an unwritten constitution. While
deliberation and consent form the primary framework for many Enlightenment theories about regimes, Maistre develops his political soteriology from a Neoplatonic model, derived from Origen, that sees
human political arrangements as a reflection of divine order.
Neoplatonic notions of divine unity allow Maistre to refute the Enlightenment idea of popular sovereignty. Even so, Maistre's view of the
relationship between church and state demonstrates affinities with that
of other Enlightenment thinkers.

Before turning to Maistre, it will be helpful to lay out a few specifics
about Origen's political theology and its relationship to the broader
Christian tradition. The conventional wisdom about Origen suggests
that as he mainly addresses metaphysical and cosmological questions of
Providence, sin, redemption and human freedom, he 'offers little
reflection on society or its structures'.[107] While Origen generally ignores
political topics, his theology does have an implied political dimension –
one that comes to the fore at the end of *Contra Celsum*, where he speaks to
Celsus' accusations that Christians subvert the authority of the Roman
Empire. Here, Origen's response is complex, but also suggestive of his

---

107. Oliver O' Donovan, *The Desire of nations: rediscovering the roots of political theology* (Cambridge,
     1999), p.39-40.

third-century context. As Gerard Caspary has argued, two tropes emerge. First, that of the empire as demonic and opposed to the Church: this is the empire that demands that Christians sacrifice to the emperor and martyrs them when they refuse. In this scenario, the Christian response is that of radical pacifism. Christians' only service to the empire is via obedience to authority, as Paul admonishes in Romans, and as a nation of priests, who wage spiritual warfare through prayer. For Origen, Christians should neither take up arms for the empire nor become its civil servants.[108] However, the more common trope is what Caspary terms the Christological trope, wherein the empire has a role in providential history. Origen acknowledges that the unity of the Roman Empire allowed for the easy transmission of the Gospel, and on a more abstract level, 'the victory of monarchy over polyarchy can be seen [...] as a reflection of the defeat by monotheism of the polytheistic principalities and powers'.[109] Moreover, the peace of the Roman Empire advanced the Gospel by allowing Christians to be pacifists. Conversely, 'the existence of many kingdoms would have been a hindrance to the spread of the doctrine of Jesus' because the 'Gospel doctrine of peace' could not be spread with 'men everywhere engaging in war and fighting on behalf of their native country'.[110] Celsus asks Origen what would occur if the empire were Christianised (of course, still a speculation in the third century), and Origen replies that 'if as Celsus suggests, all the Romans were convinced and prayed, they would be superior to their enemies, or would not even fight wars at all'. Origen goes on to provide 'an expansive political eschatology, in which the conversion of the empire accompanies its extension to the whole world with a single language and the dawning of a universal rule of reason'. However, he almost as quickly dismisses this vision, suggesting that such unity remains impossible in this life. For Origen these two disparate tropes, of Empire as Devil and Empire as Church, find union in the recognition that even the devil is a servant of divine Providence. Furthermore, a third trope, which Caspary finds in Origen's exegetical works, maintains a careful balance between the two. This trope finds a secular role for the state, 'appointed primarily for the utility of those who do not yet belong [...] to the People of God'. In this secular approach, '[w]hat is stressed is no longer the heroism of eschatological struggle but the 'bourgeois' virtues of noninterference and of give-and-take'.[111]

---

108. Gerard E. Caspary, *Politics and exegesis: Origen and the two swords* (Berkeley, CA, 1979), p.129-30; Origen, *Contra Celsum*, 7.73-5.
109. Caspary, *Politics and exegesis*, p.132.
110. Origen, *Contra Celsum*, 2.30.
111. Caspary, *Politics and exegesis*, p.141, 180.

Out of Origen's theology, then, come three strands of thought on the state, the demonic, the divinely appointed, and the secularly useful, which he held in careful tension, and which come to represent paradigmatic types for later Christians, though they do not necessarily derive them from Origen. The vision of Church opposed to the state is least frequently picked up in later Christian history, though the Anabaptists, John Howard Yoder, and Stanley Hauerwas provided noted exceptions. Under this type, the ultimate political act of the Christian is pacifist martyrdom.[112] After the Constantinian revolution, Eusebius of Caesarea drew specifically on the sacralising dimension of Origen's political theology. He emphasised the parallel between Christ and the emperor and contrasted the Christian monarchy with pagan polyarchy, just as Origen did. Further, Eusebius intimated the salvific potential of this Christian imperial polity. Importantly, in his work on Neoplatonic political philosophy, O'Meara identifies this divinising trope with Neoplatonist political theory. Thus, Origen and Eusebius are here Christianising a trope that goes back to Plato's philosopher-king and the 'intelligible paradigmatic city' of the forms. Like the Neoplatonists, Eusebius finds the earthly polity to be an imitation of divine order and thus a means of reaching it.[113] While for Origen, this Neoplatonic divinising and theocratic element is just one strand, for Eusebius, it is the prominent feature, and through him, it becomes the quintessential feature of the political philosophy of the Eastern Church. Conversely, Augustine rejects Neoplatonic political philosophy entirely and develops a political theology that develops the secular strand of Origen's thought. For Augustine, 'no political community on earth, pagan or Christian, can represent a preliminary stage or image of the city of God, nor can its ruler, even a Christian one, act as the saving mediator between God and humanity'.[114] Rather, the city of man serves to order the daily secular, temporal interests of both Christians and non-Christians, even as Christians still remain pilgrims in the earthly city awaiting the full coming of the city of God. Thus, in Origen's thought one can identify three attitudes toward the state: they can be called the separatist, the Neoplatonic and the Augustinian views.

The strong soteriological dimension to Maistre's political philosophy demonstrates his debt to the Neoplatonist, theocratic strand of Origen's political theology, and it also explains his distance from Augustine's

---

112. O'Donovan, *The Desire of nations*, p.216.

113. Of course, this 'intelligible paradigmatic city' goes back further than the Neoplatonists to Plato's *Republic*. Dominic J. O'Meara, *Platonopolis: Platonic political philosophy in late antiquity* (Oxford, 2003), p. 145-58. Also, see Lester L. Field, Jr., *Liberty, dominion, and the two swords* (Notre Dame, IN, 1998), p.220-28.

114. O'Meara, *Platonopolis*, p.157.

political theology. Like the Neoplatonists, Maistre sees politics as an imitation of divine order, and thus, 'a stage in the hierarchical assimilation of the soul to god'.[115] Providence provides the model for all order, including that of political regimes. Thus, following the Neoplatonists, Maistre understands political arrangements to be determined by metaphysical and theological concerns. As summarised by O'Meara, Neoplatonist political philosophy asserts that 'political order is monarchic in structure'; 'the monarch, the political "first cause", is transcendent' and 'power is exercised through a system of mediating ranks'.[116] In places, Maistre expresses a similar affirmation of the grounds of monarchy: 'Dieu fait les Rois', and royal 'familles sont les dépositaires du feu sacré'.[117] Consequently, the French Revolution is a disruption of the divine order, though this is of course not a problem for the divine economy, which will bring restoration through the pain and bloodletting of Jacobinism. The Restoration, however, will be the opposite of the revolution, as it partakes of, rather than works against, the divine political order: 'Au lieu de ces commotions violentes, de ces déchirements douloureux, de ces oscillations perpétuelles et désespérantes, une certain stabilité, un repos indéfinissable, un bienaise universel, annonceront la présence de la souveraineté'. Using a Christ-like image, Maistre describes how the 'roi touchera les plaies de l'Etat d'une main timide et paternelle'.[118] Thus, the monarch exercises an inviolable sovereignty derived from 'hors de la sphère du pouvoir humain'.[119] And from the monarch's divinely given sovereignty, the monarch grants honour in proper 'nombre, poids et mesure, sur les ordres et sur les individus'.[120]

However, Maistre's endorsement of monarchy did not entail a worldwide empire, as Eusebius or Origen envisions. Maistre's political thought works within the paradigm of modern nation-states, rather than ancient empire. Unsurprisingly, though, for Maistre, the origins of diverse nations lie in the hand of Providence: 'Le Créateur a dessiné sur le globe les limites des nations' endowing them with 'une *âme* générale'.[121] In this world of distinct, providentially ordered nations, Maistre allows for the possibility of regimes other than monarchy, depending upon the charac-

---

115. O'Meara, *Platonopolis*, p.151.
116. O'Meara, *Platonopolis*, p.179.
117. *Essai sur le principe générateur*, p.366; *Considérations sur la France*, p.272. Both in Glaudes (ed.), *Maistre: Œuvres*.
118. *Considérations sur la France* in Glaudes (ed.), *Maistre: Œuvres*, p.276.
119. *Essai sur le principe générateur*, p.382; *Considérations sur la France*, p.272. Both in Glaudes (ed.), *Maistre: Œuvres*.
120. *Considérations sur la France* in Glaudes (ed.), *Maistre: Œuvres*, p.239.
121. Darcel (ed.), *De la Souveraineté du peuple*, p.106.

ter of the nation. Yet, he finds that the historical record demonstrates that monarchy is the most stable, long-lasting and salutary of the regimes. Moreover, even the rare cases of democracy are due not to the exercise of popular sovereignty, but rather to providential design. While Providence provides unity to each nation, in the form of its 'genius'[122] and exemplified most often by a monarch, the ultimate manifestation of divine unity occurs in papal sovereignty over all Christendom.[123] What the monarch is to the nation, the pope is to the world. This explains why Maistre conflates papal infallibility with unappealability: he draws on a Christian Neoplatonist tradition in which earthly sovereignty mirrors the rule of God over the universe.[124] The salient point rests not in the individual abilities of the monarch or pope, but in the way in which his rule approximates and imitates the divine order. Thus, for Maistre, as for the Neoplatonists, polyarchy – or in Maistre's schema, democracy and religious pluralism – is a violation of the divine unity. However, for Maistre, this unity operates on two levels – that of the nation with its king, but ultimately that of Christendom with the pope.

Notions of providential order and unity also pervade Maistre's discussion of constitutions. Maistre emphasises humanity's inability to create, and this is particularly true with respect to constitutions; Providence has 'circonscrit au moins l'action humaine, au point que dans la formation des constitutions les circonstances font tout, et que les hommes ne sont que des circonstances'.[125] Most often the formation of constitutions results from a gradual, providentially guided development; thus, 'les lois écrites ne sont jamais que des déclarations de droits antérieurs', and not the result of deliberation.[126] Of course, Rousseau's lawmaker does make an appearance, '[l]orsque la Providence a décrété la formation plus rapide d'une constitution politique'. He demonstrates a 'puissance indéfinissable' and 'a genius who acts instinctively',[127] by perfectly joining 'des éléments préexistants dans les coutumes et le caractère des peuples'.[128] Such a lawmaker is uniquely able to perceive the divine plan for each nation. In the absence of a legislator, however,

chaque nation s'agite et tâtonne, pour ainsi dire, jusqu'à ce qu'une certain réunion de circonstances la place précisément dans la situation qui lui

122. See the article by Darrin McMahon, 'The genius of Maistre' in this volume.
123. See the article by Emile Perreau-Saussine 'Why Maistre became Ultramontane' in this volume.
124. Maistre in Lovie and Chetail (ed.), *Du Pape*, p.27; Hayward, *After the French Revolution*, p.58.
125. *Considérations sur la France* in Glaudes (ed.), *Maistre: Œuvres*, p. 232.
126. *Considérations sur la France* in Glaudes (ed.), *Maistre: Œuvres*, p.232, 263.
127. Armenteros, 'Parabolas and the fate of nations', p.235.
128. *Considérations sur la France* in Glaudes (ed.), *Maistre: Œuvres*, p.233.

convient: alors elle déploie tout à coup toutes ses facultés à la fois, elle brille de tous les genres d'éclat, elle est tout ce qu'elle peut être, et jamais on n'a vue une revenir à cet état, après en être déchue.[129]

For Maistre, the trajectory of a nation is modelled 'by a parabola'. Armenteros describes Maistre's view as one of combinatorial mathematics: 'A nation interacts blindly with chance and circumstance according to its character, until it finds the situation most expedient'. At one point, the nation's singular character is maximised by Providence's randomly thrown historical circumstances, and the nation experiences a golden age. Maistre recognises that the attaining of this peak rests on the 'suitability of a particular government to the character of the nation it governs'.[130] For Maistre, there are certain predetermined divine patterns or forms, which bring human flourishing. Again, Maistre departs significantly from contractarian thinkers. Constitutions come about through the hand of Providence, not through deliberation. Further, the flourishing of a civilisation is not within the province of human actors.

Interestingly, while Maistre's discussion of monarchy and constitutions draws on Neoplatonist political philosophy, he supports his claims through appeals to the empirical evidence of history. As with his providentialism, and his belief in human sinfulness and redemption, Maistre places his political theology within reach of an Enlightenment audience by appealing to the historical record. In the Neoplatonist tradition, the more common appeal is to nature. The cosmos provides 'a closer, more accessible, visible source of inspiration' than the divine forms for political arrangements. As the divine made immanent, the cosmos is also 'a *polis*' writ large.[131] Certainly, Maistre makes similar appeals to nature, but he also finds that 'Dieu s'explique par son premier ministre au département de ce monde, *le Temps*'.[132] Thus, he challenges his readers: 'Ouvrez l'histoire, [...] vous ne verrez pas une institution quelconque, pour peu qu'elle ait de force et de durée, qui ne repose sur une idée divine'.[133] At one point, he explicitly asserts that 'si le raisonnement glisse sur nos esprits, croyons au moins à l'histoire, qui est la politique expérimentale'.[134] Even if his readers cannot apprehend through reason the divine order of the universe, Maistre remains confident that they can discover the same conclusion through an analysis of history. Thus, Maistre boldly predicts the fall of the French republic,

129. Maistre in Darcel (ed.), *De la Souveraineté du peuple*, p.278.
130. Armenteros, 'Parabolas and the fate of nations', p.247-49.
131. O'Meara, *Platonopolis*, p.97.
132. *Essai sur le principe générateur* in Glaudes (ed.), *Maistre: Œuvres*, p.382.
133. *Considérations sur la France* in Glaudes (ed.), *Maistre: Œuvres*, p.260.
134. *Considérations sur la France* in Glaudes (ed.), *Maistre: Œuvres*, p.275.

using the image of fortune constantly throwing a die. History demonstrates that 'on a vu toujours la monarchie et quelquefois la république', thus, 'nous sommes autorisés, par la théorie des probabilités, à soutenir' that there is no such thing as a large republic because one has never existed.[135] Maistre confidently believes that only those political arrangements that imitate the divine will persist; thus, he need not appeal to revelation or esoteric wisdom to demonstrate his theories of government. History also demonstrates the political workings of Providence.

Maistre's appropriation of Neoplatonic thought causes divergences with Enlightenment views on regimes, sovereignty and national constitutions. Yet, Maistre's adaptation of Neoplatonism prompts him to arrive at similar conclusions regarding the role of religion vis-à-vis the state as key Enlightenment thinkers do. Maistre finds that human fallibility mitigates against forming 'une volonté une et régulière à la place de ces myriades de volontés divergentes et coupables'.[136] Thus, a 'gouvernement seul ne peut gouverner', but rather has need 'comme d'un ministre indispensable, ou de l'esclavage, qui diminue le nombre des volontés agissantes dans l'Etat, ou de la force divine, qui, par une espèce de greffe spirituelle, détruit l'âpreté naturelle de ces volontés'.[137] Thus, for Maistre, religion performs an important civic and political purpose. Here again, Maistre follows a Neoplatonic tradition for which '"Church" is a state institution, at the service of the political goals of the community'.[138] Of course, Maistre's understanding of Christianity as a civic religion represents a distinct departure from Origen's full understanding of Church and society.[139] Yet, it does develop one aspect of Origen's thought.

Maistre's conflation of the sacred and the secular follows in the Christian Neoplatonist tradition and finds a parallel in the thought of many Enlightenment political philosophers. Government and religion are intertwined: 'Le gouvernement est une véritable religion: il a ses dogmes, ses mystères, ses ministres'.[140] Maistre suggests that the political and the religious are coterminous: 'La politique et la religion se fondent ensemble; on distingue à peine le législateur du prêtre; et ses institutions publiques consistent principalement *en cérémonies et vacations religieuses*'.[141] Like Hobbes, Maistre understands that a stable society requires a Lev-

135. *Considérations sur la France* in Glaudes (ed.), *Maistre: Œuvres*, p.219-20.
136. Maistre, *Les Soirées*, p.734. Garrard, 'Rousseau, Maistre', p.105.
137. Maistre in Lovie and Chetail (ed.), *Du Pape*, p.235.
138. O'Meara, *Platonopolis*, p.119.
139. On Maistre's idea of civil religion, see Carolina Armenteros' article in this volume, 'Maistre's Rousseau's'.
140. Darcel (ed.), *De la Souveraineté du peuple*, p.148.
141. Maistre, *Considérations sur la France* in Glaudes (ed.), *Maistre: Œuvres*, p.233-34.

iathan that encompasses both religious and political authority.[142] Garrard argues that in this respect Maistre is also very close to Rousseau.[143] In *Emile* (1762), Rousseau acknowledges that '[q]uant au culte extérieur, s'il doit être uniforme pour le bon ordre, c'est purement une affaire de police'.[144] Moreover, at the end of *Du Contrat social* (1762), Rousseau approvingly surveys: 'dans le paganisme [...] chaque Etat avait son culte et ses dieux'. The trouble came with Jesus 'séparant le système théologique du système politique'. Rousseau believes 'Hobbes est le seul qui ait bien vu le mal et le remède', that is, to 'réunir les deux têtes de l'aigle'.[145] Maistre too comprehends the problem, but he differs, believing 'that Christianity is a civil religion'.[146] In a poignant passage, Maistre sets out his political and religious vision:

> Le christianisme est la religion de l'Europe. [...] la croix est sur toutes les couronnes; tous les codes commencent par le symbole; les rois sont des *oints*, les prêtres sont des *magistrats*, le sacerdoce est un *ordre*; l'empire est *sacré*; la religion est *civile*; les deux puissances se confondent; chacune emprunte de l'autre une partie de sa force, et malgré les querelles qui ont divisé ces deux sœurs, elle ne peuvent vivre l'une sans l'autre.[147]

Thus, the political implications of Maistre's religious thought demonstrate more of a resonance with thinkers like Rousseau and Hobbes, than with Augustine, for instance. In *The City of God*, Augustine draws the very distinction which Maistre, along with Rousseau and Hobbes, desires to erase – between the City of God and the City of Man: 'the earthly city, whose life is not based on faith, aims at an earthly peace, and it limits the harmonious agreement of citizens concerning the giving and obeying of orders to the establishment of a kind of compromise between human wills'. However, those of the heavenly city obey their earthly sovereign insofar as needed, but they are ultimately 'pilgrim[s] in a foreign land': their hope and peace rests in the transcendent heavenly city.[148]

Maistre, though he ends up at the same conclusion about Church and state as key Enlightenment figures, does so for a different reason. For Rousseau, as well as Hobbes, Adam Smith, David Hume and others, the overriding preoccupation about religion rests in its ability to destabilise the political order. Again and again, Enlightenment thinkers demonstrate a wariness of religion, which they frequently cast as a sort of superstition or enthusiasm, because of its political consequences. One

142. Garrard, 'Rousseau, Maistre', p.116.
143. Garrard, 'Rousseau, Maistre', p.116.
144. Rousseau, *Emile*, p.362.
145. Rousseau, *Du Contrat social*, ed. Georges Liébert (Paris, 1978), p.358.
146. Garrard, 'Rousseau, Maistre', p.112.
147. *Sur le Protestantisme* in Glaudes (ed.), *Maistre: Œuvres*, p.312.
148. Augustine, *City of God*, XIX.17, p.877.

common aspect of their various political solutions is the attempt to mitigate or eliminate religion as a politically divisive factor. Rather, they want to craft a religion that brings unity to multiplicity of wills in a state. Maistre appears to offer a similar political prescription – that of uniting the sacred and the secular. Yet, for him, the reason is different. For Maistre, Christianity is simply the truth, and thus, the inevitable foundation of all human structures. Of course, earlier pagan faiths participated to greater or lesser extents in that truth, but for Maistre, that only serves to demonstrate that truth is universal. To put it differently, Maistre comes to his political prescription via a Christian Neoplatonism, rather than an Enlightenment materialism. While Rousseau is concerned with what qualities in a religion make it healthy for the state, and Hobbes wants to ensure that all follow the religion of the sovereign, Maistre seems to think that there simply is true religion, and because it is true, it creates cohesion. Enlightenment thinkers, such as Rousseau and Hobbes, are concerned primarily with the functional value of religion (at least in their discussions of civil religion). Maistre, however, in the Christian Neoplatonist tradition, posits the truth of religion as a given, and then seeks to ascertain what political structures best exhibit the divine pattern.

## Conclusion

Clearly, Maistre's religious thought demonstrates complex impulses. He spent his intellectual career engaging with the Enlightenment and seeking to address its deficiencies. Yet, for all his vitriol against Rousseau and the *philosophes*, Maistre's religious thought owes much to the Enlightenment. He consistently frames his religious thought in terms of natural religion, refusing to appeal to revelation as such. Most often, Maistre defends his views by appealing to the empirical record of history. Like his Enlightenment colleagues, his notion of Providence focuses on temporal justice; his understanding of soteriology emphasises the role of political, rather than transcendent, factors; and his understanding of the relationship between Church and state establishes the need for a civil religion. However, while Maistre's thought bears the marks of the Enlightenment and its preoccupations, he also finds its philosophy to be inadequate, particularly in the face of the violence and upheaval of the French Revolution. In this endeavour to correct the deficiencies of Enlightenment, Maistre finds Origen's Christian Neoplatonism to be useful and illuminating. For Maistre, the Enlightenment's notions of Providence, evil and political legitimacy are deficient and deeply problematic. Origen's Christian Neoplatonism provides an answer as to how Providence deals with the serious crimes of humanity. Further, it finds redemption in the violence that is a perennial part of human history. Finally, it enables him to expose the weaknesses of those that propose the rational construction of governments of consent.

This analysis has several important implications for understanding religion in the Enlightenment and in Maistre's thought and the relationship between the two. First, it suggests that religion was not absent from the Enlightenment, but is rather an important aspect of understanding its philosophical project. Thus, to suggest that Maistre was both highly religious and indebted to the Enlightenment is not a contradiction. Also, Maistre's affinities with Rousseau are unsurprising given that they both stand in the modern Neoplatonist tradition. Where they differed was in how they appropriated that Neoplatonism. Maistre found Rousseau's schema to be ultimately unconvincing in grappling with evil and with comprehending political sovereignty. It is at these points that his debt to Origen is the clearest. But, in other respects, Maistre and Rousseau remain remarkably similar in their concerns. Thus, perhaps it is unsurprising that Maistre poured so much vitriol on a foe whose thought stands so close, and yet so far, from Maistre's own system.[149]

Moreover, this analysis demonstrates the complexity of Christian thought and helps to clarify Maistre's relationship to it. It goes some way towards explaining how Maistre can be both a staunch defender of the Catholic faith, even while in his own day and currently, he finds little acceptance within that fold. If this examination is correct, it would suggest that Maistre is properly understood within a more Eastern Christian tradition, rather than among the Latin Augustinian tradition. Maistre drew on the ancient faith of Origen to address what he perceived to be the inadequacies and problems of the Enlightenment and its incarnation in the French Revolution. It is a testament to his intellectual stature that he found resources in the third-century theologian to address the issues, both religious and political, of his day.[150]

149. For an elaboration of this argument, See Carolina Armenteros' article in this volume, 'Maistre's Rousseaus'.
150. I want to thank Richard Lebrun, Carolina Armenteros, Richard Boyd and Douglas Hedley for all their helpful and detailed comments and encouragement with this project.

# The pedagogical nature of Maistre's thought

ÉLCIO VERÇOSA FILHO

There is such a vast array of more or less reasonable interpretations of Joseph de Maistre, regarding one, many or all of the myriad subjects dealt with in his long career as a writer and publicist, that one is likely to become bewildered in trying to find a common ground between them. Even if one knows that there must be such a thing as a common ground, since all interpretative enterprises relate to the same basic phenomena – Joseph de Maistre's life, words, and ideas.

Religion, politics, society; anthropology, cosmology, language, history: speaking in a straightforward manner, as Maistrian scholarship stands, how can one conceive of that common ground? Beyond the reality of Maistre as a historical person who actually authored all the views under discussion, how can one venture to state a point of convergence, a central, unifying issue or concern underlying, if not all, at least the bulk of his intellectual efforts?

First of all, a few words about the pertinence of the question. We happen to live in a time in which unifying perspectives of whatever kind on whatever subjects have become suspect. In general, we have grown increasingly suspicious of the 'global account', of the 'great narrative', and we are not at ease with what might be regarded as a little more than old-fashioned conceit. Our contemporary creed goes rather the way of the 'multiple' and the diverse, deriding as it were as 'illusory', 'platonic' or even 'totalitarian', every perspective of unity.

Yet aiming at unity is just the way Joseph de Maistre proceeded in his thought, regardless of what his well-established reputation as a 'pamphleteer' and 'intellectual militant', as a writer of 'œuvres d'occasion', would easily lead one to believe. So this is the way I have chosen to approach his wealth of diverse interests and the bewildering variety of his work.

By way of introduction, I shall venture a provisional answer to my question about the possibility and definition of the common ground of Maistre's thought, by claiming that almost all that he wrote, at least everything which can be considered as of major value, attests to a *concern for man*. This is what, I believe, one finds at the core of every major piece that Maistre wrote on politics, society, religion, education and history. In all these works, man was both his subject matter and his aim.[1]

This claim may seem curious, because if we look at the matter closely and attentively enough, we will find that a concern for man is the one thing that most interpreters have *not* attributed to Maistre. Maistre is far from being perceived, even by his most ardent admirers, as an obvious 'humanist' in this wide (and loose) sense of someone who has a special concern for man. Just the opposite, he has often been seen as one of mankind's most violent critics, if not its outright enemy. And it must be granted that there is some truth in this perception. For Maistre's concern with or for man is certainly not of the regular, common type; most certainly not what we, influenced by the anthropology and the historiography of the Enlightenment, would be willing to take as the proper concern of the humanist, and that is why from a particular point of view, the widespread perception of Maistre's anti-humanism is probably right. However, on the other hand, if we strive to see things from his own perspective, if we search for the principles on which this perspective is grounded, and on which, therefore, he based his own concern for man, we cannot but challenge the accepted view, we cannot but arrive at a quite different understanding of the very definition of humanism (or concern for or with man), as well as to a fairer appreciation of Maistre's immense display of intellectual resources in developing those principles towards a grandiose vision of man and his world.

Let me now turn to Maistre's writings for a better understanding of what I mean. We shall see there that his vision is quite clear from the very start, the start meaning chiefly Maistre's first writing of some breadth, the *Mémoire au duc de Brunswick*, but also the 'first principles' from which he starts, the foundations upon which everything else, the whole Maistrian building, depends. In my view, the *Mémoire* is important because it offers a privileged view of Maistre's original, 'spontaneous' concerns, since the piece is not determined by the 'empire of circumstances' that would be dominant in his later works.

This rather peculiar text on the nature of Freemasonry begins by providing an answer to a question posed by Duke Ferdinand of Brunswick, the top authority for the lodges of the S.O.T. (*Stricte Observance Templière*), of the Scottish Reformed Rite, to which Maistre's own lodge in

---

1. The word 'man', with an inclusive meaning embracing men, women, children and the so-called third sex, is used throughout instead of the more gender-neutral 'human being' for reasons of consistency with the author's use of the term. Maistre, and the spiritual tradition in which I claim he based his thought on Human Things, consciously avoided this latter, more modern use because of its naturalistic *pathos*, which points to the so-called human condition as a fact of nature, of mere biology, the opposite, therefore, of Maistre's view of both men and women (as well as the third sex) as spiritual creatures.

Chambéry (*Parfaite Sincerité*) was subordinated: 'what is the true end of the Masonic institution?' Maistre does not hesitate a moment to reply: it is, he writes, the 'true science of Man'. His personal perspective on the subject is already clearly stated in Persius' words, attached as an epigraph to the *Mémoire*: 'Learn, O miserable ones! Learn the reason of things around you! Who are we? Why were we brought into this world? What is thy place, O Man, among things?'[2]

How is this science and this instruction that Man is summoned to take to be defined? For Maistre it is 'knowledge of man's origin and destiny'.[3] The primary object of the Masonic institution should be to direct its members towards this knowledge, allegedly its 'principal base', with a view to 'fixing and propagating' the 'sublime verities' thus found 'within the order and for the happiness of Mankind'. In a word, Maistre thinks of Freemasonry, whatever its true historical origins, as a society for the *education* or the *enlightenment of Mankind* on the truth about itself: in order to bear fruit, concern for man is expected to flourish in an education of man. In Maistre's conception, then, Freemasonry as a movement or institution should act with a view to an end that, in general terms, is surprisingly similar to the end of that general Enlightenment that Maistre fiercely fought. However, the difference between them is really a difference of kind; it lies in the outlook and nature of the science to be pursued and the truth thereof, so that their models of concern and of education have to be classified as competing ones.

According to this same text, one way to achieve such knowledge as is required to fulfil the (true) Enlightenment's task is the study of the writings of the ancients, the consultation of the Wise of the past who have first set the standards of perfection for Western humanity. If man's origin is a mystery – and why would one search for knowledge of him if he was not essentially unknown? – perhaps the ancients, who stood nearer to the origins, hold the key to what is obscure in him. And one of the first things one learns from reading them is their boasting of a knowledge of secret things that is supposedly hidden from the profane. Nevertheless, says Maistre, this knowledge is but an illusion. In spite of their quite laudable common sense, if one looks more closely one will

2. *Disciteque ô miseri! Et rerum cognoscite causas! Quid Sumus? Et quidnam victuri gignimur?... Ordo Quis datus?... Humana qua parte locatus in re?*, 'Mémoire au duc de Brunswick,' in Rebotton (ed.), *Ecrits maçonniques*, p.78. For an account of the background to the work see Rebotton's 'Introduction' to this edition; for Maistre's career as a Freemason see Lebrun, *Maistre: intellectual militant*, p.53-60, J. L. Darcel, 'Des pénitents noirs à la franc-maçonnerie: aux sources de la sensibilité maistrienne' and J. Rebotton, 'Joseph de Maistre, *alias* Josephus a Floribus, pendant la Révolution: repères et conjectures', both published in *REM*, nos. 5-6, 1980.

3. Rebotton (ed.), *Ecrits maçonniques*, p.88

find that all they had were vague ideas about man's degraded state and his future regeneration, which are but 'more or less fragile remains of a primitive tradition to be found in all nations of the universe'.[4] At any rate, Masonic legends that speak of a secret knowledge of man's origin and destiny derived from ancient pagan initiation are something that one cannot reasonably count on. For Maistre, the true 'science of man' lies elsewhere; it is a gift to be found in the word of the revealing God. 'Prouvons que nous ne sommes pas des *hommes nouveaux*, mais faisons nous une généalogie claire, et digne de nous. Attachons nous enfin à l'Evangile, et laissons là les folies de Memphis. Remontons aux premiers siècles de la loi sainte, fouillons l'antiquité ecclésiastique, interrogeons les Pères l'un après l'autre; réunissons, confrontons les passages, prouvons que nous sommes chrétiens.'[5] Yet, this Maistrian understanding of the Gospel injunction to *search the Scriptures* (John 5:39) indicates that the science of Man provided by revelation is, just like man himself, anything but clear and should not be taken for granted. In Maistre's view, it can only be the result of great effort, patience and a great deal of research and textual erudition – all this is necessary to grasp what he calls the 'revelation of the revelation', the hidden meaning of the sacred text. 'All is mystery in both Testaments', he writes, 'and the elect of one and the other are but true initiates. We have to question venerable Antiquity [i.e., Biblical Antiquity] and ask her how to understand the sacred allegories'. For the young Maistre, true knowledge of man, conceived of as the first fruits of the human intellect, is essentially the product of an esoteric reading of Sacred Scripture[6] and, as we shall see, of the human world in the light of Holy Writ, so that according to the *Mémoire* the true science of man is indeed a religious science of man (or a Christian science of Man, with 'Christian' taken in a 'transcendental' sense) that should be consolidated and propagated for the happiness and illustration of mankind.

As one can already see in this early work, this is the sense in which Maistre can be defined as a humanist. However, if by 'humanist' is meant, as it is today, 'someone who has faith in humanity but no faith in God',[7]

---

4. Rebotton (ed.), *Ecrits maçonniques*, p.93.
5. Rebotton (ed.), *Ecrits maçonniques*, p.97.
6. Immediately after the passage just quoted he writes: 'Allons même plus loin. La vraie religion a bien plus de 18 siècles. *Elle naquit le jour que naquirent les jours.* Remontons à l'origine des choses, et montrons par une filiation incontestable que notre systême réunit au dépot primitive les nouveaux dons du grand réparateur', Rebotton (ed.), *Ecrits maçonniques*, p.97.
7. See John O'Malley, 'From the 1599 ratio studiorum to the present: a humanistic tradition?', in Vincent Duminuco (ed.), *The Jesuit ratio studiorum: 400th anniversary perspectives* (New York, 2000), p.127.

Maistre was definitely not one. It is important to notice that this particular, 'negative', so to speak, conception of humanism is inherited from the eighteenth-century *Lumières*, a movement that Maistre fought his entire life, and with which his own version of enlightenment, as we just saw, is bound to compete. Maistre's humanism is perhaps closer to the one actually professed in the historical Renaissance, for Renaissance humanism, as it emerges from the most recent scholarship, was essentially a Christian enterprise of research into what it means to be a human being.[8]

Indeed, if one may regard Christian Renaissance humanism as a more or less fortunate mix of pagan wisdom and the revealed word of God, and if it is certain that the so-called 'question of Man' was at its peak in that age, it is no less certain that the ultimate standard to settle the question, the origin as well as the goal of all the resources directed towards it, was viewed in the light of the Biblical text (Genesis 1:26): 'And He said: "Let us make man in our image, after our likeness"'.[9] One may say that for the typical Renaissance humanist Man was a riddle that could not be solved or find his way into himself apart from God, 'God' meaning chiefly – though not exclusively – the Word by which He revealed his ways and, most of all, his vision (that is, his judgement) of Man. It is as if the Bible was, as a famous Jewish philosopher once put it, a piece of 'God's Anthropology',[10] destined as it were to be the major source not only of judgement but also of true enlightenment for mankind.

This is what one finds at the very core and inspiration of what I am calling Maistre's humanism, which strikes me as being the common ground of his thought: in order to be grasped in their own terms, man and his world must be seen *from the point of view of God*. Here, a clarification is in order. Jean-Yves Pranchère draws attention to the fact that Maistre reproaches the Enlightenment, and especially Montesquieu, for precisely adopting the *point of view of God*, for God's point of view is ultimately inaccessible to humanity, except in rare flashes of insight.[11] This is correct, strictly speaking, and that is why Maistre is not Hegel, or Lessing or the like. His critique of the titanic character of many of the claims of the philosophical enlightenment is directed to the ambition of attaining some kind of divine view of man and world in purely philosophical, that is, systematic terms, with no room for mystery or

8.   See, for instance, Charles Trinkaus, *In our image and likeness: humanity and divinity in Italian humanist thought*, 2 vol. (London, 1970), and P. Oskar Kristeller, *Renaissance concepts of man and other essays* (New York, 1972).

9.   See specially Charles Trinkaus, *In our image*, p.xiii-xxvii.

10.  A. J. Heschel, *God in search of man* (New York, 2001), p.129.

11.  See Pranchère, 'Montesquieu', in Darcel, Glaudes and Pranchère, *Dictionnaire Joseph de Maistre*, in Glaudes (ed.), *Maistre: Œuvres*, p.1230.

indetermination (i.e. with no room for Providence understood as divine action), as modern philosophy, specially its politics and philosophy of history, had continuously tried to do, an attitude that for Maistre would mean that man is striving to replace God, to deify his own vision, and not to be uplifted to God's perspective (to be *deified* instead), as he is expected to do when his grasp is 'captured' by the divine text. Despite the identity of the expression in both cases we are speaking of two diametrically opposed things. In fact, approaching concrete, historical man from the perspective of dogma and revelation is actually seeing him as it were from the point of view of God, all theories of prophetic insight and inspiration put aside.[12] For if man is made in God's image, and if he furthermore is commanded to perfection by the actualisation of his likeness to the divinity, one can conceive of no such thing as pure humanity or humanity as such. All that is human is of God's concern. This is why one may venture to say that Maistre's humanism, like all true humanism, is God's humanism, for, according to this vision, only God has a true concern for man or for the truth that lies within him. In effect, my contention is that it is in this spirit that the *Mémoire* sets the standard for the whole of Maistre's work, qualifying his concern for man at the same time as a religious and pedagogical enterprise, fashioning it after what one knows or can speculate about God's concern for mankind. Here Scripture is central. And Scripture shows that the Biblical God is a God who cares, in other words a provident God.

Providence is indeed only the technical, conceptual term for the Good, Omnipotent and Wise God whose name cannot be pronounced by mortal lips. Most of all we should expect that this God would be a God of Wisdom, providing man with the necessary knowledge of his nature and purpose, according to his capacity, as the Bible says, 'in measure and number and weight' (Wisdom 11:20). In fact, according to this account, the provident God is humanity's teacher, the true educator of mankind. This was already Plato's idea of the cosmic God: *ho theos paidagogei ton kosmon* – 'God is the pedagogue of the whole world'.[13] For Plato, education, in Greek *paideia*, means the process of complete formation of the whole of man according to his nature and end, with the soul understood as the seat of man's divinity or of his kinship with the divine.[14] It is in this sense that Plato's famous definition of philosophy as 'assimilation to God' has been traditionally understood. Although there has been a good deal of controversy about the pertinence of attributing to Plato a fully

12. That is precisely what I mean by drawing from Rabbi Heschel's daring and insightful observation.

13. *Laws*, X, 987b (trans. Bejamin Jowet, *Dover philosophical classics* (New York, 2006)).

14. On the Greek notion of *paideia* or education, see Werner Jaeger's monumental study *Paideia: the ideals of Greek culture* (Oxford, 1986), especially Book III.

developed concept of a providential deity, what is certain is that for him the divine intelligence that rules the cosmos truly educates and forms man, pushing him towards the imitation of the beauty and regularity of the movements of the divine stars so that he can achieve his perfection as a spiritual and rational being in the conduct of life, in the making of laws and the creation of polities and, ultimately, in the after world where his present 'life' (his *bios*) shall be judged and the next determined (or chosen) on account of what he has done with his soul.[15]

Sometime around the third or second century B.C., some of these notions about the educational intent of the divinity towards mankind passed on to Alexandrian Hellenised Judaism, influencing much of the so-called Wisdom literature produced within this new religious and cultural context. This is not to deny that the notion of the Biblical God as man's teacher was already present in the Hebrew Scriptures, as some examples drawn from the book of Deuteronomy would be apt to show.[16] However, it acquires its full meaning only in the texts of the Greek Bible, the Septuagint, where the concepts of the Greek philosophical tradition found their way into Biblical thought. There we find a vast array of interpretations of God's care for mankind and especially of his dealings with Israel. It seems clear that such interpretations are not publicised at random by the Biblical authors, but rather that they attend to a certain hierarchical pattern, with some of them being asserted as worthier than others when it comes to what is expected of a wise and good God. In fact, representations of God's judgement in the Wisdom literature range from simple revenge, as was common in more ancient texts of the Hebrew Bible, to higher concepts of caring, embodied in representations like the provident mother, the shepherd who has a concern for his herd and so on. It has been argued that this noticeable shift from the Hebrew to the Greek books was mainly caused by a heightened sense of God's worth derived from Greek thinking, which had actually, by that time, developed high standards with which to judge the morality of divine actions, and which even had a term to indicate that standard, that the Greek philosophers called *theoprepes*.[17] Having incorporated this new sense of the divinity, so the argument goes, the Hellenised Biblical authors and translators, challenged by the many passages of the Law and the Prophets in which the God of Israel is

---

15. See specially *Republic*, VII 614b-621b (the myth of Er), Lisbon, 2004; and *Laws*, 904 b-c, New York, 2006.
16. See Deuteronomy, 4:12-16; 8:1-18; Isaiah, 30:2-21, and Heschel, *The Prophets* (New York, 2001), p.233.
17. For the development of this concept (which means 'that which is worthy of God') in Greek philosophical theology, especially in earlier times, see Jaeger, *The Theology of the early Greek philosophers* (Oxford, 1947).

described as a divinity of ambiguous morality (displaying low, anthro-
pomorphic emotions like jealousy, wrath, revenge, etc. towards his
creatures), had to come up with accounts of His harsh actions that met
the higher standards they now upheld, and that is how the educational
interpretation of Providence is assumed to have been brought into
Biblical thought.[18]

Whatever the value one may be willing to ascribe to this particular
theory of its origins, the fact is that, in the Bible, the pedagogical account
of God's caring toward man appears in the guise of an esoteric theory of
God's action, as a theological interpretation of his intent, indeed as the
highest understanding one can have of divine activity, the one which is
proper only to the perfect or the initiate (the *theleiós*).[19] Moreover, and
this is quite relevant to my argument on the true character of Maistre's
picture of Providence, this higher account is not intended to exclude the
lower, less spiritual or more carnal pictures of the divinity's care (that
speak about hell, chastisement and God's revenge), for this would be a
rather unwise course of action, since these depictions are suitable for the
multitude of less perfect and more simple ones (*tá pollá*, the 'many'),
whom Origen used to call *simpliciores*, and who cannot be 'saved' or
'properly educated' without them. For the provident God is a Wise God
who communicates with men with a view to their ability to understand
the Word: to children he speaks the language of children; grown men he
feeds with the solid 'food' of the incarnate word, and thus He leads
humanity by the hand through the various stages of history, first in
created nature, then in the revealed Law and finally in the Incarnation,
to be formed in the divine knowledge of that truth which saves, a truth
that humanity could not reach by itself without God's loving assistance.
This is, in a few words, the Patristic account of God's Providence and its
revealing action in time, the first sketch of a theology of history that was
proposed as a divine education of mankind.[20] According to this view,
anyone who is willing to educate his brothers in the highest Wisdom (i.e.,
divine wisdom) is bound to imitate the ways of the divine and thus to
speak to each one according to his capacity, even if this means – as it

---

18. This argument is championed by the same Jaeger in his *Early Christianity and Greek 'paideia'*
    (Harvard, CT, 1961).
19. See Deuteronomy, 4:12-16, where the particular interpretation of God's revelation seems
    to stem from the prophet's wit or secret knowledge, being uttered not as 'God's words'.
    For a contrast that confirms my reading, see Wisdom 6:22 when the author claims he is
    going to entirely disclose divine wisdom not leaving any secrets hidden for keeping
    secrets is not the way of the truly wise man. In any case what is important to notice is the
    status of the doctrine of providential *paideia* as an interpretation, even if an enlightened
    one, and not as revelation strictly speaking.
20. This is particularly the case in the theology of Irenaeus' *Against heresies*.

often does – to speak in public (and of course to write) only esoterically, conveying one and the same message in various layers of meaning.

But there is more to the need to preserve the harsher, more violent accounts of God's action that prevailed in ancient times. On a more basic level, they have to be preserved simply because they are true, because God actually judges, punishes and chastises hard-hearted, stiff-necked man, even if this can be seen (and indeed must be seen) as a trait of His Wisdom and Mercy, as a pledge of divine love. Indeed, what I think is most important to retain as regards the new view of God's action in the Greek, more recent, Biblical books is that the tough character of the education ministered by the Holy Spirit – the *paideia* of the Holy Spirit or the 'Holy Spirit of education'[21] – is apparent in almost every pertinent passage, with God's love and care towards mankind being pictured as constantly punishing, whipping and striking, and with man, as a consequence, being constantly subjected to frustration, pain, suffering, tears, loss and desperation in order to make him 'bow his head' and 'accept the burden' of as it were God's education.[22] So much so that the term *paideia* as it appears in the Greek Bible is more often than not translated as God-ministered 'correction,' 'chastisement' or 'discipline', conveying a falsely simplistic meaning that has led many good commentators astray.[23]

This harsh picture of God's education has, of course, much to do with the Biblical contrast between God as the most holy and man as a fallen, sinning and self-centered creature, so that God is tough on man because man's wicked ways have to be converted to God's ways of justice, and on that account God is bound to lead estranged man back to good ways as a shepherd does with his sheep. But, and here is a point I would like to put particular stress on, in spite of the apparent violence displayed by the divinity in the achievement of this goal, this driving back of devious mankind to the ways of the divine presupposes a free decision on the part of man, an acceptance of God's holy sovereignty, for (although many people do not realise that) the notion of a forced education is absolutely meaningless. That this coming back originates in man's free obedience to God's call, in his free acceptance of providential education, is indicated by a classic term in both Jewish and Christian theological (but also

---

21. *Hagion pneuma paideias*, Wisdom 1:5.
22. Thus, Ben Sira says (Sirach 6: 23-25): 'Give ear, my son, receive my advice, and refuse not my counsel. And put thy feet into her (i.e. *paideia* of wisdom) fetters and thy neck into her chain'. See also the rather violent exhortation to wisdom with which he concludes the book (Sirach 51:26): 'Put your neck under the yoke and let your soul receive instruction [*paideia*]'.
23. I'm referring to Jaeger, *Early Christianity*, and Marguerite Harl, *La Bible grecque des Septante. Du judaïsme hellénistique au christianisme ancien* (Paris, 1994), and *Le Déchiffrement du sens. Etudes sur l'herméneutique chrétienne d'Origène à Grégoire de Nysse* (Paris, 1993).

Platonic, with a different meaning) traditions: it is *metanoia*, repentance, conversion and return (*epistrophé*) to God through pain and penitence.[24]

But apart from the factor of sin as well as the ontological abyss between creator and creature, there is still another meaning, perhaps even more important for my purpose, to the tough character of divine pedagogy, a meaning that points to man's greatness rather than to his baseness, to the presence of something immortal within him. For God's education of mankind, being intended for man's salvation, is concerned with the life of the soul because, as Maistre states after Plutarch following both the Platonic and late Biblical and Christian traditions, man's 'I' is the soul, and it is for and because of the soul that man is divinely educated in the first place.[25] If it were not for the soul, that divine, immortal part of man, the divine in man, what interest would the Most High have in educating him? What would be the point of His concern? For if man is divinely educated, it is primarily because he is a spiritual creature and as far as he is a spiritual creature. This, according to Maistre's completion of and commentary on Plutarch's text, is the sole reason why God shows an unceasing concern for man, without ever failing to 'nous instruire, de nous menacer, de nous écarter du mal, de nous rappeler au bien, de châtier nos vices, de récompenser nos vertus'.[26] In view of the soul and the life of the soul, which is eternal, it matters little what misfortunes may descend upon us in *this* life, whose 'goods' are but a shadow; this is the reason why, says Origen with an intense spiritualistic *pathos*, God does not 'rule the soul with a view to, say, the average fifty years of the present life, but to an unlimited time', the *ton apeiron aiona* or 'the world without limits' in which a divinised human being is supposed to dwell.[27]

I shall soon return to the details of Maistre's Origenist picture of the world as a *locus* of education. At the moment, my contention is that Maistre's Providence should be understood in the light of the *paideia* tradition that I have just been describing, as his reading and knowledge of such authors as Plato, Plutarch and Origen most strongly suggests. In

---

24. See specially Sirach 4:17-19, 26 and 18:13-14.
25. *De la Traduction d'un traité de Plutarque sur les délais de la justice divine* (henceforth *Sur les Délais*) in *OC*, para.XXXI, vol.5, p.414. It must be noted that the first Biblical reference to a doctrine of the immortality of the soul – the first occurrence in the Bible of the Greek *athanasia*, which use had always been privative to the gods – comes in together with the pedagogical interpretation of God's action. See Wisdom 2:23 and 3:4.
26. *Sur les Délais* in *OC*, XXXII, p.417. From my edition of Maistre's translation of Plutarch's essay I cannot be sure if these words are uttered by Maistre or by Plutarch, but it really does not matter: the fact is that they show how close and deep was Maistre's awareness of the tradition of providential *paideia*.
27. *De Principiis*, III, 1, 13.

effect, because they have completely overlooked Maistre's knowledge of and affiliation with this venerable tradition, most commentators have been led to interpret his rather violent depiction of the ways of Providence, especially in the *Considérations sur la France* and *Les Soirées de Saint Pétersbourg*, in an anti-humanist sense. In fact a lot of nonsense has been said about Maistre's vision of Providence: prophet of the past, worshipper of a bloodthirsty, Old Testament Deity as opposed to the gentle and meek Christian God and so on. But the fact is that one cannot understand the outlook of Maistre's providential discourse without having recourse to its theological sources, which are scarcely hard to find. It is not by chance that his translation of Plutarch's dialogue on Providence, *Sur les Délais de la justice divine*, along with the *Eclaircissiment sur les sacrifices*, a veritable showcase of Origen's esoteric thought, have been published time and again as appendixes to *Les Soirées*. For the keys to Maistre's concept of Providence, not only in *Les Soirées*, but also in the rest of his work, lie in these two minor writings.[28]

Likewise, the harsh impression left by some Maistrian representations of God's action are adequately accounted for by the pedagogic line of interpretation that I have just introduced. Here, the important feature is the 'inverted' picture of 'life' and 'death', and therefore, of 'good' and 'evil', on which the whole pedagogic, spiritualistic tradition is based.[29] This is quite apparent in many passages of *Les Soirées* as well as in Maistre's comments to his translation of Plutarch. At a certain point of the latter work he asks, as in a dialogue with that ancient Platonist who, for him, knew the true doctrine of Providence better than any other pagan writer, including Plato:[30] 'who would believe that, *in spiritual medicine, that is, in divine punishments*, there can be anything *good* but what cures the vices, which are the illnesses of the soul?'[31] For the soul, says Plutarch in Maistre's translation, is the 'veritable root of life that

28. For only a few examples of the almost direct transposition of Plutarch's arguments to Maistre's masterpiece, compare *Les Soirées de Saint-Pétersbourg*, in Glaudes (ed.) *Maistre: Œuvres*, p.485, with Plutarch, *Sur les Délais* in *OC*, XXX, p.413-14 (on original sin); *Soirées*, p.595 with Plutarch, *Sur les Délais* in *OC*, X, 385-6 and XXI, p.401-402; *Soirées* p.468 with Plutarch, XXI, p.401-402 (on freedom and moral order); *Soirées*, p.498 and Plutarch, VI, p.382-3 (the *paideia* of the cosmos); *Soirées*, p.728-29 (where there is talk of the universal prejudice regarding hereditary merit in analogy with the belief in divine justice exerted over the criminal's posterity) and Plutarch, XVII, p.394.

29. I write 'inverted' between quotation marks because this is indeed the traditional, multi-secular view on life and death and their mutual relation. In the wider perspective of the history of ideas or mentalities, our perspective of life as the *primary* 'good', the one on which all other goods are thought to depend, and, consequently, of death as the biggest enemy, which dates back to Hobbes in the seventeenth century, is the inverted one.

30. See Preface, *Sur les Délais* in *OC*, p.370.

31. *Sur les Délais* in *OC*. XXXI, p. 414.

some day shall flourish in eternity'.[32] Accordingly, in the ninth dialogue
of Les Soirées, the harshness of God's way of punishing is compared to the
tough techniques used by the surgeon to restore health to the body by
extracting evil through pain – perhaps the most classic image of the
divine educational action, one that suggests that divine chastisements
form a kind of therapsiquê, a therapy for the sinning soul.[33] The presence
of this particular interpretation of God's chastisements, and hence of
divine Providence and justice, is furthermore most apparent in that
supreme moment of the same ninth Soirée, where Maistre speaks of the
sufferings of the righteous as something whereby 'Dieu le purifie de ses
fautes passées, le met en garde contre les fautes futures, et le mûrit pour
le ciel'.[34]

Indeed, there are many other, more powerful indications of the
pedagogical character of Maistre's Providence throughout Les Soirées,
ones which would actually serve to clarify the use of the single pedagogic
analogies to Providence just described. But here it will suffice to discuss
the one appearing as a kind of early climax at the end of the fifth entretien.
To me it is by far the most important, because it has the virtue of
revealing the pedagogical nature of the entire work (and hence of
Maistre's thought as a whole) conceived as a discussion of God's providential ways in the government of the world. After having enumerated
several ways in which divine chastisement (violent death, diseases, etc.)
can be seen as a pledge of God's love and mercy towards suffering
mankind, as a way of cure and correction, he concludes with a rather
mysterious utterance to the effect that, however, one must beware not to
cross a certain line 'beyond' God's mercy lest one fall (deservedly) into
eternal death. At first glance it seems fair to say that with these remarks
he is referring to the Church's dogma of hell. However I believe there is
much more to it, and this 'more' lies in the even more mysterious
explanation that he provides: 'Toute instruction vraie', the Count says,
'mêlant donc la crainte aux idées consolantes, avertit l'être libre de ne
pas s'avancer jusqu'au terme où il n'y a plus de terme'.[35]

'All true instruction should combine fear with consoling ideas' – what
precisely does Maistre mean by these words? My guess is that he is
indicating rather clearly to the 'adept' that – though it seems harsh not to
grant the sinner the possibility of a last hour repentance – what he is
really doing is offering, as he calls it, a 'double doctrine', that is he is
saying something for the spiritual benefit and edification of his more

32. Sur les Délais in OC, XXXII, p. 328.
33. Les Soirées de Saint-Pétersbourg, in Glaudes (ed.) Maistre: Œuvres, p.713-14.
34. Les Soirées de Saint-Pétersbourg, in Glaudes (ed.) Maistre: Œuvres, p.712.
35. Les Soirées de Saint-Pétersbourg, in Glaudes (ed.) Maistre: Œuvres, p.596.

simple-minded readers. One may argue that if this is so, there should be no reason why he could not have made clear what he meant, as Origen himself did in his work. To this we can reply that in Origen's time the esoteric meaning of a text could quite easily be kept hidden from what he called the *simpliciores*, the simple faithful, since they almost always corresponded to the illiterate, to that class of people for whom Origen's writings, or for that matter any writings whatsoever, would be forever out of reach.[36] As we know, things were quite different in Maistre's time. Then, because of the incomparably greater number of literate people, simple-mindedness or lack of spiritual sensibility had 'ascended' to the world of letters and reached another level: a good deal of Origen's *simpliciores* eventually learned how to read. The result is that the readership for *Les Soirées* was far wider than the one that Origen's works would have had. In addition, Maistre had to take into account the formidable power of the established Church, which he furthermore sought to defend. So the necessity of hiding the deeper strata of his discourse from the profane was even more urgent.

However, what is important to notice is how the passage we have under consideration points quite sharply to the real nature or intent of Maistre's intellectual enterprise, which is disclosed with particular clarity in the theology of *Les Soirées*. What is really at stake here is the correct understanding of the notion that is central to the whole work, the Temporal Rule of Providence, which, as the book's subtitle clearly indicates, is stated as the main theme of *Les Soirées, ou Entretiens sur le government temporel de la Providence*. Let us, then, be reminded of its first enunciation in the book. It occurs right after the characters' opening considerations, where the Chevalier prompts his older, more experienced companions to instruct him on the ways of divine justice. Right from the start, the young man shows some resistance to the classical argument derived from the punishments and rewards of the afterlife, demanding from his wiser companions a more 'solid' and 'convincing' explanation for the use of the more worldly folk. The Senator's answer to this query is classic and deserves to be quoted in full:

> [i]l y a beaucoup de danger à laisser croire aux hommes que la vertu ne sera recompensée et le vice puni que dans l'autre vie. Les incrédules, pour qui ce monde est tout, ne demandent pas mieux, et la foule même doit être rangée sur la même ligne: l'homme est si distrait, si dépendant des objets qui le frappent, si dominé par ses passions, que nous voyons tous le jours le croyant le plus soumis braver les tourmens de la vie future pour le plus misérable plaisir. Que sera-ce de celui qui ne croit pas ou qui croit foiblement? Appuyons nous donc tant qu'il vous plaira sur la vie future qui répond à

---

36. With the obvious exception of his many homilies, conceived for oral communication.

toutes les objections; mais s'il existe dans ce monde un véritable gouvernement moral, et si, dès cette vie même, le crime doit trembler, pourquoi le décharger de cette crainte?[37]

There can be little doubt that the argument presented by the Senator displays an intense pedagogical outlook. The precise outline of this pedagogical nature of what is arguably the key notion of Maistre's providential thinking is further clarified by Plutarch in a passage on the belief in hereditary chastisements that must be regarded as perfectly parallel to the one just quoted. Let us hear what he has to say:

> C'est donc absolument la même chose qu'il y a une Providence et que l'âme humaine ne meure point; car il n'est pas possible que l'une de ces verités subsiste sans l'autre. Si donc l'âme continue d'exister après la mort, on conçoit aisément qu'elle soit punie ou récompensée, et toute la question ne roule que sur la manière. Or, cette vie n'étant qu'un combat perpétuel, c'est seulement après la mort que l'âme peut recevoir le prix qu'elle aura mérité: mais personne ne sait ce qui se passe dans l'autre monde, et plusieurs même n'y croient pas; de manière que *tout cela est nul pour l'exemple et pour le bon ordre du monde*: au contraire la vengeance, exercée d'une manière visible sur la postérité des coupables, frappe tous les yeux et peut retenir une foule d'hommes prêts à se livrer au crime.[38]

Indeed the whole argument for providential justice in *Les Soirées* deals with the ways in which God rewards virtue and punishes crime in this *visible order of things*, setting the example for the good order of the world and actually enforcing this order with its interventions and laws. In contrast to what some writers of 'the good party' have thought, perhaps led by an excess of spiritualistic zeal, the argument derived from the rewards and punishments after death, although perfectly reasonable and acceptable in itself, *should not*, as the Senator clearly states, exclude the temporal rule of Providence, for the latter is addressed to an entirely different audience for which it has a value of its own. 'Why then', the Senator goes on to ask in this same passage of the third *Soirée*, 'make admissions *(faire des aveux)* that are not necessary?'[39] Two different but complementary considerations of great import to further defining the outline of Maistre's pedagogical account of Providence as it appears especially in *Les Soirées* find their way at precisely this point: the first one relates to the intended audience of the book and therefore to the object of the education that it is designed to provide; the second concerns the question of how we should value this utility or convenience standard that

---

37. *Les Soirées de Saint-Pétersbourg*, in Glaudes (ed.) *Maistre: Œuvres*, p.460.
38. *Sur les Délais* in *OC*, XXXV, p.417-18. The emphases are all mine.
39. *Les Soirées de Saint-Pétersbourg*, in Glaudes (ed.) *Maistre: Œuvres*, p.538.

an opinion about Providence, like that of its temporal rule, is supposed to meet.

I shall deal with both considerations in an interconnected way. The first one is actually a restatement, from another point of view, of what I said earlier about Maistre's 'double doctrine' or his use of esoteric discourse. For from the quotations just cited on the pedagogical intention of the doctrinal statement of a Temporal Rule of Providence the question arises as to who are those readers in need of a harsher, more 'visible' representation of God's moral government of the world and human affairs. The texts just quoted are quite clear; they correspond not only to the classic unbeliever, but particularly to the more sensual, to the ones whose faith is fragile, whose view is limited and hence who are reluctant to accept the idea that justice is only possible in another world. Accordingly, these find it difficult to sense the presence of the divine or the spiritual in its most refined forms and thus tend to overlook God's providential government of the world to indulge in the secular perspectives of *this* life or even of their everyday petty concerns. So they often need to be reminded of the reality of God's justice through fear of chastisement in a graphic way. And that is exactly what, on a first level, Maistre sets out to do with his exposition on the temporal rule of Providence.[40]

I have pointed to the identification of these primary subjects of providential education with Origen's *simpliciores*, and furthermore to the differences of context and readership between the Alexandrian master and his Savoyard pupil, claiming that in Maistre's time Origen's *simpliciores* had ascended in life, forming what has been labelled in recent socio-historical scholarship as the public opinion of the Enlightenment. In effect, it must be noted that, as far as the spiritual understanding of religion is concerned, almost everyone in Maistre's time had become a *simplicior*, since the spiritual account of the world and man's life and, furthermore, the doctrine of God's 'particular providence' toward mankind, had been undermined by at least 150 years of intense attack from various fronts ranging from outright atheism to scientism and deism. This was the generation that Maistre had to deal with; it was this new class of readers, in many ways a product of the European Enlightenment, which he sought to reach. So it is my contention that this new spiritual situation is artfully and deliberately embodied in the character of the Chevalier and hence that, pictured as a pupil or would-be student of God's Providence, he must be seen as a mirror of the book's intended readership.

In fact, it is the Chevalier who gives rise to the whole set of conversations with his question about the different fates of the righteous and

40. Bear in mind the portrait of the executioner in the second *Soirée*.

the criminal; it is he who points to the necessity of forsaking ordinary modes of argument (that is, the belief in rewards and punishments in another world) when it comes to describing the action of God's justice; it is he who finds it particularly hard to believe in miracles or at least to accept the explanation of their possibility against the tenets of modern natural science; it is the Chevalier who cites Voltaire, Locke or Bacon as authorities, thus providing the other two senior speakers with the opportunity to challenge the 'idols' of the times; finally, it is he who, drawing on Voltaire, raises the objection taken from the suffering of the innocent or the just, which will eventually lead to the presentation of the reversibility of merits in the ninth *Soirée* as the ultimate solution to all objections against God's justice in His providential government of the world. What, I believe, is likely to lead many a reader of *Les Soirées* astray on this point is, on the one hand, the assumption that, because the Chevalier is often depicted, if not as a faithful Christian, at least as someone good-willed toward religion, he should necessarily be viewed as a representative of a religious tradition and hence as an intransigent opponent of the Enlightenment just like his other two friends; and, on the other hand, the expectation that an adept or follower of the Enlightenment, as he, in this case, would be supposed to be, should of necessity unqualifiedly reject all tenets of revealed religion as if he were a minor Diderot or Voltaire. This is not to deny that there were, as there continue to be, such extreme, archetypical cases. But the fact is that things must not of necessity be that way. In fact, these expectations are probably but prejudices that do not correspond with the actual outlook of the readers Maistre must have had in mind in view of the historic situation in which he wrote. If one looks closely enough into the features of the Chevalier as a dramatic character, one is likely to find that things are much more complicated than that. So, at this point, the one thing to do is to search for the information the book provides about him.

We are told that he is a young man (in his thirties or younger)[41], of French origin,[42] military by profession,[43] and that he was raised as a Christian.[44] He is further characterised as a man of the world inclined towards 'useful ideas' and 'practical things',[45] who can be defined as a believer by nature and inclination.[46] In spite of his having this naturally pious soul (an *anima naturaliter Christiana?*), as the dialogues progress we

---

41. *Les Soirées de Saint-Pétersbourg*, in Glaudes (ed.) *Maistre: Œuvres*, p.463.
42. *Les Soirées de Saint-Pétersbourg*, in Glaudes (ed.) *Maistre: Œuvres*, p.483.
43. *Les Soirées de Saint-Pétersbourg*, in Glaudes (ed.) *Maistre: Œuvres*, p.463.
44. *Les Soirées de Saint-Pétersbourg*, in Glaudes (ed.) *Maistre: Œuvres*, p.485.
45. *Les Soirées de Saint-Pétersbourg*, in Glaudes (ed.) *Maistre: Œuvres*, p.464.
46. *Les Soirées de Saint-Pétersbourg*, in Glaudes (ed.) *Maistre: Œuvres*, p.749-50.

are informed that his intellectual upbringing was heavily influenced by the authors of the French *Lumières*,[47] who, although not being depicted as his 'heroes', are respected as figures of intellectual and perhaps moral authority,[48] as would be naturally expected of the men who presided over the education of his generation.[49] We are also informed that the recent successes in the various fields of the natural sciences, as well as the solid reputation of the metaphysical ideas of the Enlightenment invested with the authority of these authors of his youth, had implanted in his mind seeds of doubt as to the validity of some of the truths in which, as a Catholic Christian, he would (or should) be inclined to believe.[50] However, the fact that the Chevalier was raised on the critical or dissolving *ethos* of the Enlightenment does not mean that he is simply an atheist or that he takes sides with 'philosophy' as understood by the times against the beliefs of his ancestors; this plainly means that his religion is no longer the same, that it tends irresistibly (and, in his case, insensibly) towards deism or something of the kind, and that the would-be 'adepts' who, like him, are naturally inclined towards faith, do not find, in the thought and ideology of their time and environment, the 'tools' that are required for its defense or vindication, since revealed religion had lost the epistemic authority and respectability it once had.[51] In short, this means that this willingly religious young man needs and wants[52] to be *re-conformed* to the seminal representations of his native tradition, which have been obfuscated by the philosophic propaganda of the *Lumières*. And thus, keeping in mind this outline of the Chevalier as a character, we find that Maistre's last work and masterpiece, the book into which he 'poured his head' and everything he knew, was designed to meet the standard set in one of his first writings, that of conveying enlightenment and education to man (here concrete men) from the perspective of the religious humanist tradition.

As far as the pedagogic nature of *Les Soirées* is concerned, what is likely to be a major cause of confusion for some readers is the assumption that 'education' must demand a positive project or programme, that it cannot be proposed as a 'reaction' as it is in Maistre's case. But the fact is that, for Maistre, the 'programme' for the education of the Chevalier/reader was, as rightly perceived by Jean-Yves Pranchère, presupposed from the very

47. See *Les Soirées de Saint-Pétersbourg*, in Glaudes (ed.) *Maistre: Œuvres*, p.507, 468, and 471.
48. See *Les Soirées de Saint-Pétersbourg*, in Glaudes (ed.) *Maistre: Œuvres*, p.610, 621, and 632-33.
49. *Les Soirées de Saint-Pétersbourg*, in Glaudes (ed.) *Maistre: Œuvres*, p.508 and 589.
50. See *Les Soirées de Saint-Pétersbourg*, in Glaudes (ed.) *Maistre: Œuvres*, p.484 and 554-55.
51. Note that the entire fourth *Soirée* is a commentary as well as a severe critique of the new religiosity tainted with philosophic deism.
52. See *Les Soirées de Saint-Pétersbourg*, in Glaudes (ed.) *Maistre: Œuvres*, p.552.

start, corresponding to the religious humanist tradition first set by the
Christian humanists of the Renaissance and then developed in the
seventeenth century by the pedagogical enterprise of the Jesuits
(Pranchère calls this tradition presupposed in Maistre's critique of the
Enlightenment by the rather vaguer expression of 'le système chrétien' or
'la philosophie chrétienne' which he rightly identifies with the social
system and intellectual culture of seventeenth-century France).[53] In
general terms this tradition was characterised by the 'union of science
and piety', 'knowledge and gentlemanship' that for Maistre was the
distinctive mark of France's *Grand Siècle* as well as the major sign of its
superiority as compared to the century of the *Lumières*. The typical
product of the seventeenth century was the so-called *honnête homme*, who
stands for Maistre's concrete ideal of human perfection, as the profiles of
the very characters of *Les Soirées*, typical of the society and culture of the
old regime, are apt to demonstrate.[54] So, as far as this particular point
about the education of the Chevalier is concerned, it was rather a matter
of re-establishing as authoritative what he regarded as a successful
human and educational 'standard' which was in the process of being
replaced by a new, revolutionary one.

In *Les Soirées* the first step towards this aim, the properly propaedeutic
step, is to destroy the prestige of this obfuscating so-called *philosophie*
over the Chevalier's youthful and inexperienced mind, by ravaging
mercilessly the idols of the time and thereby challenging the authority
they exert. This is the main reason why, in my view, Maistre launched
such a violent attack on Voltaire.[55] Furthermore, it is Maistre himself,
through the mouth of the Count, who makes clear that this process of re-
conformation to the religious tradition corresponds roughly to what
happens to the Chevalier throughout the book. Talking about the
superiority of Louis Racine over Voltaire as far as the education of
children is concerned, an issue raised by the Chevalier who is said to have
listened to the poet's verses on the lap of his mother as a baby, the Count
says:

53. See Pranchère, 'Ordre de la raison, déraison de l'histoire', in Barthelet (ed.), *Maistre*:
    Dossiers H, p.370.
54. On the other hand, the typical offspring of the Enlightenment was the *esprit fort* that
    Maistre scorns throughout *Les Soirées* as well as the rest of his works. See, in particular, *An
    Examination of the philosophy of Bacon*, trans. and ed. Richard Lebrun (Montreal and
    Kingston, 1998), p.270-77 and *Cinq lettres sur l'éducation publique en Russie* in *OC*, vol.8,
    p.163-232.
55. *Les Soirées de Saint-Pétersbourg* in Glaudes (ed.) *Maistre: Œuvres*, p.555-58. This is also the
    reason why, in a famous *boutade*, he writes to the editor of *Du Pape*, Guy Marie de Place,
    that one can do nothing against the ideas if one does nothing against the people who hold
    them.

Rien ne peut remplacer cette éducation. Si la mère surtout s'est fait un devoir d'imprimer profondément sur le front de son fils le caractère divin, on peut être à peu près sûr que la main du vice ne l'effacera jamais. Le jeune home pourra s'écarter sans doute; mais il décrira, si vous voulez me permettre cette expression, une *courbe rentrante* qui le ramènera au point dont il était parti.

And then the Chevalier ironically asks him right away: 'Croyez-vous, mon bon ami, que la courbe, à mon égard, commence à rebrousser?' The Count replies:

Je n'en doute pas: et je puis même vous en donner une démonstration expéditive: *c'est que vous êtes ici.* [...] Pourquoi, dans ce moment, m'entendez-vous avec plaisir? c'est que vous portez sur le front ce signe, dont je vous parlais tout à l'heure. [...] Votre esprit, je le sais, semble encore se refuser à certaines connaissances; mais c'est uniquement parce que toute vérité a besoin de préparation. Un jour, n'en doutez pas, vous les goûterez.[56]

Moreover, that the literary characterisation of the Chevalier corresponds roughly to the description I made of the generation that was partially formed on the ideas and principles of the Enlightenment, is quite clear from the very words of the Chevalier. At a central juncture of the eighth *entretien*, with a view to justifying his interest in putting into writing and eventually publishing the seven first dialogues, he says: 'Je connais beacoup d'hommes dans le monde, beaucoup de jeunes gens surtout, extrêmement dégoûtés des doctrines modernes. D'autres flottent et ne demandent qu'à se fixer. Je voudrais leur communiquer ces mêmes idées qui ont occupé nos soirées, persuadé que je serais utile à quelques-uns et agréable au moins à beaucoup d'autres'.[57] Further and clearer evidence of the deliberate pedagogic character of the dialogues as far as the character of the Chevalier is concerned is given in the following utterance addressed to his younger friend by the Count near the conclusion of the tenth *entretien*, when the education provided by the two senior companions is likely to approach completion:[58] 'Lorsque vous aurez notre âge, hélas! nous ne vous entendrons plus; mais d'autres vous entendront, et vous leur rendrez *la culture* que vous tenez de nous. Car

56. *Les Soirées de Saint-Pétersbourg* in Glaudes (ed.) *Maistre: Œuvres*, p.534.
57. *Les Soirées de Saint-Pétersbourg* in Glaudes (ed.) *Maistre: Œuvres*, p.686.
58. Of course this 'completion' shall be taken in a relative sense, because one cannot hope to achieve it as regards the depths of divine Wisdom, the subject matter of the education ministered in *Les Soirées*. This point is made perfectly clear by the unfinished (and unfinishable) condition of the dialogues (see 'Introduction' to *Les Soirées de Saint-Pétersbourg*, in Glaudes (ed.) *Maistre: Œuvres*, p.433). On the other hand, and after due qualification, the education provided to the Chevalier by his two older and more experienced friends indeed approaches completion, as all human education is expected to reach a final term.

c'est bien nous, s'il vous plaît, qui avons donné le premier coup de bêche
à cette bonne terre'.[59]

No matter the perspective from which one looks at it, it seems quite
reasonable to assert that these 'many young men of the world' who are
'disgusted with the modern ideas' they were brought up in, and who shall
be given another 'culture' by the two representatives of the European
religious and humanist tradition, are the 'real' model for the literary
characterisation of the Chevalier and hence the intended readership of
*Les Soirées de Saint Pétersbourg*. They are the subjects of the education, of
the divine education that Maistre wants to provide.[60] They are the good
earth in need of 'preparation', the ones who must be reoriented towards
certain truths in which they will eventually delight. Even the best among
them have naturally to start as *simpliciores* before being elevated, as it
were, according to their spiritual capacity, to the most sublime truths.
Here, just as it happens in the Greek Bible, fear is the beginning of
Wisdom.[61] Fear works for the salvation of the 'many', as the latter are
rustic of mind, and furthermore sensual and materialistic – they believe
only what their eyes can see, a feature as it were of the human condition
tainted by original sin. But, side by side with fear, Maistre's dialogues
supply his readers with other more sublime representations of the
divinity and its justice aimed at those who indeed are better soil, whose
souls are capable of being uplifted from their original sensual inclination
to a higher understanding of divine things so they can ascend step by
step from fear to love towards perfection.[62]

It seems to me that this notion of spiritual progress from the exoteric
to the esoteric, from the apparent and low to the hidden and sublime,
points to the overall plan or scheme of *Les Soirées*, being the key to the
book's underlying structure. Indeed, it is quite noticeable that Maistre
articulates the wide array of representations of divine justice that appear
in *Les Soirées* according to a *progressive pattern* going from the harsher or
more impressive (the eulogy of the executioner, diseases as punishments,

---

59. *Les Soirées de Saint-Pétersbourg* in Glaudes (ed.) *Maistre: Œuvres*, p.749-50. The emphasis is
    mine.
60. Here a clarification must be made to the effect that my identification of Maistre's
    intended readership with the youth of his time in no way intends to do away with the
    possibility, suggested by Darcel, that *Les Soirées* was originally intended for the education
    of a particular prince, Alexander I of Russia, for Alexander's religious and ideological
    profile and background is perfectly in line with almost all of the features I have just
    described For Darcel's suggestion, see '*Les Soirées de Saint-Petersbourg* de Joseph de Maistre.
    Image contrastive d'une œuvre et d'une ville', in Barthelet (ed.), *Maistre*: Dossiers H, p.140-
    41.
61. *Arché sophias phobestai toú Kyriou*. Psalms 111:10.
62. This ascending from fear to love by understanding that love is the ground of fear is
    already present in the Greek Bible. See Sirach 1:12.

etc.) to the higher and more intellectual ones (chastisement and suffering as spiritual medicines and, eventually, in the dialogues dealing with war and massacre in the seventh and ninth *Soirées*, even violent death as a means of universal regeneration), amassing a variety of actual, historical and Biblical as well as non-Biblical accounts of divine Providence into a general picture of what one may call the religious heritage of mankind. This thoroughness is stressed rather than enfeebled by the dialogical structure of the book, with instruction being provided in an informal, pleasant and open way by the Senator and the Count profiled as the representatives of the two classic statements of European philosophical and religious thought, of West and East, Orthodoxy and speculation, authority and freedom, complementing and amending one another's insufficiencies and biases, and thus uniting at the dawning of the Age of Reason against pure secular thought.[63]

Indeed with all this it is as though Maistre was imitating the divine pedagogical strategy of revelation by making the wealth of this religious and humanist heritage available for the future generations with a view to preserving the means necessary for them to achieve salvation and grow as spiritual creatures,[64] namely, divine knowledge of their origin and end.[65]

Still, the variety of accounts of Providence exposed in *Les Soirées* raises the question of whether for Maistre the doctrine of divine chastisements, primarily vindicated as it were by arguments of pedagogical convenience or utility, is anything more than a pious fraud. This issue, often raised in the course of Maistrian scholarship,[66] can be formulated as follows: is there a necessary relation between the convenience or utility of an opinion and its cognitive status? Is a useful opinion of necessity also true? All Maistrian scholars know by heart Maistre's response to this question, which is however much more subtle than some would like to have it.[67] In

63. In the eighth dialogue the Count says to the Chevalier that a conversation is better than reading a book as far as 'instruction is concerned, because it makes room for interruption, interrogation, and explanation'. *Les Soirées de Saint-Pétersbourg* in Glaudes (ed.) *Maistre: Œuvres*, p.686.

64. Here we are confronted with the very same scope or educational project of Pico della Mirandola's 900 theses, landmark of the spirit of Renaissance letters and scholarship. See Giovanni Pic de la Mirandole, *Œuvres philosophiques* (Paris, 2004).

65. This point regarding the sheer variety of religious representations present in Maistre's masterpiece appears to have been more or less clearly grasped by the Jesuit theologian P. Vallin in his assessment of the theology of *Les Soirées*. See '*Les Soirées* de Joseph de Maistre: une création théologique originale', in *Revue de sciences religieuses*, 74, no.3 (Paris, 1986), p.362. What Vallin has not grasped perhaps clearly enough was its distinctly pedagogical character.

66. Most recently by American scholar Owen Bradley, in *A Modern Maistre*.

67. *Les Soirées de Saint-Pétersbourg*, in Glaudes (ed.) *Maistre: Œuvres*, p.625: 'Nulle erreur ne peut être utile, comme nulle vérité peut nuire'.

fact the alternative has much more to do with our own way of thinking than with Maistre's, who, remotely inspired by the convertible character of the so-called transcendentals, the true, the beautiful and the good, took for granted the identification between the terms. It is we who, under the influence of modern scientific skepticism and the pessimist metaphysics of existential thought, find it hard to accept his supposedly naïve point of view, which is nevertheless the cornerstone of the whole classic, Socratic-Platonic way of philosophising.

But be that as it may, when it comes to the strictly pedagogical utility of a theological idea, as is the case here, and in the absence of a direct statement by Maistre to that effect, the answer must be sought in the writings of the undisputed father of the pedagogical tradition as regards divine Providence, namely, Origen, as recorded in Maistre's *Registres de lecture*.[68] There, comparing Jesus, the divine legislator, to Solon, the Athenian law-giver, Origen writes:

> As a certain legislator replied to the question of one who asked him whether he had enacted for his citizens the best laws, that he had not given them absolutely the best, but the best which they were capable of receiving; so it might be said by the Father of the Christian doctrine: 'I have given the best laws and instruction for the improvement of morals of which the many [*tá pollá*] were capable, not threatening sinners with imaginary labours and chastisements, but with such as are real, and necessary to be applied for the correction [*paideia*] of those who offer resistance, *although they do not at all understand the object of him who inflicts the punishment*, nor the effect of the labors'. For the doctrine of punishment is both attended with utility [*opheleia*] and is agreeable to truth, and is stated in obscure terms with advantage. [...] For we speak regarding Him [i.e. God] both what is true and what appears to be clear to the multitude, but not so clear to them as it is to those few who investigate the truths of the Gospel in a philosophical manner [the Christian *philosophoi*].[69]

In his work Origen deals at length with the issue of *opheleia* as it relates with the requirements of *paideia* or the divine education of man. It surely has to do with discourse, as it has been treated here, and at this level the useful is always identified with the true. And as far as the emendation of man's conduct and the care for his immortal soul is concerned, belief in a divine moral order is at least as important as this moral order itself. For if man does not believe in God's presence and action, if he is not *impressed*

---

68. 'Extraits A', p. 567. *Archives de Joseph de Maistre et de sa famille*, CD-ROM du fonds de Maistre (1996), Archives départementales de la Savoie.

69. *Contra Celsum*, III, 79, p.747-48. Italics are mine. In this same page of his *Registres*, Maistre reproduces another text by Origen which reference I was not able to trace. It reads thus: 'Nous croyons les peines dont nous menaçons les hommes nécessaires et peut-être utiles à ceux qui les souffrent'.

by the efficiency of His laws and decrees, how will he strive to change his ways as he is required to do? Moreover, the doctrine of divine chastisements is not, as already suggested, in any way incompatible with the pedagogical view, the latter being rather its interpretation, its highest interpretation as far as the understanding of God's intention in punishing is concerned. The plain notion of pious fraud, invented by the philosophers in their struggle with the religion of the polis and appropriated, in modern times, by the Averroist and Machiavellian traditions of the critique of religion,[70] is simply not applicable here, for wisdom – the command to speak to each one according to his capacity – can never be severed from the command of the truth.[71] The underlying idea is that truth has several, ever deeper layers and thus can be apprehended 'fully' in several degrees (or interpretations) by different kinds of persons in different stages of perfection.

Yet, there is still another level of meaning to the notion of *opheleia* or utility as applied to the pedagogical account of God's action, one that may serve to clarify the proper relation between the notion of a temporal rule of Providence and the spiritualistic perspective – divine education as the education of the soul – of which I spoke with regard to Plutarch and Plato. It has been hinted at a few pages earlier and has to do with the idea that God's chastisement in this life, being absolutely real, is *useful* in the highest possible degree for the perfection and elevation of spiritual, though sinful man, purifying and preparing him for life in the world to come. The representation of life in this world as a sorrowful, terrible reality, and of the so-called human condition as a most agonic (in the Greek sense of the word) experience, is familiar to every reader of Maistre's works. Everyone knows how dreadful, in the eyes of the Savoyard, life can be in this fallen state of things where 'all is violent and against nature', and many have chosen the easy way of blaming Maistre for what he thought he could not avoid seeing, confounding the sight with the object it grasps. Many have charged him with having perversely transformed the stage of human and natural existence into an ocean of blood and evils with a view to using it for the purposes of his authoritarian ideology; others have seen in his harsh picture of human existence as well as in his reflections on punishment and bloodshed either the signs of a disturbed and obsessive mind or of an oppressive childhood background, marred by constant representations of death, sin and guilt.[72] Few, however, have looked for the presence of an articulate

---

70. See especially Leo Strauss, *Spinoza's critique of religion* (Chicago, IL, 1997) and *Thoughts on Machiavelli* (Chicago, IL, 1978).

71. Jesus' parabolic way of speaking is one chief example of this.

72. For this background of Maistrian 'sensibility' see the important article by Darcel, 'Des

philosophy of the human condition that could clarify the intention behind Maistre's most terrible passages and even fewer, perhaps, have wondered whether this darker side of Maistre's reflections on human as well as natural history has anything to do with his concern for man.[73]

But this is just what we are likely to find when we look at Maistre from the perspective of the theological tradition to which he belongs. This claim has already been made in relation to the issue of Maistre's affiliation with the pedagogical spiritualist thought of Origen and Plutarch. Now it is time to dig further in our search for the deeper spirit of the theology of *Les Soirées*. Indeed it is my belief that as far as its theological content is concerned, this book must be read as a kind of modern restatement or re-elaboration of Origen's masterly attempt at developing a thorough theology of history from the point of view of God's revelation, being a re-enactment of the Alexandrian's speculations about the process through which all things fell to their present state from an initial unity in God and the ways in which a final return to unity shall be effected. I am referring to Origen's treatise *De principiis*. There is a host of strong indications of Maistre's intimate relationship with this work throughout his writings and *Registres de lecture*, but I believe that one key instance is sufficient to establish my point. Among the many citations from Origen in *Les Soirées* and the *Eclaircissiment sur les sacrifices* there is one in the tenth dialogue dealing with 'the end of all things' that stands apart for the similarity of argument and meaning it bears with its Origenist counterpart. In effect it is Maistre's appropriation of Origen's pedagogical and eschatological *pathos* in this key passage of the tenth *Soirée* that led me in the first place to look into the works of the great theologian of the third century for the key to Maistre's notion of the providential government of history.

Coming after an exposition by the Count in the ninth dialogue, about the inner *rationale* of sacrifices as reversibility of merits, that is the righteous paying for and therewith regenerating the sinner, the mystical Senator engages in an excursus on men's obsession with the idea of unity, speculating about the hidden solidarity of the human kind (as the ground of the reversibility) and picturing what it would be like at the end of all things, when 'God shall be all in all'. According to his expressed view,

---

Pénitents noirs à la franc-maçonnerie: aux sources de la sensibilité maistrienne', already cited.

73. The only one to my knowledge that nevertheless does mention it is Darcel, who says, against Berlin, that the harshest passages of the Savoyard writer 'should rather be interpreted within the framework of a Christian gnosis that is made up of orthodoxy and free intellectual speculation'. 'The roads of exile, 1792-1817', in Lebrun (ed.), *Maistre: life thought and influence*, p.29.

human history and even creation (that is, natural history), dispersed and fragmentary in the present state of affairs, would thus tend to a final unity in God brought about by edifying virtue and Christ's subjection of all things to the father, with humanity being built on the model of the body of Christ.

For the sake of both completeness and clarification, here is the full sequence of Maistre's eschatological argument taken from Paul and Origen as expressed in his endnote 14 to the tenth dialogue:

> Tous les hommes doivent donc croître ensemble pour ne faire qu'un seul corps par le Christ, qui en est la tête. Car nous sommes tous les membres de ce corps unique qui se forme et *s'édifie* par la charité, et ces membres reçoivent de leur chef l'esprit, la vie et l'accroissement, par le moyen des joinctures et des communications qui les unissent, et suivant la mesure qui est propre à chacun d'eux. (Ephesians 4:15-16, with many adaptations by Maistre).

'Et cette grande unité', Maistre goes on to say,

> est si fort le but de toute l'action divine par rapport à nous[74] '*que celui qui accomplit tout en tous, ne se trouvera lui-même accompli lorsqu'elle sera accomplie*'.[75] Et alors, c'est-à-dire à la fin des choses, *Dieu sera tout en tous.*[76] C'est ainsi que saint Paul commentait son maître; et Origène, à son tour, se demande ce que signifient ces paroles: *Dieu sera tout en tous*; et il répond: 'Je crois qu'elles signifient que Dieu sera aussi *tout dans chacun*, c'est-à-dire que chaque substance intelligente, étant parfaitement purifée, *toutes ses pensées seront Dieu*; elle ne pourra voir et comprendre que Dieu; elle possédera Dieu, et Dieu sera *tout en tous*; ainsi la fin des choses nous ramènera au point dont nous étions partis [...], lorsque la mort et le mal seront détruits; alors Dieu sera véritablement TOUT EN TOUS'.[77]

If one takes this picture as Maistre's last word about the end of history, in conceptual or theological – rather than historical – terms, one finds that *Les Soirées* recounts the whole history of the world and of the human kind in the Origenist fashion as a threefold process of unity, dispersion and, finally, return (*exitus/dispersio, conversio, reditus*) of all things to God. In technical terminology, history as the object of God's concern and the temporal rule of Providence is the process of *epistrophé* or return/conversion of fallen man and, with him, of all things back to the state of

---

74. Origen calls it God's *indesinenti opere*, the goal unceasingly pursued by the divinity. *De principiis*, I, 3, 8.
75. Ephesians 1:23.
76. I Corinthians 15:28.
77. *De Principiis* III, 6, 3 (Maistre misquotes as III, 4) quoted in *Les Soirées de Saint-Pétersbourg*, in Glaudes (ed.) *Maistre: Œuvres*, p.755 (n. 14) This passage from Origen is reproduced in Maistre's *Registres de lecture* together with other interesting considerations on the so-called 'last things'. See 'Extraits G', p.352, 355.

wholeness they had at the beginning when they were united with God. And if we return to Origen's *De principiis* (but also to the Greek Bible), where Maistre certainly drew his inspiration to compose *Les Soirées* as a theology of history,[78] we discover that this cosmic and historic process of return to primeval unity is really a divine education of mankind to be effected through suffering and pain. Because of the way things are (i.e., because of the fallen state of things) suffering and pain are conducive to perfection, to the realisation of that aim which is the end of both history and man.[79]

Indeed in his work *De principiis* Origen goes so far as to make the very principle of this 'life', the 'living principle' (the *psiquê*, which he sets apart from the rational soul or *nous*), the dreadful result of man's fall from his original condition as a purely disincarnate spiritual creature (a *logikon*, as he has it), something that defines without a shadow of a doubt the nature of 'life' in the world as the result of God's judgement over sinful, self-loving man.[80] No wonder that Maistre, after identifying life (*psiquê*) with blood in the *Eclaircissiment sur les sacrifices*, states, following 'ancient traditions', that the principle of life is guilty in itself and must thus be purified by the effusion of blood.[81] In this, as in many other instances, he is merely following the rationale of Origen's historical and cosmological account. The process of divine *paideia* is thus interpreted as essentially a *via purgativa*, a series of painful events by which God attempts to call man back from his estranged ways for the redemption of the whole world.[82] In spite of the widespread perception of Origen as a gentle humanist, in his account there is no redemption outside pain. For him it is as if pain were the natural byproduct of the soul's being progressively refined back to its 'natural' heavenly place by being severed from corporeal things. And the ultimate model for man's cooperation with this process, the ultimate divine teacher (in this particular sense) is, of course, Christ, whose subjection to the will of the father by the acceptance of a painful God-

---

78. This seems quite apparent to me although I reckon that only a thorough knowledge of both Origen's treatise and *Les Soirées* is able to entail full conviction about this point. This joint reading of both works was just what I did in my doctoral thesis 'Paidéia divina: formação e destinação do homem em Joseph de Maistre', Pontifícia Universidade Católica de São Paulo (PUC-SP), 2008.
79. See for instance *De Principiis*, II, 10, 6.
80. According to Origen, Man's fall was brought about by a defection of love towards God, described as a representation of man's self as the source of life while God is the veritable source. Thus he would have fallen from being a spirit (*nous*) to becoming a soul (*psiquê*) through a process of *cooling*, an interpretation attained through the analysis of the popular etymology of the word 'psiquê'. See *De Principiis*, II, 9, 6.
81. *Eclaircissiment sur les sacrifices* in Glaudes (ed.) *Maistre: Œuvres*, p.811.
82. The notion of cosmic redemption put forward by Maistre both in the *Eclaircissiment* and *Les Soirées* is distinctly Origenist.

designed destiny is the paradigm of human perfection. Indeed, as both the Pauline and the Origenist passages quoted by Maistre in the tenth dialogue clearly indicate, the end of all things will be brought about as a work of subjection of all things in Christ to the father. All things must subject themselves freely to Christ[83] as he himself obediently subjected himself freely to the father out of love so that 'God shall be all in all' and the beginning may resemble the end.[84]

It is in this deeper, more sublime sense of Origen's *apocatastasis* (i.e. the final restoration of all things) that one should understand Maistre's emphasis on voluntary sacrifice as the most powerful means for the collective redemption of the world, a means completely worthy of God, indeed the ultimate instance of divine *paideia*, for it is an appeal addressed to human freedom to grow back in love with God and accept the way things are as the result of his holiness, Wisdom and good will.[85] To make the pedagogical analogy complete, it suffices to point to the similarity between the example of Christ's self-subjection in the Incarnation and Passion and the Greek Bible's picture of the divine *paideia* on man's part as accepting the God-given yoke, an analogy which stresses even more the role of Christ as the supreme paradigm of man's education, in which model of submission and obedience rebellious humanity is summoned to realise its likeness to the creator and providential God.[86]

Assuming this kinship between Maistre's and Origen's theology of history leads to a more adequate understanding of the most controversial passages of *Les Soirées*, as well as of Maistre's theory of sacrifices and its place in the book's representation of human history. Accordingly, by assuming the pedagogical account of God's action as the general frame of Maistre's work, one is likely to arrive at a much more faithful representation of his rather sophisticated intellectual undertaking, of his attempt to draw a grandiose picture of the human condition that is

---

83. As according to Origen the stars and all heavenly bodies were supposed to have done.

84. See *De Principiis*, III, 5, 6. The fact that Maistre quotes *De Principiis* III, 6, 3 in a note to the tenth dialogue and hence that he accepted as authoritative Origen's account of the end of all things, may lead one to wonder whether he did not accept the other features of his predecessor's account about the beginning, like the notion of the pre-existence of souls, of corporeal existence as chastisement and so on. Indeed, in my view *Les Soirées* makes sense in theological terms only in the light of these most controversial tenets of Origen's thought. See *Les Soirées de Saint-Pétersbourg*, in Glaudes (ed.) *Maistre: Œuvres*, p.750.

85. And, conversely, of our base, fallen, sinful state. Moreover, it is at this point that the tradition of divine *paideia* meets with the so-called baroque spirituality of abandonment of oneself to God's Providence and imitation of Christ. On the influence of this spirituality on Maistre's background, see Darcel, 'Des Pénitents noirs à la franc-maçonnerie: Aux sources de la sensibilité maistrienne', already cited.

86. The fact that Christ was sinless and that he is himself God only puts further stresses on the greatness and wisdom of his *opus* to be followed by man.

unified and made meaningful from the 'point of view of God', that is by reference to mankind's divine origin and destination as derived from an esoteric reading of Holy Writ.

It would surely be excessive to try to develop here all the consequences of this Maistrian vision in all of his works. Still, I believe this much has to be said: Maistre's understanding of the workings of Providence in history as divine *paideia* is not only theological in the strict sense that points to salvation, but it provides him with a principle by which light he can read the whole of the human world – society, politics, language, public edu-cation – in a perspective that one might call, for lack of a better word, *theonomic*, meaning literally that God is taken as the measure of all things.[87] For Maistre, the belief that the *nomos* or the law of the human world is God-given implies more than the establishment of a so-called 'heter-onomy'. Because the divine *nomos* is also within man, corresponding, to a certain degree, to his true 'I', as Maistre says paraphrasing Plutarch, it is that 'I' that he must search in God's rule, as in a mirror. According to this view, fallen man must think of himself and his life in the light of a divine standard which is both within and beyond his own self.

Roughly speaking, this is the meaning of Maistre's 'theonomy'. It means God's rule not only of nature, but of society, of politics, of language, in a word, of history, of which the most apparent expression is constitution-making or the creation of the *human cosmos* around a centre that, as Plato saw it, must be divine to perseverate in being and is therefore only limitedly open to man's discretion.[88] And this creation of the human cosmos through God's often silent, but sometimes (as in the French Revolution) also *epoch-making* action over history corresponds actually to the creation of concrete, historical man, of this and that people or nation with their unique outlooks, which are designed to serve a providential purpose (again, such as France in the 'European' revol-ution) of which God only, in the unfathomable depths of His wisdom, is expected to know. As far as concrete, historical man is concerned, it suffices to learn that things in the world are really like that, that they attend to this divine pattern of continual creation, and that man, as God's image, is to *co-operate* instead of competing with Him, for only God is sovereign and all true power of creation comes from Him.[89]

In fact, by exploring Maistre's thought from the perspective of its

---

87. See Plato's *Laws*, IV, 716c.
88. In *metaphysical terms* the empire or sovereignty of the divine *nomos* in the human world must be understood in light of the doctrine of God as the unique source of being and thus the only one apt for true creation, as both the *Considérations sur la France* and the *Essai sur le principe générateur* everywhere suggest.
89. I deal with this historical formation of concrete man through society and its institutions in the second part of my thesis, named 'Providence and the forms of social power'.

pedagogical nature one is likely to challenge some of the most wide-spread and crystallised views about him such as the supposed irrationalism of his historical view of society, the 'obscurantism' of his Russian opuscules, and the perception of him as an enemy of human knowledge and science derived from his fierce attacks on modern scientism.[90] In a word, one is likely to discover a humanism in Maistre, a humanism in which man cannot, however, be the supreme measure. Take, for example, his insistence on order. As far as I can see it means chiefly that man is a God-like spiritual creature that should live in an order that is fit to his nature and destiny, a sacred order where he can be enlightened as to the truth, the whole truth about his origin, present state and end, a providential order that is supposed to be able to lead individual men and mankind as a whole to their fullness and ultimate perfection – which is to be close to God, to hold on to him through the divine seat in man, man's *logos* or rational soul. Thus, Maistre's obsession with order can be viewed as being in full harmony with the pedagogical account of his thought, and as another dimension of his attempt at educating his own 'disenchanted' times.

That Maistre conceived of an Enlightenment of his own out of his concern for man and his attachment to the notion of a religious tradition seems evident from this perspective. And if it can be seen as a 'Counter-Enlightenment', it is certainly not in Isaiah Berlin's terms, but in the sense of a religious, particularly Christian Enlightenment as opposed to the philosophic one which Maistre would rather call obfuscation, for in his view it 'debases' and 'degrades' man (degrading his 'celestial', meta-physical intelligence, as mere 'reason'), making him forgetful of his nature, of his true origin and end.

In view of all this one cannot help but find ironic the common view that associates Maistre's stress on politics and social thought with plain Machiavellianism on account of its allegedly 'experimental' nature. For whatever the value one may wish to attribute to the particular tenets of his thought, the notion of an elevation of man in the model of the God-man Christ understood as the divine *logos* in nature, society and history – as the Wisdom in which God created the world, the Word through which He spoke to the prophets and the Justice with which He rules both nature and history – this notion of man's elevation, as was already the case with the Christian humanists of the Renaissance, is absolutely central to the message that Maistre as a pedagogue sought to convey to the unknown pupils who were awaiting him in a brave new world.

90. Indeed it suffices to take a look at the curriculum he recommended – in his *Lettres sur l'éducation publique en Russie* in *OC*, vol.8, p.163-232 – to be sure that only those who are already convinced of the truth of the Enlightenment and of the exclusive character of modern scientific 'rationality' can characterise Maistre as an 'irrationalist'.

# Conclusion

## CAROLINA ARMENTEROS

## I

It should now be possible to begin answering two of the questions that opened this volume: how does Maistre stand in relation to the Enlightenment, the Counter-Enlightenment and tradition? What do Maistrian studies bring to the wider fields of Enlightenment and Counter-Enlightenment studies? And what is their relevance to our own day?

The articles by Darrin McMahon, Joseph Eaton and Jean-Yves Pranchère that comprise the book's first section show us Maistre as the soldier of the Counter-Enlightenment. Whether lending infernal qualities to genius, predicting that Washington would only be a phantom city or portraying history as fundamentally obscure, Maistre rebels against the spirit of his century. He is the irritating subverter of dominant paradigms; the systematic nay-sayer who exchanges hope for despair and idyllic visions for doom; the foremost expert of antithesis who seems to excel at one thing – denying enthusiastically what everyone else is only too avid to believe.

Yet, as these articles also show, the method is neither so simple nor the antithesis so pure. For Maistre's genius – uncultivated, unconscious, divinely endowed – is very much like the one Diderot described in the *Encyclopédie*; his condemnation of America's natives and foundling republic derives from the same kind of naturalistic reasoning and practical considerations that spawned Buffon's science and *The Federalist papers*; and his declaration that history is murky is indispensable to his attempt to make it rationally understandable.

*Sapere aude!* was the cry with which Kant classically summarised the Enlightenment; and Maistre always answered it with a passion. His notebooks attest that from adolescence onwards he was driven by a consuming desire to know – a desire that the Revolution turned into a desperate need and the *sine qua non* of spiritual survival. So of what, then, did Maistre's Counter-Enlightenment consist? The articles in Part I of this volume suggest that, at its core, it was a critique of a conceit that Maistre believed to be specific to *philosophie*. This variety of arrogance made two major claims. It preached, first of all, that humanity could ultimately know everything – whether it was the order of the natural world or the mechanisms of government. Secondly, it led people to believe that their knowledge sufficed to recreate society and politics anew, and perhaps even the natural world.

Against the compulsion to know everything, Maistre insists that not everything is knowable. The problem is not solely epistemological. It is not just a matter of the limitations of the human mind, of the fact that some of the knowledge objectively available in the world is inaccessible to people due to the partiality of the human condition.[1] At bottom, the real issue is ontological. People cannot know everything because some things – like history – are *intrinsically* obscure. The whole point of their being is that they cannot be fully known, under any circumstances.

And yet this is a source of hope, because the human consciousness of obscurity generates knowledge and reason. Recognising the obstacles to enlightenment, Maistre suggests, is enlightening, but in ways that – paradoxically – are at once completely removed from, and identical to, those proposed by the radical Enlightenment. The emphasis on restrictions simultaneously runs counter to philosophic transparency and converges with *philosophie*'s aims, striving to facilitate progress toward the highest kind of understanding of which humanity is capable. In revealing the paradoxes that produce history, the historical chiaroscuro improves our ability to give a rational account of history. And in insisting that our ignorance is actually constitutive of the world, it takes Enlightenment rationalism to new levels.

To counter the argument of some Enlightenment thinkers that human knowledge suffices to reorganise society, politics and nature, Maistre also critiqued reason. But he did not quarrel with reason per se, only with the *a priori* and critical variety of it prized by the *Encyclopédistes*. Unbearably narcissistic, maddeningly full of itself, this 'Reason' was a blindfolded pretender who presumed to knock down and discard the edifices built by all those who differed from itself. Setting out self-assuredly to set minds on fire, it aspired, in reality, to reduce humanity to the most savage ignorance. The logical result of so much benightedness was the murderous violence of the age.

If Maistre persisted in championing obscurity, then, it was to sharpen true reason, increase knowledge and prevent it from being used to serve a lonely and destructive pride. This was the tenor of his variety of Counter-Enlightenment. The articles in Part I of this book illustrate this in different ways. Whether in defining genius as a grace, warning against the *ex nihilo* efforts of America's Founding Fathers, or pointing out that

---

1.   Maistre also used this argument in *Les Soirées*, suggesting that each species understands the world according to the sphere it occupies in the hierarchy of being. See especially Maistre, *Les Soirées de Saint-Pétersbourg*, in Glaudes (ed.), *Maistre: Œuvres*, p.738.

only the greyness of history can make its content visible, Maistre was defending the wisdom – and the rationality – of modesty. He was reminding his readers that the path to truth is never solitary, and that we need assistance in order to discover.

## II

Critiquing the radical Enlightenment stimulated Maistre to posit his own, alternative responses to it. The *Encyclopédie*'s militant empiricism threw him into Plato's arms. The ancient alliance between Platonism and Christianity was reborn in his thought with new consequences. As Philippe Barthelet recounts, the innatism of the Cambridge Platonists became Maistre's weapon against the Baconian empiricism the *Encyclopédie* had deified. Platonism put yet another damper on philosophic hubris, on the idea that we can acquire true knowledge *ad infinitum* and utterly on our own. More importantly, Platonism made it possible to Christianise the Enlightenment. *Philosophie* was proud of itself because it could account for nature rationally. It could expel God and final causes from philosophic inquiry and re-focus attention on natural, secondary causes. A goddess reborn, nature emerged as the long-buried cause of phenomena, the benevolent force that enabled all progress once its secrets were revealed and released; while the God of traditional theology appeared as the malignant obscurer of everything that could make humanity happy and free.

The best way of defeating this narrative was to show, firstly, that Christianity was thoroughly capable of knowing nature, and, secondly, that it could do so without the Aristotelianism that had made Aquinas – and that Bacon and the *philosophes* abhorred. The Jesuits had done something similar when fighting the early radical Enlightenment with more empirically describable notions of nature and natural law.[2] But what was exciting about the Cambridge Platonists was that their Christian naturalism, indebted to Augustine and the Neoplatonists, was unrelated to Aristotle. More dangerously from a Christian point of view – yet more helpfully for Maistre's quest – this naturalism broke through the wall that Augustine had built between the City of God and the Earthly City. Reason now served not only to support faith and define dogma, but also to describe nature in a world permeated with God. Cambridge Platonism showed, in short, that it was possible to regulate nature without abandoning the Divinity – indeed, that one could draw

---

2. See Palmer, *Catholics and unbelievers*, and Catherine M. Northeast, *The Parisian Jesuits and the Enlightenment 1700-62* (Oxford, 1991).

close to God through nature; and that Christianity had long met the criteria the Enlightenment professed to have invented.

The ambition to demonstrate this drove Maistre from the beginning of his writing career, when he composed the essays on Rousseau in an anxious attempt to understand the Terror. As I try to show in my article, the Christian idea of conscience served as a bridge between divine transcendence and naturalist description for both Maistre and Rousseau. In the confession of faith of the Savoyard vicar, conscience was a form of reason, a psychological rendition of natural law. It extended to the collective to form the 'personne morale' of society, and the 'esprit' of social groups. Like individuals, the 'personne' and the 'esprit' could recognise the good, showing understanding; they could produce it, exercising virtue; or they could reject it, becoming guilty. This was Rousseau's *tour de force* – that he conjured society as a new nature, describable and accessible to reason, thus making sociology possible; but that, simultaneously, he presented it as the offspring of conscience, the producer of reason and the mover of the moral world.

More precise than the Savoyard vicar's, Maistre's conscience explicitly collapses natural reason onto the divine will. Concomitantly, the social groups that for him derive from conscience can be detailed even more exactly than Rousseau's society. In fact, they are even more Enlightened – if the empiricist impulse is a component of Enlightenment – since, varied, multiple and specific, they offer a wealth of concrete facts for analysis. The catch is that, because God now *is* nature and reason, *philosophie* is stabbed in the process – but only because it posits a departed God.

A familiar paradox ensues. Being divine, reason's power is unbounded, as the Enlightenment decreed. Yet, being natural, reason is limited by law. Yannis Constantinidès' article suggests that reason is inherent to the quasi-mystical illumination, to the divine revolution that will redeem humanity at the end of time, and that Maistre opposes to *philosophie*'s rationalistic critique. At the same time, though, the reason of illumination is constrained and subordinate to intuition. For Maistre as for Hume, reason is the servant rather than the ruler of the passions.

Since, however, intuition can apprehend truth systematically, it is actually a functional equivalent – if not another name – for *a posteriori* reason. This defense of intuition-as-reason placed Maistre in a characteristically ambiguous relationship to the Enlightenment. On the one hand, championing intuition as the ultimate reason was an insult to *philosophie*. On the other, it was a way of heeding faithfully the Enlightened urging that all truth be rational. As always, the ultimate goal was to harmonise with the century while reaching out to Christianity. If intuition was where reason and divine *voluntas* met, then one could keep *philosophie* company while sneaking away from it. Even more: one could intimate that *philosophie* was too weak to meet its own standards, because there was another reason it ignored, a reason higher, more productive and closer to the truth, than the reason of critique.

# III

Insofar as he sometimes rejected the methods *and* the goals of the Enlightenment, Maistre was a Romantic. This is what Douglas Hedley emphasises when reclaiming him for tradition and Christian Neoplatonism. Although he avoided any definitive pronouncements on the ultimate extent of evil's empire, Maistre proposed that the link between the transcendent and human experience is measurably manifested in sacrifice and the reversibility of merits. It was his way of dodging the naturalist and apophatic positions, along with the propositions deriving from them – that evil does not exist; that God himself is evil; and that God is utterly unknowable. Concomitantly, he restored a deep concern with human suffering and pain to the heart of philosophy. He did this in conscious opposition to *philosophie*'s abandonment of the problem of theodicy. But he did it also with a rationalist optimism in humanity's capacity to improve itself through time that seemed to exceed *philosophie*.

Maistre's more usual tendency to replicate the Enlightenment subversively returned in his struggle against Gallicanism. As Emile Perreau-Saussine suggests, Maistrian theocracy tried to achieve the very last thing of which anyone could suspect it: political liberation. This fact seems less counter-intuitive when considering that Gallicanism was closely associated with an Enlightened libertarianism that, in vindicating the freedom of the *parlements* and of Christian principle against king and pope, generated the revolutionary libertarianism[3] that attempted to guarantee national freedom by removing the religious sources of political authority. Maistre's originality was to realise that this supposedly emancipating elimination could render the secular state almighty – a total state, unprecedentedly despotic – by releasing it completely from the moral ties of Christianity.

From this perspective, politicising the Church and bestowing functions of constitutional revision on the papacy appear not as hopelessly delusional, reactionary propositions, but as dually rational and revolutionary attempts to check state power with new means. After all,

---

3.  See Van Kley, *The Religious origins of the French Revolution*.

historically, preventing revolution had never been the official papal task that *Du Pape* envisioned. The trick for Maistre – and, interestingly, for Saint-Simon[4] – was to restore the tenuous yet socially conserving power balance between Church and state that had characterised European culture and politics since the Middle Ages, and that the French Revolution had broken. The only means Maistre found to accomplish this was to reintroduce religion into civil society, and to ask the Pope to intervene in times of political crisis. Only so could liberty be rescued, à la Montesquieu, by setting authority against authority.

When he adapted Origen, Maistre again mobilised religion to topple *philosophie* while serving the latter's ends better than itself. Given this peculiar talent, Maistre has sometimes been reproached in Catholic circles for his dubious theology and his concessions to his century. Elaborating on this fact, Aimee Barbeau suggests that the deist overtones in Maistre's thought result not so much from a weakness for heterodoxy, or a willingness to be seduced by secularity; but from his resourceful recourse to the magnificent arsenal of intellectual weapons that Christianity had stocked across the centuries to defend itself.

The saying goes that the devil's most dangerous trick is to pretend that he does not exist; and Maistre's most effective strategy against the Enlightenment was to intimate that it was all make-believe. He loved to find traditional counterparts for *philosophie*'s pet ideas because nothing was more useful to him than to show that the radical Enlightenment had invented nothing, that it was as sterile and impotent as its destructive rage, and that all the themes it proclaimed to be its own were age-old and had found better expressions and more reflective advocates. His intellectual moves and polemical pronouncements were in perfect harmony on this point. He consistently distinguished the eighteenth century from its predecessor on the basis of their relative creativity. Concerned with metaphysics and abundant in theology, the *Grand Siècle* was a great age of invention. Its illustrious thinkers had had no need to write voluminously: sober brevity sufficed for their discoveries to make a lasting impression. The frivolous and godless eighteenth century, by contrast, was powerless to invent. Its sole ability was to dissert capaciously on the knowledge earned by prior ages, and to say that it was all its own.[5] Hence Maistre's turn to Origen[6]: for even a thinker as

---

4.  The idea that temporal and spiritual powers should combine to run society and that the 'crisis' of the nineteenth century originated in the Revolution's severing of the combination was central to the philosophy of Saint-Simon and the Saint-Simonians.
5.  See Maistre, *Examen de la philosophie de Bacon*, in *OC*, vol.6, p.455-60.
6.  On Origen's influence on Maistre, see Marc Froidefont, 'Joseph de Maistre, lecteur d'Origène' in *Autour de Joseph et Xavier de Maistre. Mélanges pour Jean-Louis Darcel*, ed. Michel Kohlhauer (Chambéry, 2007), p.109-18.

seemingly far removed from the Enlightenment as an Alexandrian Neoplatonist could offer ideas very much in tune with its claims.

Origen, the expert on divine education, re-emerges in the article by Elcio Verçosa Filho as the very key to Maistrian thought. Because, philosophically, everything, all of life, can be considered an education, divine *paideia* encapsulates Maistrian thought as an account of humanity's tutoring by Providence and schooling by established religion. The parallel with the Enlightenment is apparent when considering that, for the *philosophes*, humanity can progress morally and scientifically toward greater happiness thanks to the accumulation of experience. *Paideia* too operates progressively insofar as humanity perfects itself, learns about itself, and advances toward the good through the rewards and punishments that God allots across time, in keeping with justice and human discernment.

Maistre, then, may have been an innatist inspired by Descartes and Malebranche, but he agreed with the Enlightenment that humanity must improve itself morally through experience. The purpose of this improvement, in addition, is not only spiritual salvation, but also worldly happiness. Moral belief has to have practical yields. This anti-Augustinian concern with the world explains why Origen first appears in Maistre's notebooks in 1797, the year that he published the *Considérations sur la France* and was putting the finishing touches to his core political thought. Scion of a distant Christian family, Origen had never followed Augustine in his rejection of the world. This fact acquired new uses in the aftermath of the Terror, because salvaging Christian Europe then meant searching not only in its classics, but also in the ancient traditions that had remained foreign to its making. The radical Enlightenment had been the heir and the enemy of Augustine. To do away with it, to shatter its logic, one could hence seek out one of the Christian adversaries against whom Augustine had founded the philosophy of European Christendom. That the adversary in question loved the world that the Enlightenment purported to rescue only made him a more desirable ally. In fact, thanks to him, *philosophie* could be at once beaten and surpassed.

Whether Maistre did well or failed in this gamble is a matter of opinion. Judging, however, by the enduring interest of his solution, by its apparently endless ability to tease and play with the Enlightenment – now mimicking it, now adopting it, now subverting it, now denouncing it, now forcing it to reach its own unspeakable and unforeseen conclusions – it was a smashing success.

# IV

Maistre addresses questions urgent in our own day. The confrontation between tradition – especially religious tradition – and modernity has come to the fore again after the Cold War with the rise of Islam as the Occident's new cultural challenger, and with the influx of populations from traditional societies (Arabs, Hispanics) into the countries of the North Atlantic world. In this context, Maistre's thought suggests that the confrontation between modernity and tradition, especially religious tradition, can be, more than a reason for regret, a fruitful and creative dialogue. Although he himself presented his own relationship with the Enlightenment as a struggle between two mortal foes, yet he spoke to his foe in its own language. The great irony was that this conversation with modernity was established thanks largely to the tools provided by the Western philosophy that had the deepest roots in antiquity. The articles in this volume are the first to demonstrate that Platonism, ancient and modern, orthodox and Alexandrian, was a deep source of Maistre's thought that flowed from his pen in radically modern and powerfully polemical springs.

A master of paradoxes, Maistre had a talent for identifying the points where tradition and modernity could meet. He was gifted for reversing expectations, using modern concepts to support traditional arguments, and traditional arguments to simulate and partake in modernity. In enlisting Origen – arguably the greatest theologian of antiquity[7] – to assist him in this task, Maistre showed also that ancient and religious authors can, when adeptly reused, obtain strikingly modern voices, to the point of becoming hyper-modern. Indeed Maistre's case shows that, when examined with an eye to shared goals, the difference between tradition and modernity is not invariably discernible. After all, tradition is in a constant state of change, and modernity itself has created its own set of traditions, so that speaking of a confrontation can sometimes be fallacious, and that often the real problem is understanding how, when and where the two collapse onto one another.

What is certain is that the new philosophy that appeared on the European intellectual scene during 1797-1821 was an extremely rich synthesis that was not always what it seemed. It took the form of political opinions and mystical doctrines drawn from history, of reflections on the laws governing the development of nature and nations. It was eloquent and erudite, mystical and worldly, inspired by a wealth of sources – classical, esoteric, theological, philosophical. It was nostalgic for Stoic antiquity and the Christian middle ages, for the *Grand Siècle* and its cult of taste, appearance and moralism. It denounced the vanities of discourse and philosophy, and was everywhere followed by philosophical specu-lations straddling national, political and disciplinary boundaries. It

---

7. With Augustine being the greatest *thinker*.

presented itself as the aged, faithful keeper of a past irretrievably lost, and the avowed enemy of everything that had destroyed that past. But the guardians of tradition who warily dispersed its brilliant phrases – and the heirs of *philosophie* who used it to prophesy a future filled with promise – all somehow knew that, in its heart of hearts, it was the youngest child of the Enlightenment.

# Summaries

The genius of Maistre
*Darrin M. McMahon*

This article discusses Maistre's thinking about the important eighteenth-century concept of genius. While Maistre's own thinking about genius was in many ways consistent with received attitudes of the time, it is also shown to be innovative and prescient. With characteristic acuity, Maistre perceived the dangers of investing human beings with what, in effect, was a quasi-religious power. And though his own thought was not without a certain longing for genius of this very kind, in the end he mounts a powerful critique of the genius figure as a new type of modern idol.

'This babe-in-arms': Joseph de Maistre's critique of America
*Joseph Eaton*

Joseph de Maistre's commentary on America, though sparse, provides a window into his broader political philosophy. Rather than attributing New World inferiority to a degeneracy of nature, like his Francophone contemporaries, Maistre explained that America's indigenous peoples suffered from the immorality of an ancient chieftain, the former British colonists from the sin of republicanism. Maistre's understanding of the United States supported his views of recent European history; the fledgeling republic was no proof of the durability of republican government. Rather than forming a coherent anti-Americanism, Maistre's ideas about America were supportive of his condemnation of the French Revolution.

The negative of the Enlightenment, the positive of order and the impossible positivity of history
*Jean-Yves Pranchère*

Maistre's thought can be described as a political theology, pointing out monarchy as the only political order consistent with the divine law, denouncing the French Revolution as an insurrection against God, aiming at restoring the religious foundations of sovereignty. For such a political theology, the so-called Enlightenment, with its purely sceptical and negative contents, means a dismissal of the true powers of reason. Reason is order. It appears however that the meaning of the theological-political order is in expectation of an unpredictable divine event to come. Maistrian conservatism is grounded in the eschatological reserve of the time.

## The Cambridge Platonists mirrored by Joseph de Maistre
*Philippe Barthelet*

Joseph de Maistre read very early and with great attention the Cambridge Platonists, in particular Henry More and Ralph Cudworth. English Platonism as a source of Maistre's thought seems to have been underestimated by his commentators up to now. By re-evaluating this original and capital contribution we would like to show all that Maistre's 'integral Platonism' – as it is seen in particular at the end of *Les Soirées de Saint-Pétersbourg* – owes to the bold syntheses of his Cambridge masters (and especially to the Hebraistic cabbalist Cudworth), masters with whom he shared the same metaphysical curiosity within an indefectibly Christian perspective and the same optimistic epistemology.

## Maistre's Rousseaus
*Carolina Armenteros*

Whereas previous research has suggested that Maistre's attitudes to Jean-Jacques Rousseau (1712-1778) first formed in response to the French Revolution, this article argues that Maistre made up his mind on Rousseau long before the Terror, when he first read *Emile* (1762) as an adolescent or young adult in the 1770s. Maistre's family archives also reveal that his intellectual engagement with Rousseau centred always on religion and remained unaltered across the revolutionary divide, informing his thought from his early youth until his death. Indeed many of Maistre's core reflections, from his ideas on sacrifice and pedagogy to his final Ultramontanism, can be interpreted as the result of dialogues with the Rousseauian personas that persistently haunted his thought. This article identifies these personas with the dual purpose of enhancing our understanding of Maistre's intentions as a social, political and educational writer, and of tracing Rousseau's nineteenth-century posterity. The Counter-Revolution emerges in the process as a key preserver and transmitter of Rousseau's philosophy.

## Two great enemies of the Enlightenment: Joseph de Maistre and Schopenhauer
*Yannis Constantinidès*

Though Schopenhauer most probably did not read Maistre, his critique of the Enlightenment's generous but naïve ideals is very similar to that of the Count. Both share a disbelief in mankind and in the liberating power of reason and both highlight the role that evil plays in the universe. Their tragic worldviews include however a horizon of hope: salvation is possible for humanity on condition that it renounces its dreams of self-fulfillment. Maistre expected a divine revolution that would overcome the 'satanic' one while Schopenhauer thought that the will to live would suppress itself once it gained full consciousness of its dark essence.

Enigmatic images of an invisible world: sacrifice, suffering and theodicy in Joseph de Maistre
*Douglas Hedley*

This article analyses the concept of sacrifice within the broader concerns of Maistre's thought, especially his theodicy. In this way it offers a critique of Owen Bradley's powerful and illuminating 'modern' or post-modern reading of Maistre, but also a critique of the view that Maistre is a mere traditionalist or reactionary. Maistre is a distinctively Romantic thinker in that he exhibits both a sensitivity to cultural specificity and the significance of history (i.e. modern) and yet an insistence upon the ineluctably transcendent dimension of the human (i.e. traditional). This is a characteristically nineteenth-century combination. Hence it is quite wrong to see his thoughts on sacrifice as essentially sociological, even though Maistre is a genuine precursor of the sociologists of religion. While his work on sacrifice exhibits his interest in the historical institutions and rituals of human society, Maistre is nevertheless obsessed with sacrifice as an index of mankind's abiding dual nature and the problem of transcendence. Evil is not a hindrance to divine design and purpose but makes the divine presence clearer. It shows the necessity of sacrifice as expiation and substitution. On this account, Maistre quite naturally appeals to Origen rather than Augustine because the former is a proponent of a metaphysics of freedom. As such it contrasts with Augustine's emphasis upon arbitrary and inscrutable Divine will, a trait reinforced in his Protestant and Jansenist followers. However showing in its style, rhetoric and argumentative details, Maistre's general theodicy can be reasonably placed within a strand of Christian Platonism from Dante to Dostoyevsky, one that confronts with brilliance and verve the problem of Divine justice and innocent suffering.

Why Maistre became Ultramontane
*Emile Perreau-Saussine*

Why did Joseph de Maistre become Ultramontane? First, he thought that the Gallican separation of the temporal and the spiritual foreshadowed the Revolution. Maistre detected a real direct continuity between Gallicanism and liberalism – a continuity that he deplored with the utmost energy. Second, Gallicans had recognised the legitimacy of the state that granted the Church a privileged status. But what were the reasons for recognising a state that no longer granted such a status? Maistre thought that it was no longer possible to remain attached to Gallicanism. He went to seek in Rome the constraints and the moral direction that an apparently de-Christianised state could no longer guarantee.

### The Savoyard philosopher: deist or Neoplatonist?
*Aimee E. Barbeau*

This article addresses Maistre's relationship to the religious thought of the Enlightenment. But to adequately parse out this connection, Maistre's debt to the Neoplatonist tradition – received via Origen – must be assessed. I argue that these two influences need not be mutually exclusive, but rather serve to illuminate the complexity of Maistre's religious and political thought. Specifically, with respect to providence, soteriology, and the relationship between church and state, Maistre adapts Origen's theology to address the political concerns of the Enlightenment. To put it differently, Maistre's politicisation of Origen's theology indicates his engagement with the Enlightenment on its own terms.

### The pedagogical nature of Maistre's thought
*Elcio Verçosa Filho*

This article argues for the validity of a global interpretation of Maistre's thought from the perspective of religion, claiming that the various fields that make up his intellectual undertaking should be brought down to the common ground of a long-standing concern for man and his education as a spiritual creature. The contention is that the primary subject of Maistre's major works is the replication of God's providential education of mankind in the discussion of God's presence in the multiple realms that make up Human culture, giving rise to a religious Enlightenment designed to counter the secular Enlightenment that ravaged his time.

# Bibliography

## Primary sources

Addison, Joseph, *Spectator* 160 (3 September 1711).

*Archives de Joseph de Maistre et de sa famille*, CD-ROM du Fonds de Maistre, Archives départementales de la Savoie, 1996.

Augustine, *Concerning the city of God against the pagans*, trans. Henry Bettenson (London, 2003).

Barbey d'Aurevilly, Jules, *Œuvre critique*, ed. Pierre Glaudes and Catherine Mayaux, 3 vol. (Paris, 2004-2007).

Blacas, Pierre Louis Jean Casimir de and Joseph de Maistre, *Joseph de Maistre et Blacas: leur correspondance inédite et l'histoire de leur amitié, 1804-1820*, ed. Ernest Daudet (Paris, 1908).

Bossuet, Jacques-Bénigne, *Défense de la déclaration de l'assemblée du clergé de France de 1682* (Amsterdam, Campagnie des Libraires, 1745).

–, *Politique tirée de l'Ecriture sainte* (1709).

Brownson, Orestes, Review of 'Essay on the generative principle of political constitutions', *Brownson's quarterly review* 1 (October 1847).

Cassirer, Ernst, *Die platonische Renaissance in England und die Schule von Cambridge* (Leipzig, Berlin, 1932).

Cawdrey, Robert, *A Table alphabetical of hard usual English words* (1604), a facsimile reproduction with an introduction by Robert A. Peters (Gainesville, FL, 1966).

Coleridge, Samuel, *Biographia literaria*, ed. J. Shawcross, 2 vol. (Oxford, 1907).

Comte, Auguste, *Cours de philosophie positive* (Paris, 1975).

Crèvecoeur, J. Hector St. John de, *Letters from an American farmer*, ed. Susan Manning (Oxford, 1999).

Cudworth, Ralph, *Systema intellectuale hujus universi* (Leiden, 1773).

–, *Traité de morale/Traité du libre-arbitre*, ed. and trans. J-.L. Breteau ('Fondements de la politique', Paris, 1995).

–, *Treatise concerning eternal and immutable morality* (London, J. & J. Knapton, 1731).

Dante, *The Divine comedy*, 3 Paradiso (Oxford, 1939).

Descartes, René, *Correspondance avec Arnauld et Morus*, ed. G. Lewis (Paris, 1953).

–, *Méditations métaphysiques* (1641).

*Dictionnaire de l'Académie françoise*, 2 vol. (1694).

*Dictionnaire universel, contenant généralement tous les mots français tant vieux que modernes et les termes de toutes les sciences et les arts* (1690), Slatkine reprint edition, 2 vol. (Geneva, 1970).

Dostoyevsky, Fyodor, *Crime and punishment*, trans. D. McDuff (Harmondsworth, 1991).

Enfantin, Barthélémy-Prosper, *Economie politique et politique: articles extraits du Globe* (Paris, 1831).

Fèvre, Monseigneur Justin Louis Pierre, *Histoire critique du catholicisme libéral jusqu'au pontificat de Léon XIII* (Saint-Dizier, 1897).

Flower, Richard, *Letters from Lexington and the Illinois* (1819).

Gentillet, Innocent, *Discours d'état sur les moyens de bien gouverner* (Geneva, 1576).

Gravelle, François de, *Politiques royales* (Lyon, J. Périer 1596).

Hitler, Adolf, *Mein Kampf: Entstehung, Aufbau, Stil, Änderungen, Quellen, Quellenwert, kommentierte Auszüge*, ed. Werner Masser (München and Esslingen, 1966).

–, *Mein Kampf*, trans. Ralph Mannheim (London, 1969).

Hume, David, *Dialogues concerning natural religion* (1779).

Lamennais, Félicité, *Des Progrès de la révolution et de la guerre contre l'Eglise* (Paris, 1829).

–, *Œuvres complètes*, 21 vol. (Reprint, Geneva, 1981).

Lamartine, Alphonse de, *Les Confidences* (Paris, 1879).

–, *Cours familier de littérature* (Paris, 1859).

Leclerc, Georges-Louis, Comte de Buffon, *Histoire naturelle, générale et particulière, avec la description du cabinet du roi*, 36 vol. (Paris, De l'Imprimerie royale, 1749).

Locke, John, 'The reasonableness of Christianity', in *Readings in the history of Christianity*, ed. William C. Placher (Philadelphia, PA, 1988).

Maistre, Joseph de, *Against Rousseau: 'On the state of nature' and 'On the sovereignty of the people'*, trans. and ed. Richard A. Lebrun (Montreal & Kingston, 1996).

–, *Considerations on France*, trans. and ed. Richard A. Lebrun (Cambridge, 1994).

–, *Contre Rousseau* (De l'Etat de nature) ed. Yannis Constantidès (Paris, 2008).

–, *De l'Etat de nature*, ed. Jean-Louis Darcel, *Revue des études maistriennes* 2 (1976).

–, *An Examination of the philosophy of Bacon*, trans. and ed. Richard Lebrun (Montreal and Kingston, 1998).

–, *De la Souveraineté du peuple: un anti-contrat social*, ed. Jean-Louis Darcel (Paris, 1992).

–, *Du Pape*, ed. by Jacques Lovie and Joannès Chetail (Geneva, 1966).

–, *Joseph de Maistre: Œuvres, suivies d'un dictionnaire Joseph de Maistre*, ed. Pierre Glaudes (Paris, 2007).

–, *Lettres et opuscules inédits* (Paris, 1851).

–, *Mémoire au duc de Brunswick*, in *Ecrits maçonniques de Joseph de Maistre et de quelques-uns de ses amis franc-maçons*, ed. J. Rebotton (Geneva, 1983).

–, *Œuvres complètes*, 14 vol. (Lyons, 1884-1887).

–, *Les Soirées de Saint-Pétersbourg*, ed. Jean-Louis Darcel (Geneva, 1993).

–, *St Petersburg Dialogues*, tr. Richard A. Lebrun (Montreal and Kingston, 1993).

–, 'Sur la Philosophie de Kant (Notes de lecture), Analyse du livre de M. Villiers intitulé Philosophie de Kant ou Principes fondamentaux de la philosophie transcendantale, traduit de l'anglais de l'Edinburgh review, tome I, janvier 1803, no. 3, pp. 352 ff', ed. Yves Madouas, in Barthelet, Philippe, ed., *Joseph de Maistre*, Les Dossiers H (Lausanne, 2005), p.223-48.

–, *The Collected works of Joseph de Maistre*, ed. Richard Lebrun, (InteLex Past Masters Online Database, 2010).

Malebranche, Nicolas, *De la Recherche de la vérité* (1674-1675).

–, *Traité de morale* (1684).

Mallet du Pan, Jacques, *Mémoires et correspondance pour servir à l'histoire de la Révolution française*, 2 vol. (Paris, 1851).

Maultrot, Jabineau, *Mémoire à consulter et consultation sur la compétence de la puissance temporelle, relativement à l'érection et suppression des sièges épiscopaux* (Paris, Desaint, 1790).

Milton, John, *Areopagitica, a speech of Mr. John Milton for the liberty of vnlicens'd printing, to the Parliament of England* (London, 1644).

More, Henry, *An Antidote against atheism, or an appeal to the natural faculties of the mind of man, whether there be not a God* (London, 1652).

–, *A Collection of several philosophical writings of Dr Henry More* (London, James Flesher, 1662).

–, *Enchiridion metaphysicum, sive de rebus incorporeis succincta et luculenta Dissertatio* (London, G. Morden, 1671).

–, *An Explanation of the grand mystery of Godliness* (London, 1660).

–, *The Immortality of the soul, so fare forth as it is demonstrable from the knowledge of nature and the light of reason*, Book II, Chap.3, sect.11, p.74 in *A Collection of several philosophical writings of Dr Henry More* (London, James Flesher, 1662).

–, *Opera theologica* (London, Johan Martyn and Gualten Kettilby, 1675).

Newman, John Henry, *An Essay in aid of a grammar of assent*, edited with an introduction and notes by I. T. Ker (Reprint, Oxford, 1998).

*Nouveau dictionnaire de l'Académie françoise*, 2 vol. (Paris, J.-B. Coignard, 1718).

Origen, *De principiis*, 2.9.2, *The Writings of Origen*, trans. Frederick Crombie, 2 vol. (Edinburgh, 1895), vol.1.

Plato, *The Laws*, trans. Benjamin Jowet, *Dover philosophical classics* (New York, 2006).

–, *The Republic* (Lisbon, 2004)

Paillette, Clément de, *La Politique de*

*Joseph de Maistre d'après ses premiers écrits* (Paris, 1895).

Paine, Thomas, *The Rights of man* (Stilwell, K. S., 2007).

Paley, William, *Natural theology* (Boston, MA, 1860).

Pic de la Mirandole, Giovanni, *Œuvres philosophiques* (Paris, 2004).

Plutarch, *Moralia*, trans. and ed. Frank Cole Babbitt, 15 vol. (Cambridge, MA, and London, 2003, first published 1936).

Quinet, Edgar, *Œuvres complètes* (Paris, 1857).

–, *La Révolution* (Verboeckhoven, 1865).

Rousseau, Jean-Jacques, *Correspondance complète de Rousseau*, ed. R. A. Leigh, 52 vol. (Geneva, Madison, WI, Banbury, Oxford, 1965-1989).

–, *Du Contrat social*, ed. Georges Liébert (Paris, 1978).

–, *Emile, ou De l'Education*, ed. François and Pierre Richard (Paris, 1964).

–, *Julie, ou La Nouvelle Héloïse*, 2 vol. (Paris, 1958).

–, Letter to Voltaire, 18 August 1756, in *Correspondance complète de Rousseau*, ed. R. A. Leigh, 52 vol. (Geneva, Madison, WI, Banbury, Oxford, 1965-1989), vol.4 (1967).

Sainte-Beuve, Charles-Augustin, *Causeries du lundi*, 15 vol. (Paris, n.d.), vol. iv.

–, *Les Grands écrivains français: XIXᵉ siècle, philosophes et essayistes*, ed. Maurice Allem (Paris, 1930).

–, 'Joseph de Maistre', in 'Portraits littéraires', *Œuvres* (Paris, 1960).

Saint-Martin, Louis-Claude de, *Tableau naturel des rapports qui existent entre Dieu, l'homme et l'univers* (2 parts, Edinburgh, 1782).

Schopenhauer, Arthur, *Gesammelte Briefe*, ed. Arthur Hübscher (Bonn, 1987).

–, *Parerga and Paralipomena*, trans. E.F.J. Payne, 2 vol. (Oxford, 1974).

–, *Manuscript remains*, trans. E. F. J. Payne, 4 vol. (Oxford, 1988-1990).

–, *The Two fundamental problems of ethics*, trans. C. Janaway (Cambridge, 2009).

–, *The World as will and idea*, trans. R. B. Haldane and J. Kemp (London, 1883, tenth printing, 1957).

Sévigné, Marie de Rabutin-Chantal, *Lettres à sa fille et à ses amis*, ed. Philippe Antoine Grouvelle, 8 vol. (Paris, 1806).

Smith, Sydney, 'Statistical annals of the United States', *Edinburgh review* 33 (January 1820), p.79-80.

Tindal, Matthew, *Christianity as old as Creation* (London, 1703).

Tocqueville, Alexis de, *De la Démocratie en Amérique* (Paris, 1835).

Voltaire, 'Génies' and 'Lettres', in *Dictionnaire philosophique* (Paris, 1838).

Warden, David Bailie, *A Chorographical and statistical description of the District of Columbia* (Paris, 1816).

Whichcote, Benjamin, *The Works of the learned Benjamin Whichcote* (Aberdeen, printed by J. Chalmers for Alexander Thompson, 1751).

Young, Alfred, *Conjectures on original composition in a letter to the author of Sir Charles Grandison* (London, 1759).

# Secondary sources

Abrams, M. H., *The Mirror and the lamp: romantic theory and the critical tradition* (Oxford, 1953).

Anonymous, review of the 1851 edition of Maistre's *Lettres et opuscules inédits*, *Edinburgh review* (October 1852), 96:290.

Armenteros, Carolina, 'From human nature to normal humanity: Joseph de Maistre, Rousseau, and the origins of moral statistics', *Journal of the history of ideas* 68, 1 (2007), 107-30.

–, 'Parabolas and the fate of nations: the beginnings of conservative historicism in Joseph de Maistre's *De la Souveraineté du peuple*', *History of political thought* 28, 2 (2007), p.230-52.

–, 'Revolutionary violence and the end of history: the divided self in Francophone thought, 1762-1914', *Historicising the French Revolution*, ed. Carolina Armenteros, Tim Blanning, Isabel DiVanna and Dawn Dodds (Newcastle, 2008), p.2-38.

Augustine, *Concerning the city of God against the pagans*, trans. Henry Bettenson (London, 2003).

Barthelet, Philippe, ed., *Joseph de Maistre*, Les Dossiers H (Lausanne, 2005).

–, 'Joseph de Maistre entre Révolution et contraire de la Révolution', paper presented at *Actualité de Joseph de Maistre*, colloquium held at the University of the Human Sciences, Moscow, 20 June 2009.

Battersby, Christine, *Gender and genius: towards a feminist aesthetics* (Bloomington, IN, 1990).

Beaune, Colette, *Naissance de la nation de France* (Paris, 1985).

Becq, Annie, *Genèse de l'esthétique française moderne: de la raison classique à l'imagination créatrice 1680–1814*, 2 vol. (Pisa, 1984).

Berlin, Isaiah, 'Introduction' to *Considerations on France*, ed. Richard A. Lebrun (Cambridge, 1994), p.xi-xxxiv.

–, 'Joseph de Maistre and the origins of fascism', in *The Crooked timber of humanity: chapters in the history of ideas* ed. Henry Hardy (London, 1990), p.91-174.

–, *Two enemies of the Enlightenment* (1965, unpublished text in *The Isaiah Berlin virtual library*, http://berlin.wolf.ox.ac.uk/).

Bertram, Christopher, *Rousseau and the social contract* (London, 2004).

Betts, C. J., *Early deism in France: from the so-called 'déistes' of Lyon [1564] to Voltaire's 'Lettres philosophiques' [1734]* (Boston, MA, 1984).

Beyssade, J. M., *La Philosophie première de Descartes* (Paris, 1979).

Blamires, Cyprian, 'Berlin, Maistre and fascism', paper presented at *Reappraisals/Reconsidérations: Fifth International Colloquium on Joseph de Maistre*, Jesus College, Cambridge, 5-6 December 2008.

Blet, P. *Les Assemblées du clergé et Louis XIV de 1670 à 1693* (Rome, 1972).

–, 'Jésuites gallicans au XVIIe siècle?', *Archivicum historicum Societatis Jesu*, vol.29, 1960, p.55-84.

–, 'La religion du Cardinal', in Antoine Adam, Maurice Andrieux, Pierre Blet, Georges Bordonove, Philippe Erlanger, Georges Mongrédien, Roland Mousnier, Victor-L. Tapié, *Richelieu* (Paris, 1972), p.163-79.

Bireley, Robert, *The Counter-Reformation prince: Anti-Machiavellianism or Catholic statecraft in early modern Europe* (Chapel Hill, NC, 1990).

Bradley, Owen, *A Modern Maistre: the social and political thought of Joseph de Maistre* (Lincoln, NE, 1999).

–, 'Maistre's theory of sacrifice', in *Joseph de Maistre's life, thought, and influence*, ed. Richard A. Lebrun (Montreal, 2001), p.65-83.

Brown, Peter, *The Cult of the saints: its rise and function in Latin Christianity* (Chicago, IL, 1981).

Bürger, Peter, *Überlegungen zur historisch-soziologischen Erklärung der Genie-Ästhetik im 18. Jahrhundert* (Heidelberg, 1984).

Burson, Jeffrey, *The Rise and fall of theological Enlightenment: Jean-Martin de Prades and ideological polarization in eighteenth-century France* (Notre Dame, IN, 2010).

Camcastle, Cara, *The More moderate side of Joseph de Maistre: views on political liberty and political economy* (Montreal, 2005).

Canguilhem, Georges, *Etudes d'histoire et de philosophie des sciences* (Paris, 1989).

Caspary, Gerard E., *Politics and exegesis: Origen and the two swords* (Berkeley, CA, 1979).

Cassirer, Ernst, *Die platonische Renaissance in England und die Schule von Cambridge* (Leipzig, Berlin, 1932).

Caussy, Fernand, 'Joseph de Maistre et Schopenhauer', *L'Ermitage*, July-December 1906, p.24-42.

Challemel-Lacour, Paul-Armand, 'Un Bouddhiste contemporain en Allemagne. Arthur Schopenhauer', in *Etudes et réflexions d'un pessimiste* (Paris, 1901), p.241-323.

Chesterton, G.K., *Orthodoxy* (1908).

Church, William F., *Richelieu and reason of state* (Princeton, NJ, 1972).

Commager, Henry Steele and Elmo Giordanetti, *Was America a mistake?* (Columbia, SC, 1968).

Compagnon, Antoine, *Les Antimodernes. De Joseph de Maistre à Roland Barthes* (Paris, 2005).

Cottret, Monique, *Jansénisme et Lumières, pour un autre XVIIIe siècle* (Paris, 1998).

Cross, F.L. and E. A. Livingstone, eds., *The Oxford dictionary of the*

*Christian Church*, 3rd ed. (Oxford, 1997).

Darcel, Jean-Louis, 'Des pénitents noirs à la franc-maçonnerie: aux sources de la sensibilité maistrienne', *Revue des études maistriennes* 5-6 (1980), p.69-95.
–, with Richard A. Lebrun, *Joseph de Maistre et les livres, 1769-1821*, *Revue des études maistriennes* 9 (1985).
–, 'The roads of exile, 1792-1817', in Richard Lebrun, ed., *Joseph de Maistre's life, thought, and influence* (Montreal and Kingston, 2001), p.15-31.
–, '*Les Soirées de Saint-Pétersbourg* de Joseph de Maistre: Image contrastive d'une œuvre et d'une ville', in *Joseph de Maistre*, ed. Philippe Bartelet ('Les Dossiers H', Lausanne, 2005), p.138-46.
Darnton, Robert, *The Literary underground of the old regime* (Cambridge, MA, 1982).
Davies, Peter, *The Extreme right in France, 1789 to the present: from De Maistre to Le Pen* (London, 2002).
Dermenghem, Emile, *Joseph de Maistre mystique* (Paris, 1923).
Dronke, Peter, *Fabula. Exploration into the uses of myth in medieval Platonism*, Mittellateinische Studien und Texte (Leiden, Cologne, 1985), IX.

Field, Lester L., Jr., *Liberty, dominion, and the two swords* (Notre Dame, IN, 1998).
Figgis, John Neville, *The Divine right of kings* (Cambridge, 1896).
Froidefont, M., *Les Sources et les influences de la pensée religieuse de Joseph de Maistre* (unpublished Ph.D. thesis, Université de Chambéry, 2009).
Furet, F., *La Gauche et la révolution au milieu du XIXᵉ siècle. Edgar Quinet et la question du jacobinisme (1865-1870)* (Paris, 1986).

Garrard, Graeme, *Counter-Enlightenments: from the eighteenth century to the present* (London, 2006).
–, 'Isaiah Berlin's Joseph de Maistre', in *Isaiah Berlin's Counter-Enlightenment*, ed. Joseph Mali and Robert Wokler (Philadelphia, PA, 2003), p.117-31.
–, 'Joseph de Maistre's civilization and its discontents', *Journal of the history of ideas* 57, 3 (1966), p.429-46.
–, 'Rousseau, Maistre, and the Counter-Enlightenment', *History of political thought* 15, 1 (1994), p.97-120.
–, *Rousseau's Counter-Enlightenment: a republican critique of the philosophes* (Albany, NY, 2003).
Gauchet, Marcel, *The Disenchantment of the world: a political history of religion*, trans. Oscar Burge (Princeton, NJ, 1997).
–, 'Genie', in the *Historisches Wörterbuch der Philosophie*, ed. Joachim Ritter, 13 vol. (Basel, 1971–2007), vol.3, p.279–309.
Gengembre, Gérard, *La Contre-révolution ou l'histoire désespérante* (Paris, 1989).
Gianturco, Elio, *Joseph de Maistre and Giambattista Vico: Italian roots of De Maistre's political culture*, unpublished Ph.D. dissertation, Columbia University, 1937.
Girard, René, *La Violence et le sacré* (Paris, 1972).
Glaudes, Pierre, 'Bloy et l'héritage maistrien', in *Joseph de Maistre*, ed. Philippe Barthelet, Les Dossiers H (Lausanne, 2005), p.776-88.
–, 'Maistre et le sublime de la Révolution', *Revue des études maistriennes*, vol.14, 2004, p.183-200.
–, 'Paradoxe', in Jean-Louis Darcel, Pierre Glaudes and Jean-Yves Pranchère, *Dictionnaire Joseph de Maistre*, in *Joseph de Maistre: Œuvres*, ed. Pierre Glaudes (Paris, 2007), p.1243-45.

–, ed., *Joseph de Maistre: Œuvres, suivies d'un dictionnaire Joseph de Maistre* (Paris, 2007).

Godechot, Jacques, *The Counter-Revolution: doctrine and action, 1789-1804*, trans. Salvator Attansio (New York, 1971).

Goldhammer, Jesse, *The Headless republic: sacrificial violence in modern French thought* (Ithaca, NY, 2005).

Greer, Rowan, A., 'Introduction', *Origen* (Mahwah, NJ, 1979), p.1-40.

Griefer, Elisha, 'Joseph de Maistre and the reaction against the eighteenth century', *The American political science review* 55, 3 (1961), p.591-98.

Hagner, Michael, *Geniale Gehirne: zur Geschichte der Elitegehirnforschung* (Munich, 2007).

Harl, Marguerite, *La Bible grecque des Septante. Du judaïsme hellénistique au christianisme ancien* (Paris, 1994).

–, *Le Déchiffrement du sens. Etudes sur l'herméneutique chrétienne d'Origène à Grégoire de Nysse* (Paris, 1993).

Hayward, Jack, *After the French revolution: six critics of democracy and nationalism* (New York, 1991).

Hefelbower, S.G., 'Deism historically defined', *The American journal of theology* 24, 2 (1920), p. 217-23.

Heschel, A.J., *God in search of man* (New York, 2001).

–, *The Prophets* (New York, 2001).

Holdsworth, Frederick, *Joseph de Maistre et l'Angleterre* (Paris, 1935).

Hutin, S., *Henry More. Essai sur les doctrines philosophiques chez les platoniciens de Cambridge*, Studien und Materialen zur Geschichte der Philosophie (Hildesheim, 1966).

Isambert, François-André, *Politique, religion et science de l'homme chez Philippe Buchez (1796-1865)* (Paris, 1967).

Israel, Jonathan, *Enlightenment contested: philosophy, modernity, and the emancipation of man 1670-1752* (Oxford, 2006).

–, *Radical Enlightenment: philosophy and the making of modernity* (Oxford, 2001).

Jaeger, Werner, *Early Christianity and Greek paideia* (Harvard, MA, 1961).

–, *Paideia: the ideals of Greek culture* (Oxford, 1986).

–, *The Theology of the early Greek philosophers* (Oxford, 1947).

Janet, Pierre, *Essai sur le médiateur plastique de Cudworth* (Paris, 1860).

Kelly, George Armstrong, 'Rousseau, Kant, and history', *Journal of the history of ideas* 29, 3 (1968), p.347-64.

Kershaw, Ian, *Hitler, 1889-1936: hubris* (New York, 2000).

Kivy, Peter, *The Possessor and the possessed: Handel, Mozart, Beethoven and the idea of musical genius* (New Haven, CT, 2001).

Kobush, T., 'Die philosophische Bedeutung des Kirchenvaters Origenes', in *Theologische quartalschrift* (Erlangen, 1980).

Kohlhauer, Michael, ed., 'Joseph de Maistre, lecteur d'Origène' in *Autour de Joseph et Xavier de Maistre. Mélanges pour Jean-Louis Darcel* (Chambéry, 2007), p.109-18.

Kristeller, P. Oskar, *Renaissance concepts of man and other essays* (New York, 1972).

Krynen, Jacques, *L'Empire du Roi. Idées et croyances politiques en France (XIIIᵉ-XVᵉ siècle)* (Paris, 1933).

Latreille, André, 'Les Nonces apostoliques en France et l'Eglise gallicane sous Innocent XI', *Revue d'Histoire de l'Eglise de France* 142, 45 (1959).

Lebrun, Richard A., 'Introduction' to *Considerations on France*, trans. Richard A. Lebrun (Montreal and London, 1974).

–, 'Joseph de Maistre and Rousseau',
   SVEC 1972:88, p.881-98.
–, 'Joseph de Maistre as
   pamphleteer', in The new 'enfant du
   siècle': Joseph de Maistre as a writer,
   ed. Carolina Armenteros and
   Richard Lebrun, St Andrews studies
   in French history and culture 1 (St
   Andrews, 2010), p.19-46.
–, 'Joseph de Maistre et
   Malebranche', in Revue des études
   maistriennes 11 (1990), p.127-137,
   republished in Joseph de Maistre,
   ed. Philippe Barthelet, Les
   Dossiers H (Lausanne, 2005),
   p.290-97.
–, 'Joseph de Maistre, Cassandra of
   science', French historical studies 6
   (1969), p.214-31.
–, 'Joseph de Maistre in the
   Anglophone world', in Joseph de
   Maistre's life, thought, and influence:
   selected studies, ed. Richard A.
   Lebrun (Montreal and Kingston,
   2001), p.271-89.
–, Review of Jean-Jacques Rousseau,
   Julie, or the new Heloise: letters of two
   lovers who live in a small town at the
   foot of the Alps (Hanover and
   London, 1997), H-France Reviews,
   http://www.h-net.org/reviews/
   showrev.php?id = 2270 (August
   1998).
–, Throne and altar: the political and
   religious thought of Joseph de Maistre
   (Ottawa, 1965).
Lecler, Joseph, 'Le Roi de France
   "Fils aîné de l'Eglise"', Etudes, 5
   and 20 January 1933, p.21-36.
Lefort, Claude, 'Edgar Quinet: La
   Révolution manquée', in Essai
   sur le politique (Paris, 1986), p.140-
   61.
Lévinas, E., 'L'idée de l'infini', in En
   découvrant l'existence avec Husserl et
   Heidegger (Paris, 1982), p.171ff.
–, Totalité et infini. Essai sur l'extériorité
   (The Hague, 1980).
Lieb, Michael, Milton and the culture
   of violence (London, 1994).
Lively, Jack, 'Introduction' to The

Works of Joseph de Maistre (New
   York, 1965).
Lombard, Charles M., Joseph de
   Maistre (Boston, MA, 1976).
Lovie, Jacques, 'Constance de
   Maistre: éléments pour une
   biographie', Revue des études
   maistriennes 4 (1978), p.141-73.

Maire, Catherine, De la Cause de Dieu
   à la cause de la nation: le jansénisme
   au XVIII^e siècle (Paris, 1998).
–, Les Convulsionnaires de Saint-
   Médard: miracles, convulsions et
   prophéties à Paris au XVII^e siècle
   (Paris, 1985).
Maistre, Henri de, Joseph de Maistre
   (Paris, 1990).
Maritain, Jacques, Christianisme et
   démocratie (New York, 1943).
Martimort, Aimé-George, Le
   Gallicanisme de Bossuet (Paris, 1953).
Martin, Victor, Le Gallicanisme
   politique et le clergé de France
   (Picard, 1929).
–, Les Origines du gallicanisme (Paris,
   1939).
Mason, John Hope, The Value of
   creativity: the origins and emergence of
   a modern belief (Aldershot, 2003).
Matore, G. and A.J. Greimas, 'La
   naissance du "genie" au dix-
   huitième siècle: étude
   lexicologique', Le Français moderne
   25 (1957), p.256–72.
Matthes, Melissa, 'Nouvelle Héloïse
   and the supplement of sexual
   difference', in The Rape of Lucretia
   and the founding of republics: readings
   in Livy, Machiavelli and Rousseau
   (University Park, PA 2000), p.117-
   54.
McGrath, Alister E., A Scientific
   theology: 1. Nature (Grand Rapids,
   MI, 2002).
McGuckin, John Anthony, ed. The
   Westminster handbook to Origen
   (Louisville, KY, 2004).
McKim, Donald J., The Westminster
   dictionary of theological terms
   (Louisville, KY, 1996).

McMahon, Darrin, *Enemies of the Enlightenment: the French Counter-Enlightenment and the making of modernity* (Oxford, 2001).

Melzer, Arthur, 'The origin of the Counter-Enlightenment: Rousseau and the new religion of sincerity', *American political science review* 90, 2 (1996), p.344-60.

Merkle, Sebastian, *Die katholische Beurteiling des Aufklärungszeitalters: Vortrag auf dem Internationalen Kongress für Historischen Wissenschaften zu Berlin am 12. August 1908* (Berlin, 1908).

Miller, Samuel J., 'Introduction: Enlightened Catholicism on a European scale', in *Portugal and Rome c.1748-1830: Aspects of the Catholic Enlightenment* (Rome, 1973), p.1-27.

Miltchyna, Vera, 'Joseph de Maistre in Russia', *Joseph de Maistre's life, thought, and influence: selected studies*, ed. Richard A. Lebrun (Montreal, 2001), p.241-70.

Murray, John C., 'The political thought of Joseph de Maistre', *The review of politics* 11, 1 (1949), p.63-86.

Murray, Penelope, ed., *Genius: the history of an idea* (Oxford, 1989).

Muret, Charlotte Touzalin, *French royalist doctrines since the Revolution* (New York, 1993).

Negroni, Barbara, 'La Bibliothèque d'Emile et de Sophie: la fonction des livres dans la pédagogie de Rousseau', *Dix-huitième siècle* 19 (1987), p.379-90.

Nguyen, Victor, 'Maistre, Vico et le retour des dieux', *Revue des études maistriennes* 3 (1977), p.243-55.

Northeast, Catherine M., *The Parisian Jesuits and the Enlightenment, 1700-62* (Oxford, 1991).

O'Donovan, Oliver, *The Desire of nations: rediscovering the roots of political theology* (Cambridge, 1999).

O'Malley, John, 'From the 1599 *ratio studiorum* to the present: a humanistic tradition?' in Vincent J. Duminuco, ed., *The Jesuit ratio studiorum: 400th anniversary perspectives* (New York, 2000), p.127-44.

Oz-Salzberger, Fania, *Translating the Enlightenment: Scottish civic discourse in eighteenth-century Germany* (Oxford, 1995).

Paléologue, Théodore, *Sous l'œil du grand inquisiteur* (Paris, 2004).

Palmer, Robert, *Catholics and unbelievers in eighteenth-century France* (Princeton, NJ, 1939).

Pickering, Mary, *Auguste Comte: an intellectual biography*, 3 vol. (Cambridge, 1993-2009).

Porter, Roy, *The Enlightenment*, 2nd ed. (Houndmills, Hampshire and New York, 2001).

Pranchère, Jean-Yves, *L'Autorité contre les Lumières. La philosophie de Joseph de Maistre* (Geneva, 2004).

–, 'Ordre de la raison, déraison de l'histoire', in *Joseph de Maistre*, ed. Philippe Barthelet, Les Dossiers H (Lausanne, 2005), p.366-90.

–, 'The persistence of Maistrian thought,' in *Joseph de Maistre's life, thought, and influence*, ed. Richard A. Lebrun (Montreal, 2001), p.290-326.

Reardon, Michael, 'The reconciliation of Christianity with progress: Philippe Buchez', *The review of politics* 23, 4 (1971), p.512-37.

Rebotton, J. 'Joseph de Maistre, *alias* Josephus a Floribus, pendant la Révolution: repères et conjectures', *Revue des études maistriennes* 5-6 (1980), p.141-81.

Rémusat, Charles de, 'Du traditionalisme', *Revue des deux mondes* 9 (27th year, 2nd period), p.245, 15 May 1857.

Renaut, Alain, *L'Ere de l'individu* (Paris, 1989).

Rials. Stéphane, 'La Droite ou
l'horreur de la volonté', in
*Révolution et Contre-révolution au
XIX<sup>e</sup> siècle* (Paris, 1987).

Richet, Denis, *La France moderne:
l'esprit des institutions* (Paris, 1973).

Robertson, John M., *A Short history of
freethought ancient and modern to the
period of the French Revolution*, 3rd
ed., 2 vol. (London, 1915), vol.1.

Robertson, John, *The Case for the
Enlightenment: Scotland and Naples
1680-1760* (Cambridge, 2005).

Roger, Philippe, *The American enemy:
the history of French anti-Americanism*
(Chicago, IL, 2005).

Rosengarten, Richard A., *Henry
Fielding and the narration of
providence: divine design and the
incursions of evil* (New York and
London, 2000).

Rubin, Barry and Judith Colp
Rubin, *Hating America: a history*
(Oxford, 2004).


Saccarelli, Emanuele, 'The
Machiavellian Rousseau: gender
and family relations in the *Discourse
on the origin of inequality*', *Political
theory* 37, 4 (2009), p.482-510.

Sacquin, Michèle, *Entre Bossuet et
Maurras: l'Antiprotestantisme en
France de 1814 à 1870* (Paris,
1998).

Schmidt, James, 'What
Enlightenment project?', *Political
theory* 28, 6 (2000), p.734-57.

Schmidt, Jochen, *Die Geschichte des
Genie-Gedankens in der deutschen
Literatur, Philosophie und Politik
1750–1945*, 2 vol. (Heidelberg,
2004).

Schmitt, Carl, *Political theology: four
chapters on the concept of sovereignty*
(1922), trans. George Schwab
(Chicago, IL, 2005).

Schockenhoff, E., *Zum Fest der
Freiheit. Theologie des Christlichen
Handelns bei Origenes* (Mainz, 1999).

Schott, Georg, *Das Volksbuch vom
Hitler* (Munich, 1924).

Skinner, Quentin, *Liberty before
liberalism* (Cambridge, 1998).

Soltau, Roger Henry, *French political
thought in the nineteenth century*
(New York, 1959).

Soltner, Jean-Louis, 'Le
Christianisme de Joseph de
Maistre', *Revue des études
maistriennes* 5-6 (1980), p.97-110.

Spektorowski, Alberto, 'Maistre,
Donoso Cortés, and the legacy of
Catholic authoritarianism', *Journal
of the history of ideas* 63, 2 (2002),
p.283-302.

Strayer, Joseph R., 'France, the holy
land, the chosen people and the
most christian king', in *Action and
conviction in early modern Europe:
essays in honor of E. H. Harbison*, ed.
Theodore K. Rabb and Jerrold E.
Seigel (Princeton, NJ, 1969), p.3-16.

Steiner, George, 'Aspects of
counter-revolution', in *The
Permanent revolution: the French
Revolution and its legacy, 1789-1989*,
ed. Geoffrey Best (London, 1988),
p.129-52.

Strauss, Leo, *Spinoza's critique of
religion* (Chicago, IL, 1997).

–, *Thoughts on Machiavelli* (Chicago,
IL, 1978).

Strenski, Ivan, *Contesting sacrifice:
religion, nationalism, and social
thought in France* (Chicago, IL,
2002).


Taylor, Charles, *Sources of the self: the
making of modern identity*
(Cambridge, 1989).

Traverso, Enzo, *Le Totalitarisme*
(Paris, 2001).

Trinkaus, Charles, *In our image and
likeness: humanity and divinity in
Italian humanist thought*, 2 vol.
(London, 1970).

Triomphe, Robert, *Joseph de Maistre:
étude sur la vie et sur la doctrine d'un
matérialiste mystique* (Geneva, 1968).

–, 'Joseph de Maistre et Herder',
*Revue de littérature comparée*, 7-9
(1954), p.322-29.

Ullmann, Walter, *Principles of government and politics in the Middle Ages* (London, 1961).

Vallin, P., '*Les Soirées* de Joseph de Maistre: Une Création théologique originale', in *Revue des sciences religieuses*, 74, no.3 (Paris 1986).

Van Kley, Dale, 'Pierre Nicole, Jansenism, and the morality of enlightened self-interest', *Anticipations of the Enlightenment in England, France and Germany*, ed. Alan C. Kors and Paul J. Korshim (Philadelphia, PA, 1987), p.69-85.

–, 'Foreword' to Jeffrey Burson, *The rise and fall of theological Enlightenment: Jean-Martin de Prades and ideological polarization in eighteenth-century France* (Notre Dame, IN, 2010).

–, *The Religious origins of the French Revolution: from Calvin to the Civil Constitution* (New Haven, CT, 1996).

Verçosa Filho, Elcio, 'Paidéia divina: formação e destinação do homem em Joseph de Maistre', unpublished Ph.D.thesis, Pontifícia Universidade Católica de São Paulo (PUC-SP), 2007.

Viereck, Peter, *Conservative thinkers: from John Adams to Winston Churchill* (New Brunswick, NJ, 2006).

Watt, E. D., '"Locked in": De Maistre's critique of French Lockeanism', *Journal of the history of ideas* 32, 1 (1971), p.129-32.

Williams, David Lay, *Rousseau's Platonic enlightenment* (University Park, PA, 2007).

Wingrove, Elizabeth, *Rousseau's republican romance* (Princeton, NJ, 2000).

–, 'Sexual performance as political performance in the *Lettre à M. D'Alembert sur les spectacles*', *Political theory* 23, 4 (1995), p.585-616.

Wokler, Robert, 'Isaiah Berlin's Enlightenment and Counter-Enlightenment', in *Isaiah Berlin's Counter-Enlightenment*, p.13-32.

Wollenberg, Jörg, *Richelieu: Staatsräson und Kircheninteresse: zur Legitimation der Politik des Kardinalpremier* (Bielefeld, 1977).

Yolton, J., *Locke and French materialism* (Oxford, 1991).

Zenkine, Serge, 'L'Utopie religieuse des saint-simoniens: le sémiotique et le sacré', in *Etudes saint-simoniennes*, ed. Philippe Régnier, 'Littératures et idéologies' (Lyon, 2002), p.33-60.

Zilsel, Edgar *Die Enstehung des Geniebegriffes* (Tübingen, 1926).

# Index